Algerian Sketches

Algerian Sketches

Pierre Bourdieu

Texts edited and presented by
Tassadit Yacine
Translated by David Fernbach

polity

First published in French as *Esquisses algériennes* © Éditions du Seuil, 2008

This English edition © Polity Press, 2013

Polity Press
65 Bridge Street
Cambridge CB2 1UR, UK

Polity Press
350 Main Street
Malden, MA 02148, USA

ISBN-13: 978-0-7456-4694-7
ISBN-13: 978-0-7456-4695-4(pb)

A catalogue record for this book is available from the British Library.

Typeset in 10.5 on 12 pt Sabon
by Toppan Best-set Premedia Limited
Printed and bound in Great Britain by Clays Ltd, St Ives plc

The publisher has used its best endeavours to ensure that the URLs for external websites referred to in this book are correct and active at the time of going to press. However, the publisher has no responsibility for the websites and can make no guarantee that a site will remain live or that the content is or will remain appropriate.

Pierre Bourdieu, 'Making the Economic Habitus: Algerian Workers Revisited' *Ethnography* 1-1 (200): 17–41, translated by Richard Nice and Löic Wacquant. Reproduced with permission.

Every effort has been made to trace all copyright holders, but if any have been inadvertently overlooked the publisher will be pleased to include any necessary credits in any subsequent reprint or edition.

For further information on Polity, visit our website: www.politybooks.com

Contents

PRESENTATION by Tassadit Yacine   1
Bourdieu and Algeria, Bourdieu in Algeria   3
The Editorial Project   5
At the Origins of a Singular Ethnosociology   13

ALGERIAN SKETCHES by Pierre Bourdieu   35
Colonization, Culture and Society   37
The Clash of Civilizations   39
Traditional Society's Attitude towards Time and
    Economic Behaviour   52
The Internal Logic of Original Algerian Society   72

War and Social Mutations   83
From Revolutionary War to Revolution   85
Revolution in the Revolution   92
War and Social Mutation in Algeria   104

Workers and Peasants in Disarray   115
Uprooted Peasants: Morphological Upheavals and
    Cultural Changes in Algeria   117
The Algerian Sub-Proletarians   146
Haunted by Unemployment: The Algerian Proletariat and
    the Colonial System   162
The Making of Economic Habitus   180

The Ethnology of Kabylia   201
The Right Use of Ethnology   203
Dialogue on Oral Poetry in Kabylia   224

A Reflexive Definition of Anthropology   263
Participant Objectivation   265

Return to the Algerian Experience   281
For a Sociology of Sociologists   283
Between Friends   288
For Abdelmalek Sayad   295
Seeing with the Lens: About Photography   301

Appendices   315
Letters to André Nouschi   317
Chronology of Historical Events   323
Map of Investigation Sites   328
Publications of Pierre Bourdieu on Algeria   329

Notes   332

Bibliography   375

Index   381

Presentation

Bourdieu and Algeria, Bourdieu in Algeria

The Editorial Project

Algeria and Kabylia[1] occupy a central place in the work of Pierre Bourdieu, forming a major point of reference in his ethnographic writings,[2] even when he discusses objects outside this ethno-cultural zone. The material realization of the investigations and studies that form the foundation of these writings corresponds to a period that offers the double particularity of being situated at the beginning of Bourdieu's scientific work and in the midst of the Algerian war (1958–60). After recently graduating from the École Normale Supérieure in 1954, and destined for the career of a philosophy professor (he had just begun a thesis under George Canguilhem on 'Temporal structures of affective life'), Bourdieu, like many young men of his generation, was sent against his will to do military service in Algeria, at the very moment when the war had begun to intensify. In this exceptional context, his intellectual project was overwhelmed. For a while, he devoted all his energy to understanding the society of colonized Algeria, investigating the destructuring effects of the *sénatus-consulte* of 1863[3] on Algerian society (dispossession of inherited land and fragmentation of tribes). He used the resources of the library of the Gouvernement Général and the archival collections in Algiers. At the same time, he collected information from specialists (historians,[4] ethnologists) and began studying the consequences of the policies applied in the nineteenth century (the *sénatus-consulte*, the *loi Warnier*,[5] and cantonment[6]) on the way of life of the rural populations. He then obtained a position at the University of Algiers, where he taught sociology and philosophy,[7] while in parallel, in the context of the directorate of the Statistique Générale and thanks to the support of the progressive demographer Jacques Breil, he travelled through different regions of Algeria, particularly Kabylia, where he gathered the information that would provide the material for subsequently published works (*Le Déracinement*, *Outline of a Theory of Practice* and *The Logic of Practice*, just to mention three books explicitly devoted to these terrains either completely or in part). He wrote a certain number of texts in Algiers, including *Travail et travailleurs en Algérie*, and the provocatively titled *Sociologie de l'Algérie*[8] for the 'Que sais-je?' collection.

These publications inevitably had a political significance. Bourdieu sought to explain 'to French people, especially those on the left, what was really happening in a country that they often knew next to nothing about [. . .]' and, he continued:

> While telling myself that I was moving into ethnology and sociology, in the early stages, only provisionally, and that once I had finished this work of political pedagogy, I would return to philosophy (indeed, during the whole time that I was writing *Sociologie d'Algérie* and conducting my first ethnological fieldwork, I continued to write each evening on the structure of temporal experience according to Husserl), I flung myself totally [. . .] into an undertaking whose stake was not only intellectual.[9]

The intent of this volume is to make available to readers the articles Bourdieu wrote while he was in Algeria, along with the interviews that he subsequently gave on this period of his scientific activity. These texts are important because, written in extraordinary conditions, the author himself wondered how one could think of conducting ethnographic research in the midst of war; they are also the symptom of a double transformation. First of all, in the manner that Algeria and the 'indigenous' were then conceived and represented by 'orientalists', but above all a transformation in his own trajectory, as Bourdieu interrupted a career as philosopher in France and, rather than following the steep but predictable slope of philosophical theory and dialogue with major authors, opted for ethnographic enumeration, the meticulous description of matrimonial strategies, studies that involved both statistics and photography. This double about-turn would lie at the root of the invention and formation of a new way of seeing and conceiving the social world.

The interest in publishing these texts today is not to show how, right from the start, Bourdieu came on the scene fully equipped with perfectly thought-out and established theoretical concepts (habitus, capital, field), but rather to cast light on the first step in the development of his main concepts and intellectual instruments. It is to show how, in practice, by both a theoretical about-turn and an accumulation of empirical data, the ethnological categories of thought then prevailing were challenged and a certain number of new solutions proposed.

It should not be forgotten that the 'conversion of gaze', as Bourdieu himself put it, that he then effected – a profound biographical and intellectual conversion of the Paris philosopher into an anthropologist, ethnologist and sociologist – was set in a specific historical context and defined from the start as a committed way of doing science that would characterize the rest of his life: the social sciences were for him a political 'weapon', in the service of a social critique of forms of repression and domination.

But these texts remain contemporary for another reason as well. At a time when questions of colonization and decolonization are making a new and forceful appearance in public debate, they provide essential elements for understanding the damaging effects of the phenomenon of colonialism, in the colonizing societies as well as those colonized. In this way, they offer political instruments that are still subversive and innovatory for conceiving these effects, and – perhaps? – overcoming them. For this reason, the present collection is addressed above all to Algerians, and especially the young generations desiring a better acquaintance with their memory and culture. This is all the more necessary, given that this period has been the object of a kind of collective amnesia, in Algeria as well as in France.

The texts collected here should be read at four different levels. The first of these relates to the information and analyses devoted to a colonized society in the midst of a war of liberation, considered both in the duration of its deep structures and in the urgency of a brutal crisis (see the essays below under 'Colonization, Culture and Society' and on 'Workers and Peasants in Disarray'). A second level of reading shows the experience Bourdieu acquired in the course of this war (the studies under the rubric 'War and Social Mutations'). The third concerns the mode of intervention that would orient the whole of his work, illustrated by a return to the Algerian terrain (see also the articles 'Between friends', 'The right use of ethnology', 'Participant objectivation' and 'For Abdelmalek Sayad'). The last level relates to understanding the origin of a certain number of his fundamental concepts (see the articles presented under the rubrics 'A Reflexive Definition of Anthropology', 'The Ethnology of Kabylia', and above all, 'For a sociology of sociologists', and 'The making of economic habitus').

The Sociology of Algeria in Wartime

There are two recurrent themes in Bourdieu's writings on Algeria. The first is his analysis of a society overwhelmed by war. The articles published in 1959 study the relationships between economy and culture, and the phenomena of acculturation that are specific to that period. The relationship to money, for example, acquires its full significance on understanding what is meant by the notions of temporality, spatiality, honour, exchange, gift and loan that structure peasant thought. In a short space of time, and with little in the way of resources, Bourdieu establishes experimentally a methodology for studying a complex terrain, combining interviews, photography and statistics,[10] both among peasants and emigrants, and among the urban unemployed, and he manages in this way to reconstitute the specific economic 'rationality' of the traditional Algerian economic ethos.

The second theme is the analysis of the Mediterranean mythico-ritual system, and more generally the anthropological underpinnings of a society, an analysis that Bourdieu would return to in order to develop his theoretical work on the 'theory of practice'.[11] In two more recent interviews reprinted here, with Mouloud Mammeri and with Franz Schultheis, Bourdieu describes the break he had to make with the Eurocentric studies of ethnologists of the Algiers school before going on to distance himself fundamentally from a standpoint determined by the structuralist vision.

As a contribution to a sociology of Algeria (seen no longer as an exclusively ethnological object),[12] these texts remained in part confidential at the time they appeared, because of the political context. Focused on the world of peasants and workers, these articles broke with the practices of the Algiers school of ethnologists, which were most commonly characterized by a primitivist representation of Algerian population groups, if not by a form of racism.

All in all, based essentially on studies in the field, the articles Bourdieu produced during his stay in Algeria describe the peasant and working-class world, and bring to light the lasting structures of domination that enabled the colonial system to maintain itself for more than 130 years.

The Algerian War as Historical Moment and Individual Experience

Like many others, Bourdieu remained 'marked' (emotionally as well as politically)[13] by this war in which he participated as a young conscript and an army private, and against which he struggled with the weapons of reason and knowledge: preparing scientific tools that aimed to deconstruct the modes of operation of colonization, ambitious empirical research in a context that was particularly hard as a result of attacks, assassinations, raids, and, more generally, the 'ambient fascism'.[14] At the École Normale Supérieure, Bourdieu was one of a small left minority opposed both to the right and to a 'left' that was supportive of colonialist policy[15] (Socialists and Communists),[16] which made him an outsider from the beginning. 'The pressure exerted by Stalinism was so exasperating that, around 1951, we had founded at the École Normale (with Bianco, Comte, Marin, Derrida, Pariente and others) a Committee for the Defence of Freedom.'[17] Lucien Bianco, who was a close friend of Bourdieu, explained:

> Likewise, at the École Normale, we were unable to link up with any of the different currents. For example, we found Sartre's article in *Les Temps Modernes*, 'The Communists and peace', excessive; we did not follow him, but at the same time the argument then currently used against Camus (the beautiful soul) did not leave us unaffected. We really did not know which saint to worship, we were dissatisfied and uncertain. To illustrate our contradictions, a fellow student had visited Tito's Yugoslavia, and we were stupidly persuaded by the Communists that this was shameful; at the same time, the clearest element in our political action was our arguments with the Communists. After the foundation of a Comité d'Action des Intellectuels pour la Défense des Libertés (in 1952), I set up a section of this committee at the ENS (Bourdieu was naturally a member), and there were so many of us (even more than the Communists themselves) that they considered us rivals and were constantly starting brawls with us, accusing us of being social-traitors. We resisted them vigorously, and emphasized their bad faith: they campaigned for the release of Duclos, but not of Marty (both were in prison), which made us only demand more noisily the release of Marty. I particularly feared Le Roy Ladurie,[18] who struck me as a kind of Saint-Just, and I was always wondering what arguments he would brandish in the name of theory. I speak for myself, but Bourdieu prepared the responses to the Communists with me. I can't speak in his name, but we thought along the same lines.[19]

Scientific Texts, Political Texts

These earliest texts have a different value, bearing on the extraordinary context in which they were written, in so far as they make it possible to see at work the specifically political significance and desire behind Bourdieu's work. The Algerian conflict, as is well known, was a determining experience for a generation of French intellectuals – representing a key period in the development of their political consciousness and maturation[20] – particularly for those aged between 18 and 28 in 1954. There was little in common between Jacques Chirac, Michel Rocard, Pierre Joxe, Jacques Derrida, Olivier Todd, Yann Queffélec, Eddy Mitchell, Serge Lama and the peasant from Béarn or Berry, except the painful test of military service in Algeria. Bourdieu, like his friends at the École Normale Supérieure, did not escape this rude experience, which lay at the root of his intellectual conversion, as explained by one of his earliest students at the University of Algiers, Alain Accardo:

> It seemed to me that the Algerian war was for Bourdieu, if not the revelator, at least the catalyst of the discovery that the path of institutional philosophy was the wrong track for him, and that by continuing further in that direction, as he had made a brilliant start in doing, he could only compromise himself with the hypocrisy of the cultural *nouveaux riches* and the arrogance of the mandarins, bringing grist to the mill of the social domination whose effects he was measuring, not only in personal terms but on the scale of a whole society. What he wanted above all was to combat this domination that he had long had personal reasons to hate, and he now knew academic philosophy sufficiently well to understand that it was no more than an ornament and a display of the bourgeois imperialist order, and served only as a barrier to Marxism. Bourdieu did not explicitly claim to be a Marxist, but he had understood very well what made up ideology in general, and this academic philosophy in particular. As a result, he was seeking a scientific approach to social reality, and thus not a philosophical one. He struck out all the more resolutely on this path in that it seemed to him to make it more possible to reconcile several objectives: rigorous social critique without intellectual obeisance to any kind of dogma, personal distinction without allegiance to a patron, etc. Like many of us at that time, Bourdieu was a young man who wanted to change the world because he found it execrable.[21]

That is why, conducting scientific work in a time of war, Bourdieu was unable to avoid questioning the status of research, the position of the researcher in situations of extreme crisis, the place of ethnology and sociology in a period of armed conflict.[22] Breaking with the standpoint of ethnological works on Algeria, he managed to make intelligible the moral and material misery of a whole people, right from his articles of 1959. This problematic is found in 1963 in *Travail et travailleurs en Algérie*, a major investigation that, combining statisticians and a sociologist, opened up a wide field of studies on mechanisms of domination (induced by colonization, by war, by other forms of exploitation), particularly in the world of labour. In his analysis of temporal consciousness, Bourdieu emphasized the discordance between the economic dispositions produced in a pre-capitalist economy and the 'cosmos' that the capitalist economy imported by colonization implies, and showed how the most 'ordinary' economic behaviours (saving, wages, credit) require social and cultural conditions of possibility that are not met with in traditional societies. Part of this material was taken up again in 1977, in *Algeria 1960*, and in 'Haunted by unemployment: the Algerian proletariat and the colonial system' and 'The Algerian sub-proletarians' (both in this volume).

Elements of a Theoretical Break

The texts in this volume thus have a great interest for anyone seeking to understand the origin of the work and the elaboration of the analytic concepts that Bourdieu was later to develop in his books devoted to Algeria (*Le Déracinement*, *Algeria 1960*, *Outline of a Theory of Practice*, *The Logic of Practice*), and that would be continuously reworked, refined, and extended to other domains.[23] In fact, a large number of the concepts around which his work on the sociology of education and culture at the Centre de Sociologie Européenne was organized in the 1960s came about as a result of a generalization of the results of the ethnological and sociological work that he had done in Algeria:[24]

> I am thinking in particular of the relationship between subjective hopes and objective opportunities that I had observed in the economic, demographic and political behaviour of Algerian workers, and that I could also observe in French students or their families. But the transfer is still more evident in the interest I took in cognitive structures, taxonomies and classificatory activity of social agents.[25]

In order to mark a distance from ethnologists who avoided reality or supported the existing system by turning to the archaism of primitive societies, Bourdieu delayed the publication of his first studies, which appeared after Algerian independence. This was the case with 'The sense of honour', written in 1960 and only published in French in 1972. Inscribed in a structuralist perspective, these texts preceded the works in which – from 'The Kabyle house or the world reversed' through to *Practical Reason* in 1980 – Bourdieu took his distance from it in order to study the logics of practice, first of all in *Outline of a Theory of Practice*[26] and then in *The Logic of Practice*.[27] The latter work was the culmination of the whole series of studies he had conducted between 1957 and 1976 on two terrains: Kabylia and Béarn, used as reflexive counterpoint at the same time as he combined theoretical and empirical results obtained on the basis of the study of modern societies, their systems of social reproduction, their use of different types of capital, etc.

In this way, even if an initial sketch of the concept of habitus was formulated here, these early writings remain marked by the dominant theories of their time (culturalism and structuralism), and this gives a better measure of the road subsequently travelled before Bourdieu managed to develop the essential concepts of his sociology (we see this for example in 'The making of economic habitus' or 'The sense of honour', where the later concept of symbolic capital is sketched).

The texts collected in this volume thus follow a dual principle of selection. The first object was to gather texts that were dispersed and sometimes very hard to access, but that form a coherent and complementary series with the books that largely arose from them; and then to restore those elements that make it possible to understand the evolution of Bourdieu's work on the Algerian terrain on the basis of the material and intellectual conditions in which this was carried out.

In order to read these texts adequately, it is not unhelpful to understand the context in which they were produced, to grasp the colonial situation in Algeria at the time, and in the University of Algiers in particular. Likewise, certain biographic elements are indispensable for understanding the position from which Pierre Bourdieu started out, and the conditions in which he worked, during his stay in Algeria between 1957 and 1960.

Tassadit Yacine

At the Origins of a Singular Ethnosociology

The question I am going to examine is one that I have not ceased asking from my first ethnological works on the Kabyle to my more recent research on the world of art and, more precisely, on the functioning of artistic patronage in modern societies. I would like to show that with the same instruments, one can analyse phenomena as different as exchanges of honour in a precapitalist society, or, in societies like our own, the action of foundations such as the Ford Foundation or the Fondation de France, exchanges between generations within a family, transactions in markets of cultural or religious goods, and so forth.

Pierre Bourdieu, *Practical Reason*

1. The Algerian Context

A. Colonial Algeria

This is not the place to write the history of colonization, nor the history of French intellectuals faced with the problem that the war in Algeria posed for them. It is useful, none the less, to rehearse in broad lines the process that led to the war situation during which Pierre Bourdieu worked and wrote. French colonization in Algeria was certainly longer and more destructive than anywhere else in North Africa, owing to a settlement policy that promoted the arrival of colonists from Europe, the greater part of them Christians, to the detriment of the majority of the 'indigenous' population (Arab and Berber), of Muslim or Jewish religion. In order to attract and settle

Europeans, the colonial system dispossessed the indigenous population of both its landed property (plundering and occupation of the best lands) and its natural resources (esparto-grass, cork, mines). These measures were largely responsible for the dismantling of the social system characteristic of an Algeria that was more than 80 per cent rural. They undermined the authority of the tribal chiefs, who formed the core of its political organization, culminating in its definitive collapse with the outbreak of war (1954) and the establishment of resettlement camps.[1]

The injustice and violence perpetrated for more than a century had led to popular revolt on many occasions (in 1871, 1881, 1945, 1954), which only exacerbated the reactions of the colonists. Instead of proceeding to reforms, colonial politicians strengthened oppression, as when thousands of Algerians were murdered in the events of 8 May 1945 at Sétif, after demanding recognition of their rights.[2] This revolt prefigured the insurrection of 1 November 1954, which began a bloody war, with a drive to 'systematic and methodical destruction' on the one side, and on the other, resistance by way of guerrilla warfare and urban terrorism. Between these two tendencies, attempts at 'reconciliation' were undertaken by a number of political figures (Alain Savary, Gaston Defferre, Robert Verdier on the French side; Ferhat Abbas, Messali Hadj and Si Salah on the Algerian side), but the dominant minority, closed to any change, stuck firmly to its positions.

During the first years of the war, the Socialists (Section Française de l'Internationale Ouvrière, SFIO) were in power in France. Robert Lacoste (a Resistance veteran, trade unionist in the Confédération Générale du Travail, CGT, and several times minister under De Gaulle, 1944–50) was appointed minister in residence in 1956 by the prime minister, Guy Mollet.[3] The National Assembly granted the government special powers in Algeria, and the five leaders of the FLN's foreign delegation (Mohammed Boudiaf, Hocine Aït-Ahmed, Ahmed Ben Bella, Mohamed Khider and Mostefa Lachref) were imprisoned after the plane taking them from Morocco to Tunisia was hijacked by the French secret services on 22 October 1956, a historic first.

B. The University of Algiers, Reflection of a Colonized Algeria

In 1950s Algeria, by far the most part of the academics produced by colonization continued to embody the colonial system. The University of Algiers functioned like a state within the state: '[It] enjoyed virtual intellectual autonomy in relation to the metropolitan universities, with its own hierarchies, local modes of recruitment, and quasi-independent reproduction.'[4] According to Jean Sprecher, heirs to all the nationalist right-wing currents were found in Algeria:

> All the leaders of these right and far-right organizations or groupus-cules had established their bases in Algeria, which had ramifications in the student milieu: the Sidas brothers with Jeune Nation, Biaggi with the Parti Patriote Révolutionnaire, the heirs of Marcel Déat with the Phalange Française, Thomazo, Demarquet, Le Pen of course, Tixier-Vignancourt, Bernard Mamy and many others, always present when a conspiracy was being hatched. On top of these organizations must be added those formed at that time in Algeria, Martel's MPI3, the Pétainist movement of Dr Lefèvre, and the Front National Français (FNF) established by Jo Ortiz. And finally, we cannot avoid mentioning the secret but virulent activity waged within the army by the famous colonels who had made their mission the 'defence of the West', and who either had links with students, or were in a position to establish these at the right moment.[5]

It is possible all the same to distinguish schematically two major currents. On the one hand, a far right made up of Algerian French and French 'from France' (marginalized by the *pieds-noirs*), which dominated the Algiers faculty in the person of Philippe Marçais[6] and developed further with Roger Le Tourneau (inspirer of the colonial clan with all the Arabists: Marius Canard, Henri Pérès, Georges-Henri Bousquet, Jean Servier[7]). On the other hand, a so-called 'left' minority which was structured and dominated by the Communists of the PCA.[8] Both of these officially supported the war. Other tenden-cies were opposed to it, including the Liberals,[9] left-wing Christians, and Communists active on the ground, such as Henri Alleg, who had been tortured by the Parachute regiment and was famous for his denunciation of torture,[10] Maurice Audin, a mathematics lecturer at the University of Algiers, officially listed as disappeared,[11] Fernand Yveton, an employee of Éléctricité Gaz d'Algérie, executed by way of example,[12] and the Ph.D. student Maillot. This climate of extreme tension led to André Mandouze,[13] a historian known for his commit-ment to Algerian independence, being dismissed from the university after having nearly been lynched by his own students. The historian Marcel Émerit, a friend of Bourdieu and author of a book on Emir Abd-el Kader,[14] was hung in effigy by *pied-noir* students, for 'having demonstrated that rates of school attendance in Algeria were higher before 1830 than after'.[15] Other academics, less well known, sought to express an opinion favourable to decolonization, for example Jacques Peyrega (professor of law)[16] and Daniel Ligou (professor of history). This was the context in which Pierre Bourdieu taught, offering his students 'strong and clear ideas' that confirmed them in their progressive position: 'I kept a very vivid memory of the discussion on the Algerian question that we had with Pierre Bourdieu on the beach at Stora. In the context of the time, this was like an oxygen cylinder for us [CEALD[17] students].'

Orientalists with ties to the government were granted a monopoly on the social sciences, simply on the grounds of their knowledge of Arabic; as they saw it, familiarity with the language was all that was needed in order to understand Algerian society. The Marçais family (William Marçais (1872–1956), his son Philippe (1910–84) and his brother Georges (1876–1962) provided typical examples of these Orientalist scholars, 'without any specialist training, who ruled as masters over the Algiers faculty, distributing research topics and representing what was known as colonial ethnology'.[18] The sociologists and ethnologists, most often trained within the institution, were then almost always Arab or Berber linguists, civil administrators, army officers or priests.

The situation was described as follows by Abdelmalek Sayad, Bourdieu's future assistant, who was a psychology student at this time:

> It was a strange situation for a university. To sum up, the teachers broadly divided into two clans with separate powers: one clan that opted for intellectual power and another that leaned more towards political power. The former, more academic, looked rather towards Paris and the Sorbonne, hoping for prestigious support. The latter, more the illegitimate offspring of intellectualism and the university despite their titles, gave the impression of only being there, at the faculty, due to a vexatious compromise: they leaned towards political or administrative power, the side of the Gouvernement Général, and basically that of the colonial order as this was understood and experienced in Algiers (not even as it was represented in Paris), thereby renouncing their intellectual independence, the independence of thought, for colonial recognition as reward or counterpart for their allegiance.[19]

The double dependence on colonial power and metropolitan academia[20] made the task of constructing sociological topics relating to 'Algeria' difficult, especially in the context of a war reduced by colonial propaganda to the status of mere 'events'. Despite the political stand taken by many in the metropolis, on the spot it was impossible to express oneself on Algeria without being immediately exposed to violent reprisals. There were some who managed to conduct ethnological work on Algeria without taking the political situation into account, along the lines of Germaine Tillion[21] – despite her being directly involved in the struggle against poverty in the Aurès – with the establishment of 'social centres' in Algiers in 1955. Sociology was in the grip of some of the most conservative teachers, such as Georges-Henri Bousquet (professor of North African sociology, and leader of the far-right militants),[22] Philippe Marçais, who became a fervent supporter of the OAS,[23] or again Jean Servier (ethnologist and specialist in Berber society who was openly engaged in the service of the French army).[24]

If Jacques Berque held a prominent place[25] for his works of ethnography and sociology devoted to Morocco and Algeria, it was rather Germaine Tillion,[26] a wartime deportee, close to De Gaulle and on Jacques Soustelle's staff,[27] in relation to whom Bourdieu positioned himself in analysing the origins of underdevelopment. He chose as an example Chaouïa society (Tillion's own terrain, situated in the Aurès), which Tillion viewed as an enclosed world whose poverty was ascribed simply to cultural conditions, quite unrelated to colonial policy. Bourdieu did indeed acknowledge Tillion's 'immense merit' of having studied Algerian society in its burning actuality (*L'Algérie en 1957*),[28] because she emphasized the effects produced by rapid social and economic change, but he did not share her explanation of 'misery' in terms of the clash between a 'modern economy' and an 'archaic' culture. In order to acquire its full meaning, this analysis had to be placed in the context of colonialism, whose main policy was to undermine the traditional economy, as could be traced in the major legislation of the nineteenth century (the *sénatus-consulte*, the *loi Warnier*, etc.).

Several intellectuals and high officials[29] were in Algeria at this time, and on terms with the Gouvernement Général.[30] Despite deep disagreements with the policy being followed, certain individuals worked with it, including Émile Dermenghem,[31] archivist and historian of religions, a left Catholic, as well as Germaine Tillion and Louis Massignon,[32] an orientalist who was later elected to the Collège de France, and Vincent Monteil, ethnologist and Islamologist. The prevailing atmosphere there was one of extreme hostility towards the champions of an independent Algeria, as well as towards the great majority of the population: Arabs, Jews, Spaniards, Sicilians and Maltese. In metropolitan France, a number of intellectuals took a stand against the war, but this form of intervention did not satisfy Pierre Bourdieu:[33] 'I was appalled by the gap between the views of French intellectuals about this war and how it should be brought to an end, and my own experience; the army, the embittered "pieds noirs", as well as the military coups, insurrections by the colonizers, the inevitable recourse to de Gaulle, etc.'[34]

2. Pierre Bourdieu's Works in Algeria

A. His Trajectory

Pierre Bourdieu was 25 years old when he set foot in Algeria, in October 1955. He was posted in the Chéliff valley (150 kilometres west of Algiers), in an air force unit of the military staff of the French administration.[35] In early spring of 1956 he returned to Algiers, where he obtained a post with the Service de Documentation et d'Information of the Gouvernement Général, thanks to the intervention of Colonel Ducourneau, a member of Lacoste's staff (who like Bourdieu himself, came from Béarn and was related on the maternal side). Pierre Bourdieu worked initially with Jacques Faugères (a liberal lawyer) and Rolande Garèse, a *pied-noir* teacher who was attached to the same service, directed at that time by Ducourneau. The Gouvernement Général possessed one of the most well-stocked libraries in Algeria. It was here that Bourdieu met Émile Dermenghem and the historian André Nouschi, as well as researchers from the University of Algiers and the Secrétariat Social,[36] such as Henri Sanson.[37] In autumn 1957 he obtained a position at the University of Algeria to teach philosophy and sociology, while continuing to conduct his research on transformations of the urban and rural world, which he pursued in 1958 and 1959.

At the Gouvernement Général, Bourdieu found himself both a 'soldier' and a civilian, a delicate position in view of his status as a 'subversive',[38] since he had refused training at the École d'Officiers de Réserve (EOR), which was expected of students.[39] Nearly 2 million young men did their military service during this period. Many were of peasant and worker origin, the majority with little education.

The majority of conscripts were unaware of the real issues at stake in their mobilization, and believed this was simply an operation to restore order: from one day to the next they found themselves faced with a war situation and a morally dubious combat. For want of information[40] on the situation that prevailed in Algeria, even intellectuals – including those on the left – rallied only belatedly and slowly to the anti-colonial cause. It is true that, ever since conscripts had been sent to Algeria, several dozen young men – whether particularly well-informed or not, had been condemned and imprisoned for refusal to obey, or 'insubordination'.[41] But, as Jean-Marie Domenach explained at the time, 'whatever judgement one makes about the war in Algeria, it has been waged for five years by French governments with the approval of the nation's elected representatives'. If it was relatively 'easy for an intellectual or a political militant to criticize it or refuse it',[42] it was almost impossible for a conscript to adopt a position of refusal. Disobedience meant failing to recognize the established authority, to place oneself in a situation of rebellion against the state. 'How can an attitude that is respected on the part of a career officer be seen as a crime for rank-and-file soldiers, or even – as in Jean Le Meur's case – for conscript officers!'[43]

Whether private soldiers or officers, conscripts directly experienced the war that France was engaged in. This was the case with intellectuals of Bourdieu's generation, among others. 'We wondered what we were heading for. At the end of the day, we were conformist because we had not refused to serve as Le Meur had done, we felt disoriented and uncertain,' Bianco explained.[44] This was a very common reaction among conscript soldiers:

> I remember the time of the 'recallees'. I went out in July [1956] as a recallee. It was horrid when we boarded the train at Nancy. There were riot police all around to make us get into the carriages, as we didn't want to. [. . .] The trains were blocked at the stations, not so much by the recallees, but by civilians preventing the trains from passing. There were even some who'd deserted [. . .]. They left and went into town. The train was blocked and they went off.[45]

The only remaining option for the better informed was passivity and avoiding the battlefield. Hence the attempts to be posted to the civil administration:

> I was posted in the Ouarsenis, on a hilltop where there was nothing, the post had to be built. Basically, people had different jobs. Driving a senior officer's car, or filling in forms in an office in Algiers, was very different from finding yourself in a remote post on the Tunisian border.[46]

Certain jobs were thus sought after, including the most modest ones in the civil administration: cook, technician, bureaucrat, teacher, nurse, orderly, etc. 'Each year, 700 young doctors and 1,300 nurses, to be actively engaged in the SAS [special administrative sections], could be drawn from the conscripts.'[47] It is easy to understand why Bianco and Derrida opted for secondary education:

The colonel in command of the school was looking for a Germanist. Derrida had warmly recommended me. I hadn't done German since the *khâgne* [preparatory class for the École Normale Supérieure]. And then later, Derrida got me a place in Koléa, where there was a school for soldiers' children. From then on everything was easy.[48]

But the fact of not participating in a war that revolted them still did not dispense them from living with a bad conscience: against the war, yet forced all the same to serve a colonial state and 'horrified by the FLN attacks', such were the contradictions experienced by these intellectuals under the colours in Algeria.

B. His Position

In this situation of colonial war, Bourdieu took a stand that was both scientific and political, breaking with what was prevalent among both metropolitan intellectuals and the academics of Algiers. He rejected the cultural distance that the colonizers appealed to in order to legitimize the basically racist attitudes of the European elite. Bourdieu described the difference between these two worlds as a 'clash of civilizations' deliberately provoked by colonization, rather than a confrontation that would enable two cultures enjoying equal status to encounter one another and practise mutual exchange: 'For this traditionalist civilization, the incursion of European civilization posed a radical challenge.'[49]

In his view, the phenomena of social, economic and psychological breakdown had to be analysed as the inevitable result 'of an interaction between "external forces" (incursion of Western civilization) and "internal forces" (original structures of the autochthonous civilization)'.[50] The phenomena of acculturation and deculturation were not the result of an encounter between two civilizations but rather that 'of a particular situation, the colonial situation'. It was beyond doubt that if all cultures are capable of opening themselves to change, the problem consists in the modalities of borrowing or imposition: 'In a normal situation, modifications likely to undermine or destroy fundamental and vital values are repelled, whereas those in conformity with the specific "style" of the "recipient culture" can be accepted and adopted.'[51]

C. Bourdieu's Stance Towards Intellectuals in France

As distinct from many of those who wrote about this period from Paris, Bourdieu was not satisfied with a condemnation of colonial violence based simply on political or moral indignation.[52] His objective, at once scientific and political, was to bring to light the violence exercised by the colonial system, and the social and cultural dysfunctions that it induced. The decision 'to study Algerian society was inspired by an impulse that was civic rather than political'. French people at this time, no matter what their position in relation to Algerian independence, knew very little of the country, a fact that was heavy with consequences.[53] At the same time, Bourdieu attributed his stance to what he called a kind of 'scholastic irresponsibility', without which it would not have been possible to conduct fieldwork in such difficult conditions.[54]

On the basis of this knowledge and his own experience, Bourdieu forcefully voiced in the early 1960s his commitment against the war and in support of independence in a series of texts reprinted in this volume ('War and social mutation in Algeria', 'From revolutionary war to revolution', 'Revolution in the revolution').

The choice of scientific knowledge rather than simply compassion enabled Bourdieu to take the situation of the colonized into account without cherishing the illusions of the militants and their sympathizers (including French intellectuals), who could only see the positive dimension of the Algerian 'revolution' (i.e. the emergence of a dominated nation), and failed to take into consideration the importance of internal struggles within the nationalist camp, and the social and cultural cleavages that were undermining Algerian society from within.[55] These divergences had been manifest since the late 1940s, and their effects were heavy with consequences for the country's cultural and political future.[56] From 1954, dissensions were expressed within the national movement (FLN and Mouvement National Algérien, MNA), and within the Armée de Libération Nationale (ALN), between champions of total armed struggle[57] and those of a negotiated political solution.[58]

Bourdieu's attitude was distinct from that of the metropolitan intellectuals, in that his object was not to encourage post-colonial nation-states in their unconscious project of 'destruction' of their own culture, but on the contrary to help them to view their cultural identity differently:[59]

I would never have come to study ritual traditions if the same concern to 'rehabilitate' which had first led me to exclude ritual from the universe of legitimate objects and to distrust all the works which made room for it had not persuaded me, from 1958, to try to retrieve it from the false solicitude of primitivism and to challenge the racist contempt which, through the self-contempt it induces in its victims, helps to deny them knowledge and recognition of their own tradition. For, however

great the effect of respectability and encouragement that can be
induced, unconsciously rather than consciously, by the fact that a
problem or a method comes to be constituted as highly legitimate in
the scientific field, this could not completely obscure for me the incon-
gruity and even absurdity of a study of ritual practices conducted in
the tragic circumstances of war.[60]

D. The Reception of His Work

At the turn of the 1960s, all that the general public knew of Bourdieu
was his *Sociologie de l'Algérie*, published in 1958 in the 'Que sais-je?'
collection, and two articles brought out by the Secrétariat Social, in
a journal with very limited circulation. These last two were confidential and poorly received. Despite their scientific tone, 'The clash of
civilizations'[61] (the only study from this period that its author never
republished) and 'The internal logic of traditional Algerian civilization',[62] were published by the Secrétariat Social only with reluctance.
Bourdieu's familiarity with the terrain, and with certain Algerian
intellectuals, did not fail to attract the attention of far-right militants
(Ortiz, Lagaillarde, 'ultra' activists who had a grip on the University
of Algiers at this time): Bourdieu was threatened, and forced to leave
Algeria.[63] He had already been noticed by Raymond Aron, who
visited Algiers to preside over the baccalauréat juries. This connection
was renewed in 1959 by the intervention of Clémence Ramnoux,
professor of Greek philosophy, at the time that Bourdieu left the
University of Algiers. Raymond Aron recommended him the same
year to Julian Pitt-Rivers, to take part in an international conference
on the anthropology of the Mediterranean,[64] and took him on as his
assistant at the Sorbonne at the beginning of 1960,[65] before he joined
the faculty of letters in Lille in 1961. At the same time, Bourdieu was
working on a second edition of *Sociologie d'Algérie*, which appeared
in 1961 with one chapter omitted. This standard work which has
gone through at least eight editions, a synthetic analysis of Algerian
cultures and societies, found a resounding echo in milieus favourable
to Algeria both in metropolitan France and abroad, but it aroused
the hostility of the French 'intelligentsia' in Algeria (see 'Letters to
André Nouschi', in this volume).

This position in support of 'committed' research is manifest in
Bourdieu's first publications, particularly in his analysis of the work
of Germaine Tillion (*L'Algérie en 1957*), who also took a stand
against racial discrimination. As distinct from Bourdieu, however, she
saw the causes of what she called 'Algeria's misfortune' as lying in a
lack of education and technical knowledge on the part of its population, which 'prevented it from becoming modern'.[66]

Bourdieu marked his disagreement with the ethnological approach to cultural change developed by Germaine Tillion, writing:

> It seems dangerous to try [like Germaine Tillion] to understand all the phenomena of social breakdown that have occurred in Algeria simply as phenomena of acculturation [. . .]. Thus the major laws on land-ownership were conceived, by their own promoters, as a methodical undertaking to break down fundamental structures of the traditional economy and society. A veritable 'social surgery'[67] which should not be confused with a 'cultural contagion' that is simply the result of contact, these measures (essentially those of cantonment, the *sénatus-consulte* of 1863 and the *loi Warnier* of 1873) were undoubtedly one of the essential causes, if not *the* essential cause, of the disintegration of the traditional rural society: a major enterprise of dispossession of land (legalization, ill-judged sales, etc.), the disintegration of traditional social units (fraction, tribe), the break-up of the family unit as a result of the rupture of undivided property, the appearance of a rural proletariat living in misery, etc. To which must be added the sequestrations that deprived the local population of the best land, expropriations, the forest code; in a different domain, the action of the administration which often forgot its role of arbiter; military service, taxes, etc.[68]

As early as 1958, Bourdieu refuted the thesis of acculturation by drawing on the analyses of Georges Balandier,[69] known at this time for his arguments in support of the self-determination of colonized peoples.

> In actual fact, Balandier notes, this 'contact' is produced by a particular situation, the colonial one: domination by a society that is numerically a minority, but a 'sociological' majority, over an indigenous majority that is technologically and materially inferior; the distance between two societies that coexist without communication; 'economic satellitism'; a system of 'rationalizations' more or less tinged with racism, and designed to justify the privileged situation of the Europeans; and finally either latent tension or open conflict. If contact between a highly industrialized civilization with a powerful economy, and a civilization lacking machinery and with an archaic economy, involving what Germaine Tillion calls 'clumsy benefits and unconscious misdeeds',[70] was sufficient to bring about a disintegration of the structures of traditional society, it remains none the less that on top of these disturbances, inevitable consequence of the contact between two civilizations divided by such an abyss in both the economic and social domains, must be added those transformations deliberately and consciously provoked.[71]

Protected as she was by a past in the Resistance and a longer experience of the Algerian terrain, Germaine Tillion was able to challenge the colonial system in its logic of 'programmed' dismantling[72] of Algerian society. Although he did not hold a high position in the academic field, and did not benefit from any political support, Bourdieu linked up with the approach of Jean Amrouche, active as a journalist at this time, a committed intellectual[73] close to the pro-De Gaulle Catholics. As Amrouche wrote:

> Germaine Tillion based her description of Algeria on sociological considerations, but without any historical perspective. [. . .] This enabled her to avoid speaking of colonial aggression and imperialism, of conquests, massacres, etc. [. . .] She did not ask why Algeria, an archaic country in 1830 like France at the same time, remained archaic in the parts where the Arabs and Berbers have been concentrated: mountains, steppes and deserts. As if the Algerians had deliberately chosen such arid land by a stupid and ignorant choice. [. . .] She did not say that the conquest brought in its wake official colonization, the granting of the richest land to the colonists, the cantonment of the Arabs and Berbers on the poorest lands. The Algerian people were thus not deliberately and systematically impoverished by the colonial enterprise that M. Robert Lacoste upheld in 1957 when he offered loans at low interest to French people who wanted to settle in Algeria. The mechanism of pauperization was part and parcel of the general process set in motion by the aggression of 1830, which Germaine Tillion refuses to consider and describe as such.[74]

E. The Conditions of Investigation in Time of War

In fact, the position that Bourdieu took up owed the greater part of its strength to the fieldwork and investigations that underlay it. With the outbreak of war, the violence that Algerian society suffered took on open and visible form in the countryside, where the army proceeded to massive searches and aerial bombardment. By 1957, however, violence was no longer confined simply to the mountain regions, but reached the urban centres, as with the 'battle of Algiers', when the life of the city's population was punctuated by terrorism and repression.[75] Bourdieu drew on his relationship with Kabyle intellectuals, who practised ethnology without knowing it in the form of 'ethnographic' stories.[76] Mouloud Feraoun, a teacher and later a novelist, murdered by the OAS in 1962, was one of the first to read and annotate Bourdieu's texts on Kabylia; Malek Ouary, a journalist on the Kabyle channel of Radio Algiers, was also one of his informants. But it was Mouloud Mammeri above all, a French-speaking writer and researcher known for his work on Berber literature, who maintained a real intellectual friendship with Bourdieu from 1962 to 1989,[77] especially after independence.[78]

Bourdieu also worked together with officials of the Institut National de la Statistique et des Études Économiques (INSEE).[79] When he began to study the structural foundations of the disarray of Algerian peasants, produced by the colonial violence that was practised particularly in the resettlement camps, he focused first of all on the working and living conditions of Algerian workers in several regions of the country (Algiers, Oran, Constantine, Sidi-bel-Abbès, Mostaganem, Tizi-Ouzou), with a team of INSEE administrators made up of Alain Darbel, Claude Seibel and Jean-Paul Rivet.

Taking advantage of a conjuncture when the French state was issuing various new plans and censuses, Bourdieu carried out two major investigations. One of these focused on the notion of labour in the urban situation, and gave rise to several articles reprinted in the present collection, as well as in *Algeria 1960*, in which investigation of 'the traditional society (attitude towards time and economic behaviour)', first published in 1963, is broadly developed. The other was devoted to the 'uprooted' peasants that Bourdieu observed in the resettlement centres.[80] This study formed the backbone of the book entitled *Le Déracinement*, which takes up again an analysis of the effects of the open and hidden practices of colonial repression. Conceived as a continuation of *Sociologie de l'Algérie*, these sketches (1959–64) actually related to the 1957–63 period.[81]

In parallel with this research, Bourdieu conducted studies of an anthropological kind, the two things being inseparably connected. As he would later write, he wanted to understand the conditions of acquisition of the 'capitalist' economic habitus among people brought up and produced within a pre-capitalist cosmos, 'to resolve purely anthropological problems, especially those that the structuralist approach raised for my work'.[82] This distance he had taken from the structuralist approach was particularly marked in his studies on kinship, and would be spelled out in *The Logic of Practice*. Besides the anthropological structures of Kabyle society, he also set out to describe the social and cultural mutations brought about by the war (and by Algerian independence) ('War and social mutation in Algeria', the two dialogues with Mouloud Mammeri, 'Dialogue on oral poetry in Kabylia' and 'The right use of ethnology', 'For a sociology of sociologists', as well as 'Seeing with the lens: about photography', the interview with Franz Schultheis, all in this volume), which he continued to observe, now with a more distant view and with an emphasis on the reflexive procedure ('Between friends' (2000), 'For

Abdelmalek Sayad' (2000) and 'Participant objectivation' (2000), all in this volume).

Carried out at the request of the Association pour la Recherche Démographique Économique et Sociale (ARDES), and financed by the Caisse Algérienne de Développement, these major investigations of Algerian working life drew on statistics and official documents, but also on interviews, direct observation and photographs. Pierre Bourdieu worked on them with Algerian students, the investigators operating in pairs: an Algerian and a French person, or a man and a woman. Mlle Azi, MM. Azi, Sedouk Lahmer, Ahmed Misraoui, Mahfoud Nechem, Titah and Zekkal, Marie-Aimée Hélie, Raymond Hélie, Raymond Cipolin and Samuel Guedj took part in the first survey, while Abdelmalek Sayad, Alain Accardo and Moulah Hénine joined some of the former in the investigation of resettlement camps.

Bourdieu was convinced that the use of local languages (Algerian Arabic and Berber) was essential, if only to gain the trust of a population suspicious of any investigation on the part of the colonizers – the investigator would often be equated with the gendarme or the policeman.[83] As Alain Accardo recalls, 'Bourdieu had organized his team in pairs that always included at least one Berber speaker. He himself worked together with the sympathetic Sayad, whose smiling good humour and lively intelligence he particularly appreciated.'

On the subject of the conditions in which the study was carried out, Pierre Bourdieu wrote:

> There can be no doubt that the research would have been impossible without official approval, which was indispensable in order to avoid official inquisitions; this was provided by INSEE. Organized in an association of scientific research, statisticians and sociologists had in common the explicit and firm desire to make every effort to seek truth and make it known. It was this contract that bound the person responsible for sociological investigations with the Algerian and French investigators. From the very first day, the problem had been explicitly raised, and everyone understood that, having chosen to make this particular study rather than not do so – the only real choice – it was possible, by way of the concessions indispensable to carrying it out, to do so with all the objectiveness that was desirable. If, despite the brevity of their initiation in investigative techniques and the difficult circumstances in which they had to work, they were able to obtain such vivid and truthful results as can be read here, it was above all because they brought to the research a passionate interest, and felt an attentive sympathy towards their interlocutors. Having chosen, in a difficult and

– if you like – 'impure' situation, to conduct a research from which they expected anything but the confirmation of naive ideologies, they simply fulfilled their task as public scribes, without giving themselves the illusion of accomplishing a historic mission or a moral duty.[84]

It was in these conditions that the census of the Algerian population was begun at the end of 1959. 'Transposing the tools of statistical investigation developed in the context of developed economies', Claude Seibel explained, 'very soon raised a problem, as the underlying concepts that were to be measured (for example work or unemployment) did not have the same meaning in the traditional Algerian economy.'[85] Faced with such difficulties, the INSEE officials then appealed to Bourdieu to shed light from the sociological standpoint. As Abdelmalek Sayad confirms:

> It is a difficult task to work on figures or on the basis of figures, to produce figures, in a society, a social reality, an economy, that essentially does not lend itself to figuring, that cannot be figured and deciphered easily. Statisticians who did not want to be magicians of figuring surrendered to the evidence. We know that popular tradition said of the 'Roumi': they are counters (not to say accountants), measurers, calculators (in both senses of the term), surveyors – they have counted us, measured us, denominated us, etc. [. . .] And statisticians completely fit this stereotype. So they asked us right away to help them, to inform them, to explain to them, to help them understand and penetrate Algerian social reality (likewise that of all Third World societies).[86]

Thanks to a study carried out in the big cities (Algiers, Oran, Constantine) and medium-sized towns (Mascara, Bel-Abbès, Tlemcen), Pierre Bourdieu was able to focus on unemployed people faced with the reality of urban capitalism, and analyse the destructive effects of the war on these unemployed who lacked any control over their conditions: to make their position intelligible presupposed and demanded inquiring into 'the question of the genesis of economic dispositions and the economic and social conditions of this genesis'.[87] The question for Bourdieu was to understand their disarray in the face of a discordance between their positions and their aspirations, and to grasp the sense of disenchantment that possessed them to the point of impelling them to take refuge in the despair of tradition.[88] These peasants in rupture, whom Bourdieu called 'de-peasanted', formed a sub-proletariat crammed together in shantytowns on the outskirts of the big cities.[89] To different degrees, whether of urban origin or not, they lived in the most precarious conditions, and lacked any control over their time and their fate: 'The whole of life is spent under the sign of the provisional. Ill adapted to the urban world they have strayed into, cut off from the rural world and its reassuring traditions, without past or future, they are stubbornly set on forcing change, trying to get a grip on a present that irremediably escapes them.'[90]

Acquaintance with the urban world made it possible to reveal the origins of a sub-proletariat formed in greater part by peasants who had moved to the cities in the wake of the war. Bourdieu interviewed whole families in the kasbah or the shantytowns around the city of Algiers, and went out to the combat zones in order to meet there in the countryside people who had been forcibly resettled, and survived the disaster under military control.

> The massive resettlement of populations in centres located close to military positions was designed to enable the army to exercise direct control over them, to prevent them from informing, guiding, feeding and sheltering the ALN soldiers; this facilitated the conduct of repressive operations, permitting anyone who remained in the forbidden zones to be viewed as a 'rebel'.[91]

This was a measure heavy with consequences, as by seeking 'to prevent the *fellah* [smallholder] from swimming in the sea of the people and finding means of subsistence there, it was decided to destroy the people, destroy each of the sociological units that composed it'.[92] In fact, from 1957 on, the object was to rally populations by using the doctrine of 'revolutionary warfare' developed on the basis of the Indochinese experience and diffused among the general staff. The question now was not simply to combat the ALN, but also to act on the resettled populations in order to convince them to support France. Resettlement was no longer merely the corollary of the creation of forbidden zones, it became a weapon of war, by making it possible to organize and subject populations who were placed in total dependence on the armed forces. Psychological action services could then intervene, particularly by broadcasting messages over a loudspeaker system. As for action on health, economic and social issues, this was no longer seen as humanitarian assistance to be provided temporarily to Algerians displaced by the war, but was inscribed in a strategy aiming to obtain their support.[93]

For those who experienced it, however – more than a million in 1959 alone, people who had not only lost with this displacement their land, their flocks, their fowl, in short all their means of survival,[94] but had also been dispossessed of their whole culture, any chance of personal initiative and any possibility of understanding the world – these camps became immense places of death [*mouroirs*]: 'a child dies every other day in each camp,' Michel Rocard reported (nearly 500 children per day just in the camps that he visited). Jean Amrouche noted even larger numbers (from 1,500 to 2,000) for all the camps on Algerian territory.[95]

It was in this perspective that the resettlement centres were studied over a period of several months (during 1959, and the Easter vacations of 1960 and 1961) by the team that Abdelmalek Sayad belonged to; at this time he was still a student, and coordinated the collection of ethnographic data. His knowledge of the terrain made him a valued informant (when Bourdieu himself visited the Aghbala region in Kabylia), and it was with him that Bourdieu wrote *Le Déracinement*.[96]

As opposed to his articles on economic anthropology, the one devoted to 'Uprooted peasants' (included in the present volume), later reprinted in *Le Déracinement*, was completed at the same time but remained unpublished, owing to a content that was deemed 'explosive'.[97] It would eventually appear in *Études Rurales* in 1964, two years after Algerian independence, thanks to the support of Isaac Chiva, the journal's editor.

This text on the generalized destruction or 'social vivisection'[98] of Algerian society is fundamental for understanding the political import of this scientific research in a time of war. In this study, in fact, Bourdieu sought to shed light on a terrible policy that had been kept secret – begun in 1955 and practised systematically from 1958 – by a military power that defied the laws of the French republic and did not hesitate to wrong-foot the government in the eyes of both French and international public opinion. (The policy of resettlement camps was grossly in breach of human rights.) It was only behind the backs of the local authorities that a young inspector of finances, Michel Rocard, discovered their raison d'être, and his investigation was initially carried out completely in secret, and subsequently partially so. These are the circumstances in which he was informed of the creation and mode of operation of the resettlement camps:

One of my friends, a second lieutenant, drew my attention to 'quite dramatic things: the army is currently displacing populations without any kind of warning, without admitting it, which means that it has no funds allocated, and that tens if not hundreds of thousands of people lose all their possessions. [. . .]' It was absolutely essential to alert the government and General de Gaulle.[99]

These camps, administered entirely by the military authorities, had been kept hidden until Michel Rocard's report in 1959, an extract of which was published – thanks to a leak – in the mainstream press (*Le Monde*, *France-Observateur*), revealing to the broad public the 'deportation' of several thousands of people away from their home environment and depriving them of all their economic resources.

It would be mistaken to believe that such camps were few in number, and resulted only from the desire of zealous officers concerned to restore order. Far from being isolated cases, they were the results of a deliberate policy – to the extent that the term 'genocide'[100] ('children die by the thousand for lack of food') was used without hesitation by Michel Rocard and Jean Amrouche to describe this policy.

> Even accepting that no individual or social body conceived, intended, ordered or executed on the scale of a territory as large as France the enormous enterprise of death that the resettlement camps actually amount to, the result is the same. The enterprise was implacably conducted to the point it has reached, and everything leads us to believe that it is not yet finished. Despite Pontius Pilate-style orders. Everything happens as if it had been intended. People are not killed. They are not made to die. They are simply placed in a situation in which they can no longer live.[101]

The whole of Algeria's territory became a disaster area: by 1 January 1959, according to Ageron, there were no fewer than 936 camps.[102] Their number would rise steeply as the war intensified. For the year 1960, in fact, there were as many as 1,200 in the departments of Orléansville, Algiers, Médéa and Tizi-Ouzo alone.[103] 'The number of Algerians resettled reached 2,157,000, or a quarter of the total population,' wrote Pierre Bourdieu and Abdelmalek Sayad.[104] 'If on top of the resettlements, the exodus to the towns is taken into account, the number of individuals who were away from their usual residence in 1960 can be estimated at a minimum of three million, i.e. half of the rural population. This displacement of population is one of the most brutal in history.'[105] General Parlange himself acknowledged the policy's devastating effects:

> It has to be recognized, in fact, that resettlement often also meant 'uprooting', and was akin to a 'scorched earth' policy – its consequences are severe in human terms, as well as economically and socially, and if we are not careful they are bound to make more uncertain a future that already seemed difficult.[106]

Bourdieu and Sayad reported on these camps that were often enormous. Tamalous had 11,306 inhabitants, Oum Toub 8,000, Kerkera 7,250. They studied different local situations: Kerkera and Aïn-Aghbel (1,500 inhabitants) in the Collo peninsula, a region relatively spared by colonization but strongly acculturated as a result of emigration to France; Djebabra (944 inhabitants) and Matmata in the Chéliff, a region of major colonization; and finally, Barbacha, Djemaâ-Saharidj and Aghbala in Kabylia (the home region of Abdelmalek Sayad).

The most destructive effects of this policy attacked individuals at the deepest level of their identity, in particular destroying their spatio-temporal bearings: 'Many could only prefer the risk of sudden death to being crammed together and subjected to a slow death in straw huts, tents and shanties [. . .] These women rounded up by raids, whose *mechta*[107] were most frequently destroyed, had been forced four or five times out of their village to the camp, but they always headed back to their *douar*.'[108]

Alain Accardo, who took part in this investigation as a student, describes the scientific and political determination of the group of researchers to give an account of the everyday life of the resettled population:

> I do not know exactly what were the personal motivations of each of my companions. For my part, I saw this investigation as an opportunity to participate in an interesting, useful and educational work. I did not know very well how this work might serve the cause of the Algerian people, but I was sure that to trace a truthful picture of the condition of the resettled populations could only contribute in due course to defending their interests, and certainly in a more effective way than the well-intentioned but somewhat sterile activism to which we were reduced in Algiers. A correct view of the actual conditions of existence and work of the Algerian populations was a highly important ideological and political issue. It would certainly have needed hundreds of investigations like those undertaken by Bourdieu to defeat the crushing propaganda of the government.[109] But I was well aware that, by helping Bourdieu to shed light on an important aspect of the Algerian war, I was contributing to the emergence of a truth that was necessarily revolutionary in these circumstances. Since then, I have never believed that sociology should serve any other purpose.[110]

The camps were placed under high surveillance, and not open to the investigators.[111] It was necessary to obtain authorizations both from the administration and the military, and from the indigenous population and its invisible leaders. Jacques Breil, a left-wing Catholic

in charge of the statistics bureau in Algiers, provided the necessary
authorizations, despite certain members of the Gouvernement Général
and ARDES being hostile to Bourdieu. According to Abdelmalek
Sayad, approaches were also made in Paris to obtain scientific and
political support. A French ethnologist – even one collaborating with
members of the INSEE – could not stay in sensitive regions without
running risks (and making others run risks as well):[112] 'When they
arrived, one could say that they were ill received, because an event
took place that is still remembered [. . .]. The director of the Société
des Lièges [cork company] had been killed on the day of their arrival,
500 metres from the special administrative section.'[113]

Any interest taken in the indigenous population resettled by the
army was perceived as an intrusion, and a large-scale study such
as this required a secret mobilization of certain left-wing French
people, certain elements of the administration, such as Rolande
Garèse, and individuals in the government (even if a small minority),
as well as Algerian friends able to collaborate in this kind of undertaking[114] – all the more so as certain regions (such as Collo) had been
declared off-limits.

Any individual foreign to the resettlement centre had to be armed
with a special pass,[115] and to present themselves to the SAS com-
mander[116] who administered the sector, with orders to watch and
protect anyone entering the camp, a fortiori the investigators. The
same held for the occupants, who had to request permission to leave
the camp, and were subject to searches on their return: ' "I'd certainly
like to work my fields . . .", one of them said. But then there's the
control post! I have to leave my identity card with them in order to
leave. And if I should come across soldiers who ask me for my card,
that could be the death of me.'[117]

Proof of sympathy and support for the Algerian cause was also
indispensable if one was to approach the groups to be observed.
Pierre Bourdieu had his own contacts, without which introductions
to families would have been impossible, as official permits were not
sufficient to enjoy security, or, naturally enough, to guarantee relations of trust with those interviewed: 'Our work being officially
authorized by the SAS administrators, we were courteously received
by representatives of the population, who spread the word to collaborate with our team.'[118] In Kabylia, Bourdieu profited from the
assistance of investigators connected with the church, through the
mediation of Father Devulder, an ethnologist and linguist (at Djemâa
Saharidj), and of Abdelmalek Sayad's family (at Aghbala) and families in the Chéraia village: 'I was appointed to introduce them. Because
of my status [as the grandson of a dignitary], people trusted and

welcomed us,' Salah Bouhedja explained.[119] It was clear, as the investigation proceeded, that the implicit acceptance of the group gave a certain protection vis-à-vis the military.[120] In certain villages in the Collo region, in the absence of families prepared to receive them, the team chose to sleep in the former primary school rather than in the premises proposed by the SAS.[121]

The direct observation conducted in these regions marked strongly by the war (Collo, Kabylia, Ouarsenis) amounted to a challenge, and presupposed a developed strategy. Scientific and political authorizations were only a screen to deflect the attention of the local administrators from the real project:

> In fact, as Bourdieu explained to us, it was probably not the official members of the council established by the SAS who had taken the decision to spur their fellow-citizens to cooperate with us. These official representatives, accepted by the French administration and very often appointed by it as intermediaries with the population, actually served as a camouflage for the clandestine council, the 'underground *djemaa*',[122] which, here as in many other parts of a region closely patrolled by the French army, governed the civilian population according to the directives of the FLN. As a result of the goodwill that was extended to us, even if this was only indifference, we did not face any display of hostility at any time during our stay. That however did not prevent some of our number, aware that we found ourselves at the heart of one of the bastions of the 'rebellion', from fearing an ALN attack against the SAS. I have to admit that this would have been a rather uncomfortable situation, to find ourselves caught in the crossfire between a *katiba de moudjahidin* on the one hand and the SAS *harka* on the other. Very fortunately, we were spared this.[123]

The roads were often blocked (apart from the Algiers–Oran axis) as a result of attacks, and both vehicles and trains moved under military escort. As Alain Accardo indicates in a written testimony, relating these exceptional conditions of access to the terrain in 1960:

> When the Easter holidays arrived, the whole team was transported to the Collo region in Kabylia, where there was a major resettlement of the rural population. I do not know whether the big 'operation Jumelles' (1959–60), a broad military operation of 'pacification' which had been conducted the previous summer in Kabylia by General Challa, with enormous resources, had also 'pacified' the region to which we were going. At all events, the ALN must have still been very active in Little Kabylia, and it was only possible to move around in a convoy under military protection. Bourdieu chose therefore to gather us together first of all in Philippeville, which it was possible to reach

by fairly secure routes, and then to proceed to Collo by sea, hugging the coast on board a large motor-launch. This sea excursion, in magnificent weather, would have been really enchanting in different circumstances. But I believe that all of us were tense.

Bourdieu would later comment on these 'extraordinarily difficult (and risky) conditions', but they also had the effect of 'sharpening one's gaze, by the continuous vigilance they imposed'. Thus even the most ordinary problems that conducting the investigation constantly raised in this tragic situation spurred the team to 'a permanent reflection on the reasons and rationales of the study' and 'on the motivations and intentions of the researcher'.[124]

This research in time of war recorded a tragic situation in which there were few works of ethnology or sociology in a position to analyse such radical processes of social destruction. As Maurice Halbwachs had already written:

War does more than overstimulate national passions. War transforms society profoundly, slackening or paralyzing some of its functions and creating or developing others. In particular, it simplifies the structure of the social body and greatly reduces the differentiation of its parts, as Spencer said [. . .] This would also be true of revolutions, however, and perhaps even of periods of political agitation when, to external appearance, there has been no change in the structure of the social body. The functions, undoubtedly, remain the same and continue to hold sway. Tradesmen, workers, officials and peasants remain in place. However, their thought is elsewhere. Their lives, familial, professional, and friendship, continue, but with much more automatism and much less involvement of self. All activity that is not political in character finds itself, therefore, likewise reduced.[125]

It is these changes that the present *Algerian Sketches* analyse. They describe a world in chaos, a society whose values and representations have been destroyed in a violent fashion, and they therefore make a major contribution to the sociology of Algeria. This very particular situation (bound up with the war and its consequences) paradoxically sharpened the gaze of the sociologist who, through constraint and risk, sought to grasp the structures of a social world threatened with losing its collective memory.

Paris, 28 September 2007

Algerian Sketches

Colonization, Culture and Society

The Clash of Civilizations

For this traditionalist civilization, the incursion of European civilization posed a radical challenge. Any cultural change takes place in a particular situation, in conformity with universal laws. It is clear that the phenomena of acculturation observed among the North American Indians were radically different from those in black Africa, as far as their particular situations were concerned: the 'adventitious cultures' were no less different from one another, in their mindsets, their modes of action, etc., than were the 'recipient cultures', each of which likewise had its specific structure. Moreover, the style of relations between the two can be very varied, from the colonial situation through to simple technical aid, from a more or less thorough policy of assimilation through to the policy of 'reservations'. It is possible to propose, however, at least as a hypothesis, that the principles governing the phenomena brought about by contact are universal ones.

1. Some Methodological Remarks

Before analysing the original situation in which the phenomena of acculturation and deculturation observable in Algeria take place (i.e. the nature of the civilizations involved and the relationship between them), the concepts to be used in this analysis must be spelled out.

Redfield, Linton and Herskovits propose the following distinctions:

Acculturation comprehends those phenomena which result when groups of individuals having different cultures come into continuous first-hand contact, with subsequent changes in the original cultural patterns of either or both groups. Under this definition, acculturation is to be distinguished from *culture-change*, of which it is but one aspect, and *assimilation*, which is at times a phase of acculturation. It is also to be differentiated from *diffusion*, which, while occurring in all instances of acculturation, is not only a phenomenon which frequently takes place without the occurrence of the type of contact between peoples specified in the definition given above, but also constitutes only one aspect of the process of acculturation.[1]

Every culture allows greater or lesser room for change; the alternatives that civilizational contact proposes and generates are decided and resolved as a function of the system of values established in the 'recipient culture', with the result that, in a normal situation, modifications likely to disrupt or destroy fundamental and vital values are repelled, whereas those in conformity with the specific 'style' of the 'recipient culture' can be accepted and adopted. So long as this selection can be exercised, the 'culture' maintains its equilibrium and preserves its originality; the allogenic elements capable of being borrowed are selected and reinterpreted according to its fundamental norms. In the contrary case, the fundamental values themselves may be disrupted and the culture's vital norms shattered, leading to a more or less catastrophic disintegration of the cultural ensemble, which we shall call *deculturation*.

The general laws of the phenomena of acculturation (the laws of unequal rates of change, reinterpretation of borrowed elements, change of scale and change of frame of reference)[2] operate in an original context, that is, 'a global and plural society' whose elements (the autochthonous society, itself plural, and European society) must be studied in so far as they participate in the same ensemble where a complete reciprocity of perspectives obtains.

As a consequence, the phenomena of social, economic and psychological disaggregation must, it seems, be understood as resulting from an interaction between 'external forces' (incursion of Western civilization) and 'internal forces' (original structures of the autochthonous civilization). This interaction is effected within a field whose originality cannot be overlooked without the risk of missing, at the same stroke, the very essence of the phenomena studied. In fact, acculturation and deculturation are not simply the result of the contact of civilizations when this contact is produced by a particular situation, that of colonialism.[3]

If it is the great merit of Germaine Tillion to have been one of the first in the field of Algerian sociology not to turn her back on the contemporary situation, it still remains that her analyses, to have their full force, must be situated in the context that we have defined. No doubt the Aurès society, which is the basis of her study,[4] never knew either a doctor, a colonist or a government official, with the result that the economic and social disaggregation that is observed there may be described as the apparent effect of the clash between an archaic economy and a modern one that is highly specialized and competitive. But besides the fact that it is impossible to extend conclusions that are partially valid for the Aurès, an isolated territory relatively closed in on itself, to the whole of Algerian society, it seems incontestable that Chaouïa society, like other autochthonous societies, is caught up in the colonial situation. It is in this context that Germaine Tillion's analysis acquires its full truth.

Let us first of all recall her analysis in very summary terms. The equilibrium of Chaouïa society, based on a system of complex regulations (repetitions of the same structural schema in the different domains of the cultural system), has been destroyed under the action of a variety of factors: first among these, a demographic upsurge brought about by an increase in fertility and a decline in mortality; second, the exhaustion of cultivable land that is worked more intensely in order to feed a constantly increasing population; and finally, the transition from a barter economy to a market economy. The pendulum movement described by Marc Bloch ruins every economic equilibrium; the peasant whose needs are greater than his liquid assets is forced to sell as soon as the harvest is completed; as a result, he is prey to the seasonal fall that follows the harvest and sells cheaply – the quantity sold being all the greater, the lower the prevailing price. He is also forced to buy grain or bread in January or February, that is, at the time when prices are very high. As a victim of these seasonal price fluctuations, he is forced to get into debt or, if there is no other recourse, to sell his land and go off to seek work far away. We must add to these causes the role of the school, which embitters those who have received education and aggravates the situation of the others, unbalancing the family milieu, with women most commonly remaining illiterate, which leads to generational conflicts and the collapse of the traditional teachings that underlie the old psychological and social structures. To sum up, in this analysis all the phenomena of disaggregation are simply the result of the laws of acculturation.

In reality, other causes have also played a part: the *sénatus-consulte*, to take one example, divided the Touaba territory (Oued el

Abiod) into three *douars* (Tighanimine, Labiod, Ichmoul), and allocated the lands of the high valley to individual possession, leading to a movement of population towards Medina and Foum Toub, where groups settled down and built farms; on top of this, the facilities provided by the *sénatus-consulte* tended to transform joint possession into individual property. In the absence of an improvement in techniques and an extension of cultivable land, the transition from joint possession to individual property leads to impoverishment. Settlement and the individualization of property weaken collective ties. The collective granary (*guelâa*), which in a way symbolized the cohesion of the primary group (fraction), steadily loses its significance; more precisely, the different meanings with which it was invested tend to become dissociated. Thus, at Tabentut, the former collective store is still maintained,[5] and the spring festival is celebrated there; but despite preserving its meaning as a sacred place, it no longer receives the group's reserves as it did in the past. The family surveillance implied by the existence of the collective granary falls to individuals, who add individual grain-stores to their dwellings, sometimes reusing for this purpose beams taken from the *guelâa*. Similarly, the traditional measure, which was preserved in the collective granary and was used only within the group, is replaced by the commercial 5 litre measure. If the gradual abandonment of the collective granary, the foundation and guarantee of economic equilibrium – which in a self-sufficient and closed society could be ensured only by a real asceticism that tended to reduce needs to the measure of resources and enabled good harvests to be distributed over time – is explained partly by the transition from an exchange economy to a monetary economy in which the existence of substantial reserves is no longer necessary, it is also explained by the appearance of economic individualism, bound up in large part with the appearance of individual property, which is itself a consequence of the application of the *sénatus-consulte*, and with the weakening of collective sanctions.

Besides, if the Aurès was the centre of an especially marked particularism, it also functioned, as has been rightly remarked, 'as a sounding box in which waves sent out from any point in Berber territory were echoed, and often even amplified if the local vibrations were in synchrony'.[6] This is why the reforming propaganda of the disciples of Ben Badis,[7] which undoubtedly found favourable terrain in a society in the process of disaggregation, was able to create a real 'insurrectionary climate' in 1938 by brandishing such notions as injustice, rights, and independence. This seems enough to show that Algeria did not contain any genuine isolated part living sealed off and completely removed from the colonial situation.

2. Algeria's Particular Situation

It follows from these analyses that, if the causes of 'underdevelopment' may be purely natural (imbalance between population and resources, for example), or may lie in a lack of technical equipment or concentration of capital, what François Perroux[8] calls 'the domination effect' cannot be neglected, that is, the ensemble of economic phenomena brought about directly or indirectly by contact between two economic systems of unequal strength. This domination effect, which consists in 'an irreversible or partially reversible influence' exercised by one unit over the other, tending to place the dominated economy in a position of 'economic satellitism' at the same time as ensuring a constant improvement in the situation of the dominant economy, constitutes one of the essential aspects of the colonial situation.

But we should guard against viewing the economic domain in isolation. Any attempt at analysis would be arbitrary here: in fact, the phenomena of economic disaggregation are simply an aspect of that great movement of deculturation and disaggregation affecting Algerian society as a whole. This society, which as we have seen constitutes a totality whose elements are indissociable, all expressing the same original 'style', has been struck by another civilization that has not made its incursion piecemeal, here and there, but as a *totality*, producing upheavals not just in the economic order but also in the social, psychological, moral and ideological orders; presenting, in short, a total and radical challenge.

This creates an almost inextricable reality, in which it is impossible to isolate causes and effects otherwise than by abstraction and for convenience of analysis, since each effect becomes cause in its turn, and so on, with the result that each of the phenomena that could be described as a (provisional) 'terminal point' of the disaggregation process is the culmination of a bundle of extremely varied causes, each of which is itself a culmination.

To give one example: the emergence of the individual, removed from family and tribal units, is bound up with the disaggregation of the family and the tribe, itself inseparable from the general evolution of Algerian society; from wage-labour and the imperatives of the modern economy; from the weakening of the system of traditional values as a result of contact with the system of Western values; from schooling and generational conflict; emigration and urbanization; the new status of property, etc.

And so it is European civilization in the totality of its aspects that has made its incursion into the heart of the autochthonous

civilization. As distinct from mere technical help leading to a circumscribed and limited intervention, the colonial situation, and especially
so in Algeria, owing to the numerical importance of the European
society, brings about a confrontation of two 'styles of life', two views
of the world, two attitudes towards the fundamental problems of
existence. The European, in fact, brings his universe with him; he
imposes his own order on the outside world, as we can see, to take
only one example, in the colonial villages that reproduce those of
metropolitan France; he offers in each element of his behaviour, each
one of his words, a whole system of values, and in this way presents
the bearers of traditional civilization with unlimited alternatives; he
thus makes what had seemed necessary appear as contingent, what
had seemed 'natural' appear as an object of choice.

3. A Complex Problem

The problem of cultural change, 'with its procession of painful dramas
and bitter disappointments' (Hamza Boubekeur),[9] is extremely
complex. Yet it is only in the quite recent past that study of civilizational contact has held the attention of sociologists. The problem was
tackled in a certain way by the officials of the Bureaux Arabes,[10]
though they did not seem in a position to master its complexity.

Because of this, the essential elements in the problem of cultural
change have been ignored, along with its mechanisms and its solutions. And on top of this ignorance due to the very complexity of the
problem must certainly be added that resulting from differing and
often diverging reasons or motivations, in lived attitudes and human
relations as well as in political conceptions and measures bearing on
Algeria. Perhaps it also rests on ignorance of the fact that the world
of the Maghreb is the site of an original civilization, inspired by an
original logic.

If contact between a highly industrialized civilization with a powerful economy, and a civilization without machinery and endowed
with an archaic economy, would be enough on its own to give rise
to a disintegration of the traditional structures of Algerian society,
it remains none the less that on top of these disturbances, the
inevitable consequence of the clash of two civilizations separated
by an abyss in both the economic and the cultural domain, one
must add, without confusing them, the upheavals brought about by
the pursuit of economic interests, and those provoked by the establishment of heterogeneous institutions that pay no attention to
sociological realities.

One of the promoters of the *sénatus-consulte* of 1863 declared that the object of this measure was to 'provoke a kind of general liquidation of the land',[11] so that one part would remain 'in the hands of the Arabs, no longer as the collective inheritance of the tribe, but by way of personal property, defined and divided', the other being destined to 'attract and receive emigration from Europe'; and more profoundly, to 'disorganize the tribe', this being the chief obstacle to pacification. The laws on landownership (cantonment, the *sénatus-consulte* of 1863, the *loi Warnier* of 1873), a veritable operation of 'social surgery' which should not be confused with a cultural contagion that is simply the consequence of contact, certainly constitute one of the major causes of the disintegration of the traditional rural society. By the break-up and sale of collective property, as well as by facilitating ill-considered sales, they triggered a large-scale movement of dispossession of land, also leading to the disappearance of traditional social units (fraction and tribe), these being replaced by abstract and arbitrary administrative units, the *douars*, an approximate transposition of the municipal entity of metropolitan France, and tending to break up a precarious economic equilibrium of which joint possession formed one of the best guarantees.

Those forced to experience the effects[12] of these measures were aware that they would fundamentally undermine the essential norms of their society: joint possession, in fact, firmly maintains the community's cohesion, making it possible to defend the integrity of the family or tribal inheritance and hence the integrity of these groups against excessive fragmentation, foreign intrusion, and the absorption of small parcels of land by large farms. By uniting all the resources and forces that the group has at its disposal, joint possession makes it possible to achieve the best adaptation to the natural environment and to guarantee the subsistence of individuals who would not be able to live from the tiny plot that a break-up of common property would grant them. Finally, it protects the collectivity against individual improvidence or carelessness, by making it possible to impose a strict discipline on both consumption and production. It really is a cornerstone, and the legislation designed to destroy it inevitably set in motion the ruin of the cultural edifice as a whole.

The example of agrarian policy is particularly characteristic, as we see clearly displayed here all the ambiguities, even contradictions, inherent in certain of the measures taken in Algeria. In fact, if the basic laws were conceived (at least the *sénatus-consulte*) as a war machine designed to disaggregate political and economic units that were viewed as dangerous, there is no doubt that they could also acquire a different meaning and fit into an assimilationist and 'liberal' perspective. In the logic of the modern economy, joint possession appears as an absurd archaism, an obstacle to progress and the modernization of technique, given that it binds the *fellah* to routine by forbidding any future-oriented undertaking on the land and by discouraging credit.

The promoters of the cantonment policy, holding that private ownership with precise and clearly defined boundaries, in contrast to joint possession with uncertain boundaries, should form the basis of peasant life, thus sought to bring this about because they saw it as the condition for 'all social and agricultural improvements' and 'the most certain foundation for the assimilation of the two peoples' (Marshal Vaillant, cited by Xavier Yacono[13]). It was in the name of this doctrine, in a report of 18 May 1884, that Marshal Vaillant demanded the cantonment of tribes settled on collective lands. He saw this measure as 'an equitable transaction', since, while it removed a part of their territory from tribes viewed as holding a usufruct, it 'substituted for their mere right of usage an unassailable right of property on the part of territory that is assigned to them'. In reality, apart from the fact that the 'overabundance of space' deemed to justify seizing from the tribes a part of their inheritance was in a sense required by the traditional type of land use and constituted a key element of the economic system, it was highly dangerous to allocate private property of land to individuals deprived of the psychological structures and 'virtues' that are not only its foundation, but its very condition of possibility. Handing the *fellah* French-style property titles was to offer him the opportunity, the possibility and the temptation to give up his holding. The result was that this measure – just like the *sénatus-consulte* of 1863[14] and the *loi Warnier* – achieved a radically different purpose from that which was supposedly intended, since, aiming at creating individual possession, it became an instrument of dispossession.

4. Cultural Reality

It would be easy to give more examples of such interventions, which take no account of the coherent and concrete reality. Cultural anthropology seeks to spell out the conditions in which 'cultural transactions' are effected, and to define their laws in order to guard against the dangers of regression, disturbance and degeneration that bringing two civilizations of unequal development into confrontation threatens to provoke. It attempts to offer the means to brake and control, as far as is possible, the chain reactions that the mere introduction of new industries or new methods of cultivation can trigger.

This attitude implies that society should be viewed as a coherent and adapted system, as a positive reality, instead of bracketing it out or ignoring it. In Algeria, however, like the clumsy butcher in Plato's metaphor who cuts meat without following its natural articulations, the attempt has sometimes been made to establish an imported and imposed order without regard to the articulations, muscles and tendons that ensure the balance and life of Algerian society. It has been too much forgotten or ignored that culture forms a particular way of viewing existence, proposed from birth to each member of the community, not being the work of any one of them even though it only exists through them; that it is inspired by an original and unique 'spirit' in which all participate, at the same time as they constitute it in and by their common life; that it is inhabited by an 'intention' (or, if you prefer, a choice) laid down like a sediment, a preconscious intention, lived and acted before being conceived as such by the individuals involved, in the same way as language.

The cultural system is thus at the same time condition of existence and justification for existing. It is the *condition of existence* in so far as, while the structure and meanings of the culture may remain unknown to those who live it, and give rise to rationalizations and secondary elaborations, it models individual behaviour by proposing frameworks and patterns, at the same time as forming its condition of intelligibility; as a result, it is the mediation that permits two individuals to ascribe the same meaning to the same behaviours, and makes possible intersubjective communication by establishing a network of common meanings and relationships, independent of the differences that divide individuals. It is the *justification for existing*, in so far as every group – as is seen for example in the distinction between the 'in group' and the 'out group', the basis of ethnocentrism – posits, besides the vital values whose positing is contemporary with the very existence of the society in question (for example the values of solidarity in North African society), a system of values by which the group teaches itself and invites itself to be what it in fact is, with the result that every society worships itself in its own system of values, despite the fact that, in Mauss's expression, 'it always pays in the false coin of its dream'. When this mechanism of self-justification no longer operates, the society finds itself threatened or attacked in its most valuable possession. The incursion of a different civilization that proposes a different idea of life, a different system of values, leads to the discovery that this style of life, this cultural system that appears to itself as the best possible, the only one possible, providing each individual with the conviction that he has to be what he is, is in reality only one among a limitless number of possibilities. Hence the anxiety and disarray that haunt above all the 'marginal man', cast into the conflicts brought about by the weakening of traditional systems of sanctions and the duality of rules of life.

In sum, political action, more or less conscious, more or less blind, was exerted in Algeria *in the same direction* as the laws of acculturation whose action it precipitated and whose efficacy it increased instead of braking or moderating it. In this way, it went as it were in the direction of history, hastening the disintegration of traditional social structures and the suspending of those regulations that ensured the equilibrium of the traditionalist economy. Is it any surprise that Algerian society, which would have experienced in any case certain dangerous transformations, should have been caught up in a kind of dizzying whirlwind that becomes ever harder to control from one day to the next?

To be adequate to its object, the description of this totality in movement must be global, given that the phenomena of disaggregation and reintegration are all inseparably connected, with the result that the phenomena of disaggregation observable in the economic domain form only one aspect of a multidimensional reality. Among the factors of disequilibrium, we need only recall the demographic explosion, the dispossession of land, the competition of the modern-type economy. Hence a certain number of features too frequently described to need any insistence here: the decline of nomadism and semi-nomadism, the decline of handicrafts, the reduction in the standard of living, underemployment and non-employment, the appearance of a new kind of proletariat 'deemed both good for any jobs and unfit for any' (Dresch),[15] cast into material misery and moral disarray as a consequence of the undermining of vital values, emigration, etc. It should equally be stressed that, with the transformation of the legal regime of property that facilitates sale, all regulations that tended to preserve equilibrium on the land, 'regulating levers' such as joint possession, tend to lose their effectiveness. Moreover, the predominance of economic and particularly monetary values convulses an order based on human and personal relationships. For example, the old clientele tie that bound the landowner and the *khammès* [sharecropper] is broken: either the traditional advances made are viewed as loans for consumption and repayment is demanded, so that the *khammès*, no longer finding any advantage here, prefers wage-labour; or the old system is maintained but, although the situation is objectively identical to how it was previously, everything is changed in reality (law of change in the frame of reference).

Another important phenomenon is the appearance of wage-labour, the impersonal relationship between capital and labour. The agricultural worker freed from his family or his tribe, a character unknown in the old society, receives a regular wage in ready money, something that was previously rare. The colonist with his technology, his sense of work and of property, of land treated as raw material, private property and the notion of boundary, brings about a veritable transformation of values. The *fellah* sees the land shrink at the same moment as he discovers its price. The old values of prestige and honour are replaced by impersonal and abstract money value. Competition and adaptation in the world of the modern economy demand new psychological structures (work, money, savings, credit, etc.), lack of which leads to tremendous difficulties of adaptation. Economic individualism appears and, along with other causes, tends to break the old living solidarities and burst the community frameworks.

Closed-off economic units, which lived in almost total self-sufficiency, break up under the action of a number of causes. The contraction of economic space brings about a contagion of needs and a raising of the level of aspiration, more rapidly by far than the transmission of the techniques and psychological structures that are the foundation of modern economic activity, and more rapidly too than the increase in the possibilities of satisfying these new aspirations and needs – unequal rates of change that give rise to a situation of conflict. The same cause also arouses an awareness of inequalities and the birth of a spirit of demand or revolt. The consequence in the economic domain of the phenomena of social disintegration brought about by urbanization, emigration, proletarianization, generational conflicts, the crisis of moral education, etc. must also be emphasized.

5. The Conditions for a Restructuring

In order to be compelling, the present analysis would need to be less hasty. Yet some conclusions immediately suggest themselves. There can be no doubt that an effort limited to the economic domain is not sufficient to restore the equilibrium of a society in which economic deregulation is only one aspect of the collapse of the cultural system as a whole. François Perroux has shown[16] how a policy consisting of increasing overall expenditure with injections of funds designed to stimulate consumption and finance investment does not give the same results when applied to underdeveloped countries as can be achieved in a capitalist economy. This is because such a policy has to take account of 'structural factors' inseparable from the style of the civilization in question (for example non-employment).[17] Capital, as S. H. Frankel observes, is 'a social inheritance that depends on the institutions and the traditional modes of thought and action of individuals in a society'.[18] As a result, capital transferred from one society to another must be readapted to new types of behaviour, and its rational utilization presupposes the creation of new aptitudes and new structures.

Sociological analysis of underdeveloped countries suggests the need to develop a non-Keynesian economic theory that would be to Keynesian economics, valid for the case of the West, what non-Euclidean geometries are to Euclidean geometry.

Economics goes inherently together with a view of the world and a style of life; it would accordingly be supremely vain and dangerous to claim to govern a society or advise it without possessing a profound knowledge of its customs, its structures, and the spirit that inspires it. Secondly, an industrialization effort alone is not sufficient; on the contrary, the establishment of industries in an economically underdeveloped country and a society based on custom is likely to provoke tensions and aggravate disaggregation. It is certain, however, that reaching a certain minimum economic level that assures individuals an indispensable minimum hold on the world is the necessary condition for the psycho-cultural conversion by which they take their own destiny in hand. Pierre Moussa relates the following observation made in a North African factory.[19] Wages were increased by 20 per cent, and following the logic of the pre-capitalist mind, the employees worked a fifth less; wages were then more than doubled (i.e. to 240 per cent of the original), and the consequences of this increase were the opposite of those ensuing from the previous raise: as if a threshold had been crossed (Pierre Moussa writes of a 'threshold of modernity'), the workers showed the desire to work, to earn more, to provide for the future, to save, etc. Thus, as a function of a single feature, but essential as a necessary condition, that is, possession of a minimum of assurance concerning the future that gave freedom from an exclusive and obsessive concern for subsistence, the whole of the cultural system, and economic behaviour in particular, was totally *restructured*, along with the values and mental structures underlying it.

Should we conclude that improvement in material conditions alone is a necessary and *sufficient* condition for an overall restructuring of the cultural system that would ensure the transition from traditionalist economy to competitive economy? We rediscover here the old debate between materialism and spiritualism. Is material progress enough to arouse the aspiration to progress, or is the aspiration to progress rather a necessary and sufficient condition for progress? The answer seems to be that the progress of material conditions allows individuals to reach a threshold on the basis of which they *can* aspire to take possession of their future; but possibility does not mean necessity. We could say, distorting Aristotle's words, that 'the virtues of the competitive economy desire a certain ease'.

What is striking is that the transition from one logic to the other is not effected simply by summation and addition of cultural features accumulated in experience, but rather that the additive accumulation of experience only makes possible a restructuring that will re-establish equilibrium between man and his world at a different level. It follows from this that it is only possible to promote this restructuring by an overall assistance, involving equally the domains of economy, social life, political life, education, etc. In order for this transition, which might be compared with the 'turning' of a dye-stuff, to be made without obstacle or injury, the necessary conditions must be brought together, that is, people must be assured this minimum of power needed for them to be able to have wants, as well as the sufficient conditions, that is, the creation or development of those psychological virtues that give people the will to want.

Traditional Society's Attitude towards Time and Economic Behaviour

Despite the fact that it does not express a universal regularity of economic activity, the theory of marginal utility displays a fundamental characteristic of modern societies, the tendency to rationalization that affects all aspects of economic life. As Max Weber wrote:

> The specific character of the capitalist epoch, and – the one following from the other – the importance of the theory of marginal utility (as of any theory of value) for the understanding of this era, consists in the fact that, just as it is not without reason that the economic history of more than one past era has been called 'the history of non-economics', so, under present conditions of life, the convergence between this theory and life was, is, and as far as can be judged, will be increasingly great, and will shape the fate of ever wider strata of humanity. The heuristic significance of the theory of marginal utility lies in this *historico-cultural* fact.[1]

The recent development of Algerian society is one aspect of this historico-cultural fact; the process of adaptation to the capitalist economy that can be observed here reminds us of what reflection confined to our own societies can lead us to forget, that is, that the functioning of an economic system presupposes the existence of a definite system of attitudes towards the world and towards time. It follows that, if the description of the perfected capitalist system may be confined to its exclusively objective properties, for example rationalization and predictability, it remains true that, in the case of Algeria and societies in the course of development, where the system pre-exists the attitudes that it demands, concrete economic consciousness must be the first object of our analysis. In our own societies, because the economic system and attitudes are in almost perfect harmony, with rationalization steadily expanding even into the household economy, there is a tendency to ignore the fact that the economic system presents itself as a field of objective expectations which can only be met by subjects endowed with a certain kind of economic consciousness and, more broadly, of temporal consciousness. It follows that a situation that is defined by a conflict between a system that proposes or imposes itself, and individuals who have no preparation for grasping its underlying intention, invites reflection on the conditions of existence and functioning of the capitalist system, that is, on the structures of economic consciousness that are both promoted in fact by the system and demanded by it.

Indeed, nothing is more foreign to economic theory, which claims to be based on the attitudes of the economic subject, than the concrete economic subject: far from economics being a branch of anthropology, anthropology is seen here as no more than an appendix to economics, and homo economicus, a fictional creation endowed with faculties corresponding to the characteristic properties of the capitalist system, is the result of a form of a priori deduction that tends to find confirmation in experience, at least in the limiting case, because the economic system in the process of rationalization tends to fashion subjects in conformity with its expectations and demands. From this time on, when it is implicitly or explicitly asked what economic man has to be for the capitalist economy to be possible, the categories of economic consciousness specific to the capitalist tend to be treated as so many universal categories, independent of economic and social conditions; correlatively, there is a risk of ignoring both the collective and the individual origin of the structures of economic consciousness. Inspired by a monist rationalism, has economic theory not always been implicitly what it is tending to become, that is, a branch of a general praxeology, a formal science of choice?[2]

In societies on the path of development, discordance between objective structures and attitudes is such that the construction of an appropriate economic theory might well presuppose renouncing, in this case at least, the project of deducing anthropology from economics, the individuals from the system. Choosing to study the laborious process of adaptation of individuals to the capitalist system and their assimilation of the categories that are part and parcel of this, it is clearly impossible to ignore the fact that these phenomena only acquire their full meaning by reference to this system and to what makes for its specific character, that is, the relationship of domination that forces the colonized to adopt the law of the colonizer, whether in economics or indeed in style of life.

Adaptation to any economic and social order presupposes a set of empirical skills transmitted by education, whether general or specific, skills that are practical and implicit, like using the mother tongue, rather than explicitly conceived, and are integral with an ethos, that is, a 'wisdom' that is not established and unified as such. It is this acquisition that makes it possible for the individual to act in a reasonable way and with chances of success within his own society. This is why adaptation to an economic and social organization that tends to ensure predictability and calculability, that is, economic rationality first and foremost, requires a definite attitude towards time and, more precisely, towards the future, the rationalization of economic conduct presupposing that the whole of existence is organized in relation to an absent vanishing point, abstract and imaginary. The structure of temporal consciousness, and its corresponding ethos, appear, in the case of capitalist society, as the foundation of economic behaviour that is reasonable and capable of ensuring success. This is why it seems necessary to analyse, even summarily, the structure of temporal consciousness that is associated with the traditional economy: besides being indispensable in order to understand the process of adaptation to the capitalist economy and, more precisely, to explain its slowness and difficulties, this description, by requiring the suspension of all presuppositions, will also enable us to grasp the essential significance of the temporal consciousness specific to the man of our own societies dominated by the principle of rationalization.

Foresight and Prediction

If it is true that nothing is more foreign to Algerian society than the idea of a wide-open future, as a field of countless possibilities that it is up to human strength or calculation to explore and master, must we conclude, as is too often done, that the *fellah*, a kind of *mens momentanea* trapped in immediate attachment to the directly perceived present, is incapable of envisaging what may come about in the distance? Must we see in his submission to duration simply an abandonment to the vagaries of climate, the caprices of nature and the decrees of providence? But how to explain that distrust of any attempt to take possession of the future can coexist with the foresight needed to distribute the fruit of a good harvest sometimes over several years? How to explain that prediction and project are almost explicitly viewed as a presumption, a diabolical excessiveness and ambition, even though the whole tradition exalts foresight?

'Act as if you were to live forever, act as if you were to die this moment': that proverb captures one aspect of the contradiction that has to be understood, since it exalts at the same time both foresight and submission to duration. Can foresight be identified, in its foundation and its purpose, with prediction? Does building up reserves really mean facing the future, waging an assault on it, or rather constructing a defensive position, preparing for a state of siege? What is the meaning and the function of this accumulation? It is apparent, first, that the goods put by are above all destined for consumption. Secondly, while products of the soil, such as wheat or barley, may be treated either as direct goods, that is, offering or being able to offer immediate satisfaction, or else as indirect goods, that is, contributing to the preparation of direct goods but not being in themselves the source of any satisfaction, the peasant faced with this alternative, in the case of a surplus harvest, chooses to treat this as direct goods, preferring to accumulate additional wheat or barley rather than sow these and increase the prospect of a future harvest. Thus future production is sacrificed to future consumption, potential goods to actual goods, prediction to foresight.

We must then make a clear distinction between putting by reserves, which means subtracting part of the direct goods in order to reserve this for future consumption and implies foresight and abstention from consumption, and capitalist accumulation, 'creative saving' that leads to setting aside indirect goods with a view to their productive use. The latter only acquires a meaning by reference to a distant and abstract future; it demands calculating and rational prediction, whereas reserves as such, merely deferred and potential consumption, simply assume the aim of a concrete 'to come', virtually enclosed in the perceived present and already within reach, such as those consumption goods with which the peasant surrounds himself and which form the palpable guarantee of his security. Foresight, Cavaillès said, does not mean seeing in advance. The foresight of the *fellah*, an anticipated vision, a pre-perceptive anticipation, differs essentially from the rational prediction of the capitalist entrepreneur.

It differs first of all in its motivations. Economic decision is determined neither by consideration of the goal, nor by the quest for a rationale of action, but by the concern to obey social imperatives, to conform to models that have been handed down by tradition and to follow paths traced by experience. This is for example the way in which many rich peasants make it a point of honour only to consume the products of their own land; and the Kabyles often observe that big houses unwilling to derogate eat couscous made from barley while the poorest have couscous made from wheat. In the same way, when oxen come out ploughing for the first time, custom decrees that a meal is given to which the *khammès* is invited, if there is one, and a few neighbours; a couscous is then served containing pomegranate seeds that have been kept in store, whether or not one has pomegranate trees. Because honour decrees that it should be so, preserves are made, of salted meat for example, with a view to festivals, that is, intended for guests rather than for the family itself. This enables us to understand the contempt that is heaped on someone who lacks reserves, and particularly the townsman, about whom people say: 'What the day has worked, the night has eaten'. In short, the reasons that lead to goods being put by are traditional rather than rational. Foresight means conforming to a model handed down by ancestors, approved by the community, and in this way, deserving the approval of the group.[3] Behaviour of this kind is dictated by imitation of the past and by faithfulness to the values bequeathed by forebears, and not at all by prospective anticipation of a projected future.

It is also the point of honour, the *nif*, that very often presses the Kabyle peasant to increase or defend his patrimony, in order to leave an inheritance at least equal to what he has himself received. This is for example why land sold by a relative is bought back, no matter what the price and even if it means ruin, so that it will not fall into the hands of a different family. In a general sense, the peasant commits his expenditure, not at all like the capitalist entrepreneur as a function of expected profit, but as a function of the income provided by the previous season, the surplus being devoted first of all to the purchase of animals. With the peasants of the Tell, for example, when the harvest has been good the flock expands, sometimes beyond the available supply of water and pasturage, and it is not unusual for a harsh winter to cause the widespread death of poorly fed animals, so that the following year, for want of draught animals and money to buy seed, the area under cultivation is reduced, the balance being ensured by automatic natural mechanisms rather than by rational calculation. The Kabyle peasant buys land when he can. But until recently sales were still rare, being banned by honour. Previously a second pair of oxen was often purchased in the summer, on the pretext that this was needed for treading the corn (which implied that the harvest had been abundant), but in reality, on many occasions, simply so that at the end of summer, the period of marriages and festivals when social life reaches its highest intensity, people could say: 'That's the house with two pairs of oxen and a mule.' Very soon, the fodder that had been scarcely sufficient for one pair of oxen was exhausted, and it was not

uncommon for the second pair to be sold before the autumn ploughing, the time when they would have been really needed. But the family's reputation was safe. In the last twenty years, even fifty in the
regions where the tradition of emigration to France goes back a long
way, there has been an economic conversion: many people have
bought oil presses, motorized mills, trucks, etc. But the sentiment of
honour is still at the root of much behaviour: it was not so long ago
that competitions for prestige between the two 'halves' into which
villages are divided, or even between two big families, led them each
to purchase the same collective equipment, without even inquiring
whether this was profitable. Economic decision can thus be referred
to ends of a quite different order, without the specifically economic
purpose (as it seems in our eyes, since it is never explicitly constituted
as such) being decisively privileged.

Moreover, foresight is also distinguished from prediction by the
fact that this anticipation is born out of the very logic of the situation, and is essentially different from an external plan to which
action has to conform: it does not posit as a future the end presently
aimed at by the action in question, but understands it as a 'to come'
that is synthetically united to the present by a tie directly grasped in
experience or established by previous experience. In an agricultural
economy where the entire cycle of production can be embraced at a
single glance, products generally being renewed in the space of
a year, the peasant does not dissociate work from its tangible result,
a 'to come' that the present already bears. This is what explains,
among other reasons, the difficulties that arise when the length of
production cycles is modified, so that results do not appear with the
customary regularity and rapidity. That is why, in various regions of
Algeria, the service for the defence and restoration of lands (DRS),
which offered farmers the free construction of terraces for the plant-
ing of trees, came up right away against the resistance of the *fellah*,
whereas the European colonist took advantage of this windfall
without delay. Instructed by the concrete and palpable experience
that the success of work undertaken on European lands provided,
Algerian peasants wanted to benefit from the improvements they
had initially rejected (in the region of Benchicao). How can we
explain this initial mistrust, otherwise than by the fact that people
are unwilling to sacrifice a tangible interest within their reach (in the
present case, the pasture assured for their flocks by the land that was
to be restored) to an abstract interest that cannot be apprehended by
concrete intuition?[4]

The modern economy, where the distance separating the start and
the finish of the production process is extremely long, presupposes

the positing of an abstract goal and, by the same token, the constitution of an abstract future, with rational calculation also having to
substitute for the lack of an overall vision. In fact, however, for calculation to be possible, the organic unity that links the present of
production to its 'to come' has to be broken, a unity that is nothing
other than that of the product itself, as shown by comparison between
handicraft technique that manufactures an entire product and industrial technique based on specialization and division of labour. The
tasks of the peasant cannot so easily be broken down into little pieces.
They go integrally together with the natural world, which bears
within it its own principles of division and unification, and which,
far from allowing arbitrary divisions, imposes its own rhythms.

It follows that purely rational plans and projects often simply
arouse scepticism or incomprehension. In fact, based on abstract
calculation, situated in an order of possibility and assuming a departure from attachment to the familiar given, the plan is affected by
the unreality of a dream or the imaginary – as if between planning
and customary foresight there existed the same abyss as between a
mathematical demonstration and a demonstration by cutting and
folding. In order for an improvement project to win consent, it has
to concretely propose the kind of results that will improve the personal situation of those directly concerned, or people of their acquaintance. This is why measures introduced in the name of material
interest may be rejected, while they are accepted when proposed by
a respected personality; didn't the former schoolteacher, *chikh el
lakul*, in many Kabyle villages promote innovations inspired and
imposed by his prestige and his moral authority? It was out of personal loyalty towards a man who was esteemed, or as people say, 'for
his face', that they resolved to break the continuing and assured cycle
of tradition.

Mutual Aid and Cooperation

The same essential difference can be discerned between mutual aid,
which always associates individuals linked by ties of real or fictional
consanguinity, and which is encouraged and supported by tradition,
and cooperation, as collective work oriented towards abstract goals.
In the first case, the group pre-exists the performance in common of
a common work, even when this provides an opportunity for rein-
vigorating the sentiments that underlie the community; in the second
case, the group exists only by reference to future goals that are envisaged and conceived in common, with the result that, given that its

principle of unification lies outside of itself, in a future anticipated by the project and guaranteed by contract, it ceases to exist at the same time as the contract that creates it. Thus nothing would be more wrong than to believe that traditions of solidarity prepare the Algerian peasants to adapt to cooperative or collectivist structures. It could be that the agricultural workers in zones of major colonization, dispossessed of their lands and their traditions, are more disposed to this than the small proprietors in regions relatively spared.

Barter and Monetary Exchange

In the same way, if the Algerian peasants have long shown a lively distrust towards money, and if even today monetary exchanges remain extremely limited in many regions, this is because monetary exchange is to barter what accumulation with a view to capitalist use is to putting by in reserve. Whereas in the object exchanged the coming use to be made of it is grasped directly and concretely, being inscribed in it in the same way as its weight, smell or colour, with money this direct and concrete grasp is impossible; the future use that it signals is distant, imaginary and indeterminate. Money, an indirect good par excellence, is not in itself the source of any satisfaction. This is what the story of the *fellah* who died in the desert beside the sheepskin full of gold coins he had found there is designed to recall. An absurd distrust and incomprehension? But as Gaëtan Pirou said: 'An economic life that turns completely around monetary expressions and takes no account of the real satisfactions that commodities and services bring would be in a sense irrational.'[5]

In fact, with fiduciary money it is no longer things that are possessed, but signs of their signs. Kabyle wisdom reminds us of this, saying that 'a product is worth more than its equivalent (in money)', or again, 'acquire products rather than money'. Given that 'all money is fiduciary', the person who accepts a banknote in exchange for a sheep commits an act of faith in the same sense as the *fellah* does when he sacrifices a sheep on the foundations of the house he starts to build.

Money, an instrument that can be used by anyone, anywhere, for any exchange operation, is characterized by its indeterminate character: on the one hand, as a thing 'that has no other use than to be able to obtain things of any use', it includes an infinite range of possible and indeterminate uses; on the other hand, given that this infinity of possible uses corresponds to an infinity of moments of possible use, and that quite a long time may well elapse between the moment it is received and the moment it is spent, it constitutes the concrete symbol of an abstract future. First of all, therefore, it makes possible the definite anticipation of an indefinite use: 'If I do not know what quantity of wheat I shall be able to buy with it, I do at least know that I shall be able to buy wheat in the future; even if wheat is not what I need, I know that with gold I shall be able to feed myself, clothe myself, do something useful.'[6] And again: 'It is this power of anticipation or representation, even anticipated realization of a future value, that is the essential function of money, and particularly in progressive societies.'[7] Secondly, if it is true that it contains an infinite range of possible uses, since it can serve indifferently to buy a certain quantity of wheat, barley, or any other product, making it possible therefore to quantify expectations or hopes, it remains that the different possible employments of a given sum of money mutually exclude one another as soon as a person sets out to realize one or the other in practice: it is not possible in fact to devote the whole of this sum to buying wheat without renouncing the purchase of barley; in short, a choice has to be made, and it is not possible to want both one and the other. The use of money thus presupposes adopting a perspective of the possible, a projective attitude positing an infinity of possibilities that may equally be realized or not be realized, at the same time as an attitude of anticipation that selects a particular and particularized possibility as something that is bound to be realized, and also, something that can be realized only by excluding all other possibilities.

In complete contrast to this, goods exchanged by barter, on the basis of equivalences established by tradition, contain their potential use within themselves; they reveal their own value based on their quality of being goods of use, capable of being immediately used, and not depending, as distinct from money, on external and foreign conditions. It follows from this that it is far easier to use reserves rationally than to allocate a month's wage received over everything, or to establish a rational hierarchy of needs and expenditures; the temptation to consume everything at one stroke is far smaller than the inclination to spend at one stroke all the money possessed.[8] The Kabyles most commonly store wheat or barley in large earthenware jars known as *ikufan* (sing. *akufi*), which are generally pierced with a hole at different heights. And the good housekeeper, responsible for the use of reserves, knows that when the grain falls below the central hole, known as *timit*, the navel, it is necessary to be careful and moderate consumption. This calculation, it is clear, is done mechanically, and the jar is like an hourglass that makes it possible to measure at any moment what has disappeared and what is left.

The conversion that the use of money demands is analogous to that effected by analytic geometry. Clear self-evidence, provided by intuition, is replaced by blind evidence arising from the manipulation of symbols. From this point on, people no longer reason on the basis of objects that proclaim in an almost palpable and tangible way their use and the satisfaction they promise, but on that of signs that are not in themselves the source of any enjoyment. Between the economic subject and the goods or services that are expected, the veil of money is interposed. As a result, for individuals trained and prepared for an economy that tends above all else to ensure the satisfaction of immediate needs, the rational use of money, as a universal mediation of economic relations, necessarily presupposes an apprenticeship that is very slow and difficult. There is a great temptation to convert the wage just received into real goods, food, clothing, furniture; and it was not uncommon, some fifty years ago, to see workers spend in a few days the income of a month's work; at a more recent date, similar attitudes could still be observed among the nomads of the South, when shepherds who had formerly been paid in kind began to receive a money wage. We also know that the unfamiliarity of country people with the handling of money and their lack of adaptation to juridical rules made a great contribution to accelerating the movement of land dispossession. Thus, after condemning the policy that led to despoiling Algerians of their pastures, Maurice Violette noted:

> Expropriation is really abused [. . .]. At all events, when expropriation is necessary, it should be the case that the damage is repaired equitably, and in particular that the obligation on the administration to rehouse the expropriated, and especially the indigenous population, is respected [. . .]. Monetary indemnification has no meaning for the *fellah*. He will spend it right away, he is unable to capitalize it and use the meagre income that such an investment would provide him with.[9]

We know, moreover, how catastrophic was the experience of the break-up of joint possession promoted by the laws of 26 July 1873 and 23 April 1897. Having become holders of an authentic property title that was readily alienable, many small proprietors, under pressure of poverty, were tempted by the attraction of money and sold their land; having little familiarity with the use of money, which had formerly been so rare in the Maghreb,[10] they very often dissipated their small capital and were forced either to hire themselves out as agricultural workers, or to escape to the city.[11] Thus the rational use of a limited amount of money presupposes an extremely complex calculation that tends (1) to determine the future uses that are possible within the limit of the means available, and among them, those that are mutually compatible, given that the sum in hand must be sufficient to meet the needs of a definite period; (2) to define the rational choice or choices by reference to a hierarchized structure of ends. If we know that in our own societies, where cultural apprenticeship tends to inculcate as a matter of urgency the principles of saving, economizing and profit, the household economy still remains resistant to rationalization, should we be surprised that Algerians, and the rural population in particular, find it so hard to acquire and handle these complex techniques that are bound up with an ethos so deeply foreign to the spirit of their tradition?[12]

Credit and Exchange of Gifts

If out of all the economic institutions introduced by colonization, credit is undoubtedly the hardest to grasp, this is because it presupposes that people act in relation to an abstract future, defined by a written contract that is guaranteed by a whole system of sanctions and rational norms; also because, with the notion of interest, it brings in the accounting value of time. In this way, it is completely foreign to the logic of the traditional economy. Usury is certainly a normal element in a society that, though permitting the least space possible to monetary circulation, was all the less exempt from crises given that the fragility of its technology did not enable it to overcome the vagaries of climate; interest levels before 1830 averaged 50 to 60 per cent, according to Adolphe Hanoteau, and were still 25 to 30 per cent in 1867.[13] On top of this, however, nothing was more foreign to the traditionalist mind than to make time an object of calculation: this helps to explain the grip of usury and also of *rahnia*, a loan against landed property that was, in the hands of big Algerian families, an all-powerful instrument of dispossession, or indeed of *tsenia*, which, assuming the form of a sale, gave the 'buyer' free and legitimate disposal of the fruits although it was strictly speaking no more than a right of hypothecation.

Because it is always imposed by necessity, which rules out any discussion of conditions, and because it is generally destined for consumption, this emergency credit differs from credit designed to increase profit by way of investment, so that a loan of this kind, which is almost always direct, merges into usury. People only resort to the usurer as a final extremity, once all resources of mutual aid and family solidarity are exhausted. The person who, having the means to help, delivers a brother or a cousin into the hands of the usurer is irrevocably dishonoured. The ban on lending at interest is only the reverse of a positive imperative, that is, the duty of fraternal mutual aid. Thus community rules, sometimes codified in local collections, prescribed that assistance should be given to widows, to the sick and the poor, and that victims of a calamity should be helped: when an animal was injured and had to be slaughtered, for example, the community indemnified the owner and the meat was divided between various families. Exchange of services, friendly agreements (rather than contracts), gifts and counter-gifts, were all institutions that performed the functions that credit does in our own societies. Here again, as the specifically economic ends are not posited as such, but merge together with those set out by the morality of honour and the sense of community, rationalization in the sense that we understand it, implying that economic activity is carried out with a single end and a definite future in the context of a calculated plan, is ruled out.

Although each assumes identical functions in its own system, and both presuppose the overcoming of distrust, since with restitution being deferred in each case, the future intervenes and with it risk, institutions such as credit on the one hand, and exchanges of goods and services based on personal loyalty on the other, are divided by an essential difference.

In friendly agreement, the only guarantee is good faith, which is inseparable from respectability (*horma*) and the point of honour (*nif*) displayed towards others; assurance for the future is supplied not by wealth, but by the man who disposes of it. Credit, on the contrary, needs to guarantee its security by taking sureties, such as the solvency of the debtor. It also implies the notion of interest, inseparable from the quantification of value in time; a calculation that like accounting is foreign to the traditional economy, whether excluded by the logic of surplus generosity, or because goods have prices that are fixed by tradition, so that the seller's effort is confined to putting on sale as large quantities as possible.

The most important thing, however, is that the exchange of goods or services, and friendly agreement, establish between two individuals a tie that is more than merely economic: in fact, the deferred counter-gift is already virtually present in the interpersonal relationship that is the occasion for it, and is concretely guaranteed by a loyalty that is personal, and experienced in person by the person receiving it. This is how it is, more generally, with all such contracts. Given that these are made only between people who know one another, whether relatives, friends or allies, the future of the association is assured, even in the present, by the global intuition that each person forms of the other, known to be a man of honour and faithful to his commitments. The man of whom one says: 'this man is a word (*argaz d'awal*)',[14] is the living embodiment of the future, which his whole past and his reputation commit and guarantee better than all explicit and formal codes; credit, on the contrary, presupposes the total impersonality of relationships and consideration of an abstract future. Is it surprising, in these conditions, that the institutions of agricultural credit established by the colonial administration, being ill adapted, meet with incomprehension and sometimes hostility on the part of the *fellah'in*, who often see in them no more than a bureaucratic and impersonal reincarnation of the old-time usurer?

The Structure of Temporal Consciousness

The behaviour observed can therefore only be understood by reference to the historico-cultural structure of temporal consciousness. It is too often concluded on the basis of observations that are unchallengeable but selective, in agreement here with the stereotypes of racism, that the Algerian peasant, and traditionalist man more generally, lived enclosed in the immediate present, improvident and heedless of the future.[15] In fact, the 'to come', understood as a horizon of the perceived present, differs essentially from the *future* as an abstract series of equivalent possibilities, distributed in a reciprocal externality. *Pre-perceptive* anticipation, the object of potentialities inscribed in the perceived given, is part and parcel of a perceptive consciousness whose modality is belief, and is therefore opposed to the *project* understood as projection of imagined possibilities in a consciousness that asserts nothing about the existence or non-existence of its object. In pre-perceptive anticipation, the future is not posited thematically as future; it is integrated as actual potentiality in the unity of the perceived. This is how the wheat immediately presents itself, not just in its colour and form, but also with qualities inscribed in it by way of potentialities, such as 'made to be eaten'. These potentialities are grasped by a perceiving consciousness in the same way as the directly perceived aspects, hence in the mode of belief. Whereas consciousness of the project, imaginary consciousness, presupposes that attachment to the given is suspended, and aims at possibilities projected as things that may either happen or not happen, consciousness that grasps potentialities as 'to come' is engaged in a universe scattered with solicitations and urgencies, the very world of perception. The 'to come' is the concrete horizon of the present, and in this way it is proposed in the mode of presentation not of representation, as distinct from the impersonal future that is the site of abstract and indeterminate possibilities of an interchangeable subject. What distinguishes the future from the 'to come' and the possible of potentiality is not, as one might believe, the greater or lesser distance in relation to the present directly perceived, since the latter can also offer potentialities perceived as co-present that are more or less remote in objective time, provided that they are tied to it by the unity of a signification.

Consciousness lives and acts this distinction without making it explicit, unless in the form of self-irony. 'Where are you going?' Djeha, an imaginary character in whom Kabyles like to recognize themselves, was asked. 'I'm going to the market.' 'What! And you don't say "if it pleases God"?' Djeha goes on his way, but when he reaches a wood he is set upon and robbed by bandits. 'Where are you going, Djeha?' ask the people he meets. 'I'm going home . . . if it pleases God.'

This simple story is sufficient warning against ethnocentrism, and the inclination to describe the temporal consciousness of pre-capitalist man as divided from that of capitalist man by a difference in kind. In fact, temporal consciousness goes together with the specific ethos of each civilization. If it is true that, for want of having subjected their own experience of the world to phenomenological analysis, ethnologists have very often dug for themselves the abyss that, according to their interpretation of the facts, separates them from their object, and if it is true that the experience that the Algerian *fellah* forms of temporality is a modality of our own experience, it remains that everything happens as if each civilization encouraged and promoted, as a function of its fundamental choices, a particular modality of the experience of temporality.[16]

'If it pleases God' means at the same time that it might not please God. This expression marks, by way of contrast, that you move into a different world, governed by a different logic than that which prevails in the perceived world, the world of the future and the possible whose essential property is that it may not come to pass.[17] *Azekka d azekka*, 'tomorrow the tomb': the future is a nothing that it would be vain to try to grasp, something that does not belong to us. The person who worries too much about the future, forgetting that it essentially escapes our hold, is said to 'want to be the colleague of God',[18] and to bring him back into line he is told: 'Don't worry about what is foreign to you', or again, 'Don't see money not in your purse as treasure'. Excessiveness is the fact of forgetting that the possible may not happen or, as science does, claiming to reduce by prediction the infinity of possibilities to a single one. Joseph Desparmet tells how, fifty years ago, old Algerians liked to say, with as heavily ironic an emphasis as possible: 'The French will even conquer death.' In brief, the spirit of prediction is no more than presumption; so people avoid projects that are too remote, considering that the mere fact of prediction amounts to an insolence towards God. To say, as is often done, that 'the future belongs to God' means that any effort to take hold of it is a diabolical ambition.

Wisdom

Cultural apprenticeship and collective pressure tend to discourage everything that is encouraged in our own societies: the spirit of enterprise, the will to innovate, the concern for productivity and profit, and so on. The deep sense of dependence on nature, whose rhythms and rigours are directly experienced, inclines people to an attitude of submission to duration, a nonchalant indifference towards time passing, which no one thinks of mastering, exhausting or economizing.[19] Haste and precipitation are seen as a lack of good manners. *El ahammaq* is the person who rushes into action without thinking, who never stops talking, who runs to catch someone, but also the person who, in such haste to do his work, risks 'mistreating the earth' which 'will demand an account from him'. Impatient, insatiable and greedy, he does not know how to keep within proper bounds, he wants to 'embrace the earth', forgetting the teachings of wisdom:

> You may well pursue the world,
> No one will join you
> Oh you in such a hurry,
> Stop so you can be blamed:
> Subsistence comes from God,
> There is no need for you to worry.

(popular song)

All the peasant virtues hang on a single word, *niya* (or again, *tiâuggant*), meaning innocence, naivety, simplicity, uprightness.[20] *Niya* excludes greediness, which is called 'the bad eye', *thit*; it goes together with sobriety, that is, the art of moderating one's needs.[21] *Bou niya*, the straight and simple man, knows nothing of calculation and prediction, as he does not claim to pierce the designs of Providence and, respectful of tradition, makes sure not to eat up everything in one day. There are certain products that he does not sell to another *fellah*, in general everything that is eaten fresh, such as milk and butter, vegetables and fruit.[22] The only relationships he establishes are based on complete trust, and, as distinct from the horse trader, a specialist in the market, he knows nothing of the guarantees that surround commercial transactions: witnesses, written documents. He only speaks of what affects peasant and village life, holding any other subject to be impious, such as those subjects introduced by agricultural workers or emigrants. He maintains a relationship of real familiarity with his land and his animals, to whom he is able to talk a certain language. Opposed to the *niya* is *tiharchi*, adroitness, cleverness, and pejoratively malice, as well as *tahraymith*, impious malignity (*larham*, taboo), calculation and cunning.

The Logic of the Traditional Economy

If it is true that the economic behaviour of the Algerian peasant can only be understood by reference to the categories of his awareness of time, it remains that the latter are closely bound up, by the mediation of the ethos, with the economic foundations of the society and the entire culture. If the peasant with self-respect works without haste, knowing he can leave till tomorrow what he is unable to do today, if he is unconcerned about schedules, productivity, or the tyranny of the watch, sometimes called 'the devil's mill', this is because work has no other purpose than to directly satisfy primary needs.[23] Since life consists in surviving, that is, enduring, the purpose of technical and ritual activity is to ensure what Marx called simple reproduction, that is, the production of the quantity of goods that enables the group to subsist and biologically reproduce itself, as well as the reinvigoration of the ties, values and beliefs that make for the group's cohesion. Despite the fact that this society, like any human society, exists in a struggle with nature, it does not and cannot see itself in this way, unlike our own societies. Far from viewing themselves as a factor acting from outside on an external nature, people here feel encompassed within nature. As a result, the ambition of transforming the world by work is excluded, something that presupposes the suspension of attachment to the natural and social given and reference to an imagined and hoped-for order.[24] Traditional civilization does not form the ambition of taking a hold on the future and on chance, but simply sets out to afford them the least hold. The fear of objective disorder, capable of shaking or destroying the established order, leads to methodically keeping all unusual situations at bay (naturally without these operations being conducted at the level of individual consciousness), to maintaining, at the cost of a kind of shrinkage of aspirations, a situation that can be mastered by customary means, to reducing the unknown, when this unexpectedly arises, to the already known, to responding to new problems with old solutions. Traditionalism might be the specific characteristic of societies that, not choosing to engage in a struggle against nature, seek to realize an orderly balance by way of a reduction in their activities proportionate to the weakness of their means of action on the world. Constantly threatened in its very existence, forced to expend its whole energy on maintaining as high a perilous equilibrium as possible with the outside world, this society, obsessed by the concern to endure, chooses to accommodate to the world rather than accommodate the world to its will, to preserve in order to preserve itself, rather than transform itself in order to transform.[25]

Traditionalist society assures its future by seeking to fashion this to the image of the past by the means it has at its disposal; by seeking to reduce countless possibilities that are pregnant with unknown palpable threats to a past that is reassuring because it is completed and exemplary. The peasant's anticipations draw support from the reading of signs to which tradition supplies the key. 'If it thunders in January, take up the flute and tambourine; if it thunders in February, don't exhaust your fodder.' The present, and above all the future, can only be dominated to the extent that they can be attached and reduced to the past, appearing simply as its continuation or faithful copy. 'Follow the path of your father and your grandfather', or again: 'There is nothing to criticize in the man who resembles his father', such is the teaching of wisdom.

In a society constituted in this way, if the future is not posited as future, that is, as a site of infinite possibilities, it is perhaps because the order established by traditionalism is viable only on condition of being seen not simply as the best one possible, but as the only one possible, that is to say, on condition that all 'lateral possibilities' are discounted or ignored, these presenting the worst threat by the very fact that they make tradition, taken as immutable and necessary, appear as one possibility among others. What is involved here is the survival of a traditionalism that is unaware of itself as such, that is, as an unconscious choice.

Work, like belief in progress or revolutionary consciousness, is based on the choice of adopting the perspective of the possible, of suspending and questioning passive acquiescence and spontaneous submission to the existing order, both natural and social. The will to transform the world presupposes leaving the present behind in favour of a rational future that can be reached only by transforming the present given. To live in the belief in progress or revolutionary hope means treating the impossible as if it were possible or, better, acting in such a way that the impossible becomes possible and the inevitable becomes unacceptable.

The fact that traditional society repels the ambition to take a hold on the future does not exclude, if need be, that it does its utmost to guard against future surprises. Because pre-capitalist societies have too often been described in terms of absence, or in Marx's words, 'as the Fathers of the Church treated pre-Christian religions',[26] there has been a failure to perceive that they followed what may be called the principle of maximization of security, the stereotyping of behaviour that can be observed in all domains of existence expressing among other things the desire to reduce as much as possible the share of the unforeseen by abolishing innovation and improvisation, in other words, risk.[27]

Yet it is the organization of society itself, and particularly its temporal and spatial rhythms, strictly defined by the ritual calendar, that guarantee against the unforeseen, even while dispensing with rational prediction. Because it is both a principle of organization, with the function of defining an order of succession, and a force of integration, guaranteeing the harmonizing of individual behaviour and the mutual fulfilling of expectations of other people's behaviour, the calendar of works, festivals and rituals founds the cohesion of the group by forbidding any infraction of collective expectations, at the same time as it reduces to a minimum the share left to the unforeseen. Like scientific prediction in Bergson's analysis, tradition-alist society assures its future by seeking to deny it in its specific essence, that is, as unpredictable novelty; but whereas Promethean societies, confident in human reason, seek to ensure maximum pre-dictability, the foresight or, better, the prudence of pre-capitalist soci-eties has no other ambition than to reduce the share of the unforeseen to a minimum.

The pressure of economic necessity may impose a forced submis-sion to the capitalist economic order (subsistence being the price of this), and bring about the collapse of the models that traditionally governed economic behaviour.[28] But by prohibiting any kind of project, unemployment prohibits the rationalization of economic conduct and condemns society to the traditionalism of despair.[29]

This existence abandoned to incoherence does not obtain its full meaning either in its relationship to the logic of traditionalism or in its relationship to that of the capitalist economy. It would be a vain task to try to understand each concrete existence as a discontinuous series of acts, some of which referred to traditionalist models and others to capitalist ones. In reality, like an ambiguous form, each behaviour may be the object of a double reading, as it bears within it reference to both logics, with the result that capitalist behaviour imposed by necessity remains essentially different from capitalist behaviour integrated into a capitalist plan of life; and in the same way traditionalist behaviour as forced regression is divided from traditional behaviour by a chasm, that is, consciousness of the change of context. In this way, the day-to-day existence of the sub-proletarian or the proletarianized *fellah* differs absolutely from the existence of the *fellah* of old, hedged in by security. In the one case, the search for subsistence is the unanimously approved and sole object, guaranteed by customary rules; in the other, obtaining the minimum for survival is an object imposed by economic necessity on an exploited class. Owing to a change of context that everyone is aware of, and the fact that the economic assurance and psychological security formerly provided by an integrated society and a living tradition are now abolished, risky improvisation takes the place of customary foresight and the comfortable stereotyping of behaviour. Unemployment or intermittent employment thus lead to a disorganization of conduct which we should take care not to see as an innovation presupposing a conversion of attitude. Traditionalism of despair and lack of a plan of life are two faces of the same reality.

If possession of a minimum of security is the sine qua non for the rationalization of behaviour and, more broadly, for the systematization of attitudes and opinions, should we conclude from this that the satisfaction of primary needs is sufficient condition for the formation of a rational system of ends, the highest of which would be to maximize income, and the elective and generalized adoption of the ethos implicitly at work in the economic attitude promoted by the capitalist system? Analysis of the statistical findings in relation to behaviour, attitudes and opinions makes it possible to discern several types of economic attitude, associated with different material conditions of existence. Steady employment and regular income give access to what we may call the *security level*: for individuals with a monthly income between 400 and 600 new francs,[30] the object of economic activity remains the satisfaction of needs, and behaviour follows the principle of maximization of security. We should be careful not to see this as a pure and simple expression of the logic of traditionalism. In fact, behaviour and attitude can only be understood in relation to the existence of structural unemployment: even those people who have reached the security level continue to feel this as constantly threatened and view themselves as privileged; besides, the objective conditions of the labour market most often prevent them from a maximization of effort. Finally, obtaining a family income in the region of 800 new francs, which can be seen as the objective index of what we shall call the *enterprise threshold*, coincides with an overall mutation in behaviour and attitudes, the rationalization of conduct tending to extend to the household economy, the site of last resistance. Behaviours tend to form a system organized with a view to an abstract future, apprehended and mastered by prediction and calculation.

The Internal Logic of Original Algerian Society

1. Traditional Society as an Integrated System

Traditional Algerian society, viewed in terms of its internal logic rather than by reference to a normative ideal – which could only be Western society taken as a model – appears as a systematic and integrated totality, whose style and spirit have to be elucidated. Unless it is set within the cultural system with which it is in a relationship of mutual support, it is impossible to understand the real significance of this static and little-specialized economy, endowed with only rudimentary techniques; it is impossible to understand that it constitutes a maximum degree of adaptation to the world within the limits imposed by the precariousness of its resources for action; that it has been able to subsist to a certain degree despite major degradation brought about, among other causes, by contact with a highly specialized and mechanized economy; and finally, that this contact, combined with the action of the state authorities, has managed, by causing the disintegration of the entire cultural system, to throw into confusion populations for whom the old order (which one should also avoid idealizing) constituted, as the saying goes, not only a way of life but a genuine art of living.

The traditional economy is characterized by the predominance of the primary sector. Agriculture, with rudimentary methods and techniques, provides the great bulk of its resources. But it is easy to show that beneath the appearance of precariousness, the ensemble of agricultural activities forms a coherent whole. Xavier Yacono, describing the original style of life of the 'semi-settled' peoples living in the west of the Algerian Tell, brings out its coherence (interconnection of all elements) and compatibility (adaptation to the natural environment):

> The indigenous form of life was a whole that resulted from close adaptation to a definite environment and limited possibilities. The instability of settlement was justified: the indigenous people worked plots that were often very scattered; they had to keep the growing wheat or barley away from the teeth of their animals; they had to abandon a space rendered uninhabitable by too long a stay, as refuse mounted up; they therefore left and pitched their tents where there was grass for their flocks. So they used primitive tools? But why did the colonists often imitate them, after having tried more advanced methods? Because, given the environment, the *fellah* still produced as economically as possible, with the best prospects in terms of yields.[1]

The functional interdependence between the different elements of the economic structure, which this analysis brings out, presented a very difficult problem to the officers of the Bureaux Arabes:

> To advise the natives to build shelters for their flocks meant asking them to find, on a particular site, sufficiently abundant pasture to feed their animals during a long stay: was this possible in regions burnt by the sun for a large part of the year? Could one expect, given the often very short grass of Algerian pastures, to build up sufficient reserves of hay for thousands of animals? The development of artificial meadows would clearly offer a solution, but that would mean a total revolution, and assume that the question of water was settled [. . .] Difficulties of the same order in terms of expanding crop areas [. . .] What hasn't been said against the native plough, as being good for nothing? And yet, is it certain, first of all, that the abrupt introduction of the French plough is in every case an unquestionable benefit? The officers of the Bureaux Arabes asked themselves whether more intensive cultivation would not rapidly exhaust the soil.[2]

These remarkable analyses, in which the coherence and cohesion of an apparently inconsistent economic system are apparent, along with the force of resistance that an ensemble whose elements are closely linked and tied together opposes to any attempt at overthrowing it, deserve further reading; with the result that one ends up wondering, along with certain officers of the Bureaux Arabes, whether such a coherent totality does not have to be replaced by another totality, to avoid simply destroying the existing order without any guarantee that a better order can be established.

Any cultural system requires, on the one hand, a minimum of adaptation to the world, and, on the other hand, a minimum of coherence between its different elements:

- Adaptation to the world may be achieved at different levels; in traditional Algerian society, the balance is achieved at the highest level within the limits of technical possibilities (archaic instruments and methods, lack of capital, etc.), with the result that, given the same resources, it seems impossible to manage any better, since reaching a higher level of adaptation would require greater technical power and a genuine transformation of social, psychological and economic structures.
- But a culture can, while adapting to the world at a very low level, present a very high degree of integration and coherence; all the more so, it seems, the lower the level of adaptation and the more uncertain the balance between man and environment. This is because, among other reasons, the struggle against nature with terribly unequal weapons demands the total mobilization of efforts, and therefore a complete coherence of cultural structures, unyielding attachment to the vital norms on which the group's existence is based (solidarity and mutual aid), obstinate loyalty to an art of living that is also an art of surviving, resistance to the intrusion of dangerous novelties – dangerous because they are novelties – capable of shattering an order that is all the more valuable because it is known, at least confusedly, to be more precarious, traditionalism constituting above all a defence against 'catastrophic situations' that generate 'catastrophic reactions'.

The existence of a 'culture' implies the formulation of a system of norms and values, and, as with a biological organism, it presupposes the intervention of mechanisms of regulation and selection that tend to ensure its persistence through deformation, and at the price of deformation. Maintenance of stability, in fact, presupposes a capacity for modifying itself in response to new situations, and such modification, far from damaging fundamental values, aims to guarantee their stability. The degree of adaptability thus seems to be, on the one hand, inversely proportional to the level of adaptation, so that rigidity (as opposed to 'lability') is bound up with a very high degree of integration, and adaptability is that much greater, the lower the level of adaptation; and, on the other hand, directly proportional to the clarity and strength of the distinction between a culture's fundamental and vital values and those secondary 'elements' that may undergo deterioration without the whole of the cultural system being affected.

One of the keys to the 'Mozabite miracle' thus lies in the distinction between the domain of religion, which is vigorously defended against any tampering, and the domain of the economy, which is open to the boldest innovations.

2. The Spirit of Traditionalist Society

Having brought out, rather too rapidly, how the different elements of this 'culture', an external description of which risks presenting only incoherence and improvisation, stand in a relationship of interconnection, it is necessary to go further and try to show that all these connections are significant; in short, that all the constituent parts of the cultural ensemble are animated with the same 'spirit', the same 'intention', characteristic of a 'style of life' that we shall call traditionalist, for want of a better term.

In traditional Algerian 'culture', the economic domain is not set up and constituted as an autonomous system, endowed with its own laws and ruled by a set of original values. On the contrary, the values and principles that govern inter-human relations also apply in economic relations. This is why a number of institutions that are characteristic of Algerian society must be understood in terms of the logic of honour and prestige, and certainly not in terms of the logic of self-interest, which everything inclines us to do. Exchanges of services, gift and counter-gift, play an infinitely more important role here than the characteristic mechanisms of the Western economy, such as the relationship between capital and labour (waged work and labour market), credit institutions, money treated as abstract and universal mediation of economic and even social relationships, and as almost unique expression of value.

A. Mutual aid

Two of the most characteristic examples will suffice to bring out the original style of this economy. Mutual aid plays a fundamental role in the traditional sector of the economy, particularly among the Berber-speaking groups, constituting a response to technological poverty and the absence of a labour market, which is itself bound up with the scarcity of capital. As Hanoteau and Letourneux write about Kabylia, 'Everywhere, to different degrees, one comes across mutual support, both in the smallest matters of private life and in relationships of the family, village and tribe.'[3] Certain tasks, for example (such as house-building, weeding and hoeing, harvesting, gleaning, olive gathering, etc.), are performed collectively by the whole village. This must be seen less as a collective corvée than an exchange of services, the *touiza* actually constituting a *taoussa* of labour, that is, a gift that will subsequently be met by a counter-gift. Mutual aid continues to play a part in the emigrant community, being its very condition of possibility. In short, the essential character of this economy is that relationships between people prevail over people's relationships to things.

B. *Khammessat*

This feature appears again in *khammessat*,[4] which is far more a pact of honour between the master and the *khammès* than an association between capital and labour. Judged according to our own criteria, this contract has a strong resemblance to serfdom. The *khammès* is tied to the boss who dictates terms and who alone is secured against risks; he abdicates freedom and initiative, and receives only a very small share of the fruits of the soil; he sometimes finds himself chained by a debt that forces him to renew his contract indefinitely. In fact, however, far from seeing himself as a slave or alienated proletarian, the *khammès* shares in the integral life of the family or tribal group, sharing its concerns and sufferings, and its sporadic misery. He is assured against the uncertainties of the future, against lack of employment and total destitution, thanks in particular to the system of advances in kind. He is protected in this way against isolation, a considerable advantage in a society where the individual only exists in a certain sense through the group. On the other hand, *khammessat*, in the same way as mutual aid, makes it possible to compensate for the lack of a labour market. But the advantages for the master cannot be measured simply in terms of the logic of self-interest. In a context such as this, in fact, wealth is worth less for itself and the material satisfactions it brings than for the enrichment in terms of prestige obtained by the possession of a 'clientele'. In short, concern for economic profitability remains secondary; thus the poor *fellah*, who is sometimes scarcely less wretched than his *khammès* and would undoubtedly have an interest in cultivating his land himself in order to keep all its product, would thereby deprive himself of an immense satisfaction in terms of prestige. We may think of the hidalgo in *Lazarillo de Tormes*,[5] too poor to eat every day, too noble to work, but boasting a servant as a sign of his social rank.

In the absence of developed monetary circulation, *khammessat* and the other types of agricultural contract[6] constitute the only form of exchange possible between the person possessing land or means of production, and the worker. Money, far from being understood as purchasing power or instrument of speculation, rather plays the role of common denominator of value. Trade in prestige and honour is accordingly the form of exchange par excellence.

The primacy of human relationships over technical action, the personal character of economic relations, the recognition of a tie of solidarity between distant relatives, the fundamental role of mutual aid – all these features must be taken into consideration in any economic and social action. There can be no doubt, for example, that a deliberate and systematic effort to develop mutualist associations (such an attempt was made with the creation of the SARs and SAPs)[7] is in conformity with the deep structures of traditional society; fraternal mutual aid can potentially be transformed into an association of technical cooperation, requiring only a relatively easy conversion. A sine qua non for its success is that the technician (like the man of politics) must respect the natural articulations of the society on which he acts, and follow the paths that are in a certain sense already traced in outline.

C. Work

Another characteristic feature of the traditionalist spirit: since work aims only at meeting basic needs and ensuring the subsistence of the group that seeks to live in self-sufficiency, a rise in wages leads to a corresponding reduction in the quantity of labour.[8] In other words, the perspective of earning more is less attractive than that of working less. If the worker does not ask himself how much he could earn in a day by working as much as possible, but rather how long he needs to work in order to earn the previous wage that was sufficient for his needs, this is, as Max Weber observes, because 'man does not desire by nature always to earn more money, but simply to live as he is accustomed to live and earn what he needs for this purpose'; it is because, as distinct from our civilization that develops in the individual, from early childhood, the spirit of competition and recognition of efficiency as the supreme value, the Algerian child, besides being moulded to conform with tradition, is essentially prepared, owing to the low degree of social mobility (a society with little specialization or hierarchy), to succeed his parents, and not to raise himself in the social scale – something scarcely conceivable.

Besides, if every human society, by its very essence, has to struggle with external nature, one should not conclude that every society understands itself as being in conflict with nature, in the manner of our own society. Individual work, prescribed by the head of the family and carried out in collaboration, very often with the entire family group, is experienced as communion. The land is *alma mater* rather than *materies*, construction material, raw material. 'Magico-religious thinking knows no aggressive struggle of man with external nature, and for it, man is never delivered to a nature external to man [. . .] Man is understood within nature, he does not stand apart from it.'[9] He does not view himself as an 'active agent'. Such an understanding presupposes that man's desire goes beyond the necessary, projecting a rational future that can only be reached by transformation of what is presently given. Thus the will to transform the world presupposes a transformation of the will and attitude of man towards the world and his own future.

D. The future

'Modern society is in principle calculating, materialist and mechanistic.'[10] Calculating, in the sense that every decision, every transformation of procedures of work or organization, *every use* of available forces (human and natural), must be justified by demonstrating that the domination of man over nature is thereby strengthened, in other words that the same measurable result is achieved with a lesser expense of human energy, or that more in the way of natural forces is made available to humanity (or to the particular community) than would have been possible with previous methods. In other words, two types of economy, two profoundly different attitudes towards the future. Thus, for the peasant, the concern for productivity that leads to the quantitative evaluation of time is unknown, and it is the work to be done that governs the timetable rather than the timetable that delimits work. Besides, since agricultural work involves waiting, and the rhythm of labour is inseparable from biological rhythms, both animal and vegetable, the peasant mind implies submission to duration. Nothing is more foreign to it than an attempt to take possession of the future (by formal planning, for example). Not that economic calculation is totally absent, as proved by the existence of reserve stocks. But whereas building up stocks presupposes foresight, in other words anticipation of a concrete and in a certain sense tangible future, the 'hoarding' characteristic of the capitalist economy has its foundation in a calculating and rational prediction, that is, the constitution of an abstract future.

E. Saving

It is plain to see that the attitude towards work and the attitude towards the future arise from the same logic. The slightest behaviours of our everyday life are marked by a philosophy of existence that is deeply different from that of the traditionalist human being, and presupposes, as a condition of possibility, the constitution of an abstract and symbolic future. Thus money, an 'instrument that can be used by anyone, anywhere, for any exchange operation' (Louis Bodin), is characterized by its 'indeterminacy': it contains unlimited possibilities; and besides, from the fact that a longer or shorter time always elapses between the moment when it is received and the moment when it is spent, it implies consideration of the future, coming to constitute, in J. M. Keynes's expression, 'a bridge between the present and the future'. It is apparent, therefore, that the use of money presupposes structures whose importance and whose very existence escape us, because we possess these and handle them as something self-evident. In fact, these structures are specific to a determinate civilization, with the result that the bearers of a traditionalist civilization have to acquire them by an apprenticeship that is often laborious and painful.

Every educational effort must have as its primary purpose the creation of psychological structures that are the condition for adaptation to the world of the modern economy. Gifts alone (material aid, distribution of foodstuffs and clothing, etc.), apart from the fact that they demand less from the donor, contrary to appearances, risk establishing a relationship of 'dependency',[11] a cause of stagnation for the recipient and a source of disappointment for the giver.

To give a striking example: a Tunisian employer advised his workers to deposit with him each payday the money needed towards buying a sacrificial lamb for the Eid festival.[12] Two-thirds of the workers were convinced; the boss bought the lambs several months before the festival and fattened them up. While some workers received a sheep weighing 30 kilos, others could only buy a few kilos of meat from the butcher. The following year, the procedure was accepted, and even steadily spread with the result that one by one the workers all became creditors.

> Among the workers, there was one who had previously not even had the idea of saving, but had now already bought three cows and eighteen lambs [. . .] He set aside 20,000 to 25,000 francs, then came to withdraw this entire sum to buy a new cow; his little herd had prospered and multiplied in the meantime. He recently came and said to his boss: 'How about it? When I owned nothing under the sun, I didn't think of acquiring anything, but now that I've tasted the satisfaction of being an owner, all I think of is my next purchase to increase my possessions.'[13]

In this example, we can see that it is not just a matter of transforming or improving techniques, but above all of teaching psychological structures and a system of values, in short, the art of living that is inseparable from these.[14]

F. Credit

Like saving, and household economics, credit presupposes calculation and rational forecast, given that, with the notion of interest, it introduces the accounting value of time. This kind of calculation is absent from the traditionalist economy of North Africans, with their existence from one day to the next, which explains the cruel grip of usury, or that of *rahnia* or *tsenia*. As Jacques Berque writes:

> A person borrows, and the repayment date is a hazy idea. This is why *rahnia* and *tsenia* have always been a heavy burden on small peasant property: the time frame is short, and repayment is far from the mind. It then happens that at the due date, the lender remains in possession. *Rahnia*, in particular, where the pledge is retained, is no more than insidious possession, and most commonly transforms the former owner into a humble employee of the lender.

Usury, as in thirteenth- and fourteenth-century Europe where rates sometimes reached 80 per cent, is normally and logically inscribed in the traditionalist economic system. In fact, an economy that leaves the least possible place for monetary circulation is not necessarily exempt from crises, all the less so as the precariousness of its techniques does not enable it to master the hazards of climate. It follows that the credit resorted to here is an emergency one; the loan is such a vital and inescapable necessity that there can be no question of discussing its terms.

Should the *fellah* be accused of lacking foresight? That would make scarcely more sense than taxing him with laziness. Is it not rather, as we have seen in the previous example, that prediction, that is, the deliberate and rational effort to take a hold on the future, presupposes that one already has a minimum hold on one's own future, that is, a minimum hold on the world. Lack of foresight, in fact, may just as well be the expression of a total trust in the future, founded either on awareness of one's own strength or on ignorance of the difficulties that the world presents, or again of a total defiance of the future, an awareness that it is not possible to master and take possession of it. Has the Algerian *fellah* ever possessed that minimum in the way of assurance for the future that is the condition of possibility of prediction?

The phenomena of disintegration induced by the shock of Western civilization provide an opportunity to verify this principle. In the Aurès, for example, where economic equilibrium could only be maintained by calculations that sometimes extended over a number of years, and by a strict management of reserves, the rupture of equilibrium brought about, among other reasons, by contact with the European economy led to the gradual disappearance of the effort to master the uncertainties of the future, along with the minimum in the way of guarantees underlying it. The peasant knows that, whatever he may do, he will not manage to make ends meet, and he then accepts living from day to day:

> When resources are at an end (no matter whether this moment arrives one or two months earlier, since it is inevitable), he will have to leave, to travel a long way off in search of work and bread, while his family stave off hunger by boiling up juniper leaves; he will have to leave, unless he tries to gather *alfa* or make charcoal[15] (at his own risk and danger), or again sell his last goats, his donkey, or borrow against his land, no matter what the interest rate. This slope leads rapidly to collapse, with no recourse.[16]

In order, therefore, for people in this position to take their fate in hand, by organizing resources, establishing accounts and savings, applying techniques of capital (credit, investment, etc.), it is indispensable for them to possess a minimum grasp over their present and future. But this is only a necessary precondition. Undoubtedly, to the extent that people's power over the world increases, the scope of their aspirations increases equally; the domain of the unacceptable and intolerable extends at the expense of the domain of the inevitable, the domain of activity at the expense of the domain of fatality. However, development of technical power over the world is not enough by itself to create in a society the cult of progress or work. The spirit of progress, like the traditionalist spirit, goes hand in hand with a certain *Weltanschauung*, a view of the world. The conception of work and leisure, the attitude towards the future and the past, the style of interpersonal relationships, are located within a lived philosophy that does not make mastery of the world and earthly success the value of values.

If it is true, as we have tried to show here, that the style of the traditional economy is part and parcel of a civilization, it is understandable, on the one hand, that adaptation to the Western world presupposes not a simple transformation (or, as is said, an 'evolution') of the traditional style of life, but rather a radical change of logic, a mutation of the most everyday ways of thinking and a transmutation of the values that give existence its meaning and price; and, on the other hand, that, owing to the functional relationship that connects economy and civilization, the brusque overturning of economic techniques or practices is capable of bringing about the crumbling, not simply of an economic system, but of a world of values.

3. Traditional Algerian Society and the Notion of Underdevelopment

To conclude, Algerian society seen from outside offers an appearance of incoherence and inconsistency. Its production aims almost entirely at satisfying the needs of immediate consumption, and in the absence of a substantial surplus a bad harvest is a disaster; the circulation of capital is non-existent. In brief, judged by our criteria, it is enclosed in a vicious circle of poverty and wretchedness. Poor because, malnourished and decimated by disease, it would need enormous capital sums in order to feed itself, organize health care and instruction; yet only capital attracts capital. Poor because, attached to a traditionalist and customary social order, refractory to progress, oriented towards the past, for it to access the wealth that technological development procures it would need to break radically with a style of life to which it is vitally attached because it assures it a minimum of equilibrium with the world, and carry out a veritable social revolution – something inconceivable in a society that, making faithfulness to tradition and conformity to itself the value of values, could not deny these values without denying and rejecting itself.

It is also possible to give the notion of underdevelopment a subjective significance, and say that an economy is 'underdeveloped' when, for lack of sufficient productivity, it does not permit its agents to have a satisfactory level of consumption. But this leads us to some strange paradoxes; in fact, while the more highly developed economies see themselves as still having progress to accomplish, and can in a certain sense see themselves as underdeveloped, a society as ill-equipped in terms of technology as the traditional and original Algerian society in no way understands itself as underdeveloped, given that its needs are measured against its resources and that, because of the very 'style' of this traditionalist 'culture', the possibility of positing a better order, by reference to which the established order would be understood as imperfect, is radically ruled out. In short, it is no cause for surprise that a society that is poor only in relation to a wealth external to it that it cannot know, and moreover a wealth that it cannot discover internally, does not recognize itself as such, and is stubbornly, sometimes desperately, attached to a social order and a system of values in which a lived philosophy of existence is expressed.

War and Social Mutations

From Revolutionary War to Revolution

The end of the war of national liberation places the Algerian people face to face with itself. The questions that everyone has posed up till now in an abstract and quasi-imaginary fashion (so pressing was the urgency of the immediate objectives) are today imposed in a new context. How can the objectives of a revolution be substituted for those of a revolutionary war that were unanimously approved because imposed by a situation that was experienced objectively and collectively? How can this revision of goals demanded by the emergence of a new situation be effected?

The re-evaluation and reinvention that are imposed require an unflinchingly clear appreciation of the realities. Far from claiming to present a complete and systematic picture of the problems being raised in Algeria, I would like simply to indicate a few key points, try to combat the tendency to simplifications and mythologies – in short, to appeal to realism by evoking the extreme complexity of the real. Some of the analyses proposed here may seem excessively pessimistic; in fact, a victorious revolution is sufficiently aware of its strength for there to be no need to repeat the reasons for hope.

The most pernicious illusion is undoubtedly that which we can call the myth of the revolutionizing revolution, according to which the war somehow transformed Algerian society from top to bottom, as if by magic; resolving all problems, moreover, including those it raised by its own existence. There is no doubting the fact that the war, by its very form, its duration, and the significance it acquired in the minds of all Algerians, effected a genuine cultural mutation.[1] Nor can we doubt that many cultural resistances are bound to disappear with

the abolition of the colonial system and the establishment of a government of Algerians by Algerians. In this sense, to be sure, everything has changed. But is the old Adam dead for all that?

First of all, besides those for whom the revolution was the occasion
to carry out a genuine revolution, and was experienced in this way,
there are also all those who went through the war without understanding it, those who, expelled from their homes, forced to abandon
their traditional way of life for shantytowns or resettlement centres,[2]
could only submit and accept.[3]

Undoubtedly the war and the revolutionary situation were responsible for an expansion of political awareness in a large section of the
population and especially those able to read, and more profoundly,
for a real transformation in their view of the world. As shown by
studies carried out between 1958 and 1961, the revolutionary situation and the effort of political education promoted a uniformity of
opinions. In fields as varied as the education of children or the future
of Algeria, workers and shopkeepers, artisans and civil servants,
townspeople and country folk, all tended to agree on essentials. Yet
this uniformity of language should not be allowed to hide the diversity of attitudes. What is striking, indeed, is the distance between
opinion and behaviour, between judgements made in the imaginary
mode, the order of verbal conformity, on the one hand, and concrete
conduct on the other. These divergences and unconscious contradictions express a profound disarray as well as an unexpressed attempt
to reinvent new models of behaviour. On the subject of women's
work, for example, the same individual will justify models taken from
the West with arguments drawn from the logic of tradition, such as
proverbs and sayings, and justify traditional precepts with reasons
taken from Western logic. This kind of floating between two cultures
must be the centre of any reflection on the problems of education in
tomorrow's Algeria. The problem in fact is to help a whole people
invent for themselves a system of models of behaviour, in other words
a civilization, that is both innovative and coherent; and this requires
discovering new educational techniques as well as giving teaching a
new content.[4]

The relative uniformity of opinions is evidence of the effectiveness
of an effort of education and rational propaganda, but at the same
time of its limits. It is no small thing to impose a common language.
But we must take care not to forget that behaviour, attitudes, and
categories of thinking are very hard to change. Despite the force
of conviction it may have when it is dispensed by recognized authorities, education that takes on the task of deeply transforming
behaviour so as to adapt this to a new society and new objectives

should not minimize the obstacles it has to remove – a long and painstaking work.

The action of political commissars, the influence of radio and the press, have spread a political education whose importance should not be underestimated. In summer 1960, at a resettlement centre in the Collo peninsular, I attended a discussion at which the comparative merits of the policies of Nehru, Tito and Castro were compared. In a general sense, one is struck by the breadth of political culture and the subtlety of judgements; the behaviour of the Algerian masses following the ceasefire is objective evidence of a profound political maturity. None the less, given the manner in which this has been transmitted, it is only natural that this formation often remains superficial, and is not accompanied by a genuine revolution in conduct.

Undoubtedly the war and the suffering it has inflicted have amounted to a political education in itself. Through the trials they have experienced, the Algerian people have become aware of their real situation. But we should not ignore the fact that affective political consciousness is in advance of rational political consciousness. This is particularly true for women, who experienced the war more passively and passionately than actively and rationally. Among them, political sensibility often has no common measure with political consciousness and culture. The same goes for young people who have grown up during the war, and indeed for many Algerians to different degrees.

In particular, it is only at the cost of a distortion of reality inspired by the concern to apply classical explanatory models that the peasantry can be seen as the only revolutionary class. The peasantry is indeed a *force of revolution*, but not a revolutionary force in the strict sense. The Algerian peasants undoubtedly played a key role in the struggle, as both actors and victims. They are well aware of this. They certainly have everything to win and nothing to lose. They were certainly the first victims of colonialism, and have certainly kept a very acute memory of the expropriations and despoliations of which they were victim. 'You see over there, between the two trees, that's my land. The French took it after the revolt of 1875 and gave it to so-and-so who betrayed us.' And these old men have pinned in the folds of their burnous the act of application of Napoleon III's *sénatus-consulte* that stripped them of their property, even if they are unable to read it! The essential thing perhaps is that the peasant world in Algeria experienced particularly deep upheavals, as a result of major land laws, confiscations, and more recently war and resettlement. The effect is that there is no risk of the peasant masses playing the role of a brake on the revolution, as has happened elsewhere.

For all these reasons, the rural masses form an explosive force, but a force that is available for the most contradictory actions. Unable to define their own goals other than in an emotional and negative manner, they wait for their destiny to be revealed to them. Inspired by a deep sense of revolt, instilled with energies that are less rational than passionate, they are the easiest prey for demagogy; they can also, on condition that one knows how to lead them and steer the force that they bear, continue to play the same role of flying wing in the revolution as they did in the revolutionary war.

The same is true of the urban sub-proletariat – the unemployed, casual labourers, hawkers, petty employees, porters, messengers, caretakers, those who sell single packets of cigarettes or a bunch of bananas. Habituation to prolonged lack of employment and the most casual and poorly paid work, along with the lack of any regular employment, prevent the development of a coherent organization either now or in the future, of a system of expectations towards which all activity and existence can be oriented. For want of possessing this minimum grasp on the present that is the precondition for a deliberate and rational effort to grasp the future, all these people are prey to incoherent resentment, rather than inspired by a genuine revolutionary consciousness; the lack of work, or its instability, go together with the absence of a perspective of aspirations and opinions, the absence of a system of rational projects and forecasts of which the will to revolution is one aspect. Enclosed in a condition marked by insecurity and incoherence, their own vision is generally itself uncertain and incoherent. They experience, feel and resent the wretchedness of their condition rather than having an objective conception of it, something that would presuppose a certain distance as well as instruments of thought that are inseparable from education. It is natural too that this experience, lived as a trial, is expressed in the language of affect. The most frequent kind of expression is what can be called 'affective quasi-systemization', that is, a vision of the colonial world as dominated by an all-powerful and malign will. As an unemployed man from Saïda put it:

> The French don't want to give me work. All these gentlemen around me here have no work. They all have certificates: one is a builder, the other a driver, they all have a trade. Why don't they have the right to work? We lack everything. The French have all that's needed to live well. But they won't give us anything, not work or anything.

And another, a café owner in Algiers: 'It seems as if we're struggling against fate. A friend said to me, "Wherever I knock I am preceded by God, with a sack of cement on his back and a trowel in his hand; I open a door, and he seals tight the next one along.'" Everyday life is experienced as the result of a kind of systematic plan dreamed up by a malign will. The colonial system is perceived as a spiteful and hidden god, embodied according to occasion and circumstance by 'the Europeans', 'the Spanish', 'France', 'the administration', 'the government', 'them', 'that lot'. It's the impersonal 'they' that people refer to when they say: 'They want such and such.'

With steady work and a regular wage, with the appearance of real perspectives of social advance, an open and rational awareness of temporality can develop. At that point, the contradictions between over-ambitious expectations and available possibilities, between opinions offered on an imaginary level and real attitudes, visibly disappear. Actions, judgements and aspirations arrange themselves as a function of a plan of life. It is then, and then only, that the revolutionary attitude takes the place of escape into dreams, fatalistic resignation, or a raging resentment.

This is why we have to reject the thesis which claims that in the colonized countries the proletariat is not a real revolutionary force, because – as opposed to the mass of peasants – it does have everything to lose, in terms of its role as an irreplaceable cog in the colonial machine.[5] It is true that, in a country ravaged by unemployment, those workers assured of a steady job and regular income are in many respects a privileged category.[6] First of all, they are in a position to realize in a fairly coherent fashion their aspirations to a modern way of life: stable employment and an assured wage are the condition for access and adaptation to modern housing, and by the same token, an existence allowing for a certain basic comfort.[7] Then, because their working life puts them in touch with industrial society, they have been able to adopt and integrate techniques, forms of behaviour and ideas – in fact, a whole attitude towards the world.[8] Since all the aspects of this vision of the world, the centre of which is a certain attitude towards the future, form a coherent whole, the adoption of a 'rational conduct of life' is inseparable from the formation of a rational revolutionary consciousness.

Despite the economic dualism that characterizes colonial society, an important section of the Algerian population, especially in the towns, shares at least to a certain degree the benefits offered by the modern sector: family allowances and other social advantages, modern housing, education for their children, regular employment. Should this be seen as a poisoned chalice of colonialism? Should we consider attachment to these 'privileges' (which are claimed as rights by reference to the Europeans), and the existence of needs created by the effect of demonstration, as forming actual obstacles to the realization of a revolutionary politics? Quite the opposite, in fact; only those individuals equipped with a coherent system of aspirations and demands, able to locate themselves in the logic of rational calculation and prediction, will be able to understand and deliberately accept the inevitable sacrifices and renunciations. Only those individuals accustomed to voluntarily accepting the demands of reason will be able to unmask any demagogic claims that are made, and insist on a rational policy on the part of those responsible for their country. The success of such a policy also presupposes that, by an effort of education, the effort is made to appease or quash the magical impatience of the urban sub-proletariat and de-ruralized peasants who expect from independence everything that the colonial system had denied them.

To say that the peasants and the urban sub-proletariat are inspired by an emotional radicalism, and can be led in the most opposing directions, does not mean that they may subscribe to any kind of politics. The danger can be imagined of a fall into a contrary radicalism, a kind of technical hyper-rationalization that is ignorant of social realities. It follows from this that the first problem, whatever is done, is that of the political formation of the masses, or more precisely, of the dialogue between mass and elite.

One of the contradictions of the situation derives from the fact that the revolt of the masses has its root in the destruction of traditional social structures and culture. The wartime policy has only completed, with a kind of blind and methodical bitterness, what colonization had already started, destroying or undermining the economic foundations of the traditional society, its social structures, systems of representation and values.[9] A policy of revolutionary rationalization can only tend to accentuate the questioning of traditional culture; in this respect, the most catastrophic heritage of colonization may have a positive function, in that by having been manipulated to so great an extent, the masses will offer less resistance to the efforts of rational reconstruction of a new social order. Here again, however, reality has a double face: if it is true that the transformations demanded by an education aiming to introduce new techniques, new models of behaviour and new values will be slight in comparison with the upheavals produced by colonial policy and war; if it is true that Algeria is in a sense greatly favoured because the questioning of the traditional order has been so profound, because the new models and values that need to be introduced will never be totally new for those who have to adopt them, it remains that disintegration and disarray can supply the most favourable soil for ideologies of passion to develop, and possibly retrograde ones. To sum up, it is up to the leaders and elites, in the face of this ambiguous reality, to turn to good what could equally turn to bad.[10]

How can this emotional radicalism, born from experience and severe test, be brought into line with the revolutionary radicalism born from reflection and systematic consideration of reality? How can the gap be bridged between aspirations marked by ambiguity and incoherence of sentiment, and revolutionary rationalization? How can dialogue be established between the masses inclined to summary identifications or passionate prejudices, and a leadership that would relegate denouncing the legacy of colonialism to second place, focusing its criticism and action on the internal contradictions of Algerian society; that could only evoke the survivals of imperialism and awaken old resentments at the risk of triggering uncontrollable explosions; that would reject turning against colonialism, a scapegoat already sacrificed, the revolt of the masses frustrated with the miracles of independence; that would choose rigorous analysis of the situation and realistic confrontation with reality against mystifying escape into nationalist mystique?[11]

The most urgent problem is that of intermediaries.[12] The success of a rational politics supposes that this is understood and accepted by the greatest possible number. When the attempt is made to achieve profound transformations, one cannot rely only on the basic discipline of the time of struggle; it is necessary to convince and persuade, that is, to engage in dialogue and education. The attitude of the masses towards the elite is extremely demanding, but at the same time dismissive: 'As long as my son doesn't get the same education as you', said a worker to a student, 'your education doesn't count for me.' The people expect its elites to reveal its own truth, telling it what it is and by the same token what it has to be. And the people will be what it is provoked to be, either a force of revolution lost to the revolution, or a revolutionary force.

Revolution in the Revolution

The causes of and reasons for the war, the particular form it has taken and the consequences it has led to, all form a unity of meaning that must be grasped in the unity of an overall apprehension. If any one of these three aspects is dissociated from the whole in which it is inscribed, any understanding of this becomes impossible.

To deny that the revolutionary war is based in an objective situation would be to deny its very nature and even its existence. To claim that the war was imposed on the Algerian people by a handful of agitators using cunning and compulsion would be to deny that the struggle could possibly find its living forces and intentions in a deep popular sentiment, one inspired by the objective situation. Now the war exists and persists, and it will continue to do so. It exists and persists only as a function of the situation in which and from which it was born; but at the same time, it changes this situation by the very fact that it exists and persists.

Is it necessary to define this situation, even very summarily? The indigenous society was turned upside down, to its very foundations, by the action of colonial policy and the clash of civilizations. Moreover, the whole colonial society was torn apart by the tacit or open tension between the dominant European society and the dominated Algerian society. The development of the colonial system has resulted in a steady growth of the distance (and corresponding tension) separating the dominant and dominated societies, and this is true for all areas of existence: economic, social and psychological. The almost stationary equilibrium in which the colonial society is held is the result of forces that are ever more sharply opposed, that is, on the one hand the force that tends to increase inequalities and domination, 'founded objectively' – if one may say so – in social reality, the fact of pauperization and the breakdown of the original Algerian culture, and on the other hand the force constituted by revolt and resentment against growing inequalities and discrimination. In brief, carried along by its internal logic, the colonial system tends to develop all those consequences implicit in its very foundation, and to reveal its true image. Thus open aggression and repression by force are completely inscribed in the coherence of the system: if the colonial society is as little integrated as ever, war is an integral part of the colonial system, being its moment of self-confession.

The war brings into the full light of day the real basis of the colonial order, in other words the relation of force by which the dominant caste keeps the dominated caste under its sway. We can thus understand how peace presents the worst threat in the eyes of certain members of the dominant caste. Without the exercise of force, nothing could counterbalance the force directed against the very roots of this order, that is, the revolt against a situation of inferiority.

The fact is that the colonial system as such can only be destroyed by a radical challenge. All mutations here are subject to the law of all or nothing. This fact, at least in a confused fashion, has even reached the consciousness of the members of the dominant society, as well as members of the dominated. Those among the former who see their very existence as that of members of the dominant caste do not conceive any other possible order than the present order or their own disappearance. The members of the dominated society, for their part, understand that they should expect nothing from reforms or transformations undertaken from within and inside the system, given that such measures tend in reality to reinforce the system, or at least to preserve and protect it under the appearance of working for its destruction. It must be admitted, too, that the first and only radical challenge to the system is that which the system itself has generated, that is, the revolution against its underlying principles.

It is necessary now to define, very crudely, the particular form and significance that this war owes to the fact that it developed in this original situation. If one places oneself, as is often done, on the ground of formal legality, and accepts that in international relations violence is legitimate on both sides, whereas in domestic politics it is legitimate only for those who represent power, one is apparently justified in seeing the war as no more than a rebellion against the established order, and repression as a mere police operation, the forces of order having legitimacy on their side against criminals. It would be only too easy to show that the standpoint of formal legality implies an ignorance of sociological realities and a refusal to acknowledge the situation in which and against which the revolution broke out.[1]

Once such false questions are left behind, what is striking is that the 'hostile intent' of this war has something abstract about it. Two texts among others will serve as example: 'The Algerian revolution is not a holy war but an enterprise of liberation. It is not a work of hatred but a struggle against an oppressive system.'[2] 'The Algerian war is not a war of Arabs against Europeans, nor one of Muslims against Christians. Nor is it a war of the Algerian people against the French people.'[3] These phrases can be seen simply as propaganda. And yet they appear to express one of the essential characteristics of the war, that is, the fact that it is directed less (in its hostile intent, we have to stress) against concrete enemies than against a system, the colonial system. The demand for dignity expresses the same intent in a different language; it is the first requirement of people for whom the reality of the colonial system and the division of colonial society into castes has been concretely experienced in the form of humiliation.

This is why the revolution against the colonial system and caste division cannot be simply equated with a class struggle inspired by economic demands, even if motivations of this kind are not absent, given that differences in economic position are one of the most flagrant signs of membership of one or other caste. No more can it be equated with an international or a civil war. If the struggle against the caste system takes the form of a war of national liberation, this is perhaps because the existence of an independent nation appears the only decisive means for achieving a radical change in the situation that can bring about the definitive collapse of the caste system.

The very logic of the war has revealed the true face of the colonial system. All the pretences and ambiguities collapse; which explains, among several members of the dominant society, their fear of peace, whether conscious or unconscious, motivated by an awareness that the war has brought about an irreversible mutation, though one that can only come fully into existence by way of peace. It also explains, among certain people, the desire, openly avowed or not, for a total war leading to absolute victory, that is, the restoration of the caste order in its unaltered integrity. For the members of the dominant caste, the divorce and contradiction between the ideal France, often passionately loved, and colonial France, basing its domination on force and discrimination, breaks out into the light of day. Thus war, like repression, tends by its very logic alone, or, if you prefer, by the force of circumstances and often against the intent of those carrying it out, to reveal both its own nature, the nature of the colonial system, and France as colonial power. The veil has fallen away. War has brought the colonial system to its extremes, dissipating ambiguities. Generous action, inspired by a morality of pure intention, stands out against the background of a system of oppression as no more than a derisory palliative. The false solicitude, designed to conceal the reality of the colonial situation, appears as a contradiction or a cynical instrument of reconquest. The tricks and schemes are self-denouncing. War favours a new awareness.

Terrorism and repression tend to give the schism between castes its most radical form. The effectiveness of terrorism lies in the way that it brings about the most trenchant break between members of the two castes, by creating an atmosphere of mutual distrust and fear. And repression cannot fail to provoke the same effects. Repression cannot but view the members of the dominated caste as globally suspect, even if it seeks to discriminate among them. But by the very fact that it holds them globally suspect, it divides them from members of the other caste and develops in them an awareness of the schism. One of the objects of subversive warfare, however, is to bring about this new awareness at the same time as strengthening solidarity between members of the dominated society. Terrorism thus increases the split and provokes repression; and repression increases still further the split that its object was to prevent.[4]

It is maintained on the one hand that the war of liberation is the act of a handful of conscienceless killers led by cynical troublemakers who attempt to raise against France, by cunning and terror, populations who remained loyal, while on the other hand action is conducted in terms of the experienced sentiment, the conscious or unconscious basis of behaviour, which sees all 'Arabs' standing by one another and in solidarity with the FLN. This action, however, can only strengthen such solidarity. The generalized suspicion, the methodical searching of cars in which women are veiled or men wear *chéchias*, the everyday vexations (to mention only trivial facts), are all so many situations that display the existence of racial discrimination and force all individuals of the dominated caste to experience their opposition towards the dominant case and their solidarity with the other members of their own.

Any war, moreover, in a kind of dizzying transport, tends to go to extremes and become total war. And this is more than ever the case here, in a war in which the civilian population is both the stake and the victim, a war without front or frontiers, in which the enemy is everywhere and nowhere, in which neutrality, escape into passivity or indifference are practically impossible, in which the army charged with repression finds itself placed in a siege situation and cannot help cruelly feeling the collective complicity that it faces.

The effect of the circle of violence is that the adversaries, placed in a situation of reciprocal action, are ineluctably borne to the limitless use of all means available. Everything happens as if in a spiral movement, each increase in the forces of repression arousing an increase in tension and the forces of aggression, and so on. This spiral movement does not just lead to a quantitative increase in hostile forces and in the intensity with which these act, it also risks bringing about a quantitative transformation, that is, a mutation of intentions and sentiments. It has to be feared that the 'hostile intention', that is, the objective that the war seeks to attain, and the 'sentiment of hostility', that is, the hatred felt towards the enemy,[5] tend to develop in inverse proportion. The hostile intention, that is, the abolition of the caste system, an intention which, taken in pure terms, excludes any hatred towards those who benefit, whether they will or no, from the system that it seeks to destroy, could give way to a sentiment of affective and passionate hostility directed against this enemy who is not, as in other wars, distant and abstract, but intimate, close and familiar.

Thus the war, by its very existence as well as by its form and duration, has transformed the situation out of which it was born. The social field in which everyday behaviour takes place has been radically modified, and by the same token the attitudes of individuals placed in this situation towards the situation itself. How should we describe and understand this rapid and total change, this revolution in the revolution?

The war of liberation presents the first radical challenge to the colonial system, and – something essential – the first challenge that is not, as in the past, simply *symbolic* and in a certain sense magical. Attachment to certain details of clothing (the veil or *chéchia*, for example), to certain types of behaviour, certain beliefs and values, could be experienced as a way of expressing symbolically, that is, by behaviour implicitly invested with the function of *signs*, the refusal to adhere to a Western civilization identified with the colonial order, the will to assert a radical and irreducible difference, to deny the negation of self, to defend a besieged personality. In the colonial situation, any renunciation of the indigenous civilization would objectively have signified a renunciation of self and an accepted allegiance to the other civilization, that is, the colonial order. And this was indeed the sense that the upholders of the colonial order gave to what they called 'signs of development'. In the colonial situation, rejection could be expressed only in a symbolic manner. Thus the Algerians felt constantly under the gaze of the Europeans and acted accordingly, as is shown by certain habitual formulas that express the concern not to give a basis or pretext for pejorative judgements: 'The French will see you', or 'Don't make yourself ridiculous'. This makes it possible to understand all the resistances that have accumulated through to today, whether consciously or otherwise, all the rejections that are apparently absurd and aberrant.

Thus the existence of people who say no to the established order, the existence of a rational and lasting organization able to confront and shake the colonial system – in a word, the existence of an effective negation established at the very heart of the system, and recognized, voluntarily or perforce, even by those who would bitterly deny it – is sufficient to render vain so much of the behaviour in which the dominated caste expressed its rejection of domination. The war, by its very existence, constitutes a language, and lends the people a voice that can say no.

And so, each Algerian can take on and assume the profound borrowings he has made from Western civilization; he can even reject, without denying himself, a part of his cultural inheritance. Given that negation remains, permanent and unalterable, negation that sums up all the individual refusals, the novelty introduced by the West can be received without this acceptance expressing allegiance. 'Times have changed,' one often hears said, and it is necessary to understand that, the situation having changed, behaviours that had a sense and a function in reference to a different context have now lost their raison d'être.

This global transformation of attitudes is expressed in different domains. The most striking renunciations are those that concern traditions invested with an essentially symbolic significance, such as wearing the veil or the *chéchia*. Institutions such as teaching or medical care, which were intuitively grasped as part and parcel of the colonial system, and on these grounds aroused ambivalent and ambiguous attitudes, are no longer invested with the same significance, given that the tie that bound these institutions or techniques to the system of colonial domination has been broken.[6] In the same way, the perception that the individuals of the dominant society formed of the individuals of the dominated society has been radically transformed. The relationship between the members of the two societies operates for the greater part of the time in ambiguity and misunderstanding. The response to protective paternalism was often an attitude of dependency tinged with aggressiveness, and vice versa. Relations between the administration and those administered functioned along the same lines. The war revealed to each person that the situation of the dominant can be challenged, and by the same token the situation of the dominated. The European and his whole universe have been stripped of their aura. The discovery that the dominant caste can be defeated and the order over which it reigned can be broken has led the Algerian to reassess his own situation. What he often used to assume as ineluctable necessity, he now experiences as scandalous injustice. The shame that could be detected among certain people has made way for pride, and for a shame of having been ashamed.

The relationship between the members of the dominated society has also been changed. Because he no longer grasps his situation as an inevitable fate, but as a condition that can be abolished, the Algerian can, at the same time, assume his position as Algerian and refuse to accept himself as dominated. The feeling of being engaged in a common adventure, experiencing a common fate, sharing the same aspirations and the same ideals, confronting the same adversaries, has widened and deepened the feeling of solidarity among all Algerians, at the same time as giving this a new content, the notion of fraternity losing any ethnic or religious coloration and becoming synonymous with national fraternity.

War has provided this people, so long kept on leading reins, with the opportunity to appear as adult, conscious and responsible. It has allowed them to have the experience of a discipline freely assumed and acknowledged because imposed by their own authorities – in brief, with the experience of autonomy. Thus the war has brought about a mutation in the overall situation, and there is no aspect of the social system that has not been affected by this transformation of the context. Decolonization started with the beginning of the war.

This overall mutation has been supplemented by the disturbances and transformations that are the direct consequence of the very conduct of the war, or of the political and economic measures taken to respond to the war situation. By virtue of its form and duration, the war has affected every aspect of reality, economics and demography as much as social structures, beliefs and religious practices or the system of values.

The Algerian people today are experiencing a genuine diaspora. Movements of population, whether enforced or voluntary, have grown to gigantic proportions. According to reliable estimates, the number of people displaced is somewhere in the region of 2 million, so that approximately one Algerian in four now lives away from their customary residence. The resettlement of population is only one aspect of these phenomena of internal migration, even if undoubtedly the most significant. The break with a familiar environment, a stable and habitual social universe in which traditional behaviour was experienced as natural, leads to abandonment of such behaviour once this is cut off from the original soil in which it took root. The transformation of the space of life demands a general transformation of behaviour. But the uprooting is usually so brutal and total that disarray, disgust and hopelessness are far more common than the innovative behaviour that would be needed to adapt to radically new conditions. By a deliberate or thoughtless ignorance of social and human realities, the local authorities entrusted with organizing the resettlement villages often impose, without heed for the desires or aspirations of the population concerned, a totally foreign order, one which they are not made for and which is not made for them. In these immense agglomerations, alignments of buildings or *gourbis* arranged in a strict geometry, groups of diverse origin find themselves side by side, which tends to dissolve the old ties of community without allowing new solidarities based on common interest or participation in common work to be born. All that these people generally share are their miseries and disenchantment. Removed from their land, the peasants condemned to idleness try to adapt as best they can; we thus see the appearance, as also in the towns, of a proliferation of small shops with no clientele. A number of the resettlement villages, those seen as more 'successful', with wide streets, a well, bakery and coffee shop, have the desolate appearance of dead quarters. Those who live in them, even when they enjoy a level of comfort that they had not known before (which is indeed sometimes the case), are deeply discontented. Essentially, perhaps, because the most basic structures such as the rhythm of days and the organization of space have been broken. How can one express in a few lines, let alone feel, the thousand interwoven aspects of this fragmentation of the drama and art of life? The material poverty that often strikes observers is nothing compared with the moral misery of these people torn away from their familiar universe, their land, their houses, their customs and their beliefs – from everything that helped them to live. It has placed them in a situation in which they cannot even form the thought of inventing a new way of life to try and adapt to a world that remains totally foreign to them.

The internal migration also takes the form of an exodus to the cities, which appear to the country people as a refuge against misery and war. The shantytowns grow ever larger. Those who have been here longer receive relatives from the countryside. What is important from the sociological point of view is the process of 'urbanization' in which the whole of Algeria is caught up – or rather, if the neologism is permissible, a 'shantytownization'. Resettled, emigrants, refugees from the cities, all are brutally thrown into an unknown universe, unable to ensure them work, let alone those forms of security that could give stability and equilibrium to their existence. The man from a rural background, tightly bound by ties of community, closely steered by his elders and supported by the whole apparatus of tradition, gives way to someone only loosely linked to others, isolated and disarmed, torn from the organic unities in and through which he existed, cut off from his group and his home territory, and often placed in a material situation in which his old ideals of honour and dignity are no more than a memory.

In brief, the war and its sequels have simply precipitated that movement of cultural disintegration that the contact of civilizations and colonial policy started off. Moreover, this movement now extends to a territory that up till now was relatively spared and sheltered from the colonizing enterprise, especially in the mountainous regions that are being particularly affected by the war, where small rural communities, withdrawn on themselves in stubborn fidelity to their past and tradition, were able to preserve the essential features of a civilization that can now be spoken of only in the past tense.

No one can fail to be aware that a deep chasm separates Algerian society today from its past, and that an irreversible movement has been accomplished. What counts is less the rupture itself, and more the sense of rupture. The result is a suspension and questioning of the values that previously gave a meaning to existence. The experience of a life that is permanently suspended and threatened makes traditions and beliefs that were held as sacred now appear vain. The most solemn prohibitions are broken. The revolutionary situation also shatters the old hierarchies associated with the outdated system of values, replacing these with new men whose authority rests most often on quite different foundations than those of birth, wealth, or moral and religious superiority. The old values of honour crumble before the cruelties of war. The ideal self-image and the values associated with it have been put to the most radical test.

Like an infernal machine, the war has flattened social realities to the ground; it is pulverizing and scattering traditional communities – village, clan or family. Thousands of men are in the maquis, in internment camps, in prison, or else refugees in Tunisia or Morocco. Others have left for the cities of Algeria or metropolitan France, leaving their families in the resettlement centre or village; others still are dead or missing. Whole regions have been almost emptied of people. In the deserted villages it is questionable whether even the memory of old traditions survives. The transmission of traditional civilization, which adherence to the new values tends to desacralize in the eyes of the young, is interrupted by separation. Only women and old men remain in the village with the children. The young, thrown into urban life, no longer learn from their elders the precepts, customs, legends and proverbs that form the soul of the community. This teaching gives way to the political education conferred by those able to read. The maintenance of tradition supposed continuous contact between successive generations, and a reverential respect towards the elders. The patriarchal family, a primordial community which – in the countryside far more than the town – had escaped disintegration and remained the cornerstone of the entire social edifice, is dispersed and often torn apart by the conflict between generations, expression of the conflict between old values and new.

The young people of the big cities escape traditional controls and the pressure of public opinion, based essentially on the order of the village community. On top of this, the absence of father or elder brother leaves them almost completely to their own devices. A number of young men, above all in the towns, find themselves today in the situation of those whom the Kabyles call 'sons of the widow', in other words that of a man without a past, without traditions, without a self-ideal. The authority of the father, if still very much alive, has often been undermined. The head of the family has ceased to be in every case the basis of all values and the governor of all things. War has overthrown the scale of values that gave the elders precedence and authority. Revolutionary values are the values of the young generation. Formed in the war, oriented to the future, and ignorant of a past in which the older generation, whatever they do, remain rooted, these adolescents are often inspired by a radicalism and negativism that divides them from their elders. The part they play in the revolutionary war is evidence of this.

The mutation that has taken place in the relationship between the sexes should also be analysed. To the extent that the villages are emptied of men, women are steadily more involved in the war. In several cases, they find themselves bearing responsibilities that traditionally fell to men. Very often, they have to see to the family's subsistence even when they receive help from a brother, a brother-in-law or an uncle. The extremely confined space of life that they had is now widened. They circulate in the European town, enter the big stores, take the train to go and visit their brother or their husband, they see to administrative procedures and formalities. From their enclosed and secret world, they break out into the open space that was formerly reserved for men. They share the concerns and political aspirations that were the preserve of men in traditional society. Engaged in the war, whether directly or indirectly, whether actor or victim, borne by the force of circumstances to assume totally new roles, Algerian women have acquired a greater autonomy at the same time as a more vivid and proud sense of their tasks and responsibilities.

Thus, together with other influences such as that of education, which strengthens the pressure of the young people and their desire for emancipation, the cultural contagion furthered by internal migrations, urbanization and the mass politicization that brings about an expansion of the 'intellectual space', the war situation has transformed the whole of the cultural system and especially the system of relationships between the members of the Algerian family. The torn family is in the process of becoming a disintegrated family, if it does not find a new equilibrium. The fact that the effects of the war have been able to affect Algerian society so strongly at its very core, something that had previously relatively escaped such disintegration because of the very fact of its functional significance, shows how radical and total the challenge is.

To express the present state of things, older Algerians often say: 'We are in the fourteenth century . . .'[7] The fourteenth century is that of the end of the world, when everything that was the rule becomes the exception, and everything that was prohibited is now permitted, when for example children no longer respect their parents, women go to the market, and so on. Popular consciousness expresses in this way its experience of a world turned upside down, in which everything is inverted; it sees in the surrounding disorder and chaos the world of the end that heralds the end of the world. And we in Algeria are present at this end of the world. At the same time, this is experienced as proclaiming a new world.

Algerian society for the last 130 years has experienced as deep an upheaval as possible, and continues to do so today. There is not a single field of life that has been spared. The pillars of the traditional order have been shaken or destroyed, first by the colonial situation and now by the war. The urban bourgeoisie has been scattered and dispersed; the values that it embodied and preserved were carried away by the eruption of new ideologies and the appearance of new hierarchies, often issuing from the common people. The feudal magnates, often compromised by the support they granted – and still grant – the French administration, and thus associated in the eyes of the masses with the system of oppression, have lost in most cases both their material power and their spiritual authority. The mass of peasants, who opposed the innovations proposed by the West with a lively traditionalism and conservatism, have found themselves dragged into the maelstrom of violence that is abolishing the very vestiges of the past. Islam, by being dissociated from the magical and mythic practices and beliefs that anchored it to the land, and being used for a moment more or less deliberately as a revolutionary ideology able to mobilize the masses and engage them in struggle, has steadily changed its significance and function. In brief, the war, by its very nature, its particular form and its duration, has been accompanied by a radical revolution.

Of all the countries of North Africa, if not Africa as a whole, Algeria is certainly the place where the influence of Western culture, technique and ideology has been most intense. It is not a matter of indifference that, in the last five years, Algeria reads the answers to its questions in French newspapers and books, and formulates its problems, anxieties and revolts in the very logic of Western thinking. Finally, it is not irrelevant that the revolutionary situation should arouse political consciousness and by the same token the hunger to learn, to understand and be informed. Algeria has opened itself decisively to the world. It feels concerned by the adventure of all formerly colonized countries. The Chinese undertaking, most often poorly understood, arouses ambivalent attitudes, in which distrust is mingled with interest.

A society so thoroughly overturned will force the invention of revolutionary solutions, and mobilize the masses torn away from their traditional discipline and universe, thrown into a world of chaos and disenchantment, by offering them a new way of living, based no longer on undisputed submission to the rules of custom and the values handed down by ancestral tradition, but on active participation in a common task – before all else, that is, the building of a harmonious social order.

War and Social Mutation in Algeria

The sociological consequences of the war can be ranked in two very different orders, which one should be careful not to confuse: on the one hand, the sociological mutations brought about simply by the very existence of the war; and on the other, the transformations and revolutions induced by the conduct of the war itself, by the cultural clashes it has provoked and by the political and military measures taken to confront the war situation.[1]

The first kind of transformation needs to be considered first. The very existence of the war, in fact, has led to a radical transformation of the situation, that is, of the sociological field in which behaviours took place, at the same time as a mutation in the attitude of those individuals who are part of this situation towards the situation itself. From the sociological point of view, this is undoubtedly the most important event that has happened in Algeria in 130 years. It is as if this society, which more or less consciously chose to be stationary and closed in on itself, which put up a thousand invisible and impenetrable barriers to any incursion of novelty, has suddenly opened up, suddenly begun to move. How should we interpret this kind of sudden and total mutation, attested to by a thousand details?

The fact is that the war constitutes the first radical challenge to the colonial system and, what is more important, the first challenge that is not, as in the past, *symbolic* and in a certain way magical, but real and practical. We have seen how several cultural features, such as attachment to certain details of clothing (the veil, for example, or the *chéchia*), to certain types of conduct, beliefs and values, could appear as a way of expressing symbolically, that is, by behaviours invested with the function of *signs*, a refusal to join Western civilization, identified with the colonial order, a desire to remain oneself, to assert a radical and irreducible difference, to deny the negation of oneself, to defend an individuality that was threatened and besieged. In the colonial situation, any abandonment of these cultural traits endowed with the value of symbols would have signified, objectively, the abandonment of oneself and a voluntary allegiance to the other civilization.

The essential sociological fact, perhaps, is that the war, in and of itself, establishes a language, that it lends the people a voice, and a voice that says no. As a result, between the members of the dominated caste and those of the dominant there is always another presence, which Raymond Aron has somewhere called the 'third man'. From this point on, the spell of the tête-à-tête is broken; the relationship of dominant and dominated can no longer be practised in its essential purity. The logic of humiliation and contempt is suddenly shattered.

From the moment that radical negation is established at the very heart of the system, real, concrete and fearsome, able to cause a great country like France genuine concern, to give rise to disquiet and anxiety on the part of Europeans previously sure of themselves and unshakeable, to provoke ministerial crises, debates at the United Nations, programmes, conferences and speeches, visits from ministers and foreign observers – from the moment that the whole world finds itself forced to recognize the existence of this negation, all the magic negations and symbolic refusals lose a large part of their function and their meaning.

Every Algerian, accordingly, can now admit both inwardly and publicly the profound borrowings he has made from Western civilization; he can even admit to himself and others, as one of them told me with a smile, that he is 'integrated'; he can proclaim, without falling into contradiction, that he adheres to the values of Western civilization and even to its style of life; he can even reject, without denying himself, a part of his own cultural heritage. Negation remains permanent and inalterable. Colonial traditionalism essentially performed a symbolic function, playing objectively the role of a language of refusal. Now that negation exists in the objective circumstances, a negation that is the sum of all individual refusals, the innovation brought by the West can be welcomed without its acceptance expressing allegiance.

Perhaps the most evident renunciations, and also the most spectacular ones, are those that concern traditions invested with an essentially symbolic value, such as wearing the veil or the *chéchia*. The

traditional function of the veil is now supplemented by a new function, referring to the colonial context. Without pressing the analysis
too far, we can see that the veil is first and foremost a defence of
intimacy and a protection against intrusion. The Europeans, for
their part, have always perceived it as such, if only in a confused
way. By wearing the veil, the Algerian woman creates a situation
of non-reciprocity; like an unfair player, she sees without being
seen, without putting herself on view. And it is the entire dominated
society which by way of the veil rejects reciprocity, which sees, views,
penetrates, without letting itself be seen, viewed, penetrated. It is
common to hear from Europeans indignant expressions against this
kind of unfairness, this refusal to play the game, which means that
Algerians have access to the intimacy of Europeans while forbidding
them any access to their own intimacy. The veil may thus be considered a symbol of being closed in on oneself. Over the last few years,
however, one may observe, among young women and girls, a very
marked tendency to abandon the veil, which slowed down or regressed
with the events of 13 May 1958;[2] wearing the veil took on once again
its sense of symbolic negation, and its abandonment could be objectively taken as a sign of allegiance – although now there is again a
very clear resumption of the trend, particularly noticeable in the
countryside.

   This global transformation of attitudes is also apparent in other
domains. Certain institutions were rightly or wrongly understood by
members of the dominated caste as part and parcel of the colonial
situation, and accepted only with great reticence. This was true of
education and medicine. The relationship between the sick person
and the doctor, or between student and teacher, was exercised in the
context of the colonial situation, and acquired its meaning from this.
The prescriptions of the doctor and the teaching of the schoolmaster
or assistant could be intuitively felt (without the foundations of this
feeling necessarily rising to consciousness) as so many efforts to
impose the norms of a foreign civilization.

   This resistance and reticence has given way, in the last few years,
to an extraordinary thirst for learning, which is apparent in the
school situation and signalled in a thousand other ways.[3] It is a well-
known fact that, despite the major effort made to expand classes and
recruit more teachers, the number of children who do not find a place
in school remains considerable. And all teachers, particularly in the
towns, have experienced strong pressure from parents who come and
demand the enrolment of their children. The education of girls, which
until recently met with very marked resistance, is now the object of
deep interest alongside that of boys.

But the essential fact is perhaps that what was previously felt as an imposed constraint or a gracious gift is now demanded as a due. This is evident in the behaviour of parents who come and request their children's enrolment on the school register, or of those women pressing at the doors of the social centres each morning. The attitude of the petitioner coming humbly to solicit a voluntary gift has given way to a mental disposition that is demanding and self-assured, coming to claim treatment and services as its due.

The attitude of devoted submission was confusedly bound up with an attitude of resignation motivated by the avowed or unavowed feeling that the European was inimitable and could not be equalled, either in law or in fact. The members of the dominated caste could sometimes accept, if not in their conscious desires then at least in their attitudes, that differences in status expressed differences in kind. Was this not natural when the social order was such that, for the individual of the dominated caste, experience of the relationship with one's superior, whether the boss, the doctor, the schoolmaster or the policeman, was superimposed on and confused with experience of the relationship with the European as such?[4] As a result, the Algerian tended to construct a personality of 'Arab for the French'. Anyone going in search of a job from a French employer knows that he has to express himself in a certain way, to arrive punctually, to guarantee a certain performance, and so on. All that the European sees of him is this mask and this role. It often happens that this attitude is clumsy and borrowed, that the Algerian wears his personality like a badly cut suit and, out of a concern to be irreproachable and conform to what is expected of him, gives rise to the accusation of dissimulation and falsehood. A single example will illustrate this analysis: in a French home, the son of the Algerian domestic was invited one day as a guest; during the whole of the meal, his mother behaved like a servant – silent, active and busy. When it was time for coffee, she changed her attitude completely, just like an actor going off-stage. She appeared full of dignity and distinction; she took part in the conversation; her whole being was transformed, even the way that she sat on the chair, held her head or smiled.

The attitude of abusive protection that leads to dispossessing a society of concern and responsibility for its own future tends to develop in it an attitude of resigned passivity, retreat into itself and indifference towards its own destiny. This is why the paternalistic policy of aid has the effect even in the best case of placing those who are its object in the position of irresponsible and heedless children, freed from any worry about their own fate and by the same token indifferent or, if you like, ungrateful towards those who are 'doing so much for them'.

Here again, the war has changed a great deal. It has in fact offered this people, held on reins for so long, the opportunity to appear to others and to themselves as adult, conscious and responsible; it has also enabled them to have the experience of a freely assumed discipline, in short, of autonomy. It is well known, for example, how repudiation of wives was extremely common in Algeria and, according to an official publication, 'it is in this domain that the intervention of a measure of authority would be salutary, as it does not seem that Muslims are greatly disposed, at the present time at least, to renounce this privilege'.[5] Yet it only needed the Armée de Liberation Nationale, in a number of regions, to issue precise directives, for a very marked decline in the number of repudiations to be observable. In other domains too, the authority of the ALN was able to achieve in a few days what 130 years of 'civilizing action' could not. It is reported that in many places, legal cases that had dragged on for years, with both sides partly to blame, could be settled in a few minutes by the arbitration of ALN fighters. The experience of a freely accepted discipline, imposed on Algerians by Algerians in the name of a common interest, broke down many other examples of resistance that was commonly held to be insurmountable.

It is particularly important, however, that the greater part of the discipline thus imposed was completely identical in content to what the French administration had always sought to enforce. The ALN raised taxes, took charge of civic records, sometimes opened schools, etc. In the same way, the techniques introduced were specifically Western, in the diverse fields of medicine, public health, law and administration. Thus, by itself adopting institutions and techniques that popular consciousness saw as indissociable from the colonial system and that accordingly aroused ambivalent attitudes, by imposing advice and directives analogous in their content and formulation to those that the French administration might have decreed, the FLN seems to have broken the intuitively felt link that bound these institutions and techniques to the system of colonial domination. By this fact alone, they underwent a change of sign.

As a result of the change of context, the relationship between members of the dominant caste and those of the dominated caste was also modified. The war revealed to each person that the situation of the dominant could be challenged, and by the same token that of the dominated. Decolonization began with the start of the war.

The war was initially somewhat sporadic, something that Algerians each experienced at a particular time and in the context of their own village. Gradually, by exchanging information and comparing experience, each person came to understand that the same events were happening in different places. The sense of being engaged in a common adventure, experiencing a common fate, sharing the same concerns, confronting the same adversaries, gave rise to an expansion of social space; the village that was turned in on itself, the closed microcosm in which the rural population lived, opened up; the sense of solidarity expanded to the boundaries of Algeria. This deeply felt solidarity was expressed in a thousand ways: moneylenders almost totally disappeared, either becoming the object of very popular sanctions, or because, in the name of this new sentiment, loans were granted without interest. Demanding repayment of a debt incurred before 1954 was viewed as dishonourable; when a dispute occurred, it was generally enough for a mediator to intervene and invoke the principle of solidarity between all Algerians, for the conflict to be resolved. Fraternity had previously been felt as a matter of belonging, in reality or fiction, to the same social unit (larger or smaller), or at most to the same religion. Today, the word 'fraternity' is becoming synonymous with national solidarity, and losing any ethnic or religious coloration.

And so the war, by its very existence and by the new consciousness it has aroused, has been enough to bring about a genuine sociological mutation. Added to this overall phenomenon are the disturbances and transformations that are the direct and immediate consequences of the conduct of the war, among which we can list, in order of importance: the phenomena of internal migration whether voluntary or forced, generalized insecurity, the measures taken by the administration and army, and finally, the considerable intensification of cultural contagion.

The Algerian people are living today in a genuine diaspora. Displacements of population, whether enforced or voluntary, have grown to gigantic proportions. According to estimates, the number of displaced persons is somewhere between a million and a million and a half, the latter figure being closer to reality. It can be maintained without risk of error that one Algerian in four is living away from their customary residence. The phenomena of internal migration are in reality very complex and take very diverse forms. The resettlements are thus only one aspect. It is very common, for example, for villages abandoned by their inhabitants who have left for the city to be occupied by people coming from less calm or more impoverished regions,[6] this being the case especially in Great and Little Kabylia.

Internal migration also takes the form of exodus to the towns, which the rural population see as a refuge against misery or insecurity. 'It is heaven here,' you often hear people say in Algiers, 'you are away from the storm.' Men working in France often have their family move to a town, to live with a brother or parent, when they are unable to bring them to France. They sometimes take a few days' holiday and come to collect them themselves. The shantytowns are constantly growing. The former inhabitants of the kasbah who have been able to find lodgings elsewhere, to escape controls and searches, are replaced by crowds from the countryside who huddle in precarious conditions.

On the other hand, the wretched situation of the greater part of the resettled population is well enough known. Several of the resettlement centres are nothing more than 'centres of misery' – to use an expression taken from an official study – or if you prefer, *rural shantytowns*. According to this study, it seems that only a third of the resettlements are viable; in this case, the people resettled have access to their lands or else have the use of lands granted them; there is no problem of subsistence, and housing is adequate. One may conclude that for the other two-thirds, there is a problem of subsistence, which is particularly serious in those resettlements (a third of the total) carried out in order to meet operational imperatives and 'intended to disappear as soon as security is re-established'.

The mere fact of a change in residence – whether this takes the form of resettlement, leaving for the city or for France – is bound to bring about a complete mutation in attitude towards the world. Living in a new environment leads to a break with tradition, which is completed, in the majority of cases, by the impossibility of returning to one's customary residence – no matter whether this impossibility is seen as provisional or definitive. This can be seen by examining a single case, a woman around 60 who had lived in the city from the age of 14, but had always maintained close relations with her native village in Little Kabylia, returning there to spend several months of the year. In 1955, return to the village became impossible. This definitive break in her attachment to the traditional family milieu, a break that fifty years in the city had never managed to completely effect, led to an overall change in her attitude towards the world, and particularly towards Western techniques. Whereas previously she had been happy to do heavy work, except for work involving Western techniques, she now concentrated on knitting and ironing. Up till now she had never tasted an unfamiliar dish, listened to the radio or taken any interest in political events. In short, it was quite as if her new awareness of the break (rather than the break itself in the strict sense) had induced in her a sense of having to adapt to a new world to which she had remained foreign up to then.

Community man is replaced by the man in the crowd, uprooted, torn away from the organic and spiritual units in which and by which he existed, cut off from his group and his native terrain, often placed in a material situation in which it is impossible even to remember the old ideal of honour and dignity. The war and its consequences, the resettlements of population and the rural exodus, only precipitate and strengthen the movement of cultural disintegration that the contact of civilizations and the colonial situation set in motion. Besides, this movement now extends to the domain that had been relatively spared because it remained sheltered in part from the enterprise of colonization and because small rural communities, closed in on themselves in a stubborn loyalty to their past and their tradition, had been able to safeguard the essential features of a civilization that can now be spoken of only in the past tense. A cluster of highly structured small communities has given way to a cloud of individuals, lacking attachments and roots.

The old values of honour crumble away on contact with the cruelties and atrocities of the war. An old Kabyle man said: 'There is not one man who will be able to say at the end of all this, I am a man.' The ideal self-image and the values associated with it have been put to the cruellest test. There are rapes and abductions of women, scenes in which the husband is interrogated, pushed to the ground or struck in the face in the presence of women. I was told how, in one village in Great Kabylia, soldiers went to accompany women to the well that was a little outside the built-up area, in order to protect them. On return, some women went to drink coffee with the soldiers, or invited them home. 'A young soldier comes to the house. The old man, defender of honour, who has been charged by the exile with watching over his wife or his daughter, knows that he can say nothing. He suffers and keeps silent in his corner. One day, the soldier arrives with some food. The old man takes his share and says nothing. He is ruined.'

Like an infernal machine, the war makes a clean slate of sociological realities; it crushes, grinds up and scatters the traditional communities of village, clan or family. Thousands of adult men are in the maquis, in internment camps, in prison, or refugees in Tunisia or Morocco; others have left for cities in Algeria or France, leaving their family in the village or the resettlement centres; others are in the French army; others again are dead or have disappeared. Every family is dispersed and torn apart. Entire regions, in Kabylia for example, are empty of men. In a clinic run by nuns, close to Chabet-el-Ameur, there have been no babies born for several months.

A mutation is under way in the de facto relationship between women and men. Many women, and not only widows, find themselves charged with responsibilities and tasks that formerly fell to the husband. Very often, the woman has to assure the family's subsistence, even if she receives help from a brother or an uncle. Her living space, which had previously been very reduced, is now widened. She moves around in the European town, goes into department stores, takes the train to visit her husband or a brother, and deals with administrative formalities. Leaving her closed and secret world, she breaks into the open space that was previously reserved for men. Engaged in the war either directly or indirectly, either as actor or as victim, she is compelled by circumstances to assume a new role; Algerian women, whether married or not, have acquired greater autonomy over the last few years. The break-up of the family bloc leads each member of the group to become aware of his or her individuality and, at the same time, their responsibilities. Young people in the city escape traditional controls and the pressure of public opinion, the essential foundation of the village community. It can happen, moreover, that the absence of the father throws them completely on their own resources. Many young people, especially in the towns, are today in the situation that Kabyles call the 'widow's son' (even when their father is still alive), that is, lacking a past, tradition, a self-ideal, abandoned to themselves. The authority of the father is often undermined, even if he is still living. It is no longer seen as the foundation of all values and the root of all decisions. The majority of young men and women follow a new system of values, in the name of which traditions are challenged. This is true above all for young people between 15 and 20: growing up during the war, and with the radicalism typical of adolescence, facing the future and knowing nothing of a past in which their elders, whatever they might do, are still rooted, they are often inspired with a spirit of rebellion and a negativism that can divide them from the older generation. And this psychological schism is often aggravated by a separation in fact. Maintenance of tradition presupposes continuous contact between successive generations and reverential respect for the elders. In the village communities, the influence of the old men is felt well beyond childhood, with the adult man continuing to submit to the authority of his father so long as he lives in the same house. With the dispersion of the family, the continuity of tradition itself is fundamentally compromised.

And so, together with other influences such as that of education, which increases the pressure from young people and their desire for emancipation, or of the cultural contagion that tends to set the lifestyles and value systems of different generations against each other, the war has overthrown the system of established relationships between the members of the Algerian family. The torn family is on the way to being a broken family if it does not find a new equilibrium. That the effects of the war have managed to affect Algerian society so strongly at its very core demonstrates how radical and brusque the challenge provoked by the war has been.

'We are in the fourteenth century . . .'[7] A century of the end of the world, when everything that was the rule becomes the exception, and everything that was prohibited is permitted. Children no longer respect their parents, women go to market, and so on. Popular consciousness expresses in this way the experience of a world turned upside down, where everything goes against the grain; it sees in the surrounding disorder and chaos the latter days that herald the end of the world. And it is true that in Algeria we are seeing the end of the world. But the end of this world is also experienced as the announcement of a new world.

Algerian society is undergoing the most radical upheaval possible. There is no single domain that is spared. The pillars of the traditional order have been shaken or demolished by the colonial situation and the war. The urban bourgeoisie has disintegrated; the values it embodied have been swept away by the eruption of new ideologies. The feudalists, often compromised by the support they gave the colonial administration and thus associated, in the eyes of the people, with the system of oppression, have most often lost both their material power and their spiritual authority. The rural masses, who opposed the innovations proposed by the West with a stubborn conservatism, have been caught up in the whirlpool of violence that makes a clean break with the past. Even Islam, because it is used more or less deliberately as a revolutionary ideology, has gradually changed its meaning and its function. In short, the war, by its nature, its duration and its amplitude, has brought about a radical revolution. It is predictable that the return of peace will reveal an Algeria quite different from the Algeria in which the war began, an Algeria deeply revolutionary because deeply revolutionized.

Conducting a sociological analysis of the consequences of the war, therefore, does not simply mean counting the ruin and damage it has wrought. In fact, the radical mutation that is presently under way in Algeria does not just present negative aspects. The lesson of the facts offers the elements of a policy capable of turning this catastrophic experience of social surgery to good effect. It seems that, contrary to what had always been maintained, everything is possible in Algeria on condition that these masses, whom the colonial situation and the war drove into action by destroying the community ensembles in which they were rooted, are able to take their own destiny in hand with complete freedom and responsibility. The aggregate of disoriented and tossed-around atoms will perhaps give way to a new type of social unit, based not at all on organic attachment to values handed down by centuries-old tradition, but rather on active, creative and conscious participation in a common work.

Workers and Peasants in Disarray

Uprooted Peasants:
Morphological Upheavals and Cultural Changes in Algeria

The day that we learned the words 'good evening',
We got a blow on the jaw:
We were locked up in prison.

The day that we learned the words 'good morning',
We got a blow on the nose:
That was an end to our blessings.

The day that we learned the words 'thank you',
We got a blow on the neck:
The lamb inspires more fear than we do.

The day that we learned the word 'pig',
A dog's honour was worth more than ours:
The *khammès* bought a mule.

The day that we learned the word 'brother',
We got a blow on the knee:
We walked in shame to the yoke.

The day that we learned the word 'devil',
We got a blow that drove us mad:
We became carriers of dung.

If the resettlement policy fosters – or, better, *authorizes* – an acceleration of change, this is above all because it places the group in a more
defenceless state. In fact, because of the interdependence between the
organization of space, the structure of social groups and the type of
sociability, the upheaval in the morphological foundations affects
and undermines every level of social reality. In this respect, change is

sudden and total: a swarm of little units based on genealogy, strongly integrated and of modest size, scattered in space and established at the heart of their own territory – the *zribat* in the Collo region and the extended families that form *farqat* in the Chéliff – is brusquely replaced by agglomerations that are sometimes quite enormous, bringing populations of different origin together in a restricted space.[1] The convergence of groups that were previously separated in space, the increase in size of the social unit, the new organization of habitat and the network of displacements – these are the most important and most constant features of the upheaval affecting the morphological substratum of the groups. The ensuing upheavals, however, vary in their form, extent and intensity, according to the form and extent of the transformations in the morphological substratum.

From the Clan to the Household

First of all, the intervention of the authorities and the simple fact of contact between groups that differ in their history and their degree of acculturation give rise to an acceleration in the process of cultural change. The action of those in positions of authority was inspired by the intention, either implicit or explicit, to make the Algerian populations 'evolve' towards social structures and attitudes of a Western type: the clan or family unit with a genealogical basis was to be replaced by the village unit with a spatial basis; the extended family made up of several generations and marked by collective possession was to be replaced by the household in the Western sense. In several places, therefore, the resettled populations have been forced to build as many houses as there were households; some people have had to build a house for one or other of their emigrant relatives, and sometimes the emigrant himself has had to come and fulfil this obligation.[2] The separate habitation accentuates and accelerates the weakening of family ties that had already begun; each family now has its own cooking pot and its own budget, just as most often it already had its own land.[3] Besides, the convergence of different groups, the fragmentation of communities, the dissolving influence on these arising from the shantytown situation and the precariousness of living conditions all tend to weaken customary ties and give rise to the appearance of *solidarities of a new type, based above all on an identity of conditions of existence.*

In this domain too, resettlement only precipitates a movement already begun. Thus in many Kabyle villages the geographic unit, that is, the village, had gradually taken over the political, economic and ritual functions that had formerly fallen to each of the clans (*idherman*, plural of *adhrum*): for example, the collective sacrifice that each clan used to perform separately had by 1950 become common to the whole village. The same causes work towards the crumbling of the family unit: the spirit of calculation, introduced by the generalization of monetary exchange and by emigration, undermines the sense of fraternity that underpinned the family community and develops individualism in every domain. Collective possession in its various forms is an increasing burden on individuals, and is more frequently broken up. The inherited land cultivated in common is no longer sufficient to satisfy the demands of the group that it used to unite, and that now it tends to divide.[4] Each person would like to be able to disassociate his own share, less because he feels he is exploited by the others than because it is hard for him to tolerate being chained to the others by the intermediary of the common land. The authority of the 'master of the house' has been undermined by the new spirit, and can no longer maintain the unity it used to safeguard. Breaking with collective possession, a kind of desperate wager, appears the only way to free oneself from the group and seek one's own fortune. It fosters the illusion of breaking with the common poverty, whereas dividing this poverty only makes it worse. The break with the peasant community seals the break with the peasant condition: a man sells his share and goes off to the town, or else he becomes a *khammès*, in the hope of regular employment. When it survives (or is maintained), collective possession is no more than a pretence made by the family to both the group and itself. In the same way that people continue working the land because it is an inheritance that it would be dishonourable to abandon, collective possession and the common life of family members is perpetuated because a point of honour bans letting the ancestral name perish; like agriculture, which is a routine sacrifice, a forced collective possession that is maintained solely for the intention of others means a negation of the 'unity of the house' (*zaddi wukham*) that ruled out the very idea of division. A bus driver from Djemâa-Saharidj, who stopped work on the land a long time back, explains in this way the fact that his family are one of the rare few to maintain collective possession:

> I would certainly like to sleep in a bed and not on the ground, but if I buy a bed for myself, I have to buy one for every man in the family [. . .]; I would like to eat differently, to have a butane stove in the house, but how can you use butane when you have to cook for thirty-six people? No! All that is impossible, if we want to continue all living together [. . .] I don't know any more what kinship connection there

is between Dj– and me, but we can't go on sharing. We are a large house, the last big house that remains in our clan; everywhere you hear the same – with the Aït M– there is only now the house of Aa–. If we separate, it's the end; we won't be anything, none of us would be able to raise an ox by himself! We were *akham* [a house]; we'll become like the other families, *thikhamin* [maisonettes]. And that's the end of our whole clan, while the clan opposite still counts two *idzhin* [undivided] families, and being cleverer than us, they are trying to strengthen themselves still more.

Certain families, because they follow the logic of honour, abolish collective possession 'within' (*bat't'u n dakhal*: internal sharing), but by a kind of fiction, they outwardly maintain the illusion that unity remains (*zaddi n barra*). Though new walls divide the house, though all the furniture and the stocks have been divided, though the pair of oxen have been appraised along with the rest of the herd, though the property has been secretly divided between the heirs and all that remains is to plant tufts of grass along the demarcation lines to show the break-up of collective possession, nothing betrays the separation of the household to outward view. The same man continues to speak in the name of the whole family that he is responsible for to *thajmaâth* [the village council] and in the market; the same pair of oxen and the same flock continue to cross his threshold. But devoid of their original meaning, all the demonstrations by which the community recreated and strengthened itself prove incapable of reviving the sentiment or even the illusion of true community.

The Confrontation of Differences

In a general way, resettlement tends to accelerate the cultural contagion from which some groups were protected by their isolation; as a tremendous movement of enforced descent to the plains, resettlement has everywhere brought together populations that were divided by both wealth and status, by their cultural traditions and above all by their recent history and the *degree of their adaptation* to the modern economy. Thus the inhabitants of the mountain *zribat*, pure peasants who had only rare and brief connections with the town, find themselves in direct and daily contact with natives of the Aïn-Aghbel *zribat*, who seem like townspeople in their eyes. By virtue of its situation (at the centre of a cluster of isolated hamlets, and two hours' walk from Collo), Aïn-Aghbel was predisposed to play the role of a link between the rural and the urban worlds: and in fact, the inhabitants of the piedmont *zriba* combine the products of a relatively rich agriculture (very much so, since the average size of a property here was as much as 75 acres) with the wages obtained from regular employment (jobs as forest warden or cork worker) or from seasonal work, as well as cash income from the sale of wood, charcoal, heath plants and vegetables. Owing to its central position, Aïn-Aghbel served as a commercial link between the surrounding rural *zribat* and the town: playing the role of intermediary in both directions, its shopkeepers sold products bought in Collo or left on deposit by shopkeepers from there, at the same time as they collected and distributed almost all the products marketed by the surrounding peasant population, from cattle supplied by pastoral *zribat* to baskets of vegetables and fruit, jugs of milk and whey, eggs and fowl.[5] Given that some twenty inhabitants of this *zriba* also travelled each day to Collo to work either for the government or in factories (a factory making corks for bottles and other cork products, sawmills, sardine canneries), it is clear that the natives of Aïn-Aghbel maintained constant contact with the small town of Collo, a market and workplace as well as a centre of religious life, whose mosque was attended for Friday prayers, on the eve of Ramadan and for other major ceremonies. This population also owed its semi-urban character to the fact that, possessing one of the oldest schools in the whole region, it enjoyed a high level of school attendance.[6] The 'village of those who've been to school' thus naturally came to be invested with the role of intermediary in all relationships with the administration, in all acts requiring the use of French, and above all, in all circumstances where resort to writing and paper was necessary: why go to Collo to have a letter to a son or brother written by a public scribe, when you can get this done more cheaply in Aïn-Aghbel?[7] In fact, despite all the differences, solidarity forbids the person able to write from profiting from a skill that he owes to exceptional circumstances; in any case, when it is a question of confronting a 'son of the town' (*wald blad*), people prefer the help of a 'son of the mountain' like themselves, rather than resorting to the mediation of another 'son of the town'.

And so, with resettlement, peasants attached to the traditional system of values find themselves placed in continuous contact with peasants who have already taken certain liberties with tradition; the enforced leisure promotes comparison of behaviours, confrontation of opinions and the discovery of unknown representations in the economic, social and political fields. Under the olive tree where the men customarily gather, by the marabout shrine among the grass-covered tombs of the old cemetery, it is no longer, as in earlier assemblies, the oldest and wisest who speak loudest, but rather the returned emigrants, rich in their experience of work in the urban context and above all in their knowledge of the modern world and its 'civilization'; it is the literate man, an Astrakhan hat on his head and a French weekly paper under his arm, who speaks surrounded by solidly rural peasants listening in silent approval.

This expansion of consciousness and knowledge of the world reaches the very core of the traditionalist mind, which presupposes, if not total ignorance, at least a refusal of other ways of living and thinking, rejected as incompatible with the peasant state. Contact with a different world has an exceptional contagious force here. Everything used to protect the peasant who went to the town to make purchases or sell the products of his land from the seductions of urban existence; everything around him reminded him of his peasant condition, making him feel uneasily the strangeness of this world to which he was indeed completely foreign. With resettlement, the whole transplanted group finds itself continuously mingling with people who are certainly peasants, but who have broken with peasant values and traditions and embody, if not urbanity, at least de-ruralization. The new awareness of differences leads in this case to a reflection on previous existence.

In Kerkera, for example, where because of the size of the resettlement, the diversity of the groups gathered there is still greater, the mountain people who had very little connection with the town, or even with the *zribat* of the foothills, find themselves placed in contact with townsfolk from the Kerkera *zriba*.[8] And a mountain man from the El-Bir *zriba* spells out very clearly the opposition between the 'mountain people' and the 'plains people', an opposition that had long been consecrated by tradition, but that he discovered in a new guise by comparing himself to his neighbour, a native of the Kerkera *zriba*:

> We are men of the mountain; we cannot live in this place [the valley of *oued* Guebli]. We are used to water and trees.[9] We are *fellah'in* and the only thing we know how to do is work the land and live off the land. We eat millet and we live in *gourbis* made of mud and branches. We have no need for stone houses. [. . .] While they [the people from the Kerkera *zriba* and other foothill *zribat*] are close to Collo, they go there in the morning and come back three or four hours later. They all have jobs [outside of agriculture], they work in the Collo factories, they are shopkeepers, they are all builders. They live in stone houses, while we live in mud *gourbis*; they grow wheat and barley, they have a school. You see, in the resettlements they have shops, cafés, jobs in the offices, permanent houses, while we are parked away from the road, on 'terraces' [allocated by the DRS] that hold water. They go to

Collo by bicycle, they have all the cars and lorries from the centre. For our part, we've lost our donkeys. [. . .] How would my son marry one of their daughters? [. . .] They took wives from here, but we never asked for their daughters. A son of the mountain marries a daughter of the mountain; a daughter from the plain in a mountain family would mean the ruin of that family. Would we have to give her millet to eat? Whereas a daughter of the mountain can only be content living with them; wheat for her is welcome, she is used to millet.[10]

Resettlement has only accentuated the differences between the groups it brings together. In Djebabra, the Djebabra *farqa*, who arrived first, occupied the upper part of the site, which, apart from being in a better position, offered more favourable conditions of habitation (the gentle slope aiding the run-off of water) and enabled farmers easily to watch over their lands located further down. At the time of the study, in 1960, the upper part of the centre stood out by its red tile roofs: before leaving, the Djebabra who occupied this had been able to collect the roofs of their former dwellings that were located close by. The Merdja, on the other hand, who arrived more recently, had to establish themselves lower down, in *gourbis* that were highly precarious. Forced to leave in a hurry habitations located at the heart of the forbidden zone far from the resettlement site, compelled to make several successive moves from one provisional resettlement to another, they were scarcely able to rescue any of their most valuable possessions.[11] In the eyes of the Djebabra, the Merdja are mountain folk. Their lands, located on the first range of foothills, are poor, unsuitable for cereal growing and planted with trees (olive and fig); they draw some of their resources (wood and charcoal) from the patches of forest scattered across their territory, while the presence of springs sometimes makes gardening possible on small plots of irrigated land. Because the interdiction affecting the Merdja lands, which are more distant and difficult of access, spares those of the Djebabra that are closer and more fertile, the Merdja find themselves placed in a relationship of dependence towards the Djebabra, their 'hosts'. Their only recourse would be to become their sharecroppers or agricultural labourers. But they are bound to reject the present situation and, by the same token, all behaviours that tend to sanction it; hence their refusal to cultivate the only lands accessible to them, those of other people. And the oldest of the *farqa*, whom the families recognize as head by calling him *Sidi*, can say, looking at the crests on the horizon where he had his fields, his garden and his house: 'We are here, but our hearts are up there.'

An immediate grasp of the differences that resettlement accentuates, and particularly the economic and social inequalities, is often complemented, especially among the younger, by a rejection of their previous existence.[12] 'When peace returns', says a butcher from the Touila *zriba*, 'I will not return to the *zriba*, I'd rather go to Tamalous or another town, but not to the *zriba*. I'll be at home wherever I find work. We've had enough "hard", we want "gentle" and "easy". If someone wants the mountain, let him go there, it's there for him.'

Comparison between experiences, however, is only a small part in discovering the fictitious character of agricultural work in its traditional form. Despite the reduction in the standard of living brought about by resettlement, and even when nostalgia for the earlier life breaks through in statements or behaviour, disaffection with work on the land is forcefully expressed. The demand for a decent income and the aspiration to a genuine trade, previously rejected as overly ambitious, can be proclaimed in broad daylight, because peasant society is no longer sufficiently confident of its fundamental values and norms to restrain or condemn deviations.

The Broken Group

If the transplanted group provides a favourable terrain for cultural contagion, and if it is more generally the site of accelerated cultural change, this is in fact because it is too deeply disorganized and transformed to be able to exert its regulatory action. The change of habitat promotes the fragmentation of old social units, either because the new settlement separates and disperses members of the same family or clan, or because the move offers an opportunity to leave for the town. Before being resettled in Draâ-Driyas (Djebabra), the Merdja had been evacuated to a number of different places, including Sidi-Benazzouz, Saharidj 'Manival', close to a lake (Sahridj) located on the farm of a colonist, for the Laouad, Touafria, Abderrahman, Megran, Kharoubi and other families, as well as the Aalia families from Djebabra; to 'La Ferme', another estate belonging to a colonist, for the Zaouali-Bouzar, Bâa, Bouabdallah, Abed and Kebaïli families, as well as the Athman family from Djebabra. The only families directly resettled on the site of the present centre (which originally was simply another temporary assembly point) were those that shared the Draâ-Driyas territory, that is, the Medjdabi and Rouabah families from the Merdja *farqa* and the Merzoug, Djebouri and Haboui-Zitouni families from the Djebabra *farqa*. In the course of these successive displacements, groups dwindled and fragmented, many families migrated to the colonization centres of the Mitidja (Bou Medfra, Meurad, Hamman-Righa, Bourkika, Marengo, etc.), many healthy men went off to find work on a permanent basis with colonists on the plains, and others, unable to escape to the town, ended up in the surrounding resettlements. With the Merdja, for example, out of a total of 193 households (or twenty patriarchal families) that lived in the *farqa*, no more than 110 were to be found in Djebabra. Only five large families (forty households) remained complete in the resettlement: five others completely disappeared, two lost two-thirds of their members, six lost more than half, one other nearly a half and the last one nearly a quarter. Out of the thirty families that the Rouabaha (from Merdja) comprised, only fourteen are in the resettlement. A large number of family heads have been killed. Out of the five Mekki families, four have abandoned Aïn-Sidi-Mekki, where they cultivated 20 hectares of land, and are refugees in Hammam-Righa. Only one has remained in the resettlement. The large family of the Medjdabi, divided into several branches – the Medjdabi, the Bezzaz, the Belabbès and the Abbaci – relatively escaped this scattering: settled in a familiar environment, as the resettlement occupied part of its own territory, it has kept twenty-eight of the thirty-four small families that it previously counted,[13] nine families (out of thirteen) of the Kharoubi from Aïn-Taffah, four families of the Touafria; four families belonging to the Ghoraïfa, the Megran, thought they could escape resettlement by migrating to the town, but they were resettled in Msissa.

Among the Djebabra, there is no large family that has remained entirely in the resettlement: three families have completely disappeared; one has lost more than three-quarters of its former members, only two have lost less than half, and only one has kept more than three-quarters of its members. The marabout family of the Sidmou, who occupied the best lands in the region, at Guelaâ-Sidi-Malek, is scattered between Meurad, Bourkika, and Bou-Medfa.[14] The Bouchrit family has migrated to Bou-Medfa, apart from two of its eleven family heads.[15] Those families closest to the resettlement site have not escaped dispersion: half of the Djebouri are in Meurad and Bourkika, half of the Merzoug in Marengo, and there are no Dahmani here at all. In the Collo mountains, the Djenan-Hadjem *zriba* (resettled in the Ghedir) has undergone a similar fate. Faced with imminent resettlement, more than 300 individuals (out of 500 that the *zriba* counted) fled to Philippeville in 1957, while 86 (or twenty families) went to Kerkera and 113 (twenty-four families) to the Ghedir. Apart from three *harki* families, and seven others who are too suspect in the eyes of the military authorities to enjoy freedom of movement, the resettlements only contain families who did not have relations in the town able to accommodate them (sixteen families, ten of which were without their head, who had been killed or imprisoned), or families whose head was too old, sick, disabled or poor to be able to move. To give some more examples, half the population of Aïn-Bouyahia in the vicinity of Carnot (i.e. some 3,986 individuals) have been dispersed between three resettlement centres (975 in Aïn-Tida, 1,234 in Louroud and 1,777 in Bouarous), not to speak of those families whose men have all fled the *farqa* and who are now established in town. The Chemla *farqa,* situated on the plain and bordering on the main road, was partly resettled far from its land (385 families) and partly in Carnot (258 families). Finally, the very large marabout family of the Ouaïl, which occupied an immense territory in the Cherchell municipality, was totally expelled from its territory, which was declared a forbidden zone, and dispersed between the Dar-el-Caïd resettlement (twenty-two families, 124 individuals), that of Sidi-Lakehal (twenty-seven families), the Lavarande CAPER (thirteen families), and the towns in the region: Duperré, Marengo and Affreville (seventeen families).[16] Everywhere, resettlement has brought about a scattering of families and clans; everywhere, the able-bodied men who could do so have fled to the towns. As an old man in Matmata put it, 'those who still had wings strong enough to fly left, and all that remain are birds with broken wings.'[17]

From Familiarity to Anonymity

Another fact is that the convergence of groups that were previously separated in a single space, and the increase in size of the elementary social unit, have a direct effect on social life and forms of sociability. The resettlements of Kerkera and Matmata are immense rural shantytowns that have brought together individuals who were not absolutely foreign to one another; inhabitants of the same *âarch* maintained intermittent connections on the occasion of markets, pilgrimages, marriages and journeys, and the classificatory, indirect and expert knowledge that they had of one another was completely different from the familiarity (in the strong sense) that united members of the same clan and, to a lesser degree, the same village (in Kabylia, for example).[18] The increase in the size of the group fosters the appearance of a new type of sociability.[19] For example, when you meet someone in the street, you generally greet them as is done in the town, at a distance, with a simple nod of the head or a word: *s'ah'a, s'ah'it* (greetings to you). The honorary greeting, addressed to a whole group of men (*salam âalaykum*) has fallen into disuse. This greeting addressed to *thajmaâth* used to mark the entry of an adolescent into

the world of adults, in the same way as participation in certain agricultural tasks (ploughing) and the fulfilment of certain religious obligations (fasting). It was logical therefore for it to be addressed to
men, excluding women and children.[20] Today you can hear, instead
of *salam*, such incongruous phrases as *bunjur âalik, bunswar fellak,
adyu* and even *tchaw*. Shaking hands, which was unknown in traditional society, where the whole group was present at all times to each
of its members, now opens and closes almost all encounters. Marks
of civility tend increasingly to be extended to women, at least older
women: it is extremely rare now to see an old woman kiss the hand
or the head of a man, as in the traditional custom; instead they briefly
shake hands, uttering the same expressions that men use among
themselves.

In the same way, the café (and the type of sociability associated
with it) is replacing the *jamâa* [assembly]; the customers and staff of
the Kerkera cafés (eleven in number), which are located on the main
street just as in town, seek to reproduce the behaviour and attitudes
of townsfolk: games of dominos and cards, sitting on a bench if planning to drink, and on the ground (without touching the wall) if not
ordering. When the traditional *jamâa* still survives and has not been
completely absorbed by the *café maure*, long viewed as a more or
less scandalous institution (tolerated only when it was held in the
open air away from the village, and only for celebrations or before
the Ramadan fast), it is never the same people that frequent the two
places. Conversation in the café is different from that in the *jamâa*;
traditional conversation is a kind of ritual exchange, both its form
and its content being regulated by imperatives of propriety and by
peasant morality, which forbids tackling frivolous subjects of an
urban character, good only for café chatter. Finally, and above all,
the café is a kind of neutral ground where, as distinct from the *jamâa*,
which is strictly reserved for members of the clan or the village, there
is a place for everyone, young or old, rich or poor, stranger or 'son
of the country'.[21]

Another sign of transformation in the style of social relations is
the appearance of the veil for women. In previous rural society,
women who did not have to hide themselves from members of their
clan were supposed to follow distinct itineraries, to go to the well
(and secondarily to the fields) at times that were fixed by tradition:
protected in this way from the eyes of strangers, they did not wear
the veil and were free of *alh'ujba* (an existence confined to the house).
In the resettlement, as in town, there is no longer space for each social
unit, and on top of this, the men's space and the women's space
overlap; finally, the partial or total abandonment of agricultural work

condemns men to spend the whole day in the village or at home. It is impossible therefore for women to continue going out so freely without bringing disdain and dishonour on the men of the family. Unable to adopt the veil of the townswoman without denying her peasant identity, the rural woman transplanted to the town has to take care to appear only on the threshold of her own doorway. By creating a characteristically urban social field, resettlement leads to wearing the veil so as to make it possible to move among strangers.

In the long run, moreover, it is bound to promote a reinterpretation of the role traditionally ascribed to women: even before resettlement, in fact, women tended increasingly to stay at home, to devote themselves to household tasks and abandon agricultural work; or, more precisely, many peasant men, following the urban example, were increasingly reluctant to associate their wife with the work on the land that they themselves performed forcibly under constraint. In the Aïn-Sultan CAPER, those inhabitants who refuse to let their women and children work (i.e. 95 per cent of the former agricultural workers who also cultivated land on their own account, and 70 per cent of former *fellah'in*) are overwhelmed with work, the *cultural* space having been determined on the assumption of female participation in the family's labour-power (460 working days per man, a third of these being performed by women and children, that is, 120 days of women's work and 300 days of children's work). Awareness of the condition of wage-earner, and the change in attitude towards the land, authorize and encourage the change of attitude towards women's work.[22] In this context, women's participation in agricultural work seems like a swindle: 'I'm paid a wage,' one man says, 'and one worker is enough for this wage. I'm not going to have my wife work as well!' Is an attitude like this not almost inevitably bound up with discovering the low profitability of agriculture?

Resettlement prevents women from performing the greater part of their traditional tasks. First of all, the authorities' intervention is in some respects focused on them, since in the eyes of the military, as of the majority of naive observers, the condition of the Algerian woman was the most evident sign of the 'barbarism' that was to be struggled against by all means, direct or indirect. On the one hand, almost everywhere the army set up women's circles and workshops; on the other, they sought to abruptly destroy everything that they saw as standing in the way of 'women's liberation': in Kerkera (as in many other centres), the houses were not supplied with courtyards; the well and the wash-place are almost everywhere placed right in the centre of the quadrilateral. More generally, military action and repression subjected the morality of honour that governed the division of labour and relations between the sexes to a terrible test.[23] Everywhere, this policy met with a very strong resistance: in Matmata, the women's circle set up in January 1959, not in the premises that had initially been reserved for it at the centre of the village, but in the dispensary buildings 'away from the view of the men', was only regularly attended by three girls who had been appointed to this role. Everywhere, women have suffered particularly from resettlement. It is the men and the children who do the shopping and go to collect water from the well: in Kerkera, the men bring the water back in buckets or barrels loaded on donkeys, sometimes even in large earthenware jars that women set down and collect at the corner of their house, without crossing the road. Located lower down in the resettlement, however, far from the main road and out of sight of the men, accessible only by indirect paths, the traditional well of Aïn-Boumaala, used by the Kerkera *zriba*, still attracts women who come there to wash clothes, bedcovers, sheepskins; many women continue to draw their water there (despite the proximity of new wells), simply because it gives them the opportunity to chat for a while. In Djebabra, nostalgia for the old home and the earlier social life is expressed differently: women come in groups to spend the afternoon in their old houses, a quarter of an hour's walk away for those nearest, half an hour for those who have furthest to go. These efforts to continue the old way of life attest to the depth of disarray experienced by women in the resettlements. If we bear in mind that as well as these specific and direct influences there are also all those acting on the economic and social life of the group as a whole, this gives the measure of the transformation in the role that the group traditionally conferred on women.

In parallel with this, *a new type of solidarity* tends to develop, resting no longer on kinship ties but, as in the urban shantytowns, on the feeling of sharing *the same conditions of existence, on awareness of a common misery and a common revolt against this misery*. We thus see the resurgence of behaviours and attitudes analogous to those that can be observed within the primary groups of clan or village, but invested now with a quite different meaning and function. In Djebabra, for example, where the Djebabra *farqa*, the richest one, assists members of the Merdja *farqa*; in Kerkera, where every family that can cooks an abundance of couscous and sends children to take a dish to destitute neighbours. Mutual aid is no longer inspired by customary imperatives; this solidarity among the poor, sharing the same unhappiness even if it is unevenly distributed, is detached from the body of traditions that inspired the old solidarity based on a sense of fraternity. Awareness of sharing the same fate is a sufficient basis for the semi-personal relationships established in the café or in the village square: a community of experience replaces the experience of community.[24] The other is no longer necessarily perceived as member of a lineage, the son of so-and-so: 'Now everyone is alike. There are no longer people from here and people from there; no longer the sons of one family and the sons of another. We are all in the same situation, all going through the same thing' (resettled man, Kerkera). The habit spreads of designating or addressing other people, including relatives and friends, by the official patronymic that has been recently coined, often with an ironic intention, and rarely takes the name of the clan. The entrenched opposition between relatives and strangers has been abolished, and one's neighbour may be at the same time familiar and foreign – meaning that familiarity is emptied of its significance: 'Before,' says an old man from Djebabra (75 years old), 'everyone was fine in their own home, cultivating their fields. Now we are all together, and if fire catches one of us, it will burn everyone. Now it's "as the sheaf, so the stack". No one can refuse to help another. If the sheaf burns, the whole stack will burn. Before, the fire just struck a single house, now it spreads to all, as we all have to live together.'

The ambiguity of discourse precisely reflects the ambiguity of experience: if the highly intense participation in the restricted and isolated group of familiars (household or *farqa*) is described nostalgically as isolation, this is because it is opposed to the twofold and contradictory feeling of being both crushed and isolated in an anonymous crowd. Surrounded by strangers (i.e. by non-relatives), each head of family in the resettlement infringes the rule that traditionally prohibits the 'solitary' (i.e. an isolated man with no male relative, among a foreign group) from having a family.[25] The optimistic solidarity that was assured by the kinship community has given way to a pessimistic solidarity (as expressed above in the image of the fire), that is, a solidarity of misery imposed by promiscuity. Piling together in the resettlements, or in the shantytowns on the edge of small communities, brings together relatives who were previously separated. In Carnot [now El Abadia], where nearly half of the sparse population of the municipality are refugees (i.e. 44 per cent of the different *farqat*: Ababsa, Chekaknia, Cheurfa, Harartha, Mehabile and Ouled Aïssa), a fifth of the former rural population are supported by families already established in the town; in almost all cases, these are fairly distant relatives, mere *allies* (which goes against the traditional logic), even friends who help meet the needs of the refugees they have welcomed under their roof. If the solidarity imposed by the emergency situation may be exercised beyond the traditional boundaries of family, clan or village, this is because its meaning has changed. The artificial character of these temporary unions is clear to all, everyone having an all too acute awareness of their situation as helped or helper: sharing the same roof and the same cooking pot without sharing the same land and taking part in collective work and responsibility means lacking the morality of honour on which the old collective possession was based. These groups that reconstitute themselves under the pressure of necessity thus cannot provide individuals with the feeling of security that the peasant family previously ensured for its members: experienced as arbitrary and sometimes even illegitimate, the continuous coexistence with 'strangers' appears more as promiscuity than as participation in a resettled and redrawn community. This explains the paradoxical fact that the increase in material density does not lead to an increase in what Durkheim would call 'moral density', but quite the opposite.

If they weaken old solidarities and traditional oppositions, resettlement and the economic action of the army foster the appearance of antagonisms based on economic difference. In the first place, in a quasi-urban situation those groups or individuals whose previous history had brought them into contact with the modern economy and society find themselves in a favoured position. The most basic education, a certain familiarity with urban life acquired by emigration or the experience of wage-labour, provide considerable advantages in economic competition. Following the principle that work sticks together, jobs in the modern sector are monopolized by a few families, precisely those whose head has a job in this sector. In Kerkera, for example, the interviewees included five manual workers, four of whom were family heads, employed full-time by companies in Collo (building contractors, the government's highways department), or in local services in the resettlement itself. Semi-permanent workers who are prioritized for re-engagement by their former employers can be counted in the same category. Alongside these privileged ones, there are all those who have been able to obtain a temporary job of some kind, either in the centre itself, or in Collo. These are above all men working in the traditional sector (grocer's and butcher's assistants, waiters, artisan's mates, etc.) who, because they are often related to the employer, may be viewed as family manpower and are poorly paid. Also the builders and labourers who are temporarily engaged in works undertaken by the Section Administrative Spécialisée or the town hall: as the only possible employers are the public services (since family houses are built by people for themselves), they are dependent on the good will of the

SAS or the town hall, and the intermittent experience of paid work only heightens their awareness of unemployment.[26] The differences between these categories are very marked: workers in Collo, whether permanent or casual, earn twice as much as permanent workers in Kerkera, and among those working there, the permanent earn eight times as much as the non-permanent.

In the same way, at Aïn-Aghbel, there are significant differences among the resettled *zribat*: the most acculturated *zribat*, owing to the high level of emigration and the intensity of their contact with the town, have more wage-earners – permanent ones in particular – working in Collo than do the mountain *zribat*, more attached to the peasant tradition and less well equipped in economic competition. The workers employed in Collo all originate (in order) from Aïn-Aghbel, Lahraïch and Mekoua; Bekoura and Yezzar only have workers in Aïn-Aghbel itself. The other *zribat* (Beni-Bellit, Bourarsen, Yersan, etc.) do not have anyone (in the sample) in waged employment. Jobs in Collo, as we have seen, are more stable, even when intermittent (certain workers being employed each year by the same company), and twice as well paid.

The opening to the modern world acquired by emigration or by earlier experience of wage-labour, as well as formal education,[27] are not the only advantages in economic competition. We must also take into account the intervention of the authorities. The strengthening of the administrative apparatus led to the creation of a relatively substantial number of jobs. The SAS and the town hall, which alone can offer permanent jobs in the centre, allocate these as a function of the candidates' past record, their relationship with the authorities, and the services they can render. In Kerkera, for example, a former *ouaqaf* (a traditional notable who represents the population of his village to the *caïd* [meaning a government official]) is employed to do petty tasks in the town hall. His elder son is a *harki*. Another, a builder by trade, has been given a permanent job as a foreman. The K. family, originating from the Ghedir, include a secretary at the town hall (a former *khodja* [trustee] of the Kerkera *caïd*), a bookkeeper with the SAS, a post office employee, a grocery wholesaler who supplies the shops in the region and a baker. The mayor, a former official of the Constantine tramway company, readily confuses the management of municipal business with that of his own interests. He stubbornly defends the resettlement project at 'Kilometre 19', that is, close to his native *zriba*, at a site that his family and himself can control. He has a share in most of local businesses (in twenty-six, to be exact); it is he who allocates the commercial premises built by the SAS, and deals with enrolment on the commercial register. Any candidate who does not involve the mayor in his business is rejected.

Similarly, in Barbacha, jobs allocated by a public service (the municipality, the SAS, the highways department, the DRS,[28] etc.) are the reward for services rendered. A former miner from Draâ-Larbâa, for example, with a monthly pension of 130 francs, receives on top of this a salary of 160 francs as site superintendent for the local subdivision of the highways department, for having agreed to be a docile municipal councillor. The son of another municipal councillor earns 200 francs per month as a worker for the municipality. In this way, certain families, because they are better off or collaborate with the authorities, tend to monopolize waged employment and various other advantages: small handicraft businesses (transport, taxis, bakers, grocers, etc.) are also often helped by the authorities and run by people occupying official positions (as in Kerkera).[29]

Given the scarcity of cash and permanent sources of money income in general, not to mention that the majority of economic advantages, and particularly jobs in the modern sector, become the monopoly of a few, two social strata (themselves stratified) tend to form within the rural world, differing not only in their sphere of work and their incomes, but also in their consumption habits, which express their whole attitude towards the world.

Despite the apparent uniformity of conditions, differences in this field are as sharp as they could possibly be, since, in Djebabra for example, the lowest daily expenditure (on food) is 0.40 francs and the highest is 6 francs, the coefficient of variation being in the order of 75 per cent.[30] Renouncing the ascetic ethos of the old society and adopting urban consumption habits is most clearly apparent in the case of the new rich, government employees and administrative officials, secretaries and officials of the town halls, forest guards, postal employees, all of whom are very often able to add profits of various kinds to their official income, and live in the resettlement centres as people live in town, wearing the same kind of suit, occupying as comfortable houses and eating the same food.[31] This privileged minority are like a mirror that reflects to the great majority an image of their poverty: the sense of having suffered an identical misfortune, of which economic misery is only one aspect, leads to ignoring all the inequalities in impoverishment and poverty except for those that divide the profiteers from everyone else.[32] 'There are no longer poor people, and no longer rich,' said a resettled man in Kerkera; 'there are only the poor and a few individuals who profit from the general poverty.'

Urban Situation and Peasant Values

The transformation of the morphological substratum and, more pre-cisely, the increase in size of the group, create a quasi-urban situation that affects the meaning of all behaviour. This urban situation favours the 'de-ruralized' peasants, who alone are able to adapt to a certain degree, as against those stuck in their 'rurality', set on preserving peasant values, who appear out of place and even ridiculous. The resettlements are referred to as *blad*, the town, in contrast to *âarch*, *farqa* and *zriba*. Resettlement, a kind of local emigration, makes the solidly rural peasant an exile in his own land, a 'home emigrant':[33] the change of context leads to the devaluation of peasant virtues, which are useless and out of place. The old people, guardians of tradition, are most seriously affected by displacement. Being espe-cially ill-prepared to adapt to unexpected situations, owing to their age and their attachment to the traditional order, they are particularly unequipped; the quasi-urban situation created by resettlement brings about a reversal in attitudes towards traditional hierarchies: the youngest people are now no longer protected but protectors. The revolutionary context also helps to devalue the prestige traditionally attached to age. During a discussion beneath the olive tree of the *jamâa* in Aïn-Aghbel, a young man, supported by the whole assembly, replied to an old man who had previously remained silent but now spoke to ascribe the misery of the present to the abandonment of tradition: 'Oh, you old people, we know what you've done! Nothing! You're responsible for what's happening to us.'

In the same way, an old man from Djebabra explains: 'A father ordered his son to work, not to stay without doing anything, and the son replied: "You lot, you old people, you brought misery [*miziriya*] with you from birth."' And the patriarch of the Merzoug family from Djebabra, a man aged 85, describes the collapse of the old people's authority:

> Previously, when a child did something stupid, his grandfather was cited as an example, and he was told to be like him, to be as good as he'd been. It's not like that now, when everyone does what they like. Young people think the old people are crazy. Twenty years ago, old people still had authority, their wisdom was listened to. There was respect. I was already married, my younger brother was already grown up, and my older brother – he died in 1926 – came up and slapped me for not respecting him. Now, if I grumble a bit at a child, he gets annoyed and I'm forced to give in. Times have changed, people say. We can't live like we used to.

In short, it is as if, in a situation that itself gives the lie, the group can no longer impose its norms. Previously, peasant society acted quickly to make deviants – and particularly former emigrants – submit and respect the rules, but the majority then, one might say, had the whole situation going for them in guarding tradition, whereas today the whole situation constantly challenges it and puts it to severe test.

Several innovations, which are all transgressions of traditional norms, attest to the weakening of collective controls that the increase in the size of the group has brought about. For example, it is the largest resettlements, Tamalous, Kerkera, and to a lesser degree Matmata, that have particularly seen a proliferation of the 'profiteers' who, by their complicity with the military authorities, exploit the crisis situation provoked by resettlement: the commandment that banned members of the group from singling themselves out in terms of wealth, or more precisely, from using wealth to single themselves out, has become a dead letter; reprobation and contempt for individuals who do not hesitate to exploit the misery and oppression of others, making themselves accomplices of the oppressors, can no longer operate because the situation deprives it of any effectiveness: the time is long gone when fear of public opinion could force the emigrant to don his *burnous* again before returning to his village.[34]

Everything in the new situation contributes to persuading people that the break with the past is irremediable and the collapse of tradition ineluctable; innovations, and transgressions of traditional commands, simply arouse the resigned and powerless indignation of the oldest. For example, the eccentricities of former emigrants in matters of clothing (abandonment of the traditional hairstyle, wearing a tie) do not even raise a smile, and a former emigrant was even seen in the midst of a men's assembly dressed in an undershirt, with a colonial hat on his head.[35] An innovation as major as wearing the veil, which can be a sign of singling oneself out and of embourgeoisement, ends up passing almost unnoticed.[36]

The break with the old environment and the routines associated with it, the widening of the field of social relations, the very structure of dwelling space, both in the resettlement and in the home, invites urban behaviour and arouses the concerns, interests and aspirations characteristic of townspeople. Every time that the satisfaction of vital needs leaves some money disposable, this is spent on buying items of comfort, such as (in no particular order) beds, cupboards, sometimes tables and chairs, paraffin lamps that replace the old oil lamps with cloth wicks, paraffin stoves for cooking, ovens fuelled by bottled gas, radio sets, etc., as well as a greater variety of food, including new products bought in the market: wheat instead of barley, bread instead of galettes; the consumption of meat and fruits becomes more common; expenditure on clothing rises: jackets are bought for men, shoes for children and women, etc. These results of immediate observation are confirmed by the statistical study of family consumption.

Djebabra, which has remained relatively attached to peasant values, forms a contrast to Kerkera, which presents every sign of false urbanization, in a series of features going in the same direction. Although total personal expenditure varies from 100 to 194 between Kerkera and Djebabra,[37] the share of expenditure on food is lower in Kerkera than in Djebabra (i.e. 59.6 per cent as against 66.4 per cent), owing to the unequal growth of non-food expenditure. Qualitatively, the differences are no less marked: whereas there is no observable difference as far as meat consumption is concerned, a sign of genuine well-being, milk, butter and cheese make up twice as high a share of the budget in Kerkera than they do in Djebabra, that is, 2.8 per cent as against 1.4 per cent; similarly, fruit makes up 7.4 per cent in Kerkera as against 2.6 per cent in Djebabra – this is because in Kerkera a large number of small shopkeepers offer prickly pears, fresh figs and dates that are piled up and sold by volume, small melons and watermelons that are sold by the piece, whereas in Djebabra the only grocer simply sells 'real' fruit by weight: grapes, melons and watermelons. Certain types of drink which are also good indicators of urbanization are also consumed far more widely in Kerkera, in absolute and especially relative terms. These are above all drinks consumed outside the home, particularly in the café, which make up 3.5 per cent of expenditure in Kerkera whereas the figure for Djebabra is zero. Medical and pharmaceutical costs make up 8.44 per cent in Djebabra (i.e. 464 francs per family per year), as against 10.4 per cent in Kerkera (233 francs per family per year). Finally, tobacco consumption accounts for 9.9 per cent in Kerkera (the highest share among non-food items), as against only 1.3 per cent in Djebabra.

To sum up, the budget of the Kerkera resettled is close in its composition to that of the sub-proletarians in the shantytowns. Several new expenditure items flout the peasant ethos that values frugality and simplicity, requiring consumption to take second place to production; people in Kerkera care more about obtaining agreeable living conditions and providing their families with a comfort that meets the demands of modern life than about accumulating capital (if only for prestige) by buying cattle as was previously the custom. And the old peasant morality is really at an end when someone dares to say, as this resettled man in Kerkera did: 'I had an ox that I sold for 40,000 francs: I've bought a motor-scooter instead.' Consumption habits that tend to acquire a symbolic meaning certainly form the best indication of the break with the traditional ethos that strictly banned any form of 'ostentatious consumption'. Whereas it was previously dishonourable to go out and buy consumption items, and above all those least necessary – the luxuries of townspeople such as bread from the baker, vegetables and fruit – now, in those resettlement centres that are closest to the shantytowns in their morphology, the villages of the CAPER or SCAPCO,[38] it is seen almost as honourable to buy supplies in the town: as one man allocated land by the CAPER in Aïn-Sultan put it, 'it's the age of the shopping basket.'

The *gargote* [a cheap restaurant] is for the poorest what the shopping basket is for the better off: these are in fact the most evident symbols of urbanization, real or fictitious, and of the transformation of values expressed in food behaviour. In Kerkera there are two permanent *gargotes*, one fairly large, and three others that offer cooked dishes certain days in the week, such as fried sardines (20 francs for three), doughnuts, fried peppers (10 francs a piece), portions of bread and even home-made galettes.[39] Aware of practising an activity that goes against the spirit of peasant society, the owner of the largest *gargote* in the centre describes his customers as follows:

I have a *gargote*, but *there are no customers*. There are no *outsiders*, no people passing by who stop here to eat. The people here don't have money for eating. There are some who manage to eat when they are hungry, but only on credit. Those are young people. They hang around here the whole day. They don't want to come inside and ask for food; they come here, they sit down, they ask me for a dish of *chorba* [a traditional soup] or *batata* (potato stew), and a piece of bread. Am I going to refuse them? No. They eat and say to each other: 'One day or another I'll have 150 francs to give him', but I mustn't forget to ask them for it. They do the same, too, at the café when they play dominoes or cards, with the tobacco seller. It's always 'give us now, and later we'll see!' [. . .] Apart from them, I have two or three regular customers who take one or two meals here every day. They work here or on the roads, but they don't live in the region. There are the *harkis* who don't have their families here. [. . .] The local people? Why would they come and eat at my place? With the 250 francs that they spend on a dish, they would rather buy two loaves to share with their children. [. . .] But it does happen that someone who 'lives for himself' and for example cannot buy potatoes, meat or bread for his whole family, comes and eats here by himself. But that's just occasionally by chance. [. . .] I have one or two customers like that a day. All the rest [he indicates pieces of bread sold at 20 francs each, portions of cheese, hard-boiled eggs, fried peppers, etc.] is bought by children. A child is

hungry at home, he cries, there's nothing to give him, they can't buy
a loaf for 65 francs as they'd have to buy four or six to feed everyone:
his father or his brother gives him 20 or 30 francs; he comes here and
has enough to pay for a *kaskrut*.[40] Some children have got into the
habit, for example the grandson of *âmmi* Ahmed [an old man who
plays dominoes]; whenever he sees his grandfather sitting at the table
for his game, he taps him on the shoulder until *âmmi* Ahmed throws
him a 20-franc piece! But above all it's those young people who get a
bit of money here and there, running errands or selling something . . .
They come and eat here because they don't find anything to eat at
home and because there's nothing to give them at home.

Ill-judged resort to credit for food purchase, the appearance of
economic individualism, the transgression of the duties of family solidarity – all these are beginnings of the process that leads to the demoralization of the sub-proletarians of the shantytowns. Now people eat
alone, each for themselves and 'for their belly'. The sense of commen-
sality disappears with the sense of community. *Bou niya* (the peasant),
if he was invited to a special meal, would tie up in the handkerchief
along with his money the piece of meat he had carefully refrained from
eating, and take it back home for his children, an invalid or an old
person – in this way giving an ostensible sign of his sense of honour
and his abnegation, as well as of the solemnity of the occasion, the
'out of the ordinary' nature of the food offered, that is, meat.[41] Today,
such behaviour would be seen as coarse and ridiculous: meat is supposed to be eaten together with couscous, to show that, like the well-
mannered townspeople, one *knows* how to eat couscous, and besides,
that the other family members are not deprived of meat to the point
of waiting for an exceptional occasion to eat it.[42]

Formerly, the *fellah'in* would carry with them when they went to
the market, most often on foot, a piece of galette and a handful of
figs to eat on the way, when they paused in the shade by a spring.[43]
If in the exceptional case they brought back some products from the
town, for example bread or fruit, they would not eat them en route
but keep them for the evening meal taken in common by the whole
family. Today, when peasants go to market by truck and only start
off late in the morning after having coffee, they would find it highly
ridiculous to encumber themselves with provisions for the journey
when refreshments can be had in town.[44] It even happens that people
go to market just to eat a *chorba* or roast chicken; people invite
one another in advance to the *gargote* at the market; if someone is
asked to do an errand, or a family member is sent to the market, they
expect to be given the price of a meal out. And some people boast,
on their return to the village, that they ate two or three dishes at the

restaurant.[45] There is no longer the shame (this is not too strong a word) that used to surround anything touching on food. It is natural that the behaviour of those people who ostentatiously bring back a well-stocked basket of supplies (something that peasant morality explicitly banned, requiring anyone who had bought meat to conceal it) should still be more scandalous than that of those unfortunates who, impelled by need, transgress the duty of family solidarity by furtively eating a dish at the *gargote*; ostentation and abundance is perceived as a challenge not only to tradition but also to all those whom misery compels to transgress tradition. As a shopkeeper from Outaït Aïcha resettled in Kerkera puts it: 'Nowadays, you can eat cutlets every day and let your father beg. In these times, everything is possible [literally: can happen]. People are not ashamed, and no one sees anything in it to blame. All activities are permitted, stealing or begging, as long as you get money.'

'There is no longer dishonour [*âib*]': people are no longer afraid of abandoning their land or selling it to outsiders; they are not ashamed of abandoning their father or mother to poverty; they do not flinch from any expedient, any trick, to earn their living. To say that there is no longer dishonour, meaning that there is no longer honour or point of honour, is to recall that honour and dishonour are only experienced before the tribunal of public opinion, the group sure of its norms and values. In short, the crisis of the system of values is the direct consequence of the crisis affecting the group that is the guardian of values: by the scattering of social units, the relaxation of traditional social ties and the weakening of the control of public opinion, transgression of the rule tends to become the rule, there is no longer any obstacle to an individualism that is introduced along with the modern economy. In the resettlements, these immense and disparate aggregations of isolated individuals, each person feels protected by anonymity, each person feels responsible for themselves, but only for themselves and to themselves.

> These days, everyone looks out for themselves. Each person can count only on his skill. It's up to each to 'swim in his own sea' and count on his 'own knees' to earn his living. There's no longer 'my uncle' and 'my brother'. Nowadays people say 'each for his own stomach', 'everyone for himself', while previously it was 'each his own grave', because it was only there (in the afterlife) that each person was confronted with his acts. At that point, I can't do anything for you, you can't do anything for me, whereas here life is possible only by helping one another. Who can boast, today above all, that they don't need anyone? As the saying goes, 'a man [is a man] through men' [*rajal b erjal*].

Whether it is a matter of his subsistence or his honour, the individual knows that he can count only on himself, and that he does not have to give account to anyone but himself. 'Honour to you and shame on you' (*rejala lik u el âib lik*), they say: each subject is free in his actions, but he has to accept for himself the dishonour that he may attract: like the earth, like the cooking pot, honour has ceased to be a collective possession.

Space, Time and Values

A collective melancholy betrays disarray and anxiety, the weakening of old solidarities. If material wretchedness affects every individual in their most intimate core, this is because it hastens the collapse of the system of values that imposed the identification of each person with the whole group, and in this way protected him from discovering his solitude. If the group no longer manages to exert its regulatory action, this is not simply because it is unsure of its norms and values, which are belied by the situation, but also because the deepest structures have been more or less broken: forced displacement and all the arbitrary manipulations have transformed the substratum of social life, not only in its extent and size, but also in its form. Resettlement, a form of local emigration imposed on the whole group for reasons that have nothing to do with economic logic,[46] affects the whole of social life, by transforming the organization of inhabited space, the pattern that social structures project on the soil, and by breaking the bond of familiarity that ties individuals to their environment. Because the familiar world for him is his native world, because his whole *bodily habitus* is 'made' for the space of his customary movements, the uprooted peasant is touched in the deepest part of his *being*, so profoundly that he is unable to formulate his disarray, and still less to define the reason for it.[47]

In this way, the differences that separate, for example, Aïn-Aghbel from Kerkera, cannot all be attributed to density and size. In Aïn-Aghbel, the local *zribat* have been reconfigured in a space organized according to traditional logic: the men's domain, with the assembly place located in the old cemetery near the marabout shrine, is clearly distinct and separate from the women's space, around the well where different paths meet up; military geometry has had to make concessions to relief and to the former habitat, so that the monotonous alignment of the newly established dwellings is broken here and there by a house, a tree, or a rise in the ground. In Aïn-Aghbel, which they visit from time to time, the mountain-dwellers from Yersan or

Béni-Bellit find something of their familiar space; and so their disarray is less great than that of their counterparts from Oued-el-Afia and El-Bir who are resettled in Kerkera. There, space has been organized in a logic absolutely foreign and even opposite to that of tradition: the placing of shops and the width of streets, the planning of houses (lacking a courtyard) and the placing of wells, everything is made to disappoint and contradict expectations.

The structural uniformity of the *gourbi*, and still more so of the *h'awch* or *alh'ara*,[48] the projection onto the soil of the representation of the world, is replaced by the functional uniformity of the standardized unit, made up of 'two rooms and a kitchen' cells. In the *zriba*, every house had not only a courtyard, but also a wide space marked off and protected by a line of acacias; in the resettlement, the *gourbis* open directly onto the street, a street that no one knows either what to call or how to use, which is treated either as a passage between the houses, or as a 'courtyard' common to the families facing it: the *kanoun* [a clay cooking pot] is visible on the threshold; the goat and its kids, sometimes even the donkey, are tethered in a shaded corner. The transformations of habitat, normally bound up with gradual transformations in the way of life and cultural norms, have here been imposed from outside, by authorities who stubbornly refuse to recognize the models and values that govern peasant life and are expressed in the traditional habitat (fence, courtyard, absence of apertures, etc.). It is the transformation of habitat, therefore, that precedes and determines social transformations rather than the other way round, as more commonly happens. The punctilious rigour with which the smallest transformation or improvement is forbidden is evidence of the intention to impose, by way of the organization of habitat, the norms, values and style of life of another civilization.

And indeed, resettlement fosters a number of innovations, in this domain as elsewhere: as in the urban shantytowns, beds become very common, either metal beds or beds made from wooden planks set on trestles (in order to avoid sleeping on the ground, which is too damp, and to leave space for storage); a few elements of modern furniture make their appearance – kitchen cupboard, wardrobe. Traditional utensils (apart from the flat wooden board for kneading galettes and rolling couscous, and the earthenware plate on which the galettes are cooked) are replaced by an assortment of recycled objects, as ingenious as they are varied, such as tins of preserves, cardboard, wooden or metal boxes, oil cans, enamelled vessels, etc. As the ritually stereotyped furnishing of the traditional house has been abandoned, the attempt is made to imitate and reproduce, for better or worse, the storage arrangements of modern houses: planks fixed to the wall or placed on the ground on bricks, or boxes made into a kind of wardrobe, take the place of the storage holes of the *dukan*,[49] a kind of dovecot fixed to the wall; sacks, boxes and casks replace oil and grain jars, goatskins and storage pits; enamel plates replace the earthenware plates that the housewife used to place on the wall facing the door. In the same way, the lack of a courtyard, or more precisely of an outside wall protecting the courtyard, has imposed the use of curtains on the doors, and even on windows: in many cases, this is only a sack or an old sheet, but some people already use material produced for this purpose.

In short, several types of behaviour express the effort to adapt as best as possible to an unaccustomed space, which objectively demands the invention of new behaviour by its very structure. But the malaise persists:

> Between relatives, it is good to have doors facing each other, but when there are strangers, it's better not. If it had been up to us to build the village, we would have made a *mechta* for each family; now, families are dispersed in the village. Two brothers may not be close to each other. When the new houses are allocated [those under construction at the time of the study], care should be taken that all relatives are neighbours. Those people who want it can make a doorway between their houses.
>
> (Resettled man, Djebabra)

Should we be surprised that the peasants in Kerkera, in order to describe their experience, have recourse to three particular images: the image of prison to express the impression of suffocation and oppression aroused by the constriction of habitat; the image of nakedness to state the feeling of being exposed to everyone's view, at a crossroads, without any of the barriers (*zruba*) that protect the intimacy of domestic life; and the image of night-time darkness in which it is very easy to lose oneself, for lack of the customary and familiar bearings.[50]

But it is certainly the language of the body, the way of carrying oneself, of holding one's head and walking, that expresses better than words the distraction and disorientation. The wide avenues of the new villages contain only children, carrying a loaf or a jug of water; sometimes a woman hurriedly crosses. Whereas in the old habitat the whole of social life was turned inward towards the courtyard, and even the street, from which foreigners were excluded, established a tie with familiar neighbours, the new organization of space strips the house of all protection: the street pushes women back inside, and there are only their furtive glances behind doors left ajar or curtains raised.

On entering the Djebabra resettlement, built on the side of a hill, it was possible to see, already marked on the ground, a path leading from the main road up to the upper part of the village where the men gather; thus, two types of organization of space and two types of attitude towards the world are superimposed here: on the one hand, the *castrum*, intersected by two broad ways that surrender its intimacy by directly introducing the outsider into the very heart of the inhabited world; on the other hand, the closed world, the sanctuary of *h'urma* (honour) that paths joining the outside world avoid, as in Kabylia, so that the foreigner can continue on his way without entering. As if they carried in their body the pattern of their familiar movements, men never take the shortest path back to their house, that is, one or other of the broad ways; they start out on the peripheral path, inventing detours through little alleyways between the rows of houses, and making their way almost furtively, staying close to the walls.[51]

This *removal from familiar surroundings* causes an unease that reflects the disruption of the group, which is affected at its deepest level, that is, in its rhythms of space and time. By turning the organization of living space upside down, the area of technical action and that of ritual action, *resettlement disrupts the temporal rhythms that go together with this*; also, by imposing arbitrary constraints and upsetting the rhythm of daily activities, it affects the whole experience of temporality. In traditional society, the rhythm of social life, set by the periodic return of technical and ritual activities performed at the same moment and often in common by all members of the group, is both an organizing principle and a force of integration.[52]

The *fellah'in* have always known more or less lengthy periods of slower activity; but these were inscribed in the cycle of custom, fixed by tradition, and followed the rhythms of nature. Now, with resettlement, these cycles and *these rhythms have been disrupted*; as a result, what is in question is not simply the objective amount of labour performed, but the distribution of work and non-work in time. The peasant discovers time as something that can be lost, that is, the opposition between empty or lost time and full or well-filled time, notions that are foreign both in fact and in essence to the logic of the pre-capitalist economy. Empty time, experienced as boredom, can now be defined only in negative terms, as opposed to leisure time or working time. There is no longer time that simply passes, but time either lost or spent, and it is now experienced as such, because the experience that the unemployed have of duration carries an explicit or implicit reference to the capitalist view of work and temporality, a condition of awareness of unemployment. Time unemployed is empty time in contrast to the time that the economy geared to productivity sees as fully occupied, as well as to the time specific to the traditionalist economy: in effect, having no other purpose than to permit the group to endure, this could not make an experience of duration appear empty, being its own measure unto itself.[53]

The new rhythms to which peasants must submit themselves, with the curfew and the increased length of journeys, tend to supplant traditional rhythms. Temporal reference points such as the opening and closing hours of offices, the start and finish of school – which divide the day into two phases – the regular ring of the telephone in the control tower, the watchtowers and the rounds of the *harka*, the passage of the postman, the opening of the clinic and, in Matmata for example, the hours that the well is in service, replace traditional reference points such as the five daily prayers and promote a new experience of duration: rhythmic time gives way to measured time, and the watch begins to govern the life of certain categories of people.[54]

The freedom to organize one's work and define its rhythm goes hand in hand with the sense of familiarity that binds the peasant to his land. For example, when the military authorities, with a view to promoting the cultivation of land in the Merdja *farqa*, situated in the forbidden zone, decided to transport *fellah'in* there each morning by lorry, at the time the curfew was lifted, they met with a lively resistance. The fact is that agricultural activity that is subject to rhythms laid down from outside is the complete negation of traditional agriculture: 'I'm a stranger on my own property, that of my father and my grandfather; I can no longer give orders in my own house, I've ceased to be its master!' To be a peasant meant also being *master of one's land*, and thus *master of one's relationships with the land*: it meant being free to decide the conditions of one's activity, to define its moment and pace, and, among other things, to decide on all movements, on their duration and their itinerary.[55] The *fellah*'s passion for his land does not tolerate any obstacle: what use is it to be 'master of one's land' if one can no longer 'visit' it at will, but only at times and on paths imposed by others?[56] The peasants at Djebabra knew that, by allowing their activity to be restricted by regular timetables and fixed dates, they only saved the appearance of their peasant condition the better to lose it. In fact, ceasing to be a state of being, the condition of agriculturalist became a sum of tasks circumscribed in both time and space, in the same way as the work of the wage-earner.

Finally, the diversification of activities substitutes for the unique and invariable time of the old society a plurality of rhythms, matching the separate occupational lives; whereas formerly the work of the artisan or shopkeeper followed the same rhythm as that of the peasant, since it took up only the idle moments of the peasant day (during spring and summer, for example, in the morning before the men left for the fields, during the midday break, and in the evening after the return from the fields), it tends today to be differentiated from this by occupying full-time those whose work it is.[57] In the same way, in the Chéliff, the rhythm of seasonal work for the colonists has interfered with the rhythm of traditional agriculture: thus the poorest people were still out harvesting while the others were resting and feasting, the harvest being over for them. That meant an end to the identification of the individual with a collective temporality, and by the same token with the world and the group. The peasant finds himself brusquely expelled from the cycle of custom in which he was established.[58]

The groups of workers on the colonial farms represent the culmination of the movement of disintegration that resettlement has accelerated without bringing it to its natural end, first of all because the duration of the uprooted condition has been too brief for the deepest transformations to show themselves;[59] secondly, because the strong sense that this was only a temporary test weakened the effectiveness of the disturbing action. A symbol of the history of the Algerian peasantry during these last ten years may also be seen in the experience of those workers from the Aïn-Sultan CAPER who, after long being settled here, rediscovered the memory of their past in their mountain-dwelling cognates, at a time when collective memory threatened to disappear with the uprooting, fragmentation and unsettling of the group.[60]

The Algerian Sub-Proletarians

*This text is extracted from a book to be published in 1963,[1] present-
ing the results of a study carried out on the basis of interviews undertaken in 1960 in Algerian towns. The chapter from which these pages
are drawn is designed to develop a model of the process leading from
the traditionalist economic attitude to the capitalist attitude, at the
same time as objectively defining the material conditions of existence,
attitudes and ideologies of the different classes, and thereby revealing
the different kinds of adaptation to the economic order imported by
colonization. In urban society, the strongest cleavage is that separating permanent from intermittent workers (unemployed, casual
labourers, petty traders), three interchangeable conditions that very
often successively characterize the same individual. Statistical analysis, in fact, makes it possible to divide workers into two groups, those
who are stable and are then extremely stable, and those who are
unstable and similarly extremely unstable (making up one-third
of the total in 1960). Unemployment and unstable employment
place the sub-proletarians in a situation of permanent insecurity
that threatens the equilibrium of the family, compromises the individual's insertion into society, and leads, in Goldstein's words, to 'a
systematic functional disintegration' of behaviour, attitudes and
opinions, preventing any clear apprehension of a condition marked
by incoherence.*

*It is on the basis of such analysis that it will subsequently be pos-
sible for the researcher to present an overall picture of Algerian
society as this has been made – or rather, unmade – by 130 years of
colonization, and by the same token, to define both the constraints*

*imposed on the leaders of independent Algeria, and the opportunities
offered them.*

Becoming aware of unemployment is contemporaneous with a certain
manner of experiencing duration, itself inseparable from the new
meaning that is conferred on work.

Entry into the money economy is accompanied by the discovery
of time as something that can be lost, that is, of the opposition
between empty or lost time and full or well-filled time. These are
notions foreign both in fact and in essence to the logic of the pre-
capitalist economy. Time flows, paced by the divisions of the technical
and ritual calendar that lays down a moment, a duration and a particular rhythm for every activity. If, as has often been shown, paced
time is not measured time, this is because intervals lived in a self-
contained experience are not equal and uniform. Time is apprehended
in its flow by way of reference points that are so many lived experiences: either the impressionistic noting of qualitative nuances of the
world – 'when the sun touches the earth' – or a bodily experience – at
thaoulasth, that is, the hour when the chill of early morning makes
one tremble as if with fever (*thaoula*). These references are not points
of division, which would presuppose the notion of a regular and
measured interval; the islands of duration they define are not seen as
segments of a continuous line, but form so many unities, each closed
on itself and juxtaposed to the others. The week, for example, is often
called *es-suq*, that is, the period of time between two markets.

The experience of duration, being indissociable from the experience of activity, never has any other reference but itself. Evidence of
this is that, if the unit of duration is, for example, the time required
to perform a well-defined task, to plough a parcel of land with a pair
of oxen or to go to the nearest market, then space is assessed conversely in terms of duration, or better, by reference to the activity
performed during a defined period of time, the day's ploughing or
the trip to the market. The unitary experience of activity, however,
which is the foundation of all such equivalences, can only be related
to itself, and so it is its own measure, unaware of time as constraint
and a limit. It follows from this that, if this time strikes us as empty
or poorly filled, that is only because we refer it to a totally foreign
measure. If it seems to us to be time in which nothing happens, or
very little – and is this not what we have in mind when we speak of
concealed unemployment? – this is simply because nothing happens
there that we were expecting, that is, because the nature and number
of events that we consider in forming temporal sequences, and thus
their tempo, is a function of the principle of selection we implicitly

apply, in this case the idea that we have of work, and hence, of existence. We are here like the town-dweller for whom nothing happens in little villages because he rejects as trivia devoid of interest those things that fill the life of the villagers.

But isn't all this true for the time of the unemployed, or more generally, the sub-proletarians? If it seems to us empty time, isn't that because we subject it to a foreign standard? Time spent looking for work, time waiting at the employment office, can only be defined in negative terms, by contrast with leisure or working time. It is not time passed, but time wasted or expended. On this occasion, however, it is lived as such: the experience that the unemployed person forms of duration includes explicit or implicit reference to the capitalist view of work and time, a precondition for the awareness of being unemployed. The attitude of these peasants is significant in the sense of a limit, as they declare themselves to be unemployed without any decisive change having being produced in their objective situation. As the duality of their systems of reference inclines them to reflexivity, they discover their traditional activity as unemployment of which they were unaware. Time unemployed is empty time by contrast with the time that the economy geared to productivity sees as time fully occupied, and also by contrast with the time specific to the traditional economy, which, having no other purpose than to allow the group to endure, could not see as empty an experience of duration that was in itself its own measure.[2]

And so unemployment, as awareness of being without employment, is the aberrant product of a social and economic order that does not give everyone the possibility of reaching the goal that it imposes with absolute necessity, that is, obtaining a money income, and that tends to make any activity that does not attain this goal appear as time poorly filled. But as well as this, because they cannot provide the minimum in the way of security and assurance for the present and the immediate future that a permanent job with a regular wage can, unemployment, casual employment and work as a mere occupation prevent any effort to rationalize economic conduct with reference to a future goal, and enclose all existence in a fear for the next day, that is, the thrall of immediacy.

Unemployed men, illicit street vendors, people who sell a bunch of bananas or a packet of cigarettes, small shopkeepers, traditional artisans, and everyone living off charity or tips, such as watchmen, porters, messengers, are they sure enough of the present to be able to try to ensure their future? Are they not condemned to improvidence and fatalistic renunciation, as the expression of a total distrust in the future, inspired by the awareness of being unable to control the present? 'When you're not sure of today,' says an unemployed man from Constantine, 'how can you be sure of tomorrow?' And a fisherman from Oran: 'The more I earn, the more I eat; the less I earn, the less I eat.' These two striking formulas summarize the essentials of sub-proletarian existence. The only purpose of activity is the satisfaction of immediate needs. 'I earn my piece of bread and that's all.' 'What I earn, I eat.' 'I just earn my children's bread.' The old traditions of providence are finished. The town-dweller tends to resemble the image that the peasant traditionally had of him: 'What has been earned in the daytime is eaten at night . . .' Sometimes one can see a resurgence of traditional behaviour that is totally aberrant in the new context, inspired by the fear for subsistence: 'I have provisions ready,' says a small grocer in Oran who earns 400 to 500 francs a day. 'If I make nothing one day, I eat all the same.' A traditionalism of despair, as inconsistent as the day-to-day existence. But how can one hope for anything beyond the present, beyond today's bread, when even this primordial objective is scarcely satisfied? 'The wage is just enough for bread. But for anything else, no' (fishmonger's assistant, Constantine). Given that sacrifices bear first and foremost on consumption, income can rise without any savings appearing (even the very idea of saving), so greatly do needs exceed resources.[3] When they are asked whether they have savings, most of the sub-proletarians laugh or are indignant. 'Savings?', replies an Orléansville bus driver with a smile. 'When I get my pay, I feel sick, I don't know what to do. Me, I live from day to day.' People try to reduce their spending as much as possible, without ever keeping real accounts. 'It's me who goes to market,' an Oran tailor explains, 'I don't keep accounts. Whenever something is needed, I buy it, I don't keep accounts and I don't know how much I spend. I don't have any savings; if I did, I would have opened a shop [laughter]. Everything is either dear or cheap, depending on the level of one's earnings; when you have money, everything seems cheap and you spend, "you don't give a fig!"' Caught in a vicious circle of poverty, these men are all too constricted in living from day to day to be able to think of saving, the only thing that could release them from this day-to-day existence.[4]

The mode of payment, particularly in the case of day-labourers, intermittent or regular, tends to form an obstacle to the rationalization of economic conduct. 'It's better to be paid by the month than by the day,' a casual dock-worker in Algiers explains. 'By the day, you never have anything set by. You come back from work, you buy food and it's all gone. It's as if you haven't earned anything. When you're paid by the month, you can put something aside, buy things, you're calm.' Even if this were only a psychological illusion it would merit analysis, and all the more so as the insecurity created by daily payment can only increase when work is intermittent. By fragmenting income into small sums immediately exchangeable for goods intended to be consumed the same day, daily payment tends to exclude expenditure on anything durable, which can only be conceived (and amortized) over a long period, and to enclose the worker in a life from one day to the next that is synonymous with the absence of calculation.[5]

In fact, the sub-proletarians only manage to live or to survive by resort to credit. Despite their deep aversion to debt, which they owe to their peasant past, they almost all buy on credit, at least from the grocer and the baker.[6] This phenomenon is so general that it can be seen as correlative with urbanization and an indispensable condition of adaptation to urban life.[7] It is as if credit based on trust fulfilled the function that was performed in village society either by reserves, or by the exchanges of gifts and services required by solidarity.[8] It is credit that makes it possible for even the most deprived to eat every day, despite the irregularity of money income. But what about the shopkeeper? We have to cite here the explanations of a bus driver with the public transport company, very familiar with the situation of the small shopkeepers as he himself ran a dairy for several years:

> The shopkeeper continues to supply, and even supply more, and if for example someone has spent 20,000 francs, he pays 15,000; the following month, he's lucky to get 10,000 francs. That's already 15,000 francs of debts. In this way the shopkeepers are owed millions that they'll never get back; there's nothing they can do about it. If they refuse to serve, they lose their customers, they won't get the money they are owed or the little they are given. Besides, the shopkeeper does the same thing with his supplier. All this leads to bookkeeping problems, and there are only a few shopkeepers who keep proper accounts, many of them can't even write.[9]

The small shopkeeper and the sub-proletarian are more or less chained to one another; the former because he has to sell on credit if he wants to sell at all, and the latter because he can only buy on credit. The reasons that spur the small shopkeeper to grant credit are not only a matter of self-interest: someone who refuses to give credit to a man with a family to support would be dishonoured in public opinion, since beyond a certain threshold credit tends to be confused with mutual aid or support, and because the kasbah quarter or the shantytown form a mutual recognition group whose members feel tied by a kind of fraternity, and thus held to duties of solidarity. Whatever the individual reason, shopkeepers objectively fulfil an eminently social function: by agreeing to advance food in periods of destitution, and waiting to be paid when money comes in, they offer their most deprived customers a minimum of security in an existence that is haunted by insecurity. Credit makes it possible to avoid keeping accounts, since, in the absence of any calculation, it tends to make possible, in an almost automatic fashion, the extension in time of incomes characterized by irregularity. This is all the more paradoxical a mechanism as the small shopkeepers themselves scarcely ever keep proper books, they draw directly from the cashbox for the needs of their own families, are often unaware of the notion of profit and expect no more from their activity than mere subsistence. As a small shopkeeper from Sidi-Bel-Abbès put it: 'Where is the profit, then? I'm working here on credit [. . .].[10] I get goods on credit, and when I've sold them, that's when I pay the wholesaler. Sometimes I have a bit of money left over, sometimes not, then I'm forced to borrow elsewhere.' In this way, a series of incoherencies arising from the chain of credit, from the wholesaler to the retailer who doesn't calculate, from the retailer to the customer who doesn't calculate either, end up amounting to a kind of permanent equilibrium that enables the most disadvantaged strata, shopkeepers and customers, to survive.[11]

This kind of quasi-automatic regulation is one of the complex mechanisms that enable the poorest people to maintain a precarious equilibrium at the lowest level, in the absence of any calculation and any rationalization of the household economy. For example, if it is true that the imperatives of broad solidarity can sometimes present an obstacle to the formation of a capitalist class, by imposing on those who have succeeded the demand to assist others, it remains the case that fraternal mutual aid enables the uprooted peasants to overcome misery and disarray, by helping to provide them with certain indispensable forms of security, assistance in kind or in money that allows them to live during the search for employment or during periods of unemployment, sometimes even providing employment and often housing. In the same way, if the collective possession bound up with chosen or forced cohabitation often prevents modernization and long-term investment, it assures subsistence to the most deprived, the plurality of incomes pooled for a joint expenditure tending to compensate for the irregularity and low level of income. In short, everything happens as if this incoherence and uncertainty was itself its own limit: among other things, the generalized absence of regularity and rationalization, in both expenditure and income, leaves a certain room for manoeuvre; the fact that the introduction of a single regular expenditure, on rent for example in the case of families with low incomes who are rehoused in social accommodation, is often enough to destroy or undermine this perilous equilibrium provides proof of this *a contrario*.

This existence abandoned to incoherence cannot be fully understood in relation to either the logic of traditionalism or that of the capitalist economy. It would be vain to try to understand each concrete existence as a discontinuous series of acts, some of which would follow a traditionalist model and others a capitalist one. In reality, like an ambiguous form, each behaviour can be read in two ways, as it bears within it a reference to two logics: with the result that capitalist behaviours imposed by necessity remain essentially different from capitalist behaviours integrated into a capitalist plan of life, in the same way that traditionalist behaviours as enforced regressions are separated from genuinely traditionalist behaviours by the chasm that awareness of the change of context creates. This is why the day-to-day existence of the sub-proletarian or the proletarianized *fellah* differs absolutely from the previous existence of the *fellah* in a milieu of security. In one case, the quest for subsistence is the unanimously approved and sole purpose, guaranteed by customary rules; in the other, obtaining a minimum for survival is the purpose that economic necessity imposes on an exploited class. Because the context has changed and everyone is aware of this, because the economic assurance and psychological security that an integrated society and a living tradition had supplied are now abolished, hazardous improvisation takes the place of customary providence and stereotyped behavioural conformity. Unemployment and intermittent employment thus lead to a disorganization of behaviour that we should not see as an innovation presupposing a change of attitude. The traditionalism of despair and the lack of a plan of life are two sides of one and the same reality.

In actual fact, unemployment and intermittent employment have only a destructive effect. They make a clean break with tradition and traditionalism, but block the development of a rational plan of life which would be the precondition for adaptation to the capitalist economy. 'I live on *baraka* [luck],' an unemployed man says; and indeed, the existence of the majority of sub-proletarians, confined to the present day, is a continuous miracle. Everything happens as if the lack of permanent employment and the minimum regular income it assures prevented economic behaviour, and the conduct of life more generally, from being subject to rational calculation; as if, so long as the concern for subsistence is imposed, it is impossible to form a concern for survival, an ambition for providence and initiative.

What does this 'living from day to day' mean in practice? Far from the future being outlined in present behaviour, far from the present being organized in relation to an abstract future, posited by calculation and linked to the present in a rational relationship, the present day is lived without any reference to the next day, either intuitive or rational. The casual worker who receives his pay each day buys on his way home the bread or flour that he eats the same evening, without considering what will happen the next day, as his situation prevents this. The fragmentation of duration into discontinuous units tends to condemn the individual to satisfy immediate needs in an immediate fashion. The suspense of an ever uncertain tomorrow haunts the mind as a hypnotizing awareness, trapped by an objective that is imposed with absolute urgency. On this basis, the repression of an immediate response to objective suggestions and solicitations and, by the same token, the sacrifice of immediate and urgent goals to ones that are selected by rational calculation are inconceivable, since primary needs are such that their satisfaction cannot be delayed or sacrificed. What is ruled out in such conditions is establishing a rational hierarchy of goals, as a precondition for utilitarian calculation, the foundation of rational behaviour in the logic of capitalism. Saving and investment, in fact, or even the mere distribution of expenditure over time, presuppose taking a perspective on the whole set of goals of activity, or better, drawing up a plan of life, that is, the integration of the present into a coherent and hierarchized system of goals that are envisaged or projected – with the result that present activity only acquires its meaning in relation to a conceived and intended future, while reciprocally, this projected future is rooted in a present behaviour that works at bringing it about.

[. . .] If opinions that engage the future must always be hierarchized according to their modalities, from reverie through to projects rooted in present behaviour, we must be careful not to forget that the degree of commitment to a formulated opinion is a function of the degree of accessibility of the future that is aimed at. This future, however, is more or less accessible depending both on the material conditions of existence and the social status of each individual, and on the domain of existence that is involved: opinions about the future of one's children, for example, are still more disordered than are estimates of needs, since they presuppose a life plan over two generations.

It is naturally among the unemployed, petty traders and casual labourers that the incoherence of opinions about the future is greatest. An unemployed man from Constantine, for example, with no assets at all, estimates the income he needs to meet the needs of his family at 2,000 new francs per month. Questioned about the future he wants for his children, he explains: 'They would go to school, and when they were educated enough they would choose for themselves. But I can't send them to school. If I could, I'd like them to have as long an education as possible, to be doctors or lawyers. But I don't have the means. I just have to live on dreams.' The same rift between imaginary aspirations and the real situation is observed with an unemployed man from Saïda who, after saying that he fears being forced to take his children away from school for lack of resources, wants his daughter to 'go right to the end, until she's succeeded, until the *bac* [*baccalauréat*] if she can or until the certificate; like that she'll be able to work as a teacher'. Another unemployed man from Constantine says, on the one hand, 'Children need education, but for education you need money', and on the other hand, on the subject of his daughters' education, 'I'll send them to Algiers, to Paris and even further; they'll go all the way'; and finally, on a third occasion, 'You can't teach your children. When you make 400 francs a day, what can you do? I sent my daughter to a summer camp. I was forced to buy clothes for this. And I tell you that cost quite a bit.'[12] It is the same individuals who, when they are asked if they want their children to continue at school after primary level, often reply: 'Yes, all the way', or even, like an unskilled worker from Oran, 'I want the best for them.' The same absence of shadings, the same lack of realism, as in their views on women working.[13] It is actually among those individuals with the lowest incomes that we find the highest rate of sharp and absolute responses, no matter whether positive or negative. In the same way, when asked about the causes of unemployment, sub-proletarians often refuse to reply, or offer summary and contradictory opinions: 'I'm not educated', 'You're asking some odd questions', or again, 'There are too many people everywhere. Everyone is looking for a job. If I was educated, I could tell you . . . But unfortunately I can't even read the figures on a ruler. Why are you asking me this kind of thing?' (unemployed man, Constantine). These men, whose experience of work in a modern business is very often as distressing and confusing as the experience of unemployment, 'de-ruralized' country people who have to discover and learn everything at once about the technical and urban world (French language, work discipline, basic skills, measuring instruments), these perpetual underlings who can never be certain of anything, neither work for today nor work for tomorrow, these men who experience the weight of all determinisms and cannot find either in themselves, their work or their ambition reasons to apply themselves to a job that tomorrow they may no longer have – is it any surprise that they cannot forge any system of coherent opinions on a condition so deeply marked by instability and incoherence?

[. . .] The existence of the sub-proletarians can only be described as it is experienced by them, that is, in terms of lack: instability of employment and the irregularity of income resulting from it, lack of confidence about even the most immediate future, awareness of lacking all the means that are indispensable for releasing themselves from incoherence and accident, condemn them to resignation and despair, any possibility of hope being destroyed by the inflexibility of the world around them. The sub-proletarians do not envisage any escape from their condition; when asked, they most often reply with a laugh. 'I don't hope for anything,' says a casual building worker living in Tlemcen; 'my life is just the shovel and the pickaxe'. Not only is any reasonable hope of social advance outside of their reach, but the very idea of such hope: 'I work the whole year for 9,000 francs a week and 2,000 francs bonus each month. That's 40,000 francs a month. How can I live like that, with nine mouths to feed? I push the cars along, I'm not allowed to start their motors. I keep watch. That's the same thing every day, for a long time. Raise myself? You're dreaming, or you want me to dream! I don't have a trade, and you don't learn one by doing what I'm doing. Oh! If I was educated, I would have found work . . . I'd have been able to hope . . .' (garage attendant, Philippeville).

If, when they speak about their own future, the presence of the present is too pressing to allow them to forget themselves, they can escape from this for a moment if they're asked to: but does this mean forming genuine projects that could be carried out, projects with a beginning of realization in present behaviour?

[. . .] The project, to be a real option, implies a beginning of realization: it presupposes at the same time that the goal envisaged is a long way off, as something to be realized, and that it is accessible, providing that certain obstacles are overcome. The dreamy consciousness, on the contrary, can only bring the object within reach by denying the interval and the obstacles that intervene, that is, by magically suppressing the resistance of facts. And indeed, the ideology of the sub-proletarian is in thrall to magical reason.

Because he is unable to deal with the world, and his constant efforts to overcome insecurity come up against insurmountable obstacles, because the probability of his reaching the most vital goals by an active and rational attitude is extremely weak, he tends to perceive the world through the categories of magic. Life experienced as a throw of the dice, as *qmar*, gives rise to personalized forces, such as '*piston*', the *baraka* of the sub-proletarians. Far from being triggered by a freely decided project, no matter that the satisfactions it assures are symbolic and oneiric, and whether the powers with which it peoples the world are benevolent or hostile, the magical perception of the world is the only recourse of an individual faced with a universe that bans any project with a reasonable chance of success. Condemned to succumb to the arbitrary decrees of the world, even where his core values are concerned, the sub-proletarian sees the world as peopled by powers engaged in a conflict whose stake is his own fate. What they call '*piston*'[14] is not a datum of experience but one of mythical reason, that is, both an omnipresent force and a universal explanatory principle. To be convinced of this, one need only note that the greater part of the time, the notion remains as indeterminate as possible. It is in fact those who say they have never experienced its effect who speak of it the most and ascribe it an enormous role; the more favoured, whom one might suppose to have benefited from it, often deny its existence and put success down to merit alone, starting with their own.

We could see this idea of 'connections' as one of those 'functional gods' that Hermann Usener explains were characteristic of Roman religion – since it acts, like them, in everyday existence and within the familiar environment – if it were invested solely with well-determined powers, such as securing work.[15] But in fact, like a kind of *mana* or *baraka*, it appears as a force both impersonal and personalized, omnipresent and localized, that moves and inspires the whole social world. 'Nowadays, it's connections above all! Yes indeed. You can't get anywhere just under your own steam. As I see it, that's how it is, connections at work' (porter, Oran). 'We live in a particular situation where it's connections that oil the wheels' (shopworker, Algiers). 'Nowadays, everything works through connections, even machines!' (unskilled worker in a tobacco factory, Constantine). More profoundly, therefore, connections appear as the adequate expression of an existence that no reason can explain, as it is simply fatalistic, chance and arbitrary. Everything happens as if, faced with a world that claims to be one of rational meaning, but actually undermines and denounces any attempt to impose a meaning, the man who is not prepared to stop trying to decipher and explain, to seek reasons, has no other recourse than words, verbalism being the last refuge of a reason that refuses to surrender.

'What's needed above all (to get a job)? It's connections! And that depends on how things fall out. When there are twenty people seeking work, for example, and only one succeeds, it's because he's got connections. The other things don't count, children and everything. Of course, if someone's educated he finds a place, that's not the same thing: my mates are like me, they look for work and take what they find if they're lucky' (rubber worker, Oran). As soon as you try to understand, you invoke connections, a fictitious explanation of the situation, not just necessary and unavoidable, but at the same time also contingent, since those who find work are no different from those who don't. Different opinions can thus be linked together in a logic that flouts the principle of contradiction and adopts several different explanatory systems in turn. As the object is not to reason in a correct and effective manner, to reach agreement with others, but rather to save an appearance of reason, one can be satisfied with a semi-coherence and a semi-conformity with the facts of the case. The stereotype is a discourse halfway between fiction and experience, between the constructed and the fortuitous: as empty intentionality, it seems to refer to the facts despite being entirely fictitious, because automatic linkages of words take the place of authentic significations.

[. . .] Certainly, the resort to empty discourse, the echoing absence of signification that claims to make up for absent signification, is not something specific to these sub-proletarians, either as sub-proletarians or as Algerians. And yet, while inflated and puffed-up talk among the petty bourgeois often expresses simply an ignorance of their own ignorance, among the sub-proletarians it always retains a form of truth and fullness, because it is tinged with worry and despair and, like a cry for help, the sound empty of meaning dramatically expresses a dramatic experience, because it is not offered either as sufficient reason for an inexplicable existence or even as adequate expression of an inexpressible experience, but is avowedly an incoherent confession of the insurmountable incoherence.[16]

Maleficent 'connections', that is, discrimination, the colonists, the Spaniards or Italians, machinery, all these personalized and hostile powers that arise from the most concrete experience, are transfigured by magical reason. Thus the machine is described as a Moloch that swallows work: 'There are too many machines! Machines take our work!' (café waiter, Abboville [now Sidi Daoud]). 'It's the machines that take bread from our mouths!' (labourer, Constantine). 'Machines should be abolished. They're killing labour!' (watchman, Tizi-Ouzou). As interjection or exclamation, the function of this magico-mythic language is not to express or even indicate the world, but rather to express feeling.[17] The coherence of this ideological universe, therefore, does not rest on the rules of logic, but on the unity of sentiment: faced with a hostile world haunted by magical powers, is there anything else that these destitute and deprived men can oppose it with except belief in magic? The sense of the world's systematic and methodical malevolence is frequently associated with belief in the all-powerfulness of 'connections'. 'Here,' says a vegetable seller in Oran, 'it's connections!' (he strikes the ground with his stick). 'Nothing else!' ' "They" have no consideration . . .' And another man, the garage watchman in Oran: 'We're asked for baksheesh, or "they" won't give us work. Nothing! You need connections! There is work, people know how to read and write, they're given all kinds of reasons, that they are too old' (he mimics), 'all that . . . There are Europeans who are weak, thin as cats, and they're taken on. Us, we're strong and yet the government and the municipality don't give us anything.' Captive to the colonial order, which is seen as the diabolical work of an evil spirit bent on ambushing and thwarting human intentions, what can one invoke but a power of the same nature and scale? What can one expect except a miracle, when you know that all rational behaviour is condemned to failure? The expectation of a miracle, in both the individual order and the collective order, often coincides with present resignation. 'In an Islamic state,' says an Oran porter, 'there won't be baksheesh or connections. We'll walk straight. Begging will be suppressed right away, the government will see to it.' And the myth of a lost paradise, the reverse side of the expectation of a future paradise, is often also expressed: 'There is a lot of unemployment because many refugees persecuted by both sides have come into the towns. Before the events, we got everything for nothing' (a *fellah* refugee in Saïda).

[. . .] This is why an affective quasi-systematization is typical of the understanding of the economic and social world that the sub-proletarian develops. Sentiment, in fact, is the only unifying principle of a dramatic experience dominated by incoherence. Suffering and despair are never apprehended in their full light, but only form the affective colouring of awareness; thus the natural or social world, which scientific reason conceives as determined by general laws, is perceived as the bearer of emotional qualities, threats or rejections, as if inhabited by intention and inspired by will. Since it cannot be explained by necessary and objective causes, defeat, for example in the form of unemployment, appears attributable to a hostile intention, objectively embodied in the social order. This magico-mythic vision is fuelled by confrontation with the European boss or foreman, the colonist, who gives this objective malignity a face and a physiognomy, as well as a perfectly adequate language.

The sufferings imposed by such an inhumane situation are not sufficient motive for conceiving a different economic and social order; on the contrary, it is as if it is only from the moment when material conditions of existence make it possible to conceive of a different economic and social order that these sufferings can be attributed to a system that is explicitly apprehended as unjust and unacceptable. In conditions where it is impossible to grasp this, the sub-proletarians tend to experience their suffering as habitual, even as natural, an inevitable component of their existence. Their misery, in fact, imposes itself on them with such a total necessity that no escape is conceivable, all the more so as it appears to them as the common destiny of all Algerians, or at least all those they are likely to know;[18] besides, for want of the indispensable minimum of security and culture, they are unable to conceive clearly the overall change in the social order that would be able to abolish the causes of this. After inviting our investigator to visit his wretched shack and observe the destitution of his children, an Oran bus driver added: 'That's how my life is. There is only the wage, which isn't enough. The rest of us, we're made for it.' 'Everyone has his destiny', 'everyone their luck', 'that's what God has meant for me', '*Mekhtoub*', so many formulas often heard that no longer express, as they did traditionally, a confidence in oneself, but rather a resignation associated with despair or revolt. The sub-proletarians' life is one of misery and destitution, suffering and unhappiness; but they are not sufficiently detached from their condition to posit it as object.

As a result, their apprehension and comprehension of their condition are necessarily mutilated: it is as if their situation necessarily appears to them askew. This explains why they tend to attribute their defects to those in their own being, rather than to the defects in the objective order: 'Everyone has their chance,' says an unskilled worker in Constantine. 'If you're not educated you have nothing. You have trouble until you're dead and buried. That's how it is, the lives of people who can't read.' 'Nowadays,' says a builder from Saïda, 'we don't live like we did forty years ago. We live under progress. Everything depends on education. If I was educated, I wouldn't live in these conditions. I'm only a beast of burden' – '*un pauvre bourricot*', his wife repeats the last phrase in French. Awareness of the objective obstacles to obtaining a job or a sufficient income refers them to the awareness of their lacking abilities, such as the want of education and occupational training; they never arrive at an awareness of the system as responsible for their lack of education and training, that is, both for what they lack and for the lacks in their own being. As a result, failing to apprehend as such the system of which their situation is simply one aspect, they are unable to connect an improvement in their condition to a radical transformation of the system; their aspirations and demands, even their revolt, are expressed within the framework and logic of the system. This is why 'connections', as a product of the system, are taken to be the only way to inflect the system's systematic rigour. In short, if misery tends to be lived as an inevitable component of the appropriate condition of individuals whose essence is to be wanting, rather than as the effect of exploitation, it is because absolute alienation deprives the individual even of the awareness of alienation.

We should be careful therefore not to see the revolt of the sub-proletarians as the expression of a genuine revolutionary consciousness. Indignant protest against objective cruelty can be perfectly well combined with attachment to the objective order. To revolt against the established cruelty does not necessarily mean questioning the order on which this cruelty is based. Revolt and protest may be a way of accepting inferiority by confessing it. Is that not the underlying meaning of the behaviour of those people whose demands stubbornly aim at the impossible, as if to mask or compensate, by a substitute operation, for an inferiority that is at bottom recognized? This 'miserabilism' is in fact inspired by the same logic as the affective quasi-systematization discussed above. By substituting intention for necessity, one places oneself at the mercy of the arbitrary decrees of the power of which one is victim, but from which, despite everything, one expects like alms the satisfaction of vital hopes. It is the same people who say 'they don't want to give us work' and 'they don't give us enough'. A raging revolt fuelled by emotion and resentment most often goes together with resigned acceptance.[19] In fact, the sentiment of dependence, and the ambiguous attitudes it generates, take the place of the consciousness of alienation that is the foundation of a revolutionary attitude.[20] Because any individual or collective project is forbidden them, the sub-proletarians tend to form the same image of themselves as do the members of the dominant caste. 'We are made for this', they say more or less explicitly, and the others say: 'They are used to it.' Like racism, miserabilism is an essentialism.

Asking what are the conditions under which individuals can cease simply to suffer their suffering, and move on to considering and understanding it, means questioning the conditions of possibility for the positing of the possible. If there can be no doubt that material conditions of existence alone cannot determine the rise of consciousness and the apprehension of the facts as intolerable or revolting, if they even tend to prevent this, it is no less certain that establishing the present state of things as provided with this or that meaning presupposes something quite other than a kind of revolutionary cogito through which consciousness would become revolutionary by prising itself away from the world, a world in which it is present but which it cannot represent, being engulfed within it and superseded by it. If it is true that establishing the present state of affairs as intolerable and revolting presupposes the positing of a different state of affairs, absent yet accessible, it remains the case that the very positing of the possible presupposes the possibility of taking a certain distance in relation to the world. In other words, the rise of consciousness is not just the establishment of a new relationship to oneself, but fundamentally the establishment of a new relationship to the world. As a prising away from oneself and the world, culminating in the reflexive constitution of oneself and one's condition, it presupposes the possibility of freeing oneself at least to some small extent from the thrall that the world exercises. This taking of distance presupposes a distance effectively taken. To sum up, reflection requires a certain ease and, paradoxically, becoming aware of alienation is a privilege bestowed on those who are no longer so totally alienated that they cannot release themselves and take back ownership of themselves.

And so, those who are in the condition of sub-proletarians are unable to conceive it as such, because this would suppose that they could project the possibility of escape. Because it cannot but be apprehended as such, the dream of escape is simply an occasion to experience the weight of necessity still more cruelly. Prisoners in the exile of the present, these men can prise themselves away only through dreaming, which promises immediate, that is, magical, satisfactions only by establishing a sharp separation between the present of injustice and suffering, and the utopian future, bearer of all benefits: 'As for me, I don't agree that women and girls should work now. Afterwards, yes, when it's over, when the spirit of evil has disappeared and when there are gold coins on the ground, when there is an Islamic state; then she can go out, I won't say anything against it' (secondhand-clothes dealer, Oran).

Haunted by Unemployment:
The Algerian Proletariat and the
Colonial System

Algerians[1] have such a sharp awareness of unemployment that their whole existence and their whole view of existence is affected by it.[2] The awareness of not being employed can in fact inspire behaviours and orient opinions without appearing clearly to the minds that it haunts, and without their being able to formulate it explicitly. Thus, before describing the forms and degrees of consciousness of non-employment (and of the awareness of colonial domination that goes together with it), it is necessary to determine how it dominates behaviour and inspires thinking, either implicitly or explicitly.[3]

1. Personal Dependence

If the pressure of the 'industrial reserve army' is always vividly felt, it is sometimes explicitly expressed in vague and general judgements such as 'there are a lot of hands', 'the population has doubled', or else in more concrete terms, closer to a lived and still vivid experience: 'you go along the quays one morning and you'll see, there are hundreds, thousands of men waiting to get work, to work for a day to earn bread for their kids' (unskilled worker, Algiers).

A Game of Chance

In a context such as this, competition for work is the primary form of the struggle for survival, a struggle that for some people begins again each morning in anxiety and uncertainty. If this competition at

least had rules . . . But rules are just as foreign to it as to games
of chance: 'Look here, we're at a building site, for example; it's like
with *qmar* (a game of chance). Who will be taken on?' (unemployed
labourer, Constantine). Competition works without rules or restraint,
since objective methods of recruitment cannot be applied to this army
of equally unskilled hands. These, however, make up a very high
percentage of the working-class labour force.[4] Besides, only a small
proportion of the mass of workers have received any real occupational training. It follows from this that the unskilled labourer 'is
good for anything, in other words for nothing' (shop worker, Algiers).
'He's not a worker, he's a maid in the service of men' (café owner,
Algiers). 'Each person his luck [*Koul ouah'ad zahrou*], each person
his fate [*Koul ouah'ad bi maktoubou*]', these stereotyped and almost
ritual formulas express the experience of arbitrary choice that gives
one person work and leaves another unemployed.

Available for all work because not really suited to any, the unskilled
are dependent on the vagaries of hiring and firing. Consequently,
if the necessity of developing occupational training is vividly felt, the
demand for a rational organization of recruitment is also sometimes
expressed. And this is all the more so in that the competition for
employment has become that much more bitter since the war considerably accelerated the influx of people from the countryside.

The person seeking work thus has the feeling of being at the mercy
of chance. On top of this, he is often aware that the game from which
he hopes to earn his children's bread is fixed: 'You get the impression
of struggling against fatality. A friend said to me: "Everywhere
I knock, God is there before me with a sack of cement on his back
and a trowel in his hand; I open one door, and he blocks up the one
ahead"' (café owner, Algiers).

The impersonal force one comes up against, without understanding or knowing who is to blame, sometimes acquires a face. Revolt
against discrimination is then expressed, sometimes violently, without
it always being possible to draw a dividing line between experience
and stereotype:

The Europeans are favoured here. For some people being unemployed
is the natural thing, but for a European it's a scandal that no one can
tolerate, neither the administration nor other Europeans. Everything
is done to find something for them, they're discovered to have talents
and qualifications. Even if these are not real, they're discovered. So
much so that, once a European is taken on, he'll automatically find
himself at least a notch above all the Muslim staff. Impossible for him
to be a worse worker than them! That's connections at work, without
anyone identifiable being responsible; it's everyone. (Carpenter, Algiers)

Baksheesh

If workers have an acute awareness of the surplus of unskilled labour, the same goes for certain employers, who exploit the situation (or let it be exploited).

> To get a good job, you have to have connections (energetic hand gesture). You have to have strong 'shoulders'![5] You have to pay out 40,000 or 20,000 francs in baksheesh, I'm not exactly sure how much. There is another way, though. If you have a friend, a relative, he can help you get a place. But the thing that counts most is 'money-connections'. (Painter, Oran)
>
> What makes things work is 'coffee'[6] and 'shoulders'. Say that someone goes after a job. He's asked if he has five children, that means 5,000 francs. If he doesn't, he can just wait. They tell him 'We're going to move'! Only a few people are taken on, when there's urgent work. And once it's done, everyone out of the door, at least those who've not handed over money. (Casual worker, Constantine)
>
> You have to hand over 5,000 francs to get a job. (Tobacco factory worker, Constantine)
>
> If I had 5,000 francs I'd get work. (Grocer, Oran)
>
> One day I asked the boss to send two box-makers. The next day they arrived. 'Where are your tools?' 'We don't have any.' 'Go to the store and fetch them.' They didn't even know what tools to fetch. I had to teach them everything, stand behind them all the time. The poor devils didn't have any other way to earn their keep. It wasn't their fault. The next day, the site manager came and asked me not to say anything. That's the general rule. An unskilled worker is hired, they put down on his payslip 'box-maker' or skilled worker. The bloke is paid as an unskilled worker, 1,200 francs a day instead of 2,400 as skilled, and the difference disappears. When he turns up at a different company and they see his papers, he's given work that he doesn't know how to do and is thrown out; and so it goes on, until he pays to get another job. There's also the case where the worker really is skilled but is paid as a labourer. Generally speaking, you have to pay to get work, to be taken on in the building trade. You generally pay the foreman. There are many blokes who try to earn a bit of money for seven or eight months, to buy wheat, seed. They have to skip two weeks' work either at the start of the contract or at the end. Those who try to get their job back after some kind of break or interruption have to bring honey or butter, or they get the sack. Someone else has been employed in the meantime, and he's dismissed when the other returns. And he has to pay again to get another job. People double their pay like that. (Bus driver, Algiers)
>
> With us, getting anything depends on tips, even what we have a perfect right to. (Lycée caretaker, Algiers)

Acquaintances

Arbitrariness and discrimination – that would sum up the opinion of the most disfavoured classes about recruitment procedures, if it were not for the immense role played by 'acquaintances', connections. Three very different kinds of thing are included in the term 'protection': first of all, discrimination, or what one interviewee calls 'favouritism for Europeans' (machinist, Algiers); secondly, 'coffee' or baksheesh; and third, 'acquaintances' (*el maarifa*) or 'shoulders'.

To start with, recourse to connections is favoured and encouraged by the whole cultural tradition, which makes 'nepotism' in the broad sense a real obligation, in the name of the principle that insists that someone who has got on should use his own success to help others, starting with the members of his own family. Each individual is held to be responsible for several relatives, closer or less close, to whom he owes, among other things, a duty to find work by using his position or his personal connections.[7]

'Someone who's got on', says one interviewee, 'can always get by, and someone who's in the administration can "help" members of his family. If you haven't got "shoulders", it's the shovel and pick, in other words, death' (seller of sweets and peanuts, Philippeville).

On top of this, however, the importance placed on personal relationships and 'knowing people' should perhaps be understood in reference to a general conception of human relations that is in a certain sense common to both Algerians and Europeans in Algeria.[8]

Everything happens as if the effort was always made to convert impersonal relationships, formal and mediated, into direct personal relations. The necessity of this 'personalization' is felt all the more inasmuch as the quest for work is experienced, as we have seen, as an encounter with a faceless bureaucracy.

You have to go and see someone because when you go by yourself you're not taken on, even if there is work. (Waiter, Constantine)

Recourse to personal relations is thus experienced as a kind of collective defence against a globally unfavourable order; one de facto solidarity, manifest and approved, responds to another solidarity, underground and secret, to which the notion of 'fraternity' gives language and support.

If we don't help each other, who will help us? Here, the older is the brother of the younger, since basically the older is under the same sign as the younger. (Teacher, Algiers)

The belief in the efficacy of protection and personal relations is based in reality. Of those interviewed, 47.2 per cent say that they obtained their job thanks to a relative (27 per cent) or a friend (19.2 per cent), as against 14.5 per cent by direct application, 6.1 per cent through a training establishment and 3.4 per cent through an employment office. These figures are certainly not equally significant for different categories. In fact, among artisans and shopkeepers there are, on the one hand, all those who got their shop or workshop from a relative and, on the other, those who had financial help from a relative or friend. Among country people, likewise, a high proportion of peasants cultivate the land of their fathers. But, and this is the essential thing, 62 per cent of workers, day-labourers and junior employees say that they obtained their job through a relative (30 per cent) or a friend (32 per cent),[9] as against 16 per cent by direct application, 8 per cent through an employment office and 4 per cent through a training establishment. It does not therefore seem exaggerated to say that it is not really businesses that recruit, but employment is rather the result of a kind of *spontaneous cooption* among workers:

> I work here because a friend told me 'there are jobs, come and try'. I gave satisfaction, so they kept me. (Worker in a wood company, Oran)
> I got my job through a cousin; he knew the boss of the garage because he had a lorry, he did haulage. So I learnt the trade and I'm here. (Vulcanizer in a garage, Oran)

Apart from this recruitment through cooption, effected on the basis of recommendations and information supplied by workers in the business, who act spontaneously as intermediaries between the employer and the possible employee, there are only such rudimentary hiring procedures as engagement at the factory or workshop door, or even small ads. It is possible to conclude, therefore, that in the great majority of cases the labourers, workers and lower-level employees are selected by reference to their status qualities (family, relationships, etc.) far more than for their aptitudes or qualifications.

Confirmation of this emerges from the above analyses in the fact that 45.2 per cent of the subjects (52.8 per cent if we exclude the self-employed, petty street vendors, small artisans and the non-active) have family members or people from their group of origin (village or region) as fellow workers; this proportion reaches 52 per cent (and 55.3 per cent) for labourers and workers, and 45.3 per cent (55.3 per cent) for artisans and shopkeepers. Thus, alongside the major occupational clusters that sometimes have a long tradition (Mozabite shopkeepers, street-porters and vegetable dealers from the Djidjelli region, garbage collectors (former water-carriers) from Biskra, waiters from the Michelet region [now Ain-El-Hammam], dishwashers from the Sidi Aïch region, etc.), there is a whole network of small groups, born from mutual aid and cooption, which preserve in fragmentary and partial fashion, within the world of labour, a type of social relations characterized by a cultural system based on ties of kinship and mutual acquaintance.[10]

What is most indispensable for getting a job?

Response	Protection (%)	Education (%)
Labourers and workers	44	40
Artisans and shopkeepers	29.5	56.8
Executives and government employees	26.3	63.1
Total	30.8	55.4

The almost unconditional belief in the effectiveness of 'shoulders' and 'acquaintances' is both cause and consequence of this state of things. Furthermore, knowing what great store workers place on education, one can understand the importance that protection assumes in their eyes. More than members of the other social categories (for example shopkeepers and executives), they have direct experience of the effectiveness of personal relations as the only means of reducing the share of arbitrariness in the search for work. The precariousness of recruitment methods, the scarcity of skilled workers, especially the highly skilled, the surplus of general labourers, all give credit to the belief in the omnipotence of protection, not so much as an arbitrarily conferred support (which is something else again) and facilitating a dispensation, but as an indispensable adjunct to success or as a principle of selection that acts in default of any other.

There can be no doubt that the omnipotence of protection is sometimes emphatically asserted: 66.7 per cent of the subjects believe that this is enough to ensure success (as against 32 per cent who believe it is not enough), 62 per cent judging that merit is not enough; the two-thirds of those who regard protection as sufficient to ensure success state that merit is not sufficient. One-third, however, believe that protection may suffice to ensure success but merit may also, attesting therefore to a more nuanced opinion. They generally then bring up other factors in success, such as education or, in the case of shopkeepers, possession of a certain capital. Thus, with the exception of those who believe that merit is sufficient to ensure success whereas protection is not (i.e. the two-thirds of those who replied that protection is not enough), the great majority consider protection as the necessary but not sufficient condition, that is, capable by itself of ensuring success or getting a job.

Paternalism

Attachment to a trade is also a function of the style of social relations within the firm. Knowing the high value conferred on direct personal relationships in this society, it can be seen how great the aspiration can be to genuinely human relations at work. Relations of authority are often founded on the fear of dismissal, a fear that the awareness of unemployment creates. 'Personally,' explained a school caretaker (Algiers), 'I don't let myself go. The others are mainly auxiliaries and they are afraid of being sacked for the least sign of disrespect.' Most often, relations with superiors are reduced to the indispensable minimum: 'The boss is the boss, nothing more' is a common response:[11]

> I come in. I put my overalls on. Bonjour, bonjour. Bonsoir, bonsoir. (Unemployed man, Saïda, about his former job)
> Everyone says bonjour, how are you? Sometimes you shake hands [. . .] When the boss said 'I've got no more work', I said 'don't worry, it's all the same to me'. (Unemployed man, Tlemcen)

Alongside relationships of the 'bonjour, bonjour' type, which are the most usual, there are also more intense exchanges, but these are generally asymmetrical:

> When I had a boss, I asked him for advice. I invited him to festivals but he didn't want to come. He was a refugee, a Spaniard. He never gave me presents, not for Christmas, nothing at all. (Inactive, Oran)
> The boss, Monsieur T., is a friend, we even address each other in the familiar form; sometimes he asks my opinion if there are things to be done. Before, he came to see if I was tired, for example; but now he's become too rich, he doesn't bother. He gives me presents at Christmas, even a bit of money. Sometimes I've visited him with my family, sometimes by myself, but his family have never come to my house. (Salesman, Oran)

The majority of workers and employees who work in small artisan and commercial businesses that maintain professional ties of a patriarchal (or paternalistic . . .) character, say that they like their trade but are unhappy with their wages.

It's better not to work in a company. It's better to work for an artisan, as he knows his worker and his worker is important to him. My boss is like a friend for me, or like a father. I ask his advice in difficult moments, I invite him for birth celebrations and I take him presents, cakes. He does the same. It's better than being in a company where you don't know the boss. (Assistant to an – Algerian – painter, Médéa)

Very often, so as to justify their refusal to change jobs in order to earn more, employees invoke their attachment to their boss:

I refuse to change. I might end up with a boss who I don't get along with. My boss is a boss, but also a friend. He's already invited me to his house. (Bus driver, Algiers)

My boss (a cousin) is very kind to me. I couldn't leave him to earn 5,000 francs more. There are bad bosses who pay 20,000 francs, but people don't stay with them because they're bad. Someone who trusts you, that's pleasant [. . .] On holidays, if work is pressing, you can't turn down a boss like that. (Butcher's assistant, Philippeville)

I worked on one particular boat, we did loading; the boat's owner was always the same, there was a captain on board and a foreman. Oh! I got along fine with the boss, that's why he kept me for twenty-two years. I went to his house, I drank coffee and he came to my place; he was a Frenchman from France, Monsieur R– son, shipbuilder. He gave me presents for the kids. (Inactive, Oran)

I can't leave here because of the boss. He's too old: sometimes when he feels a bit tired, I stay by his bed all night. He's like a second father to us. Even my own father didn't do for us what this boss does. He even shares his food with us. My conscience would reproach me all my life [. . .] He's very kind to me and my wife. He's good. He's pure French. Even when I don't work he gives me food. Recently, the social security tried to take everything I had because I couldn't pay. It's thanks to my boss that they didn't. He paid for me. (Painter's labourer, Saida)[12]

2. Forced Labour

The Absence of Instability

It is understandable how, despite a high rate of dissatisfaction with work, and particularly with wages, occupational instability is very low: only 6.3 per cent of subjects had had three different jobs between the start of 1959 and the middle of 1960, and 3.1 per cent two jobs. More than a third of those who said that they did not like their work also declared that they would not look for anything else, some 'because they haven't time', others because they don't want to risk losing the job that they have for another very hypothetical one.

Yes, every year I make two or three applications, but I don't get any direct response and then I don't want to lose my place without having another. I send a letter, and if it happens it happens, I'm [. . .] At present, if you leave a job you're finished. It's hard to get another. (Employee in a factory making tarpaulins, Oran)

I'm not happy with my job, but I'm afraid to change. I work for 25,000 francs a month, it's better than earning nothing. (Mechanic in the merchant navy, Algiers)

Awareness of the surplus of unskilled labour means that someone who has a job is concerned above all not to lose it. Aware also of being so very easily replaceable, owing to their lack of skills and the abundance of possible candidates to replace them, the majority of labourers, workers and lower-level employees are concerned above all to keep their positions. This is shown better by the following example: 'I work too hard,' says an Oran delivery man, 'I don't get enough holiday: it's tiring. I can't have time off because I can't get a substitute; the boss would have to pay him, I'd have to train him, teach him to deliver the margarine and yeast.' A lot of confused and embarrassed explanations. But a bit further on, on the subject of overtime, he adds:

I even work Sundays, sometimes bakers come and wake me up; the goods are locked up in the truck outside my door. I never get time off. If someone was to substitute for me, and he's able to work for half the rate, then the boss will look to his interest, he won't worry that I've served him for fourteen years.

Deliberate instability is a luxury that very few workers can afford, a privilege reserved for those who, by virtue of their particular skill, are certain to readily find work. For the others, there's only a forced instability.[13]

The Lack of Social Advance

Vertical mobility in a single lifetime is also very low. Condemned to stagnation as a result of competition and the lack of prior occupational training, the majority of manual workers do not even cherish the hope of rising in their trade. Questioned on this subject, they most often replied with a laugh, the question not having the slightest meaning for them. 'I'm still on a daily basis. There aren't any grades (laughter)!' (day-labourer, Constantine). Not only is there a lack of any reasonable hope of social advance, but the very idea of such hope is absent and almost inconceivable.[14]

Do you hope to rise in your work?

'I don't hope for anything. It's just shovel and pick for me' (building labourer, Tlemcen).

'It's a stupid question, who wouldn't want to rise! If possible, I'd like to become station head' (civil servant at the Médéa prefecture).

It is significant that two individuals may laugh at the same question for diametrically opposite reasons, each seeing as inconceivable what the other finds natural.[15] It is also significant that the privilege of hope is reserved for a few.[16]

Everyone knows more or less clearly, at least among the more advantaged, that the wall blocking the horizon of their future also closes the future of everyone who shares their condition. 'Do you know anyone who's got on?' 'No, I don't.' 'No one that I know.' 'It's the same for everyone.' 'The people I know are like me.' 'I don't know; no one has risen in my trade.' And so on. The awareness of lack of employment gives rise here to awareness of a common condition. Thus the idea is often expressed that the fate of the unemployed cannot be ascribed to individual inadequacies or lack of aptitude, but rather to an objective situation. This is the basis of a new solidarity, quite different from the old, and indissociable from revolt against a shared condition.

Look, I have neighbours who say to me: 'I've run after work the whole day and not found anything.' While if I earn 1,000 francs I'm obliged to share this with them, and then we're all miserable. [. . .] Coming back from work, I discuss with my fellow workers, we discuss our worries, our misery, and then everyone goes home as we're all dead beat. (Worker in a timber factory, Oran)

'Occupations'

All the above analyses find a concrete illustration in the situation of certain petty traders, a borderline situation and in this sense highly significant. How to explain in fact the extraordinary proliferation of these makeshift petty businesses? How should we understand, taking simply the standpoint of profitability, the behaviour of those men who push their little barrow along the whole day just to sell two or three watermelons, a pair of second-hand trousers, or a packet of peanuts? Here again, it is the imperative of work at any price that leads them to do something, anything, rather than nothing.

If work means having a trade, practising it in a regular way and making a proper living from it, that's not for everyone, that's something else.

If work means doing something, doing no matter what so as not just
to sit around, to earn a loaf of bread, then it's only the lazy who don't
work. (Cook, Algiers)

So, for those who have nothing, there is always this last resort.

But what is the function of this kind of work for those who
perform it? First of all, the smallest petty commerce is the only occupation that demands no starting capital, no trade skill, no training,
no money and no premises. If we should not underestimate the
genuine importance of incomes that strike us as dismal, it seems clear
that the fact of recourse to these lines, which should be called 'occupations' rather than trades, cannot be explained simply by economic
interest. Work of this kind is not breadwinning: the material results
of the action, the profit obtained from it, do not exhaust its significance. Perhaps it should be seen as an attitude analogous to that of
the *fellah* who, in a bad year, sows after the spring ploughing knowing
that there is very little chance of harvesting anything. 'If the *fellah*
calculated,' says the Kabyle proverb, 'he wouldn't sow.' Work of this
kind is in a certain sense its own end, because it truly does not have
any adequate end outside of itself. Not that work is seen as the final
purpose of existence. Working for working's sake does not mean
living in order to work, or working in order to live. It is just as if,
being unable to access work as a means of obtaining a wage or an
income, you end up by the natural force of circumstance disassociat-
ing work from its economic result, seeing it less as tied to its product
than as something opposed to non-work. Working, even for nothing
or for a minuscule income, means, for oneself and in the eyes of the
group, doing everything within one's power in order to earn one's
living by working, in order to prise oneself away from the condition
of unemployed. The fact of trying to work (rather than working in
the proper sense) is enough to provide a justification in the eyes of
the group and in the eyes of those one is responsible for, the wife and
children, as well as in the eyes of those whom one has recourse to in
order to live. All these semblances of occupation are perhaps the last
defence against the extreme abandonment of the man 'who gets fed
by others', who lives at the expense of his relatives or neighbours.
The defence of dignity and self-respect seems to constitute the real
motivation, far more than the hope of gain. In fact, 'a dignified man
who does not want to live at the cost of others *has to* work, even if
he has to live from expedients' (cook, Algiers). The justification
obtained from the fact of making the effort to work is very important
in a society in which mutual aid is practised so intensely, in which
the unemployed person is rescued by others, relatives, neighbours or

friends. By working, if only in a symbolic manner, all these people who sell little for almost nothing attest that they are victims of an objective situation and not of their incapacity, their indolence or their laziness.

3. Disorientation

The whole existence of the most disadvantaged strata takes place under the sign of necessity and insecurity. This is particularly true of day-labourers and, more precisely, of casual workers and unemployed.

For these men, prepared to do anything and aware of not knowing how to do anything, always available and totally subject to all determinisms, condemned to live from day to day and eager for stability, deprived of a genuine trade and by this fact devoted to all the semblances of one, there is nothing solid or stable, nothing sure or permanent. The employment of daily time divided between the search for work and makeshifts, the week or month partitioned by the chances of employment into working days and days off, all this bears the mark of precariousness. No regular timetable or fixed place of work. The same discontinuity in time and space. The search for work is the only constant in this existence haphazardly swung to and fro. You look for work 'right and left', you borrow 'right and left'. You borrow from Peter to pay Paul. 'I manage by borrowing from one person or other like bits floating on water' (unemployed man, Constantine).

The whole of life is spent under the sign of the provisional. Ill-adapted to the urban world they have strayed into, cut off from the rural world and its reassuring traditions, without past or future, they are stubbornly set on forcing chance, trying to get a grip on a present that irremediably escapes them.[17]

The whole of existence is deprived of what normally constitutes its scaffolding, that is, occupational life with its temporal and spatial rhythms, its constraints, the assurances it provides, the opportunity it gives to envisage and arrange for the future. And, as one of the subjects puts it well, 'you may well say that what makes a man is work'. If the consequences of unemployment are often underestimated, it is because work is seen simply as a means of earning a living, whereas it is perhaps, if not the foundation of a way of living, at least the necessary condition for conscious or unconscious elaboration of a plan of life. For the untrained labourer without permanent employment, for the unemployed or the street vendor, for all the young people who drag out their days and who are often to be seen around slot machines or juke-boxes, the drama does not just lie in the absence of objective opportunities for work, but in the privation of a regular life of work and stability that are the guaranteed product of work.[18]

The Quest for Security

We can understand how the fundamental ambition of individuals from the most disadvantaged strata is stable employment. Every time that these aspirations are expressed, we see the appearance of terms and expressions that speak security and stability. The desire for stability, common to the great majority of labourers, unskilled workers, employees, petty artisans and shopkeepers, takes the form of the aspiration for a genuine *profession* (as opposed to a mere 'occupation'), in which the conditions of hiring and firing, of promotion and retirement, are guaranteed and regulated; in which there is protection in place against the harmful effects of unrestrained competition; in which regulations on health and safety, on hours of work, on the employment of labour, on the criteria of qualification, on remuneration, its levels, modes and types, are effectively applied. If the great majority see government employment as a kind of professional paradise, it is because all these guarantees against insecurity and arbitrariness are to be found there, even in the absence of trade-union checks.

In the absence of regular employment, what is threatened first of all is the entire psychological and – particularly – emotional equilibrium that goes together with a genuine insertion into society. It is the function of the head of the family, for example, that is called into question by unemployment, and by the same token the authority and esteem that are inseparable from it, both within the family group and outside it, among neighbours and friends. Can self-esteem survive the damage to social esteem, especially in a society like this? In this way, even the strictest cultural norms are transgressed under pressure of necessity.

> My wife has been working as a domestic. Yes, while I was without work (for eighteen months) it was my wife who worked to feed the family. (Mattress worker, Sidi-Bel-Abbes)

The reversal of functions traditionally allocated to man and woman is experienced by both the individual and the group as a final humiliation:

In the face of so much effort for nothing, good will disappears, people become discouraged and let themselves go; for some people it's despair, madness or alcohol, for others resignation. They stop making any effort, they even can't any more, they let themselves go; it's failure. Then it's the wife who works, the children who shine shoes. You stop reacting – what's the point? You're defeated. For people like this, the state should do something, as they'll never get out of this situation by their own work, it'll never be enough. The state has to accept making a loss in order to rescue them. (Café owner, Algiers)

Little by little, in this way, people settle into apathy and fatalistic resignation. It happens that street vendors end up making a regular occupation out of what was originally just a temporary makeshift. 'Many people find themselves forced to do that in order to live, to the point that now nothing would induce them to do anything else. It's bad, as what started off as a necessity becomes a form of laziness' (cook, Algiers). People adjust themselves and irresistibly become accustomed to a vegetative and parasitical existence. Totally left behind by the world, they settle into unemployment or pretend work and are satisfied with it. The objective obstacles are an excuse for resignation.

Employment and Life Plan

In the absence of regular employment, what is lacking is not only a place of work and a daily task, but a coherent organization of present and future, a system of expectations and a field of concrete ends to which all activity can be oriented. It is only on the basis of a structured and controlled present field that a future at once distant and foreseeable can be aimed at and posited in a rational project or expected. Unemployed, porters, runners of errands, street vendors, watchmen of who knows what, petty retailers of a packet of cigarettes or a bunch of bananas, and all those people whose earnings are as much alms as a tip, are not certain enough of the present moment to try to ensure themselves a future, not having that minimum grasp of the present moment that appears to be the condition of possibility for a deliberate effort and a rational attempt designed to get a hold on the future. Fatalistic improvidence and abandonment to chance are the expression of a total lack of confidence in the future, based on awareness of an inability to control the present.

The perspective of regular and steady work is correlative with the formation of an awareness of time that is open and rational; the lack of work or unstable employment, on the other hand, goes together with an absence of any perspective of aspirations and opinions, the absence of a system of projects and rational foresight. In the absence of any real perspective of social advance, for example, the majority of unemployed and labourers without regular work forge aspirations that are disproportionate and contradicted by actual possibilities. There is often an immense and unbridgeable abyss separating the level of aspiration and the level of accomplishment, imagination and experience.[19] Questioned about the future that he hopes for his children, an unemployed man from Constantine declares: 'They will go to school; when they're educated they can choose for themselves. But I can't send them to school. If I could, I'd like to have them study until they were doctors or lawyers. But I don't have the funds. I can dream.' The same man, whose present income is non-existent, estimates 200,000 francs per month to be the income he would need in order to meet the needs of his family. The same gap between aspirations lived in imaginary or dream mode and the real situation is found with this unemployed man from Saïda who, after saying that he feared being forced to remove his children from school for lack of funds, wants his daughter 'to go right through, until she's succeeded, until her *baccalauréat* if she can, or the certificate, then she can work as a teacher'. The other man from Constantine says, on the one hand, 'You need education, but to get education you need money', and on the other hand, on the subject of his daughters' education, 'I'll send them to Algiers, to Paris, even further. They'll go through to the end', and finally, on a third occasion, 'You can't educate children when you earn 400 francs a day. What can you do? I sent my daughter to a summer camp. I was forced to buy clothes to send her there and I assure you that cost something!' Another unemployed man from Constantine combines the most contradictory statements on the subject of his daughters' future: 'I'll only send the boys to school. The girls each need a guardian', and further on: 'Oh! If she's educated, she [the daughter] will have to work; she can look after herself, that's her business. But now, even if my wife and I are starving, I won't let her work.' The same contradictions and even incoherencies exist among the petty artisans and traders:

> I'd like my sons and daughters to continue their studies; they can be an engineer or manager, or else a teacher if that's impossible. For my part, I've had no professional training, I'm unfortunate; I don't want my children to suffer the same fate. [. . .] But I can't send them to school, I'm afraid of not being able to send them, as I can't afford their books. I think I'll be forced to remove my daughter. (Street vendor of vegetables, Tlemcen)

For those unable to envisage rationally a reasonably accessible future, the only thing left is to dream.

4. Forms and Degrees of Awareness of Unemployment

The simple fact of calling oneself unemployed, or grasping the existence of unemployment as such, marks a radical change of attitude towards one's own situation. In fact, what can the notion of unemployment mean for the mass of unemployed and non-employed who remain outside the circuit of the modern economy and are unfamiliar with waged work? For substantially similar real occupation rates, country people from the Kabyle communities readily declare themselves unemployed if they deem their activity insufficient, whereas the inhabitants of southern Algeria would rather call themselves occupied. This is easy to understand given that the former, by virtue of a long tradition of emigration to France and the Algerian cities, have a direct or a mediated experience of the modern economy,[20] which remains relatively foreign to the latter. In the traditional rural milieu, lack of work is not seen as unemployment, and still less as leisure. Agriculture and stock-raising have their rhythms, their alternation between periods of full work and periods of slower work. All members of the family, from the patriarch to the young adolescent, take part in agricultural work to different degrees and with different functions. They thus all see themselves as occupied, and permanently so, since there is always something to be done, no matter how little. The appearance of an awareness of not being employed marks a total change in attitude towards work and towards the world. Natural submission to an order that is natural because traditional (that is, taken for granted) gives way to an attitude that is demanding, even revolutionary. The person who declares himself unemployed, instead of calling himself occupied, views and judges his condition in relation to a new system of reference. It is because he implicitly or explicitly introduces the notion of full employment, drawn from experience of the modern economy and work in the European milieu, that he sees himself as unoccupied.[21] This is also apparent in the fact that young people between 14 and 25 who are not occupied, being more open to the modern world, declare themselves unemployed the same day. In the field of employment, as elsewhere, the demonstration effect exerted by European society has been immense. It follows that what inspires the demands of the Algerian masses is not the abstract and formal concept of abstract and universal rights, understood as the rights of man, but revolt against inequality and privilege, the desire to enjoy the same advantages as the Europeans. Demands along the lines of 'why them and not us?' precede the assertion of the legal equality of all men, and not the other way round.

Awareness of unemployment is more or less acute, more or less rational, depending on individuals and social categories. The mere statement of the fact, the simple announcement of the existence of unemployment, of lack of work or excess labour-power, is the most basic (and the most common) form of expression of the awareness of unemployment, and generally exists alongside the active awareness expressed only in attitudes. Beyond this, two types of expression of awareness of unemployment are met with, which we must take care not to confuse. Individuals from the most disadvantaged strata express and live the experience of unemployment and the colonial situation in the logic of affectivity. Revolt is directed above all against a personal authority rather than against economic exploitation, against individual persons or situations, and not against an organization that has to be totally and globally transformed. However, the systematic character of the most disparate experiences, from bullying through to unemployment, is felt in a very lively way. The belief thus develops that all these experiences are the result of a kind of plan, systematically conceived by a maleficent will.[22] 'The French', says an unemployed man from Saïda, 'don't want to give me work. All these gentlemen around me are without work. They all have certificates, one is a builder, the other a bus driver, they all have trades. Why don't they have the right to work, then? The French have everything they need for a good life. But they don't want to give us anything, not work or anything.' And the Algiers grocer: 'Someone who has work should give it, not hide it.' Unemployment is understood here not as an aspect of an economic and social conjuncture, which the colonial situation might at least partly explain, but rather as the result of a will. Necessity is replaced by intention. The colonial system is experienced as a kind of spiteful hidden god, who might be embodied, according to circumstances, in 'the Europeans', 'the French', 'France', 'the administration', 'the government'.

This spiteful god takes the place of the God of tradition in many people's minds. And by the same token, the optimistic fatalism, the sense of *mektoub* (it is written) that meant, above all, abandonment of self and trust in divine will, is often replaced by a pessimistic fatalism, based on the inner conviction that it is absurd and vain to struggle against an all-powerful maleficence. Where people used to say 'it is written', they now say 'it's intended'. And in parallel with this, a profound revolt is expressed, a 'revolt of the emotions' rather than a true revolutionary consciousness, because it attacks less the system than its manifestations, and the energies inspiring it are not so much rational as impassioned.

With permanent employment and a regular wage, education and trade unions, the existence of real perspectives of social advance, a coherent and rational view of the colonial system appears. Wage-workers in the modern sector, civil servants, the bosses of rationalized companies, might bracket out their lived experience and the passion inseparable from it and, by the same token, go beyond the phenomenal manifestations of the colonial system that certain minds focus on because these are more manifest and more charged with emotional force. For individuals possessing the material and intellectual resources indispensable for adopting a 'rational conduct of life', who are capable of placing themselves in the logic of rational calculation and prediction, who are endowed with a coherent system of aspirations and demands, revolutionary consciousness strikes its roots in everyday existence.

Inspired by a radicalism of feeling, unable to expect an improvement in their conditions otherwise than from a complete overthrow of the social order, the sub-proletarians of the towns, like the proletarianized country people, risk becoming the prey of demagogues who promise radical and magical solutions, if they do not find in a revolutionary trade-unionism not only the reasonable hope for a real transformation in their condition, but also a transformation of their way of life and their representations determined by education.

The Making of Economic Habitus

I witnessed, in Algeria in the 1960s, what with hindsight appears to me to be a veritable social experiment. Owing to the war of national liberation and to certain measures of the military policy of repression, such as the forced relocation of population carried out by the French army, this country – in which some remote and isolated mountain peoples, such as those I was able to study in Kabylia, had preserved almost intact the traditions of a pre-capitalist economy quite alien to the logic of the market[1] – was submitted to a kind of *historical acceleration* which caused two forms of economic organization, normally separated by a gap of several centuries and making contradictory demands on their participants, to coexist, or to be telescoped, under the eyes of the observer.[2]

Without repeating the details of already published analyses, and giving priority to unpublished information preserved in my fieldwork notebooks, I would like to outline briefly what appeared to me with total clarity in that quasi-laboratory situation, namely, the *mismatch* between economic dispositions fashioned in a pre-capitalist economy and the economic cosmos imported and imposed, oftentimes in the most brutal way, by colonization. This mismatch forced one to discover that access to the most elementary economic behaviours (working for a wage, saving, credit, birth control, etc.) is in no way axiomatic and that the so-called 'rational' economic agent is the product of quite particular historical conditions. That is precisely what is ignored both by the economic theory which records and ratifies a particular, historically situated and dated, case of the economic habitus under the name 'rational action theory', without any consideration of the economic and social conditions that make it possible, because it takes it for granted, and the 'new economic sociology'[3] which, for lack of having a genuine theory of the economic agent, adopts 'rational action theory' by default and fails to *historicize economic dispositions* which, like the economic field, have a social genesis.[4] It was no doubt because I found myself in a situation where I could directly observe the disarray or the distress of economic agents devoid of the dispositions tacitly demanded by an economic order that for us is entirely familiar – in which, being an embodied and therefore naturalized social structure, they appear as self-evident, necessary and universal – that I was able to conceive the idea of statistically analysing the conditions of possibility of these historically constituted dispositions.

Some Properties of the Precapitalist Economy

All the major characteristics of pre-capitalist economic practices can be related to the fact that the behaviours that we regard as economic are not autonomized and constituted as such, i.e. as belonging to a specific order, governed by laws irreducible to those that govern ordinary social relationships, especially between kin.

In Kabyle society at the end of the colonial era, exchanges between relatives or neighbours obeyed the logic of the gift and counter-gift. People of honour do not sell milk ('Would you believe it? He sold some milk!'), or butter or cheese, or yet fruits and vegetables; instead, they 'let the neighbours benefit too'. A miller with surplus flour would not think of selling a foodstuff which is the very basis of the eating regimen. The logic of gift exchange combines with mythico-ritual logic to forbid one from emptying a receptacle: what is sent back thus is called *el fel*, which means the 'lucky charm', like the provisions (eggs or poultry) given to the mason when he goes off to work outside the village. The same is true of services, which are governed by strict rules of reciprocity and non-payment *(gratuité)*, and also of loans. For example, the *charka* of an ox (in which a peasant lends an ox for a predefined period in exchange for a certain number of measures of grain) can only be set up between quasi-strangers (in other words, if kin and neighbours cannot assist) and it is enshrouded in all kinds of dissimulations and euphemizations intended to mask or repress its mercantile potentialities. In most cases, the two 'contracting parties' prefer to agree to conceal the arrangement, with the borrower trying to disguise his destitution and make believe the ox is his own, and the lender abetting him in this pretence because it is better to hide a transaction that does not strictly conform to the sense of equity, as capital could never be perceived and treated as such. Everything takes place as if the transaction becomes increasingly reduced to its economic 'truth' as the relationship between the agents involved in the exchange becomes more remote and therefore more neutral and impersonal, with the relative weight of generosity and the sense of equity within these structurally ambiguous relationships steadily decreasing in favour of self-interest and calculation.[5]

Relations reduced to their purely 'economic' dimension are conceived as *relations of war*, which can only obtain between strangers. The site par excellence of economic warfare is the marketplace, not so much the small market of the village or tribe, a place where one is still among people one knows, as the bigger markets of small towns further afield (informants cited Bordj bou Arreridj, Akbou or Maison-Carrée, for the region of Kabylia) where one comes up against strangers, including the most dangerous, the professional dealer (*maquignon*), and is consequently exposed to all the trickery and bluff of a war without quarter. And from the countless stories of the misfortunes of the market a few general principles can be extracted: when the object of the transaction is well known, unequivocal, a relation of anonymous exchange is possible and the choice fastens mainly, or exclusively, on the thing to be bought; when it is unknown, equivocal, and can give rise to deception (like a mule which may turn out stubborn or an ox that may have been artificially 'fattened' or may prove aggressive), the choice bears mainly on the vendor. In any case, one strives to substitute a personal relationship for an impersonal, anonymous one, in particular by requiring all kinds of guarantees and by mobilizing 'guarantors' and witnesses, whose role is as it were to dissolve the relationship between buyer and seller in a network of intermediaries.[6]

The strategies of honour which govern ordinary exchanges are not totally absent from the extra-ordinary exchanges of the marketplace. Thus, as also happens in marriages, after the verbal exchanges which conclude with the fixing of the price, the vendor ostentatiously returns a relatively large portion of the sum to the purchaser 'to buy meat for his children'. Informants describe many cases of purchases of land motivated by the wish to protect a relative, man or woman, from dispossession in favour of a stranger or, following another logic, to assert a group's point of honour in the face of a rival group. In short, the logic of the market, that is, of war, is never really accepted and recognized as such, and those who make the best of it – the dealer, market dues collector or usurer – are despised.[7]

A brief excursus on the relations between peasants and craftsmen, especially blacksmiths and millers, and their transformations, linked to the emergence of real commercial trades, will allow us to verify that strictly economic logic is not independent of the logic of the social relations in which it is immersed, or 'embedded', to use Polanyi's (1957) terminology.[8] In the Kabylia of the 1950s, the work of the blacksmith was the object of a non-monetary transaction governed more often than not by customary law: the village blacksmith was expected to provide each peasant with all the repairs needed to maintain his equipment in exchange for an annual levy on the harvest proportionate to the number of yokes of oxen they owned. The case of the Aghbala water mills, which I studied with Abdelmalek Sayad, shows how social and economic relationships interpenetrate.

Because the millers of Aghbala, unlike the very strongly stigmatized blacksmiths, were not excluded from the community, although they were among its most impoverished members, each mill was tied, through the interplay of the exchange of services and the back-and-forth of relationships and alliances, to a stable clientele, treated with special respect, rather like guests, and the miller levied a share (a tithe) of the grain he had handled in exchange for the service rendered. With the decline of agriculture, linked to the introduction of new activities (crafts, commerce, etc.) and the appearance of non-agricultural resources stemming from emigration,[9] use of traditional watermills decreased (people would buy milled flour rather than have their own grain milled) and motorized mills took their place, sweeping away as if by magic the whole system of conventions that governed the play of collective solidarity in the case of traditional milling.

Thus, for instance, tradition dictated that any load of grain not brought to the mill on the back of a beast of burden be ground for nothing and before any others. For it could only be the small stock of a pauper, gathered by gleaning, or the gifts of the *Aïd*, the tithe levied on the crops, or the gift of a richer relative, or the product of begging around the threshing floors: in any case a quantity too small to be reduced by another tenth and too urgently needed for its milling to be delayed. With the motorized mill, generally acquired by saving (rather than being merely a customary object that one inherits), and perceived and treated as a mere means of production (in the strict economic sense), comes the logic of investment and the calculation of costs and profits, in place of the satisfactions of autarkic performance that a peasant who owned all or part of a watermill could derive from grinding his own grain. An old *fellah* remembered having used the mill of which he was three-quarters owner for thirty-five consecutive days, which amounts to a quarter of the period of activity. The user of the motorized mill, however poor, becomes a customer and the miller behaves towards him like a businessman concerned to get a return on his investment.

This transformation of 'craft' activities – hitherto always subordinated to agricultural activity and generally performed by stigmatized categories, such as blacks, or by the poorest members of the society as a complement to the *khammessat* (the traditional form of sharecropping) – into real 'trades' and full-blown 'occupations' finds its equivalent in the domain of commerce, which could previously be no more than a supplementary activity, alongside farming (anyone who 'sat on his chair all day long', 'in the shade', would have been thought an 'idler'). Thus one took care to open up shop only in the morning, before the men set off for the fields, and in the evening after the return from work, during the summer months. The premises used for shopkeeping were part of the house and neighbours or kinsmen (or, for those who did not have a right to such familiarity, the old woman of the household) would not hesitate to call out or to enter the house to be supplied with a packet of coffee or sugar (either by the master of the house or by one of the women, or by one of the boys specifically assigned to this task).

Everything changed in the 1960s with the emergence of the full-time shopkeeper, who no longer wants to do the work of a peasant and hands over his land, if he has any, to his son, his brother, or a *khammès*. Permanently available in his shop, which is now distinct from the house, during clearly defined opening hours, often dressed differently from the *fellah*, he has the sense of doing something by running a shop (and not of wasting his time), even when, in the *regroupements*, the forced settlements produced by the fake urbanization imposed by the French army, he really has very little to do (his shop becomes in fact a meeting place where one comes to talk without purchasing anything). For the old peasants bound to the economy of good faith (*niya*), this 'rise' of the shopkeepers was one sign of the collapse of the old world, as an informant from the Aïn Aghbel regrouping explained:

> Even the butchers make fun of the cultivators nowadays. All they need is a shop, a special shirt for work, to change clothes, some labourers to slaughter [the animals], to clean up, to sell in the markets, and they are no longer butchers [a traditionally despised trade, like that of blacksmith] but 'men of wealth' *(des riches)*. It's become a *métier* [he uses the French word for an occupation, a trade]. Everything's a *métier* now. 'What's your métier,' people ask. And so everyone finds himself

a *métier*. One puts three boxes of sugar and two packets of coffee on a shelf and calls himself a 'grocer'. One who can nail four planks together calls himself a 'joiner'. Everywhere there are 'drivers', even if there are no cars: all you need for that is a licence in your pocket. Who does that feed?

To some extent it's the [French] Army that did that, giving people a *métier*. First there was self-defence, that's the first *métier*.[. . .]Then there were the *harkis*,[10] the *goumiers*, the *moukhaznt*, the *serdjan* [*sergent* – sergeant], *kabran* [*corporal* – corporal], *serdjan* major, then there was the *sakritir* [*secrétaire*: secretary] and the khodja [*cadre* – executive], not to mention el mir [*le maire* – the mayor] and his iqoun-sayan [conseillers – counsellors]. After that, the lieutenant only has to hear that such and such knows how to do this or that and he puts him down as having that *métier*.

Little by little, everyone forgot that there is the work of cultivating the land, which is being neglected. When they did the census, I heard Mohand L. protesting because they put him down as a 'cultivator', whereas they found a real *métier* for all the others on the list: 'You despise me. For all the real cultivators you've found a *métier*, but me, because I don't have a plot of land (*thamtirth*), you're making me a *fellah*. Those are cultivators, they've got land right up to their front door, and yet one is a driver and the other is a shopkeeper. I won't even mention Hocine M., who is *elkhodja gel biro* [executive in the office]! But I've got a *métier* too!

And he goes on to describe how this character set himself up as a dealer (*tadjar*) and general go-between, who, in exchange for a commission, organizes the sale of wood or supplies the village with straw or any other commodity:

Then there is work in France too, which has brought us welders and house painters and machine operatives. The mines have given us hewers and timbermen and gallerymen. All we need now is engineers. All these people stopped working a very long time ago, but they've still got their *métier*, especially if the *métier* is on their identity card: that's the undeniable proof. Those who don't have a *métier* can still be an *antriti* [*en retraite* – retired] or *anfaliditi* [*en invalidité* – on disability].

The Economic Conditions of Access to Economic Practices

This long and colourful monologue invokes, pell-mell, some of the factors, such as emigration or the classificatory activity of the French army, also a great purveyor of factitious activities, which, together with the generalization of monetary exchanges and the arrival of technical innovations, have introduced all the way into the most remote regions of the rural world the logic of the monetary economy and so-called rational economic calculation. Studying the trans- formations of economic practices in rural society enables one to grasp more clearly and more completely what they entail, namely, a whole lifestyle or, better, a whole system of solidary beliefs – so much so that one must speak, to describe them, not of adaptation but of *conversion*.[11]

To bring home to readers – who, like our economists and sociolo- gists of the economy, move like fish in water in the so-called rational economy – that the word *conversion* is not too strong, and to provoke in them the conversion of the whole mindset that is necessary to break with the universe of deeply embodied presuppositions which make us perceive the economic conducts current in our own economic world as self-evident, natural and necessary, and therefore rational, I would need to be able to evoke here the long series of often infini- tesimal experiences which made me *feel* (*éprouver*) in sensible and concrete fashion the contingent and arbitrary character of these ordi- nary behaviours that we perform every day in the ordinary course of our economic practices and that we experience as the most natural things in the world (like, for example, receiving change in a shop for the money tendered, rather than, as people would in Kabylia, arriving at the 'shopkeeper's' with the exact sum in hand corresponding to the exact price of the object to be bought).

I remember vividly spending long hours questioning a Kabyle peasant who was trying to explain to me a traditional form of the loan of livestock, because it had not occurred to me that, contrary to all 'economic' reason, the lender could feel obligated to the bor- rower on the grounds that the latter was looking after an animal that in any case would have to be fed. I also remember the mass of anec- dotal observations and statistical data that I had to accumulate before I understood the implicit philosophy of labour, based on the equiva- lency of labour and its remuneration in money, that I was engaging in my spontaneous interpretation of this world, and which was pre- venting me from fully understanding certain behaviours or the aston- ished reactions of my informants (like that of the old Kabyle discovering the proliferation of '*métiers*', quoted above): the utter outrage at the behaviour of the stonemason, back from a long sojourn in France, who asked that his wage be supplemented by the sum cor- responding to the monetary value of the meal traditionally offered upon completing the building of a house, which, in an unprecedented breach of propriety, he had declined to attend; or the fact that, for an objectively identical number of hours or days of work, the peasants of the southern parts of Algeria, less affected by emigration (and the regrouping policy of the French army), said more often that they were labouring, as peasants, than the Kabyles, who were more inclined to claim a '*métier*' or to describe themselves as 'unemployed'. I took this philosophy so much for granted that it did not occur to me that it was concealing from me the work of invention and conversion that those whom I was observing had to perform in order to break away from a vision, for me very difficult to grasp, of labour as a *socially recognized social occupation*, independent of any material sanction and which could, in the limiting case, be reduced to performance of the essential function of a man, who is not wasting his time when he talks with other men in the assembly or distributes work to the members of the household.

Just as I had to immerse myself in the logic of the Kabyle mythico-ritual system in order to be capable of committing deliberate 'solecisms' in the questions I put to them (for example, by bringing an object made with fire, such as a carding comb, into a ritual where one would expect a female object, such as water or wool) so as to provoke the denials or laughter from my female informants – who, like us in matters of language, found it easier to spot mistakes than to enunciate rules, which is the business of grammarians and not of ordinary speakers – so too, but doubtless with more difficulty, because nothing had prepared me to understand the economy, especially my own, as a *system of embodied beliefs*, I had to learn, step by step, through ethnographic observation later corroborated by statistical analysis, the practical logic of the pre-capitalist economy, at the same time as I was trying as best as I could to figure out its grammar.

It was no doubt the quasi-native familiarity with the practical logic of the pre-capitalist economy that I had acquired through ethnographic inquiry, and which, through a kind of *methodologically provoked anamnesis*,[12] had 'awakened' some deeply buried memories of my own country childhood in the Pyrénées mountains – I was often sent, with the exact change counted out into my hand, to the hamlet grocer, who had to be called into his shop by shouting 'hoo-hoo' on the threshold of his house – that enabled me to perceive the historically extra-ordinary aspect of the seemingly banal story, related in the press of 29 October 1959, of those pupils in a school in Lowestoft, England, who had set up a club to insure themselves against punishment: a paid-up member who suffered a caning would receive 4 shillings, but, in light of certain abuses, an additional clause had been instituted that excluded liability for deliberately provoked incidents.

It is also this practical understanding of an economy of practices that had become perfectly exotic that allowed me to discover and to understand that, as Henri Bergson observed, 'It takes centuries of culture to produce a John Stuart Mill'. To put it differently, everything that the science of economics takes as given, that is to say, the ensemble of dispositions of the economic agent which underpin the illusion of the ahistorical universality of the categories and concepts that this science uses, is in fact the product of a long collective history, and it has to be acquired in the course of individual history, in and through a labour of conversion which can only succeed in certain conditions. Once this 'utilitarian' was restored to his exoticism, I wanted, after many others, like Max Weber, Werner Sombart or R. H. Tawney,[13] whom I was reading avidly in those years, to contribute to understanding how he was progressively invented, in the course of history, by undertaking the explicit project of observing the process of acquisition of all the dispositions that the 'spontaneous' Stuart-Millian schoolboys of Lowestoft spontaneously engaged, such as the computation of costs and profits, lending against interest, saving, credit, investment and labour itself. I endeavoured to establish rigorously, by statistical means, the economic and cultural conditions of access to what is called rational economic behaviour.

The principle of the overturning of the vision of the world in late colonial Algeria was nothing other than the acquisition of the *spirit of calculation*, which one should be careful not to confuse with the universal capacity to calculate. To subject all the behaviours of existence to calculating reason, as demanded by the economy, is to break with the logic of *philia*, of which Aristotle spoke, that is, the logic of good faith, trust and equity which is supposed to govern relations between kin and which is founded on the repression, or rather the denegation, of calculation. To refuse to calculate in exchanges with one's 'nearest and dearest' is to refuse to obey the principle of economy as propensity and capacity to economize or minimize expenditure (of effort, 'pains', then labour, time, money, etc.), in favour of giving without counting, a refusal which can in the long run foster the atrophy of calculating dispositions. It means refusing to leave a world in which the family, and the exchanges of which it must be the site, provided the model for all exchanges, including those that we regard as 'economic', for a world in which the economy, henceforth constituted as such, with its own principles, those of calculation, profit, etc., claims to become the principle of all practices and all exchanges, including those within the family, to the great scandal of this Kabyle father whose son had asked him for a wage. It is this overturning of the table of values which gave rise to the economy as we know it, and some particularly intrepid economists, such as Gary Becker, are simply following through the implications of its logic, of which their thought is itself the un-thought product, when they apply maximization models constructed according to the postulate of calculating rationality to the family, marriage or art.[14]

It is clear that the learning of the modern economy is not reducible, as one might suppose, to its purely technical dimension (although this is not negligible). For to espouse the 'utilitarian' vision is to break with a whole 'art of living' and, by the same token, with all those who share it and feel directly threatened by what rightly appears to them to be an *apostasy*. This is never clearer than when those who manage to break free of the grip of necessity are reminded of the duties of solidarity by the members of their family. The unremitting and sometimes overwhelming pressure that they apply is no doubt one of the factors that make efforts at upward mobility particularly difficult and perilous and, more generally, that make it harder to adapt to the demands of the modern economy.[15] So long as the good-faith economy remains alive, it is the whole group which imposes obligations of honour that are perfectly incompatible with the cold law of self-interested calculation.

Thus, in rural villages of Kabylia as in the regroupings or shanty-towns surrounding Algiers, relations between shopkeepers and their customers did not have the simplicity and transparency of exchanges in supermarkets or even in the small shops that can (and must) display a sign saying 'The House Does Not Grant Credit'. Paradoxically, borrowing presupposes a relationship of trust: one does not ask just anyone; more precisely, one only asks someone who will be required to meet the expectation, in other words a member of the group within which a certain form of solidarity exists. And, even within the group, one only asks peers who are entitled and obligated to 'reciprocate' – for example, at the time of the *twiza* of ploughing, the owners of yokes of oxen, and not day-labourers, who, if they are invited, or come on their own initiative to help, must be remunerated. Likewise, one asks for credit only from someone whom one knows is obligated to grant it. The shopkeeper who is asked to give credit feels that he 'must' give it, because he is well aware of the extremely harsh ordeal inflicted on the honour of the asker, who, to meet the basic needs of his household, has to make an entreaty that brings dishonour to himself and to his whole family, which proved unable to provide him with the resources enabling him to avoid it: 'I cover myself with dishonour, do not dishonour me'. Outside of the social framework in which the answer is possible, refusal does not violate the law of exchange and acceptance takes on the meaning of alms, a gift without counter-gift set up between strangers, or genuine credit, in the modern sense of the word, which presupposes the return of what is advanced and therefore the presumed conditions which make it possible.

Entry into the urban world and into the economic economy brought about by wage-labour necessitates a decisive break with this highly ambiguous form of relationship characteristic of all the customary behaviours of solidarity. This break both presupposes and effects a very deep transformation of the most fundamental dispositions, those which define the whole relationship to the economic world, which is a world of needs and aspirations that are inextricably intertwined with duties and ethical principles expressed in the language of honour, debt, devotion, gratitude, etc.

Having thus recalled the immersion of economic things in the universe of ultimate beliefs and values, those that are bound up with the idea that each man (or woman) has of himself or herself, in his or her own eyes and in the eyes of others, it remained for me to analyse the variations in economic practices and strategies in relation to various factors, especially economic ones, and so to reveal that calculating dispositions towards work, saving, housing, fertility or education are tightly linked, through the mediation of dispositions towards the future, to economic and social conditions that are *economic and social conditions of possibility and impossibility*. Below a certain threshold defined (or, rather, identified) by a certain economic and cultural level (measured statistically by yearly income and years of schooling), rational dispositions cannot be constituted and incoherence is the principle of the organization of the existence of subproletarians. Below a certain threshold of economic security, provided by stable employment and a certain minimum of regular income, economic agents can neither conceive nor perform most of the behaviours that are presupposed by an effort to get a grip on the future, such as the calculated management of resources over time, recourse to credit or birth control.[16]

This is to say that there are economic and cultural conditions for access to the economic behaviour that tends to be regarded as normal or, worse, natural for any normal human being. Having failed to raise the (albeit typically economic) question of these conditions, economics treats the prospective and calculating disposition towards the world and time, which we know to be the product of a quite particular collective and individual history – as a universal 'given', a gift of nature. In doing so, it tacitly condemns in moral terms those who have already been condemned in reality to the fate of economic 'misfits' by the economic system whose presuppositions it records.[17]

The View of a Folk Economist

Listening to this Kabyle cook, in Algiers in the summer of 1962, just as I was completing the analysis of the statistical data, field observation and interviews that provided the empirical basis for my book *Travail et travailleurs en Algérie*, I could not but feel admiring astonishment. For this man endowed with barely an elementary education was depicting, in his own words, alternating between French and Berber, the core of what I had been able to discover about the ongoing transformation of social and mental structures wrought by capitalist expansion and colonial war in Algeria, but only by means of a long and arduous effort of data production and deciphering: the new meaning given to labour with the 'discovery' of wage work and the correlative devalorization of agricultural activities, the acquisition of new temporal habits, the economic logic of the apparently anti-economic conduct of the small street peddlers, the wide-reaching effects of wage earning on the domestic sphere and gender relations, the link between economic conditions and the working-class, petty-bourgeois and bourgeois economic ethos, the abiding thirst for material security in an economic cosmos characterized by suffusive insecurity and unpredictability, the complex intrication of fertility, matrimonial, educational and economic strategies, the close dependence of aspirations – especially as regards children's schooling – on objective chances of upward mobility and on the structure of the capital to be transmitted or acquired, etc.

In the manner of a folk economist, this cook sketched in a couple of hours an encompassing and quasi-systematic depiction, well worthy of scientific discussion, of a universe on which he had been able to adopt a viewpoint at once close up and distant, owing to the series of positions he had successively occupied within the colonial order. These positions had given him a unique point of view on Algerian society and economy, as a view taken from a point in objective social space at once central – unlike the vast majority of manual workers and clerks, he had seen the world of the Europeans from the inside – and yet marginal, because he had never broken his ties with all the companions in misfortune that he had encountered in the course of a picaresque existence. The edited transcript of this interview (recorded near the home of trusted intermediaries) allows the reader, thirty years later, to grasp the practical economic sense guiding the actions and representations of a particularly perceptive member of the emerging Algerian working class at the dawn of the country's independence. And it vividly recapitulates in biographical terms the process of collective acquisition of a properly economic habitus undergone by those members of the war generation of Algerians who had the minimal economic and cultural capital required to accede to it.

'I Tried to Work All Over the Place'

I was 13 when I ran away from my village and my family. I was still in school; my father had gone off to work in France, and so I was alone. It was 1928. A cousin, my mother's sister's son, who had already found work in Algiers promised to find work for me there. So I came to Algiers with him. I was taken on as a delivery boy in a dressmaking business, high fashion for women. I got 200 francs a month, a season ticket and a suit – a livery – in wool with the cap and badge of the firm. The firm belonged to three sisters; there were twenty-three seamstresses. I delivered the dresses. The first time I entered the Aletti Hotel, I could not believe my eyes: I was a boy from the mountains, it was the first time I had seen a big hotel, the first time I had got on a lift, the first time I had been received by a doorman. I had an evening dress to deliver, I had the client's name and her room number; she gave me a tip of 100 francs, half of my monthly wages! I earned quite good money, we worked during the season: summer, autumn, winter. Spring was the slack period. The sisters would go off and get the new season's patterns and models from Paris. I still got my monthly pay and I would do something else on the side. I sent all my money back home. So long as I was sending money, it worked out, they would have never wanted to keep me back in the village.

At first I lived with the cousin who had brought me to Algiers, then I went off to live at the place of one of the seamstresses. She was very kind. She was doing a lot of overtime; sometimes she would stay working until 11 or midnight. Then I would walk back with her. Her father was a baker. I spent two years at the fashion house. I was starting to grow, I couldn't stay in that job forever: you don't learn anything carrying dresses around. I wanted something for the future. So I went to work for the baker. I was an apprentice by night and I did the delivery round in the morning. I would set off at 7 o'clock with a basket of loaves and I would climb up to the fourth, fifth and sixth floors. I was badly paid – back then they didn't pay you a piece-rate as they do now. I started to learn the trade, but it didn't excite me. I loved the movies. I would spend the whole day at the movie theatre. I loved modern life. At night I didn't sleep, I couldn't hold out. I stayed two years with that baker.

I tried, after that, to work all over the place, doing all kinds of things. In 1935, I was a washer-up in a restaurant. Little by little, by watching the others and then trying out for myself, I learned to cook. My first boss saw that cooking interested me and he helped me. First it was a small restaurant, and there I learned to do everyday cooking, it wasn't professional yet. I learned the trade (*métier*) when I moved into the big restaurants where there are whole armies at work: a chef, a *maître d'hôtel*, a kitchen manager, a cook for the hors d'oeuvres, a cook for the sauces, a cook for the roasts, one for the vegetables, one for the fish, and so on. It's a trade that I like a lot, but it has major drawbacks: the hours. Very early in the morning, late in the evening, because the customers aren't regular in their habits. For instance, you might have no one at all from 7 to 9 and then at 10 you don't have a table free. You work close to the fire, you drink a lot. I got into the habit of drinking in that trade. Then I left the restaurant trade. I had worked mainly at the Casino de la Corniche. I wanted to do both – practise my trade and be a civil servant. I worked at the Maison Blanche. I lost my job there after the strike of 1957. In spite of all the promises I was never taken back. After that, I rented a small shop for 1,100 francs a month. I sold vegetables. I used up all my money in that shop. I closed it down and converted it into a place to live. For the past seven months I've been on sick leave.

'When You Can't Get a Sandwich, You Buy Peanuts for 10 Francs'

[. . .] During the war in 1942 I was a street trader too. I sold blocks of ice from a mobile stall on the street. I did quite well because, at the time, there wasn't so much electricity to run fridges. People didn't have as many fridges as they do now. They had iceboxes.

It's hard to make ends meet in that trade. Some manage to have some good days, others earn barely enough to eat a few scraps of food. The most wretched ones, the ones who do it just to have something to do, are the sellers of coloured water. They buy colouring and some ice and offer glasses of yellow, green or pink water for 5 francs a glass or 20 francs a bottle. Another lot who earn nothing are the merguez and kebab sellers. I'm not talking about the ones well set up in the cafés – these ones, they make money, 60 francs a kebab, 40 or 50 francs a merguez. I mean the ones on Government Square. They fry up guts and lungs, the uneatable offal that you can't even mince for merguez. They grill sardines too. These ones are also harassed by the police. The little that they earn, they make on the bread: they buy a small loaf at 35 francs, perhaps even 28 or 39, and sell it in six small pieces at 10 francs each. Lately, after they published an article about them in the *Journal d'Alger*, the riot police made a sweep of them. It was at the end of the month, there must have been people standing in line to renew their public transport season tickets, they were afraid of getting dirty or being jostled or perhaps the smoke and the smells made them feel sick, and they must have written to the paper. The *Journal d'Alger* published a virulent article about them, with photos, asking that they be arrested and convicted and not just have their equipment seized. It talked about a risk to public health, an eyesore, a disgrace to the city – so many things that mean nothing to us and especially not to the people concerned.[. . .] The day after the police raid, they were back again, just as many as before.

You have the sellers of fruits and vegetables who make money, and the peanut sellers too. That's because when money gets tight, the trade that suffers first, and hardest, is non-consumable goods, and only later is the food trade hit – first the most expensive foods, the luxuries, then when things get really bad, the basic foodstuffs, bread, flour and so on. [. . .] That's when people buy the smallest quantities, things that don't cost much, things you can buy for 10 francs, 15 francs, especially when you're hungry. When you have nothing to eat at home, you can eat for 150 francs in a cheap diner (*gargote*). When you can't, you get a sandwich on Government Square for 60 or 80 francs. When you can't do that, you buy peanuts for 10 francs. The peanut sellers, they are always guaranteed to sell; they buy them at 100 francs a kilo and sell them at 500 francs a kilo.

'It all Depends What You Mean by Work'

The sellers of vegetables do well too, because they are well organized. They all come from the same region: Djidjelli, Taher, Colla, El-Milia. That counts for something. At the wholesale market – I saw this when I used to sell vegetables – all the wholesalers without exception come from that region. There's a certain amount of swindling. Those wholesalers sell the stuff at half price to men from their region, who take it away and sell it on the street. They do that either out of solidarity or because they get a cut. The brokers don't know anything about it. In this manner the retailers are sure to get a profit margin and that enables them to sell tomatoes at 40 francs a kilo while a greengrocer with a shop has to sell them at 75 francs and a grocer or a Mozabite at 120 francs. Besides, as soon as they manage to get established, they have their own clientele, generally manual workers who live far away and come specially to stock up for the whole week. It's more economical for them.

It's easy, you can start with nothing. For 500 francs you buy a garment, a pair of trousers, say, and you sell it a hundred metres down the street for 550, 600 or 700 francs. It's that much you've made, 100 or 150 francs. And 100 francs is a lot for someone who hasn't got two francs to rub together – I don't know if you've been in that situation. [. . .] When I've got 1,000 francs, 100 francs for me is the price of a coffee, I buy a newspaper for 100 francs, I give 100 francs to a kid who's begging. But when I haven't got those 100 francs, I can assure you that to find them is hard as hell, it's more than 1,000 francs, more than 5,000 francs, more than 10,000 francs. Well, for this man it's the same thing: when that's all he's got, for him 100 francs is a fortune. Someone who has never been short of money can't know that, he can't understand that.

I've seen quite a few people in that position. The fact is, there's a lot of them now, because there are a lot of refugees [from military operations in the countryside] who have no work and who are expected to bring back money. It's the only thing left for them to do. One way or another you always manage to get on with a shopkeeper who will give you some of his goods to sell for him on the square. You can make a small profit on that. I've seen people start by selling a basket of croissants and brioches for a baker, others selling crockery, others a few yards of cloth in the working-class districts on people's doorsteps. You always manage to work.

Of course, it all depends what you mean by work. If work means a *métier* [occupation, trade], to carry it on regularly and to live decently from it, that's not for everyone and it's a quite different thing. If work means doing some-thing, doing anything so as not to sit around doing nothing, so as to earn a crust, then only idlers don't work. A self-respecting man who doesn't want to live at other people's expense must work even if he has to hustle and make do. If he can't find any work, he can still find something to sell. A lot of people have been forced to do that in order to survive, and now they wouldn't do anything else for anything in the world. That is bad, because what started off as a necessity becomes a form of laziness. [. . .]

As for the Kabyles, they have solved the problem: they didn't even try to work here, off they went straight to France, even without experience. Personally I've known two crises when there really was a lot of unemploy-ment: 1936 and the recent events, since December. I won't even mention 1936, that was the lead-up to the war. But the situation is serious now because of the hordes of cultivators who are now in the city and are asking to work. *Those people are beginning to understand what work is* and to realize that what they were doing before − tilling the land − wasn't work. So there's a lot of them now demanding work and there is less and less work to go round.

'The Civil Servant is King'

[. . .] With work, the thing that matters most is whether it is tiring or not. The least taxing work is especially the civil servants, and the professionals; and even the doctor has a great deal of moral fatigue. But the civil servant does his eight hours and goes home; he's got a guaranteed monthly salary, it's a secure life. Then come the shopkeepers: the bigger they are, the less tired they get. Then the craftsmen who work for themselves − they're like the middle-rank civil servants, skilled manual workers and technicians. Then come the unskilled workers. The fellahin are either like the biggest craftsmen who generally don't do the work themselves, or like agricultural labourers when they have to work themselves. But the worst-off of all are the agricultural labourers who work very hard, for very long hours, and earn nothing. We have two expressions that say exactly what they mean: first *Aquabach* [breaking up the earth: farm labourers] and then *Albala dou ouabiouch* [*la pelle et la pioche*: spade and pickaxe, meaning the labourers].

Nowadays, if anyone has a choice, they want to be a civil servant. There's nothing like being a civil servant, whatever the rank. When every-thing is of equal level, it is always better to be a civil servant, unless, like the doctors, you can be both at the same time − self-employed and a civil servant. They all work at the hospital and they have their own private practice. A civil servant, no matter how high he gets, will never earn as much as the lowest of doctors. And then it is the doctors who have the most prestige. More than engineers, for example. Anyway, for me, I'd rather be a doctor, it's a question of responsibility. [. . .] Engineer, doctor, these are fine jobs, lawyer too. [. . .] But then again no, the lawyers are all unemployed right now. With the same qualifications, you're better off being a magistrate: the magistrate is a civil servant and *the civil servant is king.* It used to be, the lowest of jobs was to be a message receptionist or bus conductor for the CFRA [Algiers' public transport system]. You had to go up and down the buses, jostle with people, check their tickets, sometimes argue and tussle with the passengers. Now the conductors are civil servants, they're kings; they are better off than the drivers, they have a good wage, they don't get out of their seats, they don't need to get into arguments any more, some of them make 100,000 francs a month. Say, take M., the waiter who served us, with the family allowances he gets 120,000 francs a month. He has six or seven children – but then would you believe how much children here eat?! They cost you money when they're sick or when they need new clothes. [. . .]

The lowliest of civil servants has his car and his house with a loan from the government. Look, you don't imagine that M. is any more educated than me and yet I've been a greengrocer. I ate up all my money. Because the most unfortunate of all are the small shopkeepers. They earn a lot less than workers, and most often they eat up all their money. One of the laws of business is that it's money that brings in money. Now, our shopkeepers here, they haven't got much capital, they have little money to start with, and so it's inevitable that they don't make much. They just about scrape by and, compared to the manual worker, they have more to worry about – finding customers, keeping their stock up, doing the accounts, and always the fear of going bust, whereas for the same income the manual worker does his day's work and he has nothing more to worry about, especially if he is paid monthly like a civil servant. *For a civil servant, his job is like his capital* – it isn't for a shopkeeper. The government will give a civil servant a loan, to build a house for example. A shopkeeper can't get a loan or a bank advance unless he's got security, that's to say unless he owns property. A civil servant gets medical treatment by the government if he's ill; and the shopkeeper? Nothing! All that, for what advantages? The so-called freedom of being self-employed [*le prétendu libéralisme de la profession*]? It isn't true. A profession is 'liberal' when a man can live from it, and at that point they are all 'liberal'. A shopkeeper is free to open or to close his shop in theory but when he's waiting for a customer he loses the freedom he has and he has no use for a freedom that he cannot benefit from. Even a doctor isn't that free. A doctor has to go and visit a patient at midnight if there is need, but then there's no comparison with the shopkeeper: the shopkeeper waits for the customer whereas the patient comes looking for the doctor.

'That They Wear a Clean White Shirt Every Day Doesn't Make Them Bourgeois'

[. . .] We don't have a bourgeoisie here. We like to be bourgeois a lot, but we aren't. How many people of wealth are there among the Muslims? A few names only: Tchkikene, Bensiam, Bellounich who deals in wood and ice, Tamzali who deals in oil, soap and figs, Tiar who is a big shopkeeper and industrialist, Ben Turki, Mouhoub ben Ali, etc. Those are the biggest ones, the only bourgeois we have! Note that all those people made their fortune in trade and industry, and if today they've got houses and land, it's that they've bought them up with the money they made. They're not bourgeois with land and flocks and herds and tenants living on their land. That kind of bourgeoisie doesn't exist at all in Algeria. If it did exist once – 'the Great Tents' – it is ruined now; it has lost its land.

I've got a book, I can show it to you, it's got the figures. I don't remember exactly but you don't have a tenth, a fortieth or even a hundredth of big landowners who are Muslims. And then you can't compare an acre of rocks on the slope of a mountain that you have to work with a hoe, because a yoke of oxen would fall off it, with an acre on the plains with water, ploughed with a tractor. Bourgeois who are big landowners, who do we have? I can think of Sayah, Bengana, and Ben Ali Cherif. It is mostly Oran and Constantine who have these few rich Muslim landowners. In Algiers, you have a bourgeoisie of traders and industrialists. They must be nouveaux riches, because our proverb 'Wealth comes from ploughing or inheritance' doesn't apply to them. They don't plough and they couldn't inherit anything else because land and herds were the only wealth in times past.

As for the doctors, lawyers and big shopkeepers, they aren't really bourgeois: the fact that they can wear a clean white shirt every day, change their suits, live in a villa, drive a car, eat well and spend as much as they want doesn't make them bourgeois. To be bourgeois, you have to be in the business of being bourgeois, have capital that brings in money, either to run a factory or to have a company or shares in the bank. A bourgeois has money but the money has to bring in more money and help to employ other people. A doctor, or a lawyer, or a high-ranking civil servant, they aren't bourgeois even when they have money. There will be bourgeois in Algeria when there are factories, really big money, guys who own boats, planes, railways. [. . .] The buses we have now aren't enough. When I say bourgeois, I mean rather big firm, 'corporations'. One thing that shows well that our bourgeois don't have the business sense of the real bourgeois yet is that they have personal wealth but they haven't started any corporations, they are not organized. On the contrary, they just compete with each other, they vie with one another. They tried to do it, just before the 'events', then the events came and they got afraid that business would go badly, and they were also afraid of displaying their money because people were envious and they might be asked to help out. [. . .]

'The Morality that Hunger Teaches'

In business now it is the little guy who's figured it out, the smaller fortunes – those of less than 10 million – are getting together. But it's a pity, they are Kabyle, they are jumping on cafés, after the hotels and the restaurants, it's by dint of habit. When you start out in the restaurant business, even at the level of a cheap diner [*gargote*], if you make money with that, what can you do other than opening a bigger restaurant? Now, that's how the Kabyle got started, first as café waiters and restaurant waiters.

And then, a young man from a good family in Algiers is not going to open a restaurant and do the cooking and serve at table: it's a trade people look down on. You have to be a Kabyle highlander to do that, just as you have to be a black from Biskra to be a water carrier. Oftentimes the little guys get rich because they haven't got the 'daddy's boy' mentality and they don't waver about going into business. That's why they have got ahead: they don't say 'I'm So-and-so's son', or 'So-and-so was my grandfather'. Like the marabouts from back where I come from, they almost live on begging, it's a disgrace. Anyway, now it's over with, no one gives them anything any more, they tell them: 'Your ancestor was a saint, he did deserve our piety, but you, you people are thieves. If your grandfather could speak to you now, he would condemn you and tell you, "go to work". All that is prejudice, there is no trade that is "sub-par" [*sous-metier*]. You have to be a worker! Forget your parents, they've taken everything with them – baraka, the name, the qualities and the blemishes.' That, the little guys have understood that in the face of necessity. That's why, on many things, especially now, with the war, the little guys are ahead of the established big guys in the towns. These little guys, they've decided to push ahead, throw everything out of the window, throw off the traditions, while the rich guys they still hang on to them. The little guys only ask to be helped along that way, and as soon as they've taken the first step they go the whole way.

[. . .] I started to socialize with Algiers families who swear only by their name and origin, even the married women. Between you and me, these women cheat on their husbands more often and more easily than working-class wives do, because with all the jewellery they've got, all their money and fine clothes, they get bored more than the women who look after their children and the little room that they keep clean. Right now I am with a woman from those circles, so I know a good deal about the mentality of those people. Rotten to the core! You find morality among the poorer folks, that's the morality of work, the morality that hunger teaches. When you're hungry, there's a lot of things you don't think about.

I'll give an example: right now, take the daughters of a skilled worker who earns a decent wage, has a secure job, a solid trade, who can clothe his children properly, for instance a postman, or a hospital employee, or a bus conductor. Well, the daughters of those people go to school and if they do well in their studies, the parents will do everything they can to push them as far along as possible, the same as with their sons. Even if she's 20, 22, the father thinks only of his daughter; he knows that the more education she has, the better she will earn her living and the happier she will be in her home by giving a hand to her husband – a husband that the daughter will choose for herself because if he agrees to let his daughter be educated, he knows that she'll take liberties with his authority. A rich father, he doesn't think the same way. He says to himself: 'My money is what will make my daughter happy, the man who comes to marry my daughter will want her because of my wealth, he wants her because she is my daughter, the daughter of So-and-so. But I don't want my fortune, and therefore my daughter, to go to just anyone, so I must choose my daughter's husband myself. And for that, at age 15 my daughter must be at home and wear the veil, and I must keep watch over her to marry her as I see fit.'

Parents like that worry about their money and not their children. The result is, the worker's daughter will be a teacher, or a nurse, perhaps a doctor, or simply a clerk in an office – and we need everything in Algeria. The rich man's daughter, who ought to be better placed to gain an education, will barely know how to write a letter with her primary school certificate and will become an idler, asking to be covered in jewels, growing fat on cakes and making a lot of babies. At 30 she's already old because she married at 17. She's weighing 160 pounds because she eats well and never stirs from the sofa; when she goes to the steam bath she takes a taxi. That's another side of '*l'Algérie à papa*' that we have to get rid of, like the rest. The future depends on it. The way to save Algeria is to give that mass of wretched people who have nothing, who can do nothing but unskilled labour, secure jobs like the ones of the people who don't hesitate to send their daughters to the lycée and the university. The little guys are becoming more modern, more developed, than the rich guys. [. . .]

'Modern Life Requires Everyone to Work: The Husband, the Wife, the Children Too'

Education can't do any harm. On the contrary, the 'son of a nobody' isn't a nobody if he gets an education; without an education, he would be a double nobody. I say that because for a long time people said that education is the ruin of a girl. She's done for! To send her to school, to teach her French, is to show her everything that goes on among Europeans, tempting her and giving her a taste for and a chance of escaping from the authority of the parents, and the husband, for the worse, of course. This is what people said for a long time, and this is what the rich cling to for their own daughters, being more concerned with who will inherit their wealth.

Now people are beginning to realize that going to school, on the contrary, is a necessity in life and that in addition to schooling [*l'instruction*], there's education [*l'éducation*]. With education, you can trust a woman. Before, a woman only had to be seen talking to a man, or smiling, to be castigated. But talking to a man, laughing and smiling, that doesn't mean sleeping with him. [. . .] It is because there was hatred in us that we always attributed evil intentions to our women. Fortunately, all of that is beginning to disappear. It's the war that has made it disappear. Women who had never seen the street found themselves face to face with soldiers, in the offices and in the markets. It's finished, no one can denounce them now. On the contrary, they should be congratulated if they are able to stand in for their husbands and children. Thus girls must not be excluded from schooling.

Women should work and young women must be brought up to work and not to live in the house as they used to – we are in the atomic age, it's time to build some civilization here! A woman's capacity to work depends on the household, one must always come back to that. A woman can't work like a man, for a man only has that to do, a woman has the household and children. One mustn't turn her into a man through work. The way civilization is going, sewing and health care and other occupations are fine for women. We need to develop that, and quickly, because in Algeria we are lacking everything, we have nothing, not even nurses: we need everything, from A to Z. And nowadays? Modern life requires everyone to work, not like up to now, where one person works and ten eat. The husband at work, the wife too, the children too, at school, in apprenticeship or in a job – in an office, a workshop or whatever. You need discipline, you need to respect the orders of the government. You even need a dictatorship, to force everyone to work. [. . .]

The Ethnology of Kabylia

The Right Use of Ethnology
Interview with Mouloud Mammeri

It was with the Kabyle writer Mouloud Mammeri, on the occasion of the launch of Awal *magazine in 1985, that Bourdieu returned to the importance of the relationship to the terrain and the difficulties inherent in apprehension of the object, such as the questions of taxonomy that preoccupy ethnologists more than the group studied. Naming and classifying have in effect the function of establishing a hierarchy and, by definition, attributing an identity that may or may not conform to the 'truth' of the social world, in that the latter, owing to its elasticity, is both will and representation. Participant observation reveals a number of obstacles bound up with appellations that vary as a function of groups, political situations and agents, whereas many ethnologists have a tendency to reification. The interview returns to the fact that naming is also 'to make exist', hence the importance of language and its power of designation in societies undergoing a crisis of identity. The Kabyle experience enabled Bourdieu to deduce that well-conducted ethnology functions as a social psychoanalysis whenever present and past are interwoven, as is the case with colonization in Algeria, and that it is impossible to project oneself into the future without revisiting the history that agents have a tendency to repress. By the play of self-revelation, this dialogue enables the ethnologist – originating from a dominated region in a dominant universe – to provide the other with scientific and intellectual instruments. Ethnology, from this point of view, is the appropriate discipline: it participates in the self-reflection that is indispensable to knowledge of the other.*

**Mouloud
Mammeri:**

Perhaps you remember the interview we did on Kabyle poetry, which you published in *Actes de la Recherche en Sciences Sociales* in 1978. This was on a precise subject. Thinking about it again since then, it seemed to me that this raised a certain number of questions of a more general order. I do not mean the classic problems that the ethnologist confronts, I am thinking of a more precise point. There is now an Algerian ethnology or anthropology, and in a more limited way a Kabyle or Berber one. But for someone who himself hails from Kabyle society, it is clear that this raises a particular problem. Given that it is one's own society that one is studying, I wonder what degree of validity the conclusions drawn from it can have?

Pierre Bourdieu: I could reply in two ways: on the one hand, by positioning myself on the strictly epistemological level; on the other hand, which is what I shall do, by taking a sociological point of view. I understand in fact the resistances to ethnology and ethnologists, and I am deeply convinced that it is worthwhile trying to study these and overcome them. This is the reason why I shall try to reply first of all by analogy with my own experience.

One thing I have done is basically quite analogous to what you are doing, as I have worked on a society which happens to have a great resemblance to Kabyle society, that is, the society of Béarn. What specifically characterizes the situation in which you are trying to understand a society with tools that were developed by a whole anthropological tradition for extremely different societies, in particular Melanesian or American? I must say first of all, quite frankly, that there are a certain number of questions that I would never have had the idea of posing to Béarnais society if I had not done anthropology: even for problems of kinship, despite the fact that they are extremely important for the agents themselves – in these societies, in practice, these problems are only spoken of in terms of questions of transmission of property, of inheritance, the problems posed by relationships, or conflicts between relatives, etc. – I am not certain that I would have reinvented everything taught by the tradition of kinship studies and the problematic it implies. In other words, there is a technical culture that is indispensable in order to go beyond a rather naive recording of the given as it presents itself. The import of foreign, international problematics provides a certain distance and freedom: it makes it possible not to be glued to the reality, the self-evidence, the indigenous intuition that leads to both understanding everything and at the same time understanding nothing. That is what makes the difference between the spontaneous ethnology of amateurs and professional ethnology.

As far as Kabylia is concerned, for example, it is very striking to see how until a very recent date, for complex historical reasons, Kabyle studies remained almost completely outside all intellectual currents (with some few exceptions). There was a kind of spontaneous ethnology, produced either by civilian administrators or by the military, who applied the categories that occupied their minds, that is, often juridical categories (this is clear with both Hanoteau and Letourneux). Since these categories are very inadequate, they very often saw nothing or, more exactly, they did not really see what they were seeing, because, to use Heidegger's image, they did not see the spectacles that were on the end of their nose, which enabled them to see what they saw *and that alone.*

In the case of Kabylia, as in Béarn, there was also a kind of spontaneous literature, often produced by schoolteachers who themselves came from the region: for example, a certain Tucat wrote a small monograph on his Béarnais village, and for years that was all there was on Béarn; the few ethnologists familiar with the problems of European ethnology (and there were some very good ones, such as Marcel Maget, before the renaissance of the 1960s) spoke of the *besiat* (the ensemble of neighbours, *lous besis*) as a structure typical of Béarnais society.

There was a great deal of literature of this kind in Kabylia, which was indeed not so bad, and at least supplied good descriptions. But familiarity means that there are questions that one does not even have the idea of raising, as things seem so self-evident. For example, at one time, given the role of the blacksmith in the system of ritual practices and representations in Kabylia (I had in mind the question of the difference between the spatial structure of a forge and that of a house), I looked for a good description of an old-time forge. I could only find one in the

whole literature, in Boulifa,[1] because people weren't
interested in this, for lack of a problematic. And I
am almost certain that, if Boulifa gave a description
of the forge in his textbook of the Kabyle language,
intended for teachers in the Bouzaréa, what he had
in mind was the French primary school textbooks,
where there was always a forge and a blacksmith . . .

MM: I think so too. I simply wonder if we should not give
credit to some of these spontaneous ethnologists. I
believe that none of them (expect perhaps one,
Masqueray, in his *La Formation des cités* rather than
Souvenirs et visions d'Afrique) . . .[2]

PB: Masqueray was very scholarly, but his science is
clearly very out of date.

MM: I don't think that any of them really had the project
of explaining Kabyle society. What they particularly
wanted was to get to know it, and as far as documentation goes, I must say that I personally find both
Hanoteau and Boulifa very well supplied and often
very exact. To take one particular point, for example,
they rescued poetic productions on which it is now
possible to carry out a more critical or more scholarly reflection. Another example is that of the White
Fathers . . .[3]

PB: What is interesting about most of the works of the
White Fathers is paradoxically that they did not have
a properly sociological or ethnological problematic.
I say this, of course, pressing the paradox a bit, and
on reading their transcriptions I have often found
myself regretting that they did not have the minimum
in the way of ethnological culture that would have
enabled them to press their questioning or description a bit further (for example on the house or on
ritual), instead of resting content with recording
what was said to them. That said, to the extent
that they wanted above all to collect discourse and
transcribe it as exhaustively as possible, they collected everything without distinction, without wor-
rying too much about its ethnological relevance, and
in this way they delivered a treasure of unexploited
resources, from which all professional ethnologists,
from myself onwards, have drawn much.

That is why I believe that access to an international theoretical problematic is important. I think
– I permit myself to say this because I deeply believe

it – that you have played a very important role in independent Algeria by continuing to establish a national tradition of scientific ethnology, applying tested methods and concepts. That is very important for both scientific and political reasons: the attitude that uses familiarity with the indigenous population or denunciation of colonialism in order to repudiate the whole scientific tradition has completely catastrophic effects. For my part, if I have understood anything from Béarnais society it is that, when I began studying it, I had in mind very general problems, such as the question of the relationship between kinship structures and economic foundations, as well as all my Kabyle stories: I wanted to see, for example, if matrimonial strategies varied as a function of the mode of succession, with on the one hand primogeniture and on the other collective possession with equal parts being shared.

MM: In Béarn, you have the tradition of primogeniture . . .

PB: Yes. Because this was the comparison I had in mind, I could see things that I would never have seen if I'd stayed within the relationship of indigenous familiarity. But this relationship of familiarity also enabled me to see things that I did not see when I was not in my own universe.

MM: I sometimes wonder if, for an ethnologist studying his own society, this relationship of familiarity hasn't been shattered long ago. In the great majority of cases, he has had to leave the society he came from very early on and make a new world for himself, which he generally enters by way of school. He learns very soon, at his own expense, that things that seemed to him completely familiar are precisely not so. It is curious to note how in a completely different domain, that of fiction, this phenomenon of rupture with a traditional familiarity has given rise, in both English and French, to a whole production in literature, fiction, theatre, etc., always of course in a Western language.

PB: There are extraordinary advantages in the fact of being native, on condition that one knows what this implies, that is, everything that it hides (and it hides a good deal: everything that is self-evident). One of the most difficult things for an ethnologist, for

example, is to know what is important or not important, what is serious or not serious, the correct
weighting of things.

MM: I believe that is very hard, for concrete reasons such
           as language, cultural habits, etc.

PB: I believe that often the question is not even raised.
           When I was working on Kabylia, I always told
           myself: 'If it was an old Béarnais peasant who was
           telling me this, what would it mean?' It was not
           hard for me to imagine what a Béarnais peasant
           would think of a rather naive ethnologist, full of that
           derisory good will that defines him professionally: a
           bloke from the town, pleasant, a good head on his
           shoulders, he listens to me, he's polite . . . And then,
           he is French . . . In the colonial situation, this kind
           of respect is respected . . . That said, you have a
           rather protective relationship: you explain nicely
           to him the official values of the group, honour,
           all that . . . You don't go as far as telling him anec-
           dotes that are what is really essential. (I rediscovered
           all that when I went to work on the university and
           intellectual world: what was most important was
           only revealed in particular little things, bordering on
           gossip . . .) In other words, in all good faith he tells
           rather tall stories.

MM: Perhaps simply the fact of being an ethnologist, that
           is, someone who is not directly involved and who in
           any case comes from outside, creates a particular
           kind of relationship between him and the people he
           calls his informants. In a way, he puts the informant
           in the condition, the posture, of someone who
           'responds', and it seems to me that the discourse that
           he holds with a researcher from outside, whom he
           certainly knows to be foreign and pleasant, is not the
           same as he would hold with another peasant, Kabyle
           or Béarnais, as perhaps he wouldn't emphasize the
           same things. That certainly falsifies the communica-
           tion a great deal.

PB: Absolutely! If only because the other person would
           say to him: 'That's enough, don't tell me these
           stories.'

MM: The paradox, at least apparently, is that even when
           he 'plays' at being the informant in this way, he's in
           good faith, etc.

PB: Yes, and it's partly from respect . . .

MM: He systematizes, I believe, things that are not system-
                atic in reality, as he tells himself: 'I have to tell him
                things that stand up, that are coherent, etc.' And so
                he is often making a more or less conscious case: you
                always have to put on a good front to the foreigner,
                even if, as here, in a kind of peaceable complicity.

PB: Exactly! That said, the same also happens with an
                indigenous bourgeois from the town: it also goes very
                well . . . I've often seen in Algeria young men and
                women who felt rather guilty towards the people,
                especially in a revolutionary period, who needed
                these stories, and who suddenly accepted them as
                legal tender. I think that there is a kind of exchange
                here, a two-way deception, in which neither side
                intends to deceive. The person questioned takes the
                role of ethnologist, he positions himself at a level
                where he says: 'As for honour, I'll tell you what it is
                . . .' He searches out sayings, proverbs, definitions,
                the traditional story of the man who said to his
                wife: 'If I'm dishonoured, etc.' In short, the inquiry
                situation itself arouses a whole medley of conven-
                tional discourse, which is nothing like what you get
                when you say: 'But look here, tell me the story
                of so-and-so's marriage, which made such a scandal.
                A real story, ok!' Among the Béarn peasants there
                is a tradition of sententious discourse, strengthened
                by primary school essays, which enchants rural
                (Heideggerian) philosophers. This kind of official
                discourse, designed for official exchanges, is not false.
                It's what has to be said in situations of representation;
                it forms part of the strategies of self-preservation.
                     This is true in all milieus. But what is specific to
                the populist posture, of which ethnological effusion
                is one aspect, is that it rests content with this official
                discourse. What is an informant if not this very
                respectable character whom you're directed to? You
                are always directed to very dignified old people, who
                'know a lot', who are considered wise, who speak
                with a nod of the head, seriously, who seek to make
                a good impression, for themselves and for the whole
                group whose spokesperson they more or less are. All
                this changes when you interrupt this official dis-
                course by referring to concrete cases, or showing that
                you know these little stories. That is a way of bring-
                ing things back to the ordinary, unofficial way of

speaking about the matters of life. In other words, with proper names, precise details, and not big and vague declarations about honour or dishonour in general. And then that's no longer the same thing at all.

MM: Concerning Kabyle society, what one can say about it, I believe, is that the two discourses are equally true, but in a way they do not operate at the same level of truth. The quite simple reality is of course that of ordinary discourse, but in certain circumstances even the most ordinary man knows and feels bound by discourse that is ready-made, official, etc. You could say that he is trapped. 'You acknowledge the value of this discourse, the ready-made one? Then you don't have a choice, you bring your actions into line.' That generally ends in tragedy (it's rare, but it does exist) and perhaps the greatest occurrence of one or other of these two cases depends, independent of individual temperament (something that is clearly impossible to take into account), on parameters that can be disclosed by analysis.

I believe that social status, the place where you are in the hierarchy, is one of the most important factors: the more you have a position of prestige (the big families), the more you are bound. Also the era: before colonization, the *nif* code was imperative, that is, reality was not very distant from discourse. During the colonial period, with exile, the existence of French courts, mere contact with a society with different values, there was a growing gap between conventional sophistries and actual behaviour. The war of liberation and independence has widened the gap: 'ready-made' discourse has become more rare, and increasingly appears an anachronism; it continues to be held, it is true, but I believe this is because the language has not yet developed forms of discourse that can be substituted for it. This is in the process of establishing itself around values such as the claim of identity, but that will necessarily take a certain time to be completed and thus be in a position to replace the other, to modify or coexist with it: the tribe often loses words long after it has lost the corresponding things.

All this means that the discourse of the best-advised informant always needs to be decoded, and I imagine the same holds for a Béarnais peasant, who is in some sense an authorized spokesperson, invested by his position and by others with the role of speaking, one could almost add of putting the best gloss on things, when he gives the 'dressed up' version of the *besiat*.

PB: Yes, you are completely right: the two modes of discourse are each equally part of the reality. And it would be absurd to privilege the ordinary discourse, what people say among themselves, as more true, more authentic, in relation to formal, 'proper' discourse, that of extraordinary situations, including the relationship with the investigator as a relationship with an outsider. Both are true. But the ethnologist, if he is not suspicious, has every chance of getting to know only one. That is why a whole work is needed, which presupposes a lot of preliminary information, to get out of the sermonizing about *ânaya* (honour) or *nif*. Then a lot of difficulties arise, conflicts, and also things that may be extraordinarily harsh. An old informant, whom I had asked to tell me about a dramatic case of family conflict which I had heard spoken of, about the marriage of an eldest son, told me that the father had said to his son, who wanted to 'derogate' by marrying a poor girl: 'But what does she have to offer? – Her sex!' He would never have told me this if I had not set him on the terrain of everyday realities. I believe that there is a place for an extraordinary ethnology, which would be done by people capable of going beyond normative generalities and conducting their investigation in a natural situation, in normal relations, without even having to question people.

MM: In the case of the autochthonous informant, to go in the direction that you were saying there is still an additional obstacle: it's that, when other people perceive that a guy is in the process of doing something like a study over there, they have a tendency to . . .

PB: To tease . . .

MM: They have a tendency to tease, while knowing that he knows the score, that he is very familiar with the things being spoken about. In this particular case, people considered that he had changed his role and they told him the story as it should be told.

PB: A kind of official version . . .

MM: That's it. I have precise examples of the same story that I was told, knowing who I was, etc., and then quite by chance in a bus, the same story told me, but by someone who didn't know . . . There was a world of difference between them!

PB: And what was it, this story?

MM: A question of adultery, something very tragic in Kabylia, at any rate according to the traditional code. The first version was impeccable, in conformity with the old laws: punishment was necessary, honour demanded it, etc. But when a man who was directly involved in this (he wasn't one of the participants, but very close) told me about it, without realizing, because it came up in conversation, it was apparent that there were heaps of accommodations, compromises, etc. The code of honour is very fine, but you play for high stakes, and perhaps need to take a few precautions. It's a whole game . . .

PB: I think that the ethnologist cannot escape naivety, however narrowly, unless he bears in mind that reality is infinitely more complicated, and unless, having this in mind, he is capable of obtaining and mastering the useful information. Something that is not easy, since following such complicated stories of Kabyle or Béarnais kinship is really hard work: the pertinent information lies in allusions, nuances, which are hard enough for someone to follow in their own country . . . Which makes me think that an ethnology which, strengthened by a whole theoretical tradition, would also have as well this kind of sense for nuances, subtleties, compromises, would represent a revolution and show that the distinction made between ethnology and sociology does not really exist. I think that the difference lies essentially in the fact that the relationship to the object is different.

MM: That is rather what your own work shows, your own trajectory. In particular, the fact that you have concretely lived this problem of the relationships between sociology and ethnology, which at first sight may appear simply a subject for academic debates, has certainly helped you in the solutions that you have contributed.

PB: Yes, I believe so. I have mentioned above discourse on the notion of *besiat*, the set of *besis* or neighbours.

People spoke of this as if it was a well-defined social unit. For my part, I had never heard such a thing spoken of. *Lous besis* means the neighbours. There are some circumstances in which this is somewhat formalized, as there are problems of protocol: in particular, on the occasion of burials. It is formalized in this way to avoid conflicts. (It's the same in Kabylia, people formalize so that there won't be conflicts, when there are risks, for example important marriages with an outsider.) People say: 'the first neighbour is the person opposite, the second is the one to the right, the third is the one to the left', something like that. But that only exists on paper. First of all, people have often quarrelled with neighbours, then there are neighbours by house and neighbours by land (which is not at all the same thing). And then, there is a whole casuistry. On certain occasions, you might invite this neighbour, or that one to another occasion.

As far as Kabylia is concerned, I also asked myself how the village was organized; people gave me different breakdowns, bearing different names: in one place *adrum*, somewhere else *taxerrubt*; sometimes *adrum* includes *taxerrubt*, sometimes the other way round. Faced with such incoherence, I thought that my notes must have been wrong. I wanted to reach a neat pattern, with a clear hierarchy of units from the 'house' to the 'tribe', as General Hanoteau had done. There was an article by Jeanne Favret in *L'Homme* . . . faultless! Regurgitated Hanoteau! But for my part, I always had in mind *lou bestiat*, and I told myself: 'They adapt, they reify occasional units, which exist, but not as is commonly believed.' That connects with what you were saying just now: everything is negotiable, everything is open to discussion. A marriage story can be told in thirty-six different ways, according to the person it's being told to. That is what I tried to show with Sayad about marriages: marriage with a parallel cousin is often a catastrophe, since the daughter is ugly or deformed, but someone has to be found to look after her, though it's presented as perfectly regular, as conforming to the rules. In other words, there is a whole work going on, a work that's actually political. That is really what I learned in Kabylia: people manipulate social reality, and I believe this is universal. Reality of this kind exists largely in discourse.

MM: I believe it is possible to do away with this inconven-
ience, as soon as you realize (or you accept) that
there is a kind of nominalist inflation at work in all
these group appellations. Giving something a name
both simplifies and reassures. It all depends on
knowing what each of these appellations precisely
corresponds to. Personally, my impression is – I don't
know quite how to put it . . . – that they all exist,
but in a kind of virtual state, or rather some of them
almost always and actually . . . I don't know, for
example, *axxam, taddart, laârc* (the family, the
village, the tribe) . . . but a good many others are
rather as if in limbo, waiting to exist, waiting for
what? . . . Precisely for the opportunity when they
will have a meaning and possibly operate: *adrum,
taxerrubt, ssef, taqbilt* are notions rather of this kind.
Even their meaning is imprecise, labile, and I realize
at this very moment that if I had to translate and say
exactly what distinguishes an *adrum* from a *taxerrubt*, I would be completely vexed, and then a Kabyle
can live his whole life without these entities ever
intervening in his existence, and if the occasion suggests – or forces – their reactivation, the feeling that
people have about them is so vague (because they
have not been used) that no one now knows very
well, and they call *adrum* what is elsewhere called
taxerrubt.

PB: Quite. Groups exist first of all in discourse. As soon
as you say 'the Kabyles', that exists to some extent.
And manipulation is possible on this basis. If I change
the way of naming things, I change things themselves
a bit. By telling in a different way, I tell something
different. Here we come back to the conversation we
had on another occasion, when we spoke of those
poets who were basically professionals of manipulation of the social world.

MM: Absolutely! . . . professionals of manipulating words,
and thus of society. In the same order of ideas, I don't
know what you think, but it seems hard to me to
escape the almost always unconscious temptation to
manipulate. I wonder if I can give the current example
of some Kabyle intellectuals who are trying in a way
to recuperate Kabyle society, a society, how shall I
put it, that is ideal or mythical . . . They don't really
know any more themselves, I believe . . . I know all
the problems that this simple question raises, and

they are certainly quite complex. One can always say: this picture of Kabyle society, or Béarnais, or Greek from the Homeric age, is more ideal than real. But what defines reality? It remains clear that in practice, for self-evident concrete reasons (political, social, cultural), a Kabyle intellectual today is too greatly drawn towards an ideal re-creation of his own society, particularly in reaction to the devaluing image that people who deny it try to give of it.

PB: I think that ethnology, when it is conducted well, is a very important instrument of self-knowledge, a kind of social psychoanalysis that makes it possible to restore the cultural unconscious that everyone born in a certain society has in their head: mental structures, representations, that are the root of fantasies, phobias, fears. And this cultural unconscious must include all the traces of colonization, the effect of humiliations . . . To say that ethnology is a colonial science, and therefore only good to be thrown away, is a great stupidity. When I returned to Algiers and saw what you were doing, I thought: 'What a miracle that Algeria has escaped this kind of stupid reaction!'

MM: It was very insular, and more tolerated than really accepted, let alone avowed. Unofficial ideologists, in this case duplicating official discourse, condemned ethology without a hearing. At the 24th International Congress of Sociology, which was held in Algiers in March 1974, the then minister of higher education and scientific research made a standard accusation against ethnology, on the model of a Manichean opposition: sociology = developed societies; ethnology = colonial societies, ergo to be rejected a priori. Now, you can also say that this attitude is curiously similar to that of the Kabyle or Béarnais peasant we were speaking of just now. Because I must say that, despite this declaration of principle, despite this discourse of an accepted spokesperson, this minister never put up any obstacle to the research that was being done in ethnology. For example, we were able to devote a whole debate precisely to the problem you have just brought up.

PB: Yes. To return then to our question, I think that what is at issue is the capacity to confront reality, to look the truth in the face. What can original Kabyle-ness

represent for these young people? A kind of fantasy
of return to origin, of primitive democracy?

MM: That is all both true and false, in my view. I don't
know what you think of it . . .

PB: Yes, here again, the analogy between Béarn and
Kabylia is useful. In Béarn there were in each of the
small valleys little autonomous republics, which had
their own customs, etc. There were collections of
customs, the equivalent of the Kabyle *kanoun*. There
are many other analogies: the same masculine values,
the same values of honour, very democratic assemblies, where decisions were taken unanimously, etc.
But at the same time, these societies were marked by
extraordinary harshness and violence: you had to be
tough to live in them and still survive. People would
stake their life on a word . . . an unfortunate word.
People want pre-capitalist societies to be either a lost
paradise or primitive barbarism. In actual fact, it's
very complicated: they are societies that have an
unprecedented charm, that produce quite extraordinary kinds of people, who in many respects are more
noble and sympathetic than our contemporaries. At
the same time, they are societies that are very hard
to live in, marked by extremely harsh forms of
exploitation and also extraordinary physical and
symbolic violence. That is why this kind of populist
exaltation of the past is both very understandable
and very dangerous.

MM: But don't you get the impression that it is complicated again by the fact that these societies, Béarnais
or Kabyle, are – at all events, in Algeria this is
very clear for Kabyle society – in a state of total
crisis? Then all those things people tended to
systematize, to structure, are on the way out, or
already gone. And so study of them becomes more
difficult.

PB: You are right to correct me . . . This original state,
doubtless rather mythical, has been totally abolished,
and to try to revive it today is rather mystificatory.
For example, one of the foundations of this society
was joint possession: joint possession between brothers was, I believe, the basis of the whole system. The
break-up of joint possession, however, began between
the two world wars. There were even all kinds of
strategies to disguise it. This society had been under

attack for a long time at its very foundations, because
without joint possession, it becomes very hard to
operate relationships between brothers, between
wives, the unity of the house, the authority of the
family head. And then the war, particularly with the
resettlements and all the violence, completed the
overthrow of social and mental structures. In other
words, it is completely naive or dangerous to hope
to restore the old social order, when the conditions
of its functioning no longer exist at all.

MM: Does this not raise, in your opinion, a problem
of the validity of results? It was certainly far easier
to extract from the old system a certain number
of rigorous conclusions; there was a coherence
in that society. Now, in this state of transition,
Kabyle or Béarnais society is not completely modern,
or not modern society at all. Yet it is no longer
what it was.

PB: I think that a number of important things must still
function according to the old traditions. For example,
as far as matrimonial exchanges are concerned, this
must have changed enormously (I would much like
to see now how this happens). But I think that is a
domain where, at least at the level of discourse, at
least to justify or describe it, you still have to use the
old terminology and all the representations associated with it. In the same way, mythico-ritual structures, the oppositions between dry and wet, masculine
and feminine, no longer function as they did in the
days when the great collective rituals were still practised. Having said this, they still exist in people's
minds, in language, through sayings . . . As Sayad
has shown, for example, with '*el ghorba*', even the
emigrants fall back on all the resources of traditional
thinking, like the opposition of East and West, to
conceive their totally new situation. I think that you
have to understand this logic, while knowing that it
no longer functions at all like it used to do, and that
you have a kind of ambiguous structure, between the
logic of class divisions and the traditional solidarities. You would have to study the relationships
between family structures and social structures . . .
How family units, torn apart by inequalities, manage
to survive. It would be fascinating to study a big
Kabyle marriage today, with the gathering of emigrants and people who've remained, the branches

that have grown wealthy and those that have stayed in the village, etc.

This is certainly all very far from the Berber society certain people dream about . . . Having said that, it is understandable that these people invent a Berber society as they would like it to be, as a function of their present needs.

MM: That is also what I think. There is a kind of projection of present aspirations on to the reality of the past. The Berbers are marginalized, a minority, unrecognized, illegitimate. People tend to give the old Berber society all the attributes that they clearly miss today. I don't know if I can add here that this vision is not necessarily more false than the others. I know all the arguments that can be raised against it. I tend to believe that there is an anthropological view that disenchants the world by cleaning it up, but if the enchanted world is an amplification, the cleansed world is a restriction. Those are both forms of travesty, each of which is perhaps as revealing as the other. Enchanted Kabylia is still Kabylia, as I believe it is impossible to build absolutely on thin air. A pretext is needed, perhaps simply a text. It is probable that for a sociologist such as yourself this point of view may appear not at all pertinent. I would just like to offer it in order to have your opinion on it.

PB: Yes, social sciences encounter very difficult problems, especially when applied to societies that have a hard time keeping going . . . Like the Kanak[4] today, the Berbers, etc. People who are placed in these critical situations, where their collective identity is in crisis, and in particular of course the intellectuals of these groups, are led to projections that are more or less fantastical. Berber society, as dreamed by its intellectuals, makes you think of what Feuerbach said about God: just as God is ascribed everything that we lack – we are finite, he is infinite, we are imperfect, he is perfect – so in the same way the old Berber society is ascribed everything that present-day Berber society does not have, everything that it lacks. And in this fantastical reconstruction, even the best ethnology can be used as an instrument of ideological idealization. It's a form of millenarianism . . . which is very readily understandable, but which is none the less very dangerous, since it leads to such problems as that of the unity of the Berbers.

I said just now that the Kabyles had taught me that the social world is to a large extent what people want it to be. I titled a chapter of *Practical Reason* (the chapter on marriage, I believe) 'The social world as representation and will', after the title of Schopenhauer's famous book. That is the pure limit of nominative idealism. To say that the world, meaning the social world, is my representation and my will, is not completely crazy, given that there is an elasticity of the social world due to the fact that the social world exists partly by way of the representation that the people who live in it make of it, and that the Berbers, or previously the Aït Abdeslam clan or the Aït Mengeullat tribe or anyone else, if people believe it exists, then it already does exist a bit. Consequently, the fact of developing representations, even rather delirious and including a share of mythical millenarianism, may have a political usefulness.

That means that the sociologist is trapped rather between utopianism and sociologism, as Marx put it. He may say: 'The Berbers as such don't exist. The Mozabites, Kabyles, Chaouïa, Touaregs – that's something quite different.' They are different social structures, completely different structures of kinship, not to mention the economic base or religious traditions. Naturally, they have a language in common, and yet! . . . etc. That is sociologism, and sociologism has often been used by the colonial power, which divides in order to rule. Having said that, the fact that people say that 'the Berbers are the Berbers', or 'Berbers of all countries, unite!' is a social fact: by saying that, they may help to bring it about. But they have that much more chance of bringing it about if what they say is based more in reality, if their utopianism has sociological foundations, if the Berbers or the Berber land that is dreamt of have a foundation in reality, a name, a language, a belief in the unity of origin, etc. The problem is the same for social classes: the class is also representation and will, but it only has a prospect of becoming a real group if this representation and will are not completely mad and have an objective basis in reality.

MM: I think that, if you had to give just one example, the best one would be democracy. People say: Kabyle society, or Berber society in a general sense, was democratic. I believe this is true, but people act at

the same time as if this democracy was an inseparable and necessary attribute of these societies or, what
comes down to the same thing, the result of a choice
that has been explicitly made, in the ether, without
constraints or determinations. But at least as far as
Kabylia is concerned, the Turkish state was practically non-existent there, just as was any other form
of state. Which means that, if you really try to rescue
democracy as an essential attribute of Kabyle society,
or Berber society in a general way, you also have to
want the conditions without which it is no longer
anything more than a pious vision or, in the best of
cases, a mobilizing utopia.

PB: In any case, the fact that people believe that a group
          exists, that they struggle for it to exist, contributes
          to making it exist. I could once again bring in an
          analogy, mentioning the case of Occitania. Occitania
          does not have a great deal of foundation in reality.
          The Occitans, in order to struggle against the French
          language, have created an artificial language, which
          people no longer understand.

MM: Do you mean all the people, or just some of them?

PB: 'Ordinary' Occitans do not understand their own
          languages (Béarnais, Landais, Bigourdan, etc.) when
          they read them in the unified transcriptions of
          local scholars. Can you imagine the Berber trans-
          criptions of the White Fathers? . . . Who in Kabylia
          could read them? A scholarly language is recon-
          structed. The real foundation of the unity of
          Occitania is the fact that it is a dominated region,
          whose people have been stigmatized because they do
          not have the right accent. That is already a real basis
          of unification.

MM: It's a negative definition.

PB: Yes. Besides, there are certainly some specific cultural
          traditions. Having said that, if people start to believe
          it, if they start putting 'OC' on their car, etc., it is
          not impossible that there may one day be an Occitan
          state . . . That shows the elasticity of the social.

MM: What you are saying reminds me of our interview in
          Actes. Perhaps you remember how at one point we
          spoke about *tamusni*, the Kabyle wisdom. For me,
          tamusni existed, as I myself lived in that atmosphere
          when I was young. Some Kabyles, who had read the

article, came to me and said: '*Tamusni*, we know what that is, but all those things you've surrounded it with?' . . . For me, all these things existed. But in the face of these reactions, I was led to ask myself whether I hadn't given an image of *tamusni* that was certainly faithful, but perhaps a bit . . .

PB: A bit exalted?

MM: A bit exalted . . . perhaps as a function of my expectations, I'm not sure. Yet I continue to believe it is basically true. Because something quite extraordinary happened subsequently. The same people who had criticized me for having spoken of *tamusni* in this way came to see me again some time later and said: 'You didn't tell everything: you forgot this, you forgot that . . .' In other words, the things I had mentioned were more or less as I had said, but perhaps they had not been sufficiently considered. Someone has to say them in order for them eventually to enter consciousness.

PB: Questions of words have a key importance in these matters. I don't have to teach a Kabyle that there are groups that exist only by way of the word that designates them. That is the case, in the Western tradition, with noble families. As the name is transmitted through the male line, a lineage can disappear when the last man dies without a descendant. The same happens in Kabylia. It is not by chance that in the independence struggles, that is, the struggles for 'recognition', names had such great importance. . . With the Kanak, for example, it's a matter of orthography: there is a struggle over whether the name should be written as 'Canaque' or 'Kanak'; Kanak is the nationalist form, Canaque the colonial one.

MM: That reminds me of a somewhat similar case in Algeria. Official discourse, until very recently, refused even the mere use of the word 'Berber'. The press, official speeches, the media, all bent their efforts to invent terms: Maghrebin, traditional, original, African, Libyan . . . as long as the word 'Berber' was avoided. A kind of return to the magical mentality of the nineteenth century, unreasoned fear – on reflection, not so unreasoned – the unreasoned fear that the Word would end up creating the being . . .

PB: As soon as people believe it exists, the group does
        begin to exist . . . that is the great paradox of the
        social world. In traditional society, it is exactly the
        same: the terms of kinship and political taxonomies
        (*axxam, adrum, taxerrubt*, etc.) structure the percep-
        tion of the social world, of other people, and in this
        way, the relationships one can have with them.
        Having said that, as we see in the use of terms of
        address, these structures can be made to serve differ-
        ent functions. It is this which leads to a kind of
        elasticity of the social, and *tamusni* – this I believe
        is one of its virtues – is the art of playing the possi-
        bilities offered by this elasticity of words and struc-
        tures that it simultaneously both designates and
        produces.

MM: Playing with it flexibly, that is, remaining within the
        game, within the norms, but with a certain margin
        of manoeuvre, emerging from it when necessary, but
        only when necessary . . . It must not be broken . . .
        You play with it up to the limit where what is at risk
        is not just changing the rules of the game, but break-
        ing the game itself.

PB: Yes, it's the same for the Berbers. There has to be a
        foundation, therefore a limit. If there is no founda-
        tion, it doesn't work. The person who today says
        something like: 'We're going to unite bourgeois and
        proletarians' doesn't have much chance of success.
        In wartime, as we saw in 1914, it may work. But in
        ordinary times, you have a better chance of success
        by saying: 'Workers of all countries, unite!' That's
        the problem of social units: in order for them to
        exist, there have to be objective foundations; but
        objective foundations are not sufficient for their
        existence. The Berbers can be grouped in thirty-six
        ways. If one particular grouping wins out over
        the others, it's in part because people will have made
        it exist.

MM: Or else, something I believe happens fairly often,
        because this grouping, at a given moment and
        for definite historical reasons, carries and sets in
        motion a project in which other people recognize
        themselves . . .
        I mean that particular historical conditions may
        press a particular group and almost drive it to a more
        intense reaction . . . You get the impression that it

exists in, I don't know how to put it, a more asserted fashion. But other people, who are fundamentally in the same situation, have the impression that it expresses them as well. I'm afraid I'm going out on a limb, but I would be ready to believe that once a certain number of objective conditions are combined, there will necessarily be a group to take them into account, and that group, rightly or wrongly, will give the impression that it exists in a way more than the others do.

Dialogue on Oral Poetry in Kabylia
An interview with Mouloud Mammeri

To give a purer meaning to the words of the tribe.

Mallarmé

The very notion of 'oral literature', for Pierre Bourdieu and Mouloud Mammeri, constitutes a paradox, arising from the categories of classification by means of which European scholastic thought perceives the oral productions of colonized societies. The European view of culture is itself the product of a history in which the town and the transition to writing have long since fashioned the ways of making and conceiving literature, even in popular milieus that have now long since abandoned their oral heritage – under the effect of symbolic domination.

Mouloud Mammeri, a writer, researcher, and himself initiated into tamusni, *the Kabyle wisdom, gives Bourdieu the opportunity here to investigate the conditions of possibility of a poetry that is both oral and scholarly, like that of the Kabyle bards or of Homer.*

The two authors seek to situate this verbal skill and the games it implies in the antique tradition of the Greek world, where the poet bore the name of demiergos (demiurgos, *the artisan, who is involved in practices that are esoteric or even magical).*

Beyond the role and function of these initiates in the art of speech, the present dialogue shows the important place ascribed by the Berbers to discourse and to the conditions of its broadcasting, transmission, perpetuation and codification.

Tikkelt-a ad ḥeǧǧ asefru	Finally this time I shall embark on
ar Lleḥ ad ilhu	the poem
ar-d inadi deg lweḍyat	Perhaps it will be good
	And will travel the plains
Win t-issnen ard a-t-yaru	Whoever hears it will write it down
ur as iberru	And not forget it again.
w'illan d lfahem yezra-t . . .	The wise mind will understand its
	meaning . . .
(Si Muhend-u-Mhend)	(Si Mohand-Ou-Mhand, second
	half of the nineteenth century)
Aaniǧ d bab'i-y-idaan	Is it a father's curse
iffǧ-ed felli leḥdit llil	That has condemned me to night-
	time talk?
Ibbwḍ-eḍ yiḍ medden akw	When night comes, everyone sleeps,
ttṣen	Whether they have shelter or are
ger w'idlen ḍ w'ur-endil	destitute.
Ar nek imi d bu inezman	Outside I walk, wrapped in worries
armi-diy âabbans s-elmil	And bending under the weight.
(Lḥaǧ L Moexṭaṛ At-Sâid)	(Hadj Mokhtar Ait-Saïd, first half
	of the nineteenth century)

Pierre Bourdieu: Oral poetry, and more generally what is sometimes called, in a strange combination of words, 'oral literature', faces research with a seeming paradox, which is certainly produced in large part by the categories of perception through which European thinking, long dominated even in so-called 'popular' forms by the town, writing and the school, apprehends oral productions and the societies that produce these: how is a poetry possible that is both oral and scholarly, such as that of the Kabyle bards, or of Homer? We know the antimony in which Homeric research is trapped right from the start: either Homeric poetry is scholarly, and cannot be oral; or it is oral and is not scholarly. In fact, once it is admitted to be oral, as is the case with what is known as Lord and Parry's theory, prejudices about the 'primitive' and the 'popular' prevent it being granted the properties that are granted to written poetry. People cannot conceive that *oral and popular* poetries can be the product of a scholarly quest, in both their form and their content. They cannot accept that such poetry can be made to

be spoken before an audience, an audience of ordinary people, and yet contain an esoteric meaning,
designed to be the object of meditation and comment.
It is completely ruled out that the work might be the
product of a deliberate quest, making a *second degree*
use of the codified and objectified procedures that
are most characteristic of both oral improvisation
and iteration. But perhaps we should start by locating
your own relationship to *tamusni*, Berber 'philosophy', and recall how you 'learned', and particularly
'revisited' and understood it.

Mouloud   I believe that my father was the last but one in the
Mammeri: *tamusni* lineage. He had a disciple who also died,
and after them something different began: that is
recognized by the whole group, it is not just a personal view. People say: 'There was such-and-such
and so-and-so'; they cite the whole genealogy of the
imusnawen (*amusnaw*, plural *imusnawen*, the sage
or poet) who transmitted *tamusni*. Then, when the
last one died, whose name was Sidi Louenas, that
was at an end . . . After him, this form of *tamusni*
was dead and people went on to something different.
Even if, externally, some superficial forms have been
kept, in reality everyone knows that this way of
conceiving and telling things died with that man.
Besides, it truly was a collective drama when he died,
people knew that something had definitively died
with him. And so I am not the son of the last
amusnaw but of the last but one, and I think this has
been helpful to me inasmuch as it has made me very
sensitive to this kind of thing.
    For my part, I could not be my father's successor,
given that I did not lead the same kind of life at all;
I went to university, and so I already had other points
of reference. But despite this, he was concerned
throughout his life to initiate me as much as he
could. I even wonder sometimes whether the taste
for literature that I acquired very early on did not
come to me from the ambiance in which I bathed as
a child without even being aware of it. While he
neglected to teach me the practical things of life,
which I very much needed, each time he had visitors
with whom he was going to have an exchange that
was more than trivial, my father searched me out
wherever I was. I was still very young, and he knew
very well that three-quarters of the things that were

said I could not understand. But all the same he
bathed me in that atmosphere . . .

As an adolescent, I admit that I loved this passionately; it was no longer he who searched me out
in the village, I was the one who wanted to know
whom he was going to be with . . .

PB: So you have combined the education of the 'literatus'
with the systematic and invisible education of the
amusnaw?

MM: I started to transcribe Kabyle poems at an early age.

PB: And your father knew this?

MM: He must have wondered. I found in his own papers
(he had a little education, he'd gone to school up to
the school-leaving certificate, that was the first generation of Algerians who'd had the Third Republic's
schooling) transcribed poems that I had heard him
recite orally. Besides, I had a great-uncle who himself
put together a collection of Kabyle poems (he had
gone to lycée). That said, my father acquainted me
with several of his 'peers', not only within the Aït
Yenni tribe, which I come from, but also outside this,
because these *imusnawen* make visits from one tribe
to another. When I was still a child, my father regularly took me to the markets, because the markets
were a privileged meeting-place. My father spent half
an hour purchasing, and the rest of the time he spent
meeting people and hanging out with them; they did
the same thing. This was a kind of education on the
spot, both deliberate and diffuse.

An Art and an Art of Living

MM: The apprenticeship was an apprenticeship through
practice. It was not an abstract apprenticeship. It was
also necessary to act in conformity with a certain
number of precepts and values, without which
tamusni is nothing. A *tamusni* that is not avowed,
not lived, is only a code. *Tamusni* is an *art*, and an
art of living, that is, a practice that is learned by
practice and that has practical functions. The productions it makes possible, poems, maxims, are not
art for art's sake, even if their *form*, which is sometimes very recherché, very refined, can lead people to
believe this . . .

PB: But perhaps it would be good to spell out a bit what
the speciality of the Aït Yenni tribe was, and the
particular position of your family within this tribe?

MM: We are artisans, I don't know for how many centuries: armourers, sometimes jewellers, but armourers
in particular. It is a function that is very conducive to
tamusni, since the artisan has leisure, freedom, conditions of work that are very much more propitious
than those of a peasant. The peasant, when he is in
his field, is alone with his animals, with the land. In
the armourer's workshop, many people come by: not
only men who come to have their rifle adjusted, but
also people who come in order to talk – it's a meeting
place. In winter, in particular, when it's cold outside
and much better to be in the armourer's workshop.
Heaps of people came through my father's shop. My
grandfather deliberately passed on everything he
knew of *tamusni* to my father; this was conscious,
since it was he who possessed it in his generation.
There was a kind of inheritance here that reached my
grandfather, who passed it on to my father, and my
father passed it on to a marabout in our village. But
it was like that not just in our family but in many
others, and this was undoubtedly because of the high
number of artisans in the tribe. Most Kabyle tribes
are peasants; ours included peasants, of course, but
there was a proportion of artisans that was certainly
higher than elsewhere. Above all, people came from
far afield to find the things they needed: weapons,
jewels, metal objects.

PB: You know how in Homer the poet is somewhere
described, in the *Odyssey*, by the word *demiergos*,
that is *demiurgos*, which is translated as 'artisan' and
which should properly be translated as 'initiate'; and
several indications suggest that this was a specialist,
sometimes a foreigner. Besides, in his chapter on
religious communities, Max Weber evokes the particular status of the artisan, indicating that he is
'caught up in the toils of magic', owing to the fact
that every art of an unusual, esoteric character is
considered a gift, a magical charisma, a personal gift
that is generally hereditary and that separates him
from the common run of men, that is, from peasants.
Is the *amusnaw* not a *sophos*, the master of a technique that is very practical, as opposed to an abstract
and gratuitous wisdom?

MM: *Tamusni* is simply the name of action corresponding to the word *issin*, knowledge, but a knowledge that is initially practical, technical. And so the *amusnaw* is precisely the original *sophos*.

PB: Doesn't it sometimes happen that people expect from the *amusnaw* practical skills and competence, for example medical?

MM: That happens, but even if he does not give prescriptions or care, he remains despite everything an *amusnaw*.

PB: Doesn't he practise his expertise in matters of field boundaries, the agricultural calendar, etc.?

MM: Absolutely. He was deemed to be more familiar with all this than other people; he knew exactly how work was distributed over the twelve months of the year, what had to be done before or after, how trees were grafted, etc. The last of them in date had a great reputation for his knowledge of a heap of medical remedies, which plant cured which disease . . .

The Particular Status of the Artisan

PB: Could just anyone come into the workshop? Could other specialists come, and what happened then?

MM: The people who came were of different social status. They came because they knew that it was a privileged place for this kind of exchange. It could also happen that people came who were capable of dispensing *tamusni*, and in that case, there was an exchange between them with equal weapons.

PB: A match?

MM: Not exactly. There is a current expression that says: 'Everyone learns from another' (*Wa iḥeffeḍ ǧef-fa*). There was exchange of proverbs and parables that the *imusnawen* tossed back and forth, each trying to distinguish himself. Other people were there as spectators, as apprentices in a sense. They came to seek wisdom. Without it being a place of pleasure strictly speaking, just of entertainment, but a select and superior entertainment.

The advantage is that this can continue throughout the year, since the artisan works all the time, the whole day and the whole year, without a break; whereas the peasant is ruled by the seasons, and he's alone in the fields.

PB: Another characteristic of these artisan groups is that they travelled, either to sell or to buy. They were more in contact with the town than other people, with the outside world.

MM: Absolutely. And we have precise examples of this. Generally, in the ethnological literature, it is said that before the French conquest the Kabyle tribes were cut off from one another, that the only relations between them were hostile ones, that *anaya* was needed to go from one to the other. There is some truth in this, but in fact there was a great mobility: on the part of pedlars, poets, women, *imusnawen*, marabouts, ordinary people. There was a code of friendship that bound you to friends outside the tribe, you quite simply just went there.

In my own family, one of the armourer ancestors, who lived in the second half of the eighteenth century, normally went to sell the products of his handicraft on the Kabyle coast. When you think of the conditions in which journeys were undertaken at that time – there were no roads, there was perhaps even a certain insecurity – that was remarkable: he was obliged to cross I don't know how many groups, tribes, villages. On the other side, family tradition tells that he was visited by a Turk, who had had to leave Algiers because he had killed someone and the courts were looking for him. If this Turk came all that way, he must have known that he would be welcomed . . . And so the isolation was quite relative, and artisans were certainly more open towards the outside world than a peasant could be, someone who might spend his whole life in his own village.

PB: They were predisposed to fulfilling the function of ambassador, mediator, intermediary . . .

MM: I wouldn't go so far as to say 'ambassador' . . .

PB: Bearers of news, of ideas . . .

MM: That is certain. They were men of discourse by vocation, and as such they were bearers of news. At all events, it was in their interest to be men of discourse. The man I am telling you about was renowned for this. Heaps of stories are told about him: how he extracted himself from difficult situations, precisely by discourse, because discourse truly was a weapon in his hands.

PB: Did they go and sell their products themselves?

MM: Generally people came to them to buy.

PB: That also gave the opportunity for contact with the outside world . . .

MM: Certainly, people come from everywhere to find you, you're obliged to have a number of connections that go beyond the village, beyond the tribe.

Informal Apprenticeship and Initiation

PB: To go back a moment, there was an informal apprenticeship analogous to what you yourself received. But were there not also more explicit forms of apprenticeship, more specific ones?

MM: I believe there were two things. First of all there was this informal apprenticeship. An important role in this was played by the village assembly that was held at regular intervals – for example, every other Thursday in the month – and where all village business was transacted. These assemblies were genuine schools of *tamusni*, since those who spoke there most often were naturally the most eloquent people, 'masters of speech'. But anyone could attend, even children. Personally, as a small child I attended a large number of village assemblies, and I remember very well how they went. So, there was already this kind of regular school. But there were also markets, and pilgrimages, which are particularly important occasions because they give rise to sizeable gatherings, both in the number of participants and in their diversity of origin. Now, as well as this apprenticeship which happens almost by itself, there is initiation in the strict sense, which is conscious, intended by a master, and only addressed to two kinds of person: the poet and the *amusnaw*, the first still more clearly than the second, who at least has the faculty of also learning *tamusni* in an informal way (although, at a certain degree of initiation, he is obliged to resort to consulting 'initiates' who preceded him, in a voluntary way). But for the poet it is almost a necessity.

PB: In other words, the *imusnawen* select themselves to a certain degree by going and attaching themselves to a master, who for his part chooses them. It's rather the mutual selection of two charismas.

MM: Yes, candidates ask to be initiated, and among all those who frequent him, the master judges those whom he estimates to be gifted and to deserve to continue.

The Function of the Poet

PB: Can you spell out the distinction you are making between the *amusnaw* and the poet?

MM: First of all, strictly speaking an *amusnaw* need never compose verses, he may not be gifted for poetry, despite being gifted for discourse, discourse in prose. This is already a first distinction. Among the poets, there were those who ensured mechanical transmission, who recited poems they had not made up themselves.

PB: They were professionals: was a special name given to reciters of this kind who went from village to village, to distinguish them from genuine 'creators'? Something like the contrast between the *rhapsode* who recited and the *aede* who composed, or between the *joglar* who performs and the *trobaor* as author?

MM: In actual fact, there were two terms in use among the initiates: *ameddah* and *afsih*; the *afsih* is able to create as well as just recite, and is an *amusnaw* almost by definition.

PB: Whereas the *ameddah* is only a reciter . . .

MM: The *ameddah* may very well know thousands of verses and recite them, without being otherwise personally gifted for it; what he does have is memory. But he fulfils none the less a function that is indispensable in the milieu of oral literature.

PB: He was a bit like a library, an archive: he knew things that everyone knew a bit of, but he knew more than other people.

MM:	He knew them better and he knew a large number. In general, other people knew bits and pieces, segments.
PB:	Was he able to make a living from this skill?
MM:	Absolutely. He was a professional and this was all that he did. He went from village to village, from market to market, especially at harvest time, whether it was olives, figs or grain, and practically throughout the year.
PB:	And at festivals?
MM:	No, not so much at festivals. At festivals, everyone is allowed to recite.
PB:	And the *afsih* was someone quite different?
MM:	Yes, he did not perform in this way. He rather chose his moment. When he came, it was an event . . . He didn't turn up just because the olive harvest was good.
PB:	And similarly, it wasn't a question of 'paying' him directly, openly . . .
MM:	Of course. The man who was our national poet, if I may say so, in the eighteenth century, was called Yusef-i-Kaci, he really was a very great poet in the old style. He was given oil, but a large quantity, and that wasn't because he came to a particular place, it was a kind of tribute. People said: 'On such-and-such a day we have to collect oil for Yusef-u-Kaci.' Everyone came with the quantity they wanted to give, and they went and took it to his house.
PB:	And he didn't work.
MM:	No, he didn't work. This was his function. Besides, he wasn't from our tribe but from a tribe that was distant from ours, the At Djenad, on the coast. There was a kind of choice that was made in this way. I couldn't find out properly how, coming from At Djenad, he became our poet, to the point that now we all know verses of his, whereas in At Djenad these are not very well known, even though people there also see him as a great man. They were on the border of the independent Kabyle country, between that not subject to the Dey and that subject to the Dey. This situation had its frictions, wars with the forces of the

PB: Dey, and it was always he who was sent to negotiate with the caliphate.

PB: Here he did fulfil the role of ambassador.

MM: Yes, here he really did have the role of ambassador, a political role, he took decisions. For example, during a quarrel between the Turks and the At Djenad, he asked the At Djenad: 'What shall I say to the Turkish *caïd*?' People told him: 'Say what you want, we are behind you.' And so he was vested with a kind of authority. It really was a political role.

Esoteric Discourse and Exoteric Discourse

PB: That is completely in the logic of what you were saying just now, when you said that, for your father, poetic speech always had a practical function, an ethical one. In other words, whatever the uses of this competence, they were always practical . . .

MM: At all events, it was always practical, relating to life, without thereby being utilitarian. I am not saying that the *imusnawen* did not perform among themselves the kind of gratuitous exercises that evoke pure poetry. Yes, but among themselves: 'Now that we are among connoisseurs, let us indulge to our heart's delight.'

PB: In those cases, their discourse was more esoteric?

MM: Yes, in a way it was discourse for the initiated. They had a real understanding among themselves. There were even stages, themes, a ritualization. I remember very well, towards the end of his life, when my father met with his disciple – that was even a bit dramatic, inasmuch as they were reduced, isolated . . . the end of something, and they knew it . . . What fireworks! It was very fine, but I had the impression that it was at an end. No one could follow, and they did not even permit themselves a display of such virtuosity in front of others, because they knew very well that this wouldn't go down well. So they reserved this for themselves. There was a special language (I couldn't stop them to ask: 'Yes, but what does that mean?'). But they understood one another.

PB: This kind of esoteric culture, was it developed precisely in these meetings between 'initiates', by poetic work?

MM: I couldn't say, but I believe this was how it developed. My impression was that each person had a share in it.

PB: And wasn't there always a hierarchy between the virtuosi themselves, on top of the hierarchy that you have established between the poets and the mere reciters?

MM: Yes, I believe that there was a hierarchy based, if not on absolute value, at least on value as recognized by others. People said: 'This person is at such and such a level in *tamusni*; he is at the top of the ladder. Someone else is quite close, but not quite there . . .; another person is learning . . .' As there were opportunities for meeting, for performance, the *amusnaw* was being tested almost throughout his life, all the time; you couldn't make a mistake.

PB: This was a judgement by the people, but also by the initiates.

MM: Yes, but one thing merged into the other. The judgement of the initiates could not exactly coincide with that of the people, inasmuch as pretence can have a greater effect on the people than on professionals. Among 'initiates', you can't look at one another without laughing; if someone is bluffing, the others know. Otherwise, you can bluff in the eyes of the people, but you can't do so for long.

Excellence

PB: If I understand correctly, *tamusni* was a kind of wisdom that could only be expressed in discourse if it was also expressed in practice.

MM: People accept transgressions, but on certain conditions. They say: 'If this *amusnaw* does this kind of thing, he can permit himself this but I can't. To transgress the *taqbaylit*, the code of honour, is something I can't permit myself, I can only conform to it. He can transgress: he is beyond it. With me, if I transgress it's by failing, it is that I'm not up to the sacrifices that the *taqbaylit* demands. With him, if he does so, even though he could excel, it's because he sees further.' So they knew very well that a man is a man and that an *amusnaw* can commit some irregularities because he is a man. The group accepts irregularities of this kind.

PB: They are beyond the rules, but they fulfil them by being beyond, as supreme realization of Kabyle excellence.

MM: I think that's it. People say: 'He's very good. He transgresses, but in the right direction', that is, upward rather than down.

PB: He is the person who expresses the truth of the game by playing with the rules, instead of just playing according to the rules.

MM: The Kabyles understand this. 'He has played well, he has put the problem in terms that permit him to act like this; as for me, I am obliged to conform strictly to the rule; they are for the generality, but he is beyond.' *Tamusni*, in the narrow sense, is knowledge of a body of prescriptions, values, etc. But there is something beyond this. A certain poet replied one day with a poem that begins like this: 'The understanding of things is higher than *tamusni* (*Lefhem yegleb tamusni*)' – Si Mohand. This isn't a contradiction. What it means, in fact, is that if you treat *tamusni* as merely a mechanical sum of precepts, you can learn it, all you have to do is go to an *amusnaw* who will transmit all the prescriptions. But if you want to be a real *amusnaw*, then there is something beyond the rules that transgresses them, or better, transcends them.

The Course of Initiation

PB: Continuing from what you were saying about the training of professionals, can we assume that, given that there are degrees of initiation, there is the possibility of a kind of course or progress, with successive tests?

MM: I believe that there is a kind of apprenticeship in two stages. The first is done in the same conditions as for *tamusni*: an initial apprenticeship in poetry is done by attending all the regular meetings to which the poet is constantly invited, in order to illustrate an argument, explain a concrete situation (the ordinary Berber language lacks a certain number of abstract terms, but it is possible to render even these abstract notions in everyday language, and the procedures for rendering these abstractions were either poetry or parables). This is the reason why, in Kabyle society, everyone can be a poet at one moment or another in their life, because they have felt a more intense sentiment than usual. The professional is the person from whom this is expected the whole time. If it turns out that another person invents something about an event, this can be integrated into the corpus. The difference with the professional being that he is capable of doing this the whole time.

In order to reach this kind of mastery, you have to undergo a second stage of apprenticeship which is far more formalized, institutionalized. You spend a long time following a poet, who teaches you the different procedures. There was even a kind of examination, at which the teacher gave an authorization (*issaden*) or licence. This consisted in creating oneself a poem of a certain number of lines, a hundred lines. A hundred lines is a great deal for an oral production. People said: 'He has composed as many as (*issefra-ḍ...*)', and the figure was given, generally a hundred. To give one example, the poet who was in a sense the teacher of all others, Mohammed Saïd Amlikec, had a large number of disciples, it was he who gave this investiture. To one of his disciples, El Hadj Rabah, he said one day: 'If you want me to give you the licence to be a poet, make a poem of a hundred lines.' The claimant said: 'A hundred lines is nothing . . .' He made a hundred and fifty, far more than envisaged, and it is said that the moment came when he could no longer find a word to rhyme with the previous line. He said: 'I'm sorry, I can't find a rhyme here – *dag'ur as ufry ara lemǧaz is*', and he continued. But the master said to him: 'That's fine. You've gone far beyond a hundred lines', and gave him a licence to make poetry. On the other hand, however, each time he performed somewhere, the 'licensee' had to begin with a prayer in verse that his master had made. He began with: 'As my master Mohammed Saïd has said – *akken i-s inna wemyar Si Muhend Ssâid*', which is a way of paying homage, respect: 'As my master has said . . .', which didn't

mean that he was incapable of making some verses
of prayer himself. No, it was simply the consideration, the homage paid to the master in poetry. Until
the day that El Hadj Rabah, having got above
himself, judged that he was now as competent as his
master, and perhaps even more so. He went to
perform somewhere, and said: '. . . As the child El
Hadj Rabah has said . . . – *akken i-s inna weqcic
Lḥaǧ Rabeḥ* . . .' And he said the prayer, which was
fine, as good as that of the master. But people were
scandalized: 'What! He dares to perform his own
prayer, he's a usurper! It's a sacrilege!' And the legend
adds that from this moment, his inspiration dried up,
because he'd transgressed the rules of the game. In a
certain sense, he'd betrayed. He'd broken the chain.
He continued to make verses, but no one listened to
him any more, his charisma had disappeared.

PB: That tends to confirm that, as Weber says, the art of
the poet is conceived as a magical charisma, whose
acquisition and preservation are guaranteed by
magic. But is that all there is to it? There is also a
whole technical aspect, rules of composition, procedures, etc.

MM: There were very precise rules. It was as a function of
the rules that people could decide whether a poet was
more or less expert. The poet I was telling you about,
Yusef-u-Kaci, the greatest poet of the time before the
French occupation, composed according to a certain
number of canons. I remember an anecdote: one day,
a man from the Aït Yenni sought him out. He came
from quite a long way away to ask the master to help
him to perfect his art of making verses. He arrived,
saw the poet and addressed him in verse:

A dadda Yusef ay ungal	Dada Youssef, my big brother,
ay ixf l-lehl is	master of all your peers,
Tecbiḍ ṭṭaleb l-lersal	you are like the great *taleb*
igran di Wedris	who recites the sacred texts
Ul-iw fellak d amaâlal	at the Oudriss school, my heart is sick for you,
Awi-k isâan d ccix is.	it wishes to have you for master.
(Muḥ At-Lemsaaud)	(Muh At-Lemsaaud)

The rhyme is in '*is, al*'. Yusef-u-Kaci replied in the same vein, six lines of the same form, using the same rhymes:

Cebbaġ w'ur	I say of someone who is
nekkat uzzal	not courageous
icmet wagus is	that his weapons are ugly
Am-min irefden	He is like someone
uffal	wielding a rod
d win i d leslaḥ is	and making a weapon
Ney afsiḥ deg	of it
lmital	Like the poet who does
ur nessefruy	not draw
seg-gixf is.	his verses from himself.
	(Yusef-u-Kaci)

Which means: 'There are things I can teach you, but the person who learns can be taught by anyone. It is not worth the trouble of coming to see me.'

Despite what the master might say, there was a technique, canons; but on top of this there was a wisdom. What the master says in his reply is: 'You want technique. Fine, I answer you in the same rhythm and with the same rhymes, but on top of this with a teaching, a wisdom.'

Giving a Purer Meaning to the Words of the Tribe

PB: It's this that makes Berber poetry more than a 'pure' art, in the tradition of 'art for art's sake': it supplies the means for expressing and conceiving difficult situations and experiences.

MM: That is precisely the function of metaphor or parable: to condense in a small number of words that contrast, that are striking and thus easy to memorize, an ultimate teaching. And from this point of view verses are wonderful; first of all you remember them, and secondly, when a poet is gifted, he manages to say, by a certain number of approximations, stylistic procedures, things that ordinary prose does not say.

PB: So what the poet is granted is a licence to force language.

MM: Yes, this is part of the procedures: the contrast, the act of making a word signify something rather different than what it means in current language, a slight

	shift that enables him to make it say something that it could not have said normally.
PB:	This intensive use of ordinary language makes it possible to make language 'render' the maximum, to 'give a purer sense to the words of the tribe'.
MM:	Yes. And this is easier in verse than in prose. In prose, there are limits to intelligibility. It took me years to understand certain verses that I had long been familiar with. One day, I said: 'Yes of course, that's true.' Something took place within me.
PB:	This retrospective illumination vindicates the old maxim of the majority of traditional teachings, based on memorizing: 'learn first, understand later . . .' There is something like the idea that this condensed, intensified sense will take a long time to express itself, to manifest itself; it will demand meditation and resists deciphering.
MM:	At all events, in poetry the deeper sense may not be apparent at first sight. In prose, on the contrary, the interlocutor has to understand.

The Dissipation of Meaning

PB:	The search for this intensification of language implies an advance into obscurity: the search for assonance, alliteration, shifts in the meaning of words, all this makes for language becoming obscure.
MM:	Certainly, but there is a kind of counterpart to what you are now saying. For example, I transcribed a poem that my father used to recite. A long time after, I discovered the text of the same poem at the house of a marabout who is now dead . . . I asked him whether he had any manuscripts, and he brought me a few sheets. I saw lines that weren't quite finished. I thought they might be verses: indeed they were verses, transcribed into Arabic letters. This was the poem that my father recited orally, but longer, and with more difficult language even in the part that was common to both versions, also some words had been replaced by others.
PB:	Replacement is not accidental; was this in the direction of the regular meaning?
MM:	Yes, towards regular meaning. It was a loss, and not at all an enrichment.

So much for the oral version of the poem in question. In actual fact, two versions of it were known. A clear symmetry can be noted between the two poems, but it was introduced only subsequently: classic six-line stanzas with crossed rhymes, made up of three couplets the last of which contained two heptasyllables, the two others varying. In both poems the rhymes use 'i' as the supporting vowel in the uneven lines, and a different vowel in the even ones. The first line also has the same form in both poems, with a simple but subtle variation of the day (Tuesday, Thursday), and particularly the time (the evening of defeat and the morning of victory).

First Poem: Oral Version

Win ur neḥdiṛ ass-n *ṭṭlata tameddit* *mi-d čuddu*	Oh! not to have witnessed the battle on Tuesday night!
Kul azniq la-d iṭṭeggiṛ *kul tiġilt* *la-d tfurru*	Every alley spewed out (warriors) Each hill swarmed with them
I tin ur ibġi Ṛebbi *âaddik m'atnegheḍ* *azru*	But if God does not will it can you shatter the rock?

Second Poem: Oral Version

Win ur neḥdiṛ ass *l-lexmis taṣebḥit* *mi tembweṭṭaj*	Oh! not to have witnessed the flaming (storm) on Thursday morning!
Ibda lbaṛud l-lexzin *l a yeṭṭenṭaj*	The old powder crackled
Xemsa-u-sebâin ay *geġlin* *as ġef Tewrirt* *l-Lḥeǧǧaǧ*	Seventy-five (warriors) fell for Taourirt-El Hadjadj alone[1]

The written poem is longer. I don't have it at present. But I can try to recall it. Twelve verses of it come to mind (if I remember right, the poem has thirty-five verses in all). After all, my situation is precisely the same as must have happened throughout the centuries to translators of the oral tradition. Anyway, here are the verses I remember:

A ṭṭir yufgen iâalla *Ifer ḫuzz-it*	Bird flown to the heights, Let your wings glide.
Ḥebsen leǧwad la *âaḍla* *ḥed ma n zeṛṛ-it*	Without truce, the nobles (warriors) have fortified their camp: none of them can now be seen
Tlatin ḥesbeǧ kamla *ssarden semmḍit*	I saw thirty of them, rightly counted, who, washed and refreshed,
Ay geǧlin deg ṭṭwila *ǧef teqbaylit*	Fell with their long rifles for Kabyle honour.
Kra bbwi iḫuz ḥed *lǧila* *ičča ten ttṛad* *msakit!*	All those caught by the critical moment were consumed by war, poor men!
A ttir azegza yemrin *ddu deg llyaǧ*	Shining white bird, go in the air
ǧer tâassast ggaren *aâwin* *kulyum d asraǧ*	Towards those who are commissioned to mount the guard each day saddling (their horses)
Ulac tifrat, yiwen *ddin* *ǧas ma texla neǧ* *atteggaǧ*	For there is no truce, one sole outcome: either destruction, or exile!
Ass l-lexmis may *sen zzin* *ikker waâjaj*	On Thursday, when they laid siege in the dust,
ibda lbarudl-lexzirn *le yeṭṭenṭaj*	the old powder began to crackle

Xemsa-u-sebâin ay *geğlin* *ğas ğef Tewrirt* *l-Lḥeğğağ*	Seventy-five (warriors) fell for Taourirt-El-Hadjadj alone.

(Yusef-u-Kaci, second half
of the eighteenth century)

Here is the full text of the poem as given in the manuscript. I just translate the additional lines:

Belleh a ṭṭiṛ ma d *w'iserrun* *ddu deg llyağ* *At Yanni laaz n tudrin* *Sellem at wagus meḥřağ* *Ass-l-lexmis mi yasèn zzin* *ikker waâjaj*	(3 to 6:) With the Ait-Yenni, honour of the villages: bear my greeting to the men with their belts filled with powder. When they laid siege on Thursday the dust rose
Ibda lbarud l-lexzin *la yeṭṭenṭaj* *Xemsa-u-sebâin ayg-geğlin* *ğas ğef Tewrirt l-l ḥeğğağ* *Ariḍa mazal-ten din* *i tembwṭṭağ*	(11 and 12:) They are there still tonight amid the sound of shots.
ğer tâassastr ggaren aâwin *kulyum d asrağ* *Ulac tifrat, yiwen ddin* *ğas ma texla neğ atteggağ*	
A ṭṭiř yufgen iâalla *ifer ḥuzz-it* *Ḥebsen legwad lemḍilla* *ḥed manzeṛṛ-it* *Assen ur irbiḥ sslam* *mi myugen ṭṭrad-n-twağit*	(21 and 22:) It was an unlucky day when they made a harmful war.
Tlatin ḥesbeğ kamla *ssarden semmḍit* *ay-d iqqimen deg ṭṭ wila* *ğef teqbaylit* *Kra bbwi yeṭṭef ḥed l-lğila* *ičča-tenṭṭrad msakit*	

Ttṛeġ-k a waḥed lewḥid   (29 to the end:)
a Lleh uṛ netṭis   Unique, peerless, I
daaġ-k s-eṣṣḥaba laâyan   implore you,
    God inaccessible to
    sleep
    I invoke you by the
    famous
    Companions of the
    Prophet

Aali d irfiqn-is   By Ali and his peers
Tegḍ a deg lğennet amkan   Make space for us
jmâa akka-d neṭ ḥessis   in Paradise
    All of us who are
    here to listen.

At the end of the day, there is not such a great difference: the final strophe of six lines (29–34) is the obligatory 'envoy' in this kind of poem. This is a general purpose stereotype (it can be adapted to any kind of poem: a mark of this here is the change in rhyme). In fact, I suspect that the first section of the poem (1–16) is missing a distich, as the set is classically made up of a series of six-line stanzas (one for the final section, two for the second, and usually three for the first); which would mean that a first loss of content took place already at the stage of the initial transcription.[2]

PB: Do you know of other similar cases of reduction of extraordinary language to ordinary language?

MM: Certainly, but this one is quite significant. It concerns a battle between two tribes. Two attacks were actually launched; one took place on a Tuesday and failed, the other, two days later on Thursday, was successful. The first poem (six lines) was improvised literally on the spot: the warriors returned but had failed to capture the village, they had been defeated . . . The next day, they decided on the attack for Thursday. The poet made another poem, according to oral tradition: likewise of six lines. He simply says that the attack was successful this time, that the village has been captured, etc.

    The written form of the second poem is longer, and altogether different in form. Now, there is another poem of six lines on the same subject, which my father told me, and which was remade after the model of the first six-line poem. What happened? Six lines are easy to remember. The second poem was reduced to the form of the first by completely refashioning it, to make it into a pendant of the first: the attack first failed, then succeeded. So there was a whole work of restructuring, but to the detriment not only of the length of the poem but also of its meaning and impact: the written version is fuller, more human. The primitive poem, when I found it written down, took a lot of trouble to decipher. I am not even certain that I understood it rightly, in two passages at least, whereas the other, which was dictated to me, is comprehensible and very well balanced in relation to the first. It is not completely in everyday language, but it is readily comprehensible. And so it is likely that the development that took place was in the direction of 'vulgarization'. My father recited to me a number of verses that I transcribed, and I later found blander versions of these with other people. Blander, because there were things that they left out, and that they preferred to say in everyday language.

PB: Yes, certainly the first thing to disappear is the play on ordinary meaning, the shifts in meaning, archaisms, unusual forms of vocabulary and even syntax. But don't people also engage in a work of exegesis similar to that which you have had to do yourself in order to discover the meaning of these old poems? Isn't there a struggle over the meaning of words, aiming to appropriate the authority contained in a saying, a proverb, or a verse that has become a proverb? Isn't one of the dimensions of the *licence* granted the poet precisely that of playing with the words of the tribe?

MM: I believe it is. There is a kind of everyday consumption; but there are also degrees of higher initiation when people analyse the deeper sense. And then the 'sages', when they are among themselves, do not give the same value to the same examples.

PB: Starting from ordinary meaning they produce an esoteric meaning, which the apparent exoteric commonplaceness conceals from the lay mind. Does it not follow that, even in the presence of a lay audience, they can use a language with a dual purpose, a double meaning, a *double entendre*: are there not

necessarily several *levels of interpretation*, just as
there are several *levels of expression*?

MM: That reminds me of an experience I had. In one
village, at a given time, there were two *imusnawen*,
who were the representatives of two opposing *soff*
(parties, leagues). They had been adolescents together,
they had learned *tamusni* together. And then the vicis-
situdes of politics divided them. They remained separate for years, each at the head of one of the two *soff*.
I attended the reunification of the village. The first
amusnaw, who was particularly talented, spoke, and
the other replied. What I then heard was an extraordinary amoebic chant. People listened, their impression was that they understood what was being said
very well. But this was not the case. What reached
them was the evident meaning, the apparent meaning
of this discourse, but all the rest escaped them. The
two masters visibly took great pleasure in this.
    To be able to speak at last to someone who under-
stands you, and who can reply to you in the same
terms . . . It almost turned into a specialist debate.

PB: One of the specific talents of these 'initiates' must
have been familiarity with references, the ability to
say 'as such-and-such a person said' . . .

MM: Absolutely. There is a body and a corpus of *tamusni*.
It used to be conscious; people said: 'I'm going to
learn from so-and-so.' There were schools, which
had their parables, their verses, their procedures,
their style, and above all a whole series of values,
references which had to be known, possessed. And
the more of these you possessed, the more advanced
you were in *tamusni*. This apprenticeship was deliberate on the part of the *imusnawen*: they went from
one tribe to another. They went expressly to see so-
and-so, spent the whole night with him in order to
learn from him.

PB: Weren't the great trans-tribal *imusnawen* those who
accumulated the whole of these various corpuses?

The 'Sense' of the Situation

MM: There was one who was extraordinary in this respect.
People approached him to resolve heaps of problems,

difficult problems, critical cases. He had a certain authority . . . He was able to adapt his discourse according to the tribes and places that he visited: 'These people, you have to tell them this or that, you have to act in this or that way with them.' He had the 'sense' of his audience. This wasn't opportunism. But you don't say just anything to anyone. If you want your *tamusni* to be effective in the particular case, you have to adjust it to your hearers.

PB: That is undoubtedly one of the most important characteristics of oral discourse, to have to adjust to a situation, an audience, an occasion. The real science of oral discourse is thus a science of the opportune moment, the *kairos*. *Kairos*, for the sophists, was the opportune moment, which had to be seized in order to speak to the point and give your words their full effect; but what the word originally meant, as Jean Bollack has shown, was the white of the target, and the person who has the sense of *kairos* is the one who hits the spot . . .

MM: I think it is no coincidence that the Greek and Kabyle expressions converge. In the language of *tamusni*, when the solution to a problem is being looked for in a meeting, people say: 'The right decision is like the target, you don't know *who* will hit the spot . . . – *ṛṛay am lġerḍ, ur teẓriḍ w'aa-t iḥazen.*' This is to encourage the person who hesitates to speak in the assembly, to emphasize how every performance is necessarily relative. To illustrate this 'sense' of the situation, the same *amusnaw* told me the story of two villages in another tribe that were in conflict. He was summoned to resolve the matter. On his arrival in one of the villages, he did not seek out the initiators of the conflict, but the village marabouts. And he said to them: 'You are to come with me; I'll ask you to intervene with your people and tell them this or that, but it is up to you to tell them in your own way.' The marabouts agreed, because they knew they were dealing with a remarkable *amusnaw*. They spoke until midnight. When it was his turn to speak, he did not stop until around three in the morning: he quite amazed them. Elsewhere he would have acted differently, knowing very well that the values he was going to defend were the same, but that it was necessary each time to adapt the form to his hearers.

The Power of Words

PB:	In fact, the very basis of the authority he exercises lies in his exceptional mastery of language.
MM:	Yes. The fact that the *imusnawen* have at their disposal almost a language of their own, an esoteric one, or at least a particular, deeper use of language, is understandable in this logic. I have an example in mind that particularly struck me: this was before the French occupation, at a time when the *imusnawen* intervened in a real and effective way, when they wielded an effective power. This was a quite ordinary tale. It concerned a man who had married a woman from a neighbouring tribe, and had been forced to leave his own tribe – something quite rare at that time. No one knew where he had ended up; he didn't give any sign of life. This went on for almost seven years after he left. One day, the woman's relatives came to see the husband's parents and told them: 'Our daughter has waited long enough, close to seven years. You yourselves admit that this situation has gone on long enough. Alright, either you are sure that this man will return soon, and his wife will stay. Or else, if he does not give any sign of life, we shall take back our daughter.' The others replied that perhaps the man was alive somewhere . . .

Several meetings were held. As the woman was from a different tribe, the problem could not be settled easily. At one of the meetings, a representative from the woman's tribe, very eloquent – he was a great *amusnaw* – cornered the others with a series of arguments that seemed irrefutable. He ended up by saying: 'If you are in agreement, let us conclude. This woman will come back to us.' But one of the others, who knew that one of the most remarkable speakers was absent, replied that there was no hurry, that they would meet once more, in a week, to recite the *fatiha* (the prayer). They separated. Then they met up a week later, this time with the presence of the other *amusnaw*. Scarcely had he arrived when the representative of the woman's group said: 'The matter is settled, let us recite the prayer and say: "God grant that this curse does not follow us – *Awer nawi daâussu.*"' The other replied: 'We are going to recite the prayer, but I propose that we pray instead that we do not depart from the way of God – *Awer necceḍ deg-gwebrid r̩-R̩ebbi.*' The first then said: 'Get up. Nothing is settled, we're leaving.'

On the way back, his people asked him: 'What does that mean?', and he explained: 'When I said: "Let the curse not follow us", this meant that a man who abandons his wife for so long is cursed if he does not return to her. When the other replied: "God grant that we do not depart from the way of God", from the rule, the law of God, this meant: the law of God is seven years, and seven years are not yet over; when he said those words, I understood very well what he meant: "You do not have the right to take this woman until seven years are up."' Even if this is a limiting case, it is interesting inasmuch as the same exchange over a small incident could happen for more important events.

The Ultimate Antimonies of Existence

PB: The story you have told represents the higher form of the relationships that would also take place between ordinary men, on the occasion of marriage negotiations, for example, and that at a lesser degree of refinement would give rise to similar jousts.

MM: Certainly. But I believe there is a difference almost in kind, not just in degree.

PB: The one who wins is the one who has the culture 'on his side', who has a better mastery than the other of the rules on which everyone agrees . . .

MM: Yes. But here the word is inseparable from the thing, the way of telling from what is told. In the case of marriage negotiations that you mention, people 'speak' the culture in such terms that it is comprehensible for both parties. In the other case, the level of interpretation is changed: it's Antigone and Creon. The other man could have invoked, against the letter of the law, the human right of the abandoned woman, but on condition that he found the appropriate, correct, linguistically exemplary expression. It was an ultimate problem that was posed between them, whereas for the others it was simply an oratory joust. By making a confrontation between two formulas, the *imusnawen* put their finger on a problem that is a human problem. Which is primordial: written law or 'human' right, etc.? I am sure that, without having read Sophocles or the philosophers, they raised the question of the ultimate antimonies of human existence on the basis of this simple story.

PB: And it is in the name of the intuition people had of their ability to position themselves at this ultimate level that they were given the right to be beyond the rules of morality and ordinary language.

MM: I believe it is in the name of this that they were given the right to transgress the code, at least outwardly.

I recall the act of a well-known *amusnaw* before the conquest. His tribe, at war against a hostile tribe, approached a third, the Aït Yenni, to help them against their enemy. According to the rule of *nif* (point of honour), there is no way of knowing whether the people making such a request are in the right or not. They asked for help, and it would be a serious dereliction not to grant them this. Someone went to find the first group's *amusnaw* and said to him: 'Look, we not only have the neighbouring tribe against us. The Aït Yenni are coming to their aid. So we have to divide our forces in two and send half of our men against the Aït Yenni. The *amusnaw* replied: 'No, ignore the Aït Yenni. If they come with the others, you'll be forced to fight them; but above all, don't attack them!' The reply came: 'What! We'll be seen as cowards!' The *amusnaw* replied: 'If you feel that you are in a situation of inferiority, *nif* will not oblige you to run to your loss.' And his verse became a proverb:

Treg̱ at tezmert meqqwqṛet	By your mercy, great powers
d ṣṣalḥin	sacred to the Zouaoua (confederation),
Igawawen	I swear by Jeddi Manguellet (a
Uḥeq Jeddi	saint)
Mangellat	and the saints who surround
lawleyya widen	him
i-s inuḍen	As we have Tamejjout (the
Imi d Amejjud	enemy),
nsaâ-t	We shall not draw a new
ur-d nerni lhem	mishap upon us.
iḍen	(Laarbi At Bjaaud, eighteenth century)

This statement would have seemed scandalous if proposed by someone else, in the name of the principle: 'Perhaps you'll be defeated, but you have to fight.' A well-known proverb says: 'When you fall, honour falls – *Mi teghli ighli lâa* .' But as *amusnaw*, he enjoyed a kind of freedom that was refused to others.

Poet, Literatus and Peasant

PB: But the story you were just telling, about the *amusnaw* who sought out the marabouts, told them what they had to do and imposed the solution by making use of their authority, raises the question of the relationships between *tamusni* and Koranic tradition, vested with the authority of writing and the sacred. How should we describe this kind of triangle formed by the *amusnaw*, as exemplary depositary of Kabyle excellence, *taqbaylit*, that is, the marabout, a literatus endowed with religious authority, and the simple peasant, who recognizes each of them, though of course each in a different way and with a different claim? How is the competition organized? It is possible to imagine that it has effects both on the content of *tamusni* and on the content of the Koranic message as this is actually conveyed by the marabouts. How does it happen that these two 'powers', based on very different principles, manage to agree? Is it not that fundamentally this competition is both inevitable and inadmissible, inconceivable, and so always masked and repressed by common consent?

MM: Despite my awareness that this kind of regret is useless, I have often regretted all the same that the development of Berber *tamusni* was unable to take, as was the case in Greece, the form of an autonomous and progressive development, without trauma, without the imposition of an external authority. I have often regretted that the *imusnawen* did not have the possibility of making the transition to writing without having to reckon with a kind of competition or domination coming from without. Islamic culture, despite all its qualities, is very fundamentalist, it does not admit variation; it bases itself on the authority of God, it has been revealed, it is in the text of the

Koran. It is complete, and there is nothing else to do than comment on it.

PB: In several of the examples you have cited, the *amusnaw* as layman invokes the word of God, the religious norm: from the standpoint of a priest, this is a kind of usurpation. How is the problem of the relationship between secular wisdom, *tamusni*, as deep expression of the national culture, with its own values, and the religious culture with its universal claim, revealed and endowed with the authority of the written word, raised in concrete terms?

MM: I believe that these relationships have always been experienced over the centuries as ambiguous, even if nobody said so because that would have been scandalous, unthinkable. People wanted at all costs to think that it was one and the same thing. The will of God and the text of divine law could not be contrary to *tamusni*, and conversely, *tamusni* could only stand in the straight line of revealed truth. It remains none the less that in practice there were cases of effective competition, even if this was not intended and still less claimed. I believe that the primacy of religious truth was accepted: the Koran is the Koran, no one can challenge the word of God. *Tamusni* secularizes the truth of the Koran, or else extends it in practice, in reality, in everyday life. There could still be contradictions between the one and the other. Most often these remained unheeded: the marabouts, the only people instructed in Koranic law, were even forced by their position to a certain number of compromises, they accommodated, they had to say that the Koran was compatible with the norms of their society, otherwise they would have condemned themselves. They had a 'trick': they said that law supports customs, which I believe is not always true: when the Kabyles disinherited women, they went counter to religious law . . . And so there were real contradictions. The *amusnaw* is the person who experienced these most intensely and who suffered most from them, because he had a lot of dealings with the marabouts, who were able to read in books things that he could not have access to.

PB: The best proof of this is the mass of texts of Berber poems that you discovered in marabouts' houses.

MM: Yes, it is likely that the literatus had this purely
        instrumental value of possessing a technique of
        preservation. Besides this, however, the *amusnaw*
        knew that in books there was a different wisdom,
        which he did not himself possess. The *imusnawen*
        had frequent dealings with the marabouts. But at
        the same time they lived with everyone else. And
        so they were at a kind of point of intersection of
        the two things. Both like the marabouts and differ-
        ently: because the marabout is also at a point of
        intersection of two worlds, but on the side of reli-
        gious law, whereas the *amusnaw* is on the secular
        side. He is first of all a representative of *taqbaylit*
        taken to a higher degree, which is what *tamusni*
        constitutes.

PB: The *amusnaw* is a specialist in the elaboration of
        specific values. He is a kind of expert in *taqbaylit*, in
        Kabyle being.

MM: An expert in Kablye being, but also in all the
        aspects of life: social, moral, psychological. The
        marabout, for his part, is above all the interpreter
        of the Koran and the commentaries on the Koran,
        Koranic law. The marabout is a marabout by virtue
        of birth; the *amusnaw* is an *amusnaw* by choice; he
        is obliged to avow a certain number of values and
        techniques in order to become an *amusnaw*. The
        marabout does not have a choice; he is the son of
        his father, he just has to pronounce the law. He
        may combine the two things; there are many
        marabouts who are *imusnawen*. It is rare for an
        amusnaw to have studied Arabic; that is a different
        logic, and just wasn't done.

The Censorship of the Dominant Discourse

It is certain, therefore, that there is a problem here,
and I would say that the consequences are rather
harmful for *tamusni*. No doubt *tamusni* can profit
from a certain number of things that are in books,
borrowings that it secularizes. I believe however that,
at a more general level, the development that took
place in Greek society would never have happened
in Kabyle society, because, when it had to say certain

things, when it had to move to a different register (for example, that of cosmology), it came up against something that already existed and that thereby exerted an effect of *censorship*, preventing the Kabyles from drawing responses from their own resources, their own *tamusni*.

One of the great differences between Greek and Kabyle civilization undoubtedly lies in the fact that Berber *tamusni* developed in an unfavourable environment: it is a constrained culture. Islam enjoyed a kind of symbolic privilege, which the other acknowledged: from the mere fact of the existence of this dominant culture, *tamusni* immediately faced certain limits. According to Ibn Khaldun, the Berbers had so many poems that it would fill the libraries to write them down. We are thus right in thinking that a favourable period existed when this oral culture was far more developed; that was before the invasion of Kabyle by the marabouts, starting in the sixteenth century, that is, by men who brought a civilization that was sacred, international, scriptural, and bound up with the state.

PB: The existence of a scholarly, literate culture meant that, as far as certain forms of culture were concerned, the space was already occupied.

MM: This confrontation between a scholarly culture and a popular culture is a very ancient fact in Berber culture.

PB: But it's the whole problem of Berber culture . . .

MM: Yes, and this problem has been regularly experienced, particularly on the terrain of law, because here contradiction and competition are self-evident. I believe that in the text of 1748 that disinherits women there is a preamble or a conclusion, I can't recall, that says 'the marabouts and *imusnawen* met together and, having judged that the situation was such-and-such, decided . . . and God will punish anyone who goes against the decision' . . . These people were not stupid; they knew that this went against religious law, and yet they took this decision that was anti-clerical, if I may say so, by appealing not only to God's sanction but to his actual assistance. This is said in the text in so many words.

Inside and Outside

PB: In ordinary experience, the peasant has a very ambiguous relationship to the marabout, who is at the
same time acknowledged and rejected (I am thinking
of the proverbs about the marabouts who, like rivers,
swell when there is a storm, in case of conflict). If
the marabout was not this kind of power that was
both transcendent and external, rather than being a
truly deep expression of the culture, *tamusni* would
not have enjoyed the kind of freedom that was
granted it as secular wisdom, esoteric but secular. I
mean that if the relationship to the marabout had
been a simple one, less ambivalent, *tamusni* would
have been unviable.

MM: I think that is the case. The marabout is not an
amusnaw. He is partly outside the society.

PB: The marabouts intermarry, they do not work with
their hands, they do not have to practise Kabyle
values, they are exempt from these.

MM: He is outside, which makes it possible to expel him,
and it is this very externality that means that he is
useful, that he can serve as mediator.

PB: Despite everything, there remains the need of a
person who, being inside, can reconcile the group
with itself, not only with other groups.

MM: And the person who is inside is the *amusnaw*.

PB: And this is certainly why there are cases when they
had to meet up, as in the case you cited just now,
when they were forced in a way to act together. But
for most of the time their spheres of action were
independent.

MM: The essential thing is that there is a certain independence. It was not possible to avoid interference, of
course; there were even many cases of this. But I
believe that, in actual fact, they operated in two different domains. Different things were required of
them. An *amusnaw* could very well serve as intermediary. But this function did not fall on him by delegation, by divine election, as a descendant of the
Prophet, as was the case with the marabout, even if

intellectually he was very mediocre. The *amusnaw*, for his part, has to risk his own skin.

PB: The role of *amusnaw* has something prophetic about it. It rests on people being chosen, whereas the marabout is not chosen.

MM: Within the religious group, too, there can be prophetic individuals: I have in mind for example Sheikh Mohand, who broke with the great sheikh whose second in command he was, criticizing him for applying the letter of the rules, sacrificing to a pure ritualism, without leading a real spiritual life. And so the opposition between priest and prophet exists already within the marabout group itself. It remains none the less that there is something of the prophet in the *amusnaw*: he has a prophetic style.

PB: He is the man of crisis situations, critical situations, who is able to speak and say what has to be said when everyone is reduced to silence.

Renewing Tradition in Order to Preserve It

MM: He possesses the faculty of invention, whether as a response to crisis or in ordinary times; he is the person who can make a step forward, a step to the side, right or left, an advance or a diversion. He does not simply say what is, he also says what he invents on the basis of experience or his own reflection. *Tamusni* is not a body of knowledge cut off from life and transmitted 'for the pleasure of it', but a practical science, an 'art' that practice constantly reinvigorates, to which existence constantly throws challenges. This means that the heritage only survives by constantly changing; transmission continually refashions the heritage by bringing it up to date: the role of the *amusnaw* is to make the tradition understood as a function of the present situation, the only one actually experienced, and to make people understand present situations in the light of tradition, to make this tradition pass into the group's own practice. There are the ordinary responses of codified routine, the breviary of customs and usages, accepted values, that constitute a kind of inert knowledge.

On top of this, there is the level of invention, which is the domain of the *amusnaw*, who is capable not only of putting the accepted code into practice but of adapting it, modifying it, even 'revolutionizing' it (as with the case of the two Mohands), infringing it, breaking with it – this break still being in the spirit of the ancestral *tamusni*, because betraying the outward apparatus of *tamusni* means being more deeply faithful to it. This is not always without its risks, and sometimes disasters; a well-known proverb says: '*Tamusni* is anguish – *tamusni d aġilif.*'

PB: So *tamusni* is the capacity to tell the group what it is according to the tradition it has given itself, by a kind of definition through conceptual construction that tells it at the same time what it is and what it has to be in order to be truly itself; and this in real time, on the spot, at the very moment it is needed, after a defeat or before a battle, and at any moment, which means that the *amusnaw* is always put to the test, always in the breach. So *tamusni* is also an art of improvising, in contact with the situation or with an audience. How does this contact with the audience, its responses and its approval, mark the poetry itself? Are there not cases when it all hangs on an unfortunate word, and the poet has to take care to say the word that is needed, to say what is needed?

Is there not also a theatricalization designed to give the words their full force by accenting the extraordinary character of the discourse and of the person delivering it?

The Universal in the Singular

MM: In the case of the poet, the relationship to the audience is immediate, with no intermediary; the audience are there, the poet likewise, in flesh and blood, they are face to face. And so there is immediate production and immediate reception. I believe that this makes a contribution to preventing any creation for creation's sake, a quest that is autonomous and purely formal.

PB: Does this mean that the appearances that can give the impression of a formal quest, obscurities and archaisms that evoke the most elaborate forms of poetry, are actually deceptive? It would be equally wrong to read this poetry as something by Mallarmé or to see it simply as a 'primitive' form of poetic expression.

MM: We can return to the example that I cited just now, that of the apprentice poet who seeks out the master and asks to be initiated. The six-line poem that the master addresses to him – immediately, in response – is bound up with the purely fortuitous occasion that gave rise to it. What is specific to the poet is to give an exemplary response, that is, to give a universal response in relation to a particular case; to take a particular problem, born from a particular situation, to a universal level. But the fact that this universal response was produced in relation to a very precise event is just what confers on it a reality that distinguishes it from a mere intellectual concern, internal to a certain milieu.

PB: The poet is the person able to universalize the particular and particularize the universal. He is able to respond to a particular situation and a particular audience, and in this way assure the symbolic effectiveness of his message. You brought up just now the preliminary acquaintance that the poet must have with his audience if his words are to 'take', to be *effective*.

The Enigma of the World

MM: The relationship between audience and poet is such that a poetic performance may actually be a kind of play for two characters, the poet and his audience. The poet is not alone in his creating. I believe he is impelled by his audience, by a kind of call from his audience to which he responds. To give an example: one day, a poet, the man I was telling you about just now, Yusef-u-Kaci, came to the tribe and praised the villages that had originally made up the tribe, though they had since been joined by three others conquered in war, He ended his poem, and the hearers sensed that it was reaching its conclusion. Someone came up to him, leaving the circle surrounding the poet, and said: 'Dada Yusef, that's all very well, but I think you are coming to an end. Be careful, we are not alone now, are there others?' The poet was on a mat, he had a triangular tambourine in his hands which he would strike lightly, he turned around on the mat and segued into an improvised praise for the three other villages. The audience admired this. In this case, we can say that half of Yusef's poem was dictated by his hearers. Another time, a different poet went to a village and noticed that while he was reciting, his audience were distracted and whispering. He stopped and gave them an ad hoc poem, the conclusion to which has become a proverb: 'I sing and the river carries away – *kkateg iteddem wassif'* (Aali Aamruc, first half of the nineteenth century). Here again, the poet drew something universal from a small fact.

PB: Even when he does not completely invent, as in the cases you've mentioned, the *amusnaw* always does the work of invention needed to adapt the poem to the situation. In fact, as creation is the unique application of generative patterns that are traditional and thus common, each production is at the same time both tradition (at the generative level) and unique (at the level of performance). In the limiting case, as long as there is no fixed text, no discourse fixed once and for all, there are as many variants as there are different situations of production, and thus adjustments to both the situation and the audience.

MM: As regards adjustment to the audience, I transcribed a long poem that dates from the early years of the French occupation, the years 1856–7, just before the French entered Kabylia. The Kabyles made a first attack but this was not sufficiently well prepared, and it finished indecisively around Drâa-el-Mizan. In front of the fighters who had just returned, a poet (the same one I was telling you about just now, who was seen as the master of his time) improvised a short poem that was well received and that he went on to develop further. He cited the names of the tribes, villages and men who had particularly distinguished themselves in combat. This appealed to the tribes that had actually taken part in the battle. But the poet went and gave the poem in different places. And I have found three versions of the same poem, with the names of the tribes, villages or individuals being changed.

PB: Did you collect these orally?

MM: I collected two orally and one in writing. The one I found in writing was in a notebook in which a teacher who had heard it orally had copied it. There are some interesting accommodations: for example, there was one village that did not want to take part in this war, which it saw as lost in advance. It was hard to include a fact of this particular kind, but the poet managed to find . . . certain arrangements . . .

PB: But was it the poet himself who invented the variants, or the people who themselves did the work in order to appropriate it?

MM: I'm unable to say. But I think it was him, or perhaps both sides at once. But he must have made at least one of the two modifications: I know that one of the variants was collected from the poet's own words. The other may be a re-creation by people from the place who liked the verses and arranged them so that they could apply them to themselves.

PB: But these adaptations and accommodations are favoured by the poem's *polysemy*, which means that the same discourse, with a double (or triple) meaning, may be understood in different ways depending on the audience. We just saw an example of this when the two *imusnawen* spoke in a way above the heads of their audience.

MM: One of the names of poetry in Kabyle (it's a little different in other Berber dialects) is *asefru* (plural: *isefra*), which comes from *fru*, to elucidate, make clear, something that is obscure. I think this is a very old meaning. In Latin, a poem is *carmen*, which I believe meant a spell, an effective formula that opens doors. This is the exact sense of *asefru*, and perhaps the convergence is not accidental, with these Mediterraneans for whom the word is above all an instrument of elucidation, what makes things permeable to our reason.

PB: Doesn't *fru* also mean winnowing the grain? So the poet would be the person able to distinguish and make distinct, who by his *discernment* anticipates a *diacrisis*, separating things that are ordinarily confused?

MM: The person who elucidates obscure things. One of
Yusef-u-Kaci's poems begins as follows:

Bismilleh	In the name of God, I shall
annebdu lḥaṣun	begin
a lḥadeq ṯhessis	Men of wisdom, listen to me,
kkateǧ lmaani	I sing parables, artfully
s-eṛṛzun	I arouse the people
sakwǧey lǧis	I give examples and enlighten them,
	My discourse contains a lesson and
	I arouse the people; you could say:
	I mobilize the people (*djis* is the army,
	the people who fight).
	The poet is the man who mobilizes the people;
	He is the one who enlightens them.
Ad awen-d	I shall make things as distinct to you
berrzeǧ lumuṛ	
am-m idrimen	As the coins in a purse,
di sselfa,	said the most prestigious among them.

A Reflexive Definition of Anthropology

Participant Objectivation

I do not need to tell you how happy and proud I am to receive a mark of scientific recognition as prestigious as the Huxley Medal and to enter into this kind of pantheon of anthropology that the roster of previous recipients constitutes. Drawing on the authority that you hereby bestow upon me, I would like, in the manner of an old sorcerer passing on his secrets, to offer a technique, a method, or, more modestly, a 'device' that has helped me immensely throughout my experience as a researcher: what I call 'participant objectivation'. I do mean participant 'objectivation' and not 'observation', as one says customarily. Participant observation, as I understand it, designates the conduct of an ethnologist who immerses herself or himself in a foreign social universe so as to observe an activity, a ritual, or a ceremony while, ideally, taking part in it. The inherent difficulty of such a posture has often been noted, which presupposes a kind of doubling of consciousness that is arduous to sustain. How can one be both subject and object, the one who acts and the one who, as it were, watches himself acting? What is certain is that one is right to cast doubt on the possibility of truly participating in foreign practices, embedded as they are in the tradition of another society and, as such, presupposing a learning process different from the one of which the observer and her dispositions are the product; and therefore a quite different manner of being and living through the experiences in which she purports to participate.

By 'participant objectivation', I mean the *objectivation of the subject of objectivation*, of the analysing subject – in short, of the researcher herself. One might be misled into believing that I am referring here to the practice, made fashionable over a decade ago by certain anthropologists, especially on the other side of the Atlantic, which consists in observing oneself observing, observing the observer in his work of observing or of transcribing his observations, through a return on fieldwork, on the relationship with his informants and, last but not least, on the narrative of all these experiences which lead, more often than not, to the rather disheartening conclusion that all is in the final analysis nothing but discourse, text, or, worse yet, pretext for text.

It will quickly be clear that I have little sympathy with what Clifford Geertz calls, after Roland Barthes, 'the diary disease',[1] an explosion of narcissism' sometimes verging on exhibitionism, which came in the wake of, and in reaction to, long years of positivist repression. For reflexivity as I conceive it does not have much in common with 'textual reflexivity' and with all the falsely sophisticated considerations on the 'hermeneutic process of cultural interpretation' and the construction of reality through ethnographic recording. Indeed, it stands opposed at every point to the naive observation of the observer which, in Marcus and Fisher, or Rosaldo, or even Geertz, tends to substitute the facile delights of self-exploration for the methodical confrontation with the gritty realities of the field.[2] This pseudo-radical denunciation of ethnographic writing as 'poetics and politics', to borrow the title of Clifford and Marcus's edited volume on the topic, inevitably leads to the 'interpretive scepticism' to which Woolgar refers and nearly manages to bring the anthropological enterprise to a grinding halt (Gupta and Ferguson).[3] But it does not suffice either to explicate the 'lived experience' of the knowing subject, that is, the biographical particularities of the researcher or the Zeitgeist that inspires his work (as Alving Gouldner famously did in his dissection of Parsons in The Coming Crisis of Western Sociology[4]) or to uncover the folk theories that agents invest in their practices, as the ethnomethodologists do. For science cannot be reduced to the recording and analysis of the 'pre-notions' (in Durkheim's sense) that social agents engage in the construction of social reality; it must also encompass the social conditions of the production of these pre-constructions and of the social agents who produce them.

In short, one does not have to choose between participant observation, a necessarily fictitious immersion in a foreign milieu, and the objectivism of the 'gaze from afar' of an observer who remains as remote from himself as from his object. Participant objectivation undertakes to explore not the 'lived experience' of the knowing subject but the social conditions of possibility – and therefore the effects and limits – of that experience and, more precisely, of the act of objectivation itself. It aims at objectivizing the subjective relation to the object which, far from leading to a relativistic and more-or-less anti-scientific subjectivism, is one of the conditions of genuine scientific objectivity.[5]

What needs to be objectivized, then, is not the anthropologist performing the anthropological analysis of a foreign world but the social world that has made both the anthropologist and the conscious or unconscious anthropology that she (or he) engages in her anthropological practice – not only her social origins, her position and trajectory in social space, her social and religious memberships and beliefs, gender, age, nationality, etc., but also, and most importantly, her particular position within the microcosm of anthropologists. It is indeed scientifically attested that her most decisive scientific choices (of topic, method, theory, etc.) depend very closely on the location she (or he) occupies within her professional universe, what I call the 'anthropological field', with its national traditions and peculiarities, its habits of thought, its mandatory problematics, its shared beliefs and commonplaces, its rituals, values, and consecrations, its constraints in matters of publication of findings, its specific censorships, and, by the same token, the biases embedded in the organizational structure of the discipline, that is, in the collective history of the specialism, and all the unconscious presuppositions built into the (national) categories of scholarly understanding.

The properties brought to light by this reflexive analysis, opposed in every respect to a self-indulgent, intimist return to the singular, private person of the anthropologist, have nothing singular and still less anything extraordinary about them. As they are, in good measure, common to entire categories of researchers (such as graduates of the same school or from this or that university), they are not very 'exciting' to naive curiosity. (Here one can echo Wittgenstein in the *Philosophical Investigations*: 'What we are supplying are really remarks on the natural history of human beings; we are not contributing curiosities however, but observations which no one has doubted, but which have escaped remark only because they are always before our eyes.')[6] And, above all, the fact of discovering these properties and making them public often appears as a sacrilegious transgression inasmuch as it calls into question the charismatic representation that cultural producers have of themselves and their propensity to see themselves as free of all cultural determinations.

That is why *Homo Academicus* is arguably the most controversial, the most 'scandalous' of the books I have written, despite its extreme concern for objectivity.[7] For it objectivizes those who ordinarily objectivize; it unveils and divulges, through a transgression that takes on the air of treason, the objective structures of a social microcosm to which the researcher himself belongs, that is, the structures of the space of positions that determine the academic and political stances of the Parisian academics. Those are the hidden structures that, for example, at the time of this survey, oppose Roland Barthes to Raymond Picard and, through their persons, a 'literary semiology' perceived as avant-garde and a traditional literary history in the style of Lanson on the defensive. One can take the violence of participant objectivation even further, as did one of my students, Charles Soulié (1995), who showed that research topics (masters theses and subjects of doctoral dissertations) in philosophy and sociology (the same would apply to anthropology) are statistically linked to social origins and trajectory, gender, and above all to educational trajectory.[8] This means that our seemingly most personal, most intimate, and therefore most cherished choices, namely, our choice of discipline and topics (for example, economic anthropology versus the study of kinship, Africa as against eastern Europe), our theoretical and methodological orientations, find their principle in socially constituted dispositions in which banally social, sadly impersonal properties still express themselves in a more or less transfigured form.

It will have been noted that, in speaking of participant objectivation, I have moved, without seeming to do so, from anthropology to sociology, and, more precisely, to the sociology of the academic institution as I practised it in *Homo Academicus*. I hardly need say that the French university is, in this case, only the *apparent object*, and that what really has to be grasped there is the subject of objectivation (in this instance myself), his position in that relatively autonomous social space that is the academic world, endowed with its own rules, irreducible to those of the surrounding world, and his singular point of view. But one too often forgets or ignores that a point of view is, strictly, nothing other than a view taken from a point which cannot reveal itself as such, cannot disclose its truth as point of view, a particular and ultimately unique point of view, irreducible to others, unless one is capable, paradoxically, of reconstructing the space, understood as the set of coexisting points (as P. F. Strawson might put it) in which it is inserted.

To give a better sense of what is unusual, under its appearances of banality, about the overturning that consists in taking a point of view on one's own point of view and, thereby, on the whole set of points of view in relation to which it defines itself as such, I would like to call to mind the novel by David Garnett, *A Man in the Zoo*, of which I have often thought with respect to the approach I adopted in *Homo*

Academicus. It tells the story of a young man who quarrels with his girlfriend during a visit to a zoo and, in despair, writes to the director of the zoo to offer him a mammal missing from his collection, man – himself. He is then put in a cage, next to the chimpanzee, with a sign saying: 'Homo sapiens MAN. This specimen, born in Scotland, was presented to the Society by John Cromartie, Esq. Visitors are requested not to irritate the Man by personal remarks.'[9] I should have put a similar warning at the front of *Homo Academicus* to avoid at least some of the 'personal remarks', not always very kind, that it earned me.

The reflexivity fostered by participant objectivation is not at all the same as that ordinarily advocated and practised by 'postmodern' anthropologists or even philosophy and some forms of phenomenology. It applies to the knowing subject the most brutally objectivist tools that anthropology and sociology provide, in particular statistical analysis (usually excluded from the arsenal of anthropological weapons), and aims, as I indicated earlier, to grasp everything that the thinking of the anthropologist (or sociologist) may owe to the fact that she (or he) is inserted in a national scientific field, with its traditions, habits of thought, problematics, shared commonplaces, and so on, and to the fact that she occupies in it a particular position (newcomer who has to prove herself versus consecrated master, etc.), with 'interests' of a particular kind which unconsciously orientate her scientific choices (of discipline, method, object, etc.).

In short, scientific objectivation is not complete unless it includes the point of view of the objectivizer and the interests he may have in objectivation (especially when he objectivizes his own universe) but also the historical unconscious that he inevitably engages in his work. By historical, and more precisely academic, unconscious (or 'transcendental'), I mean the set of cognitive structures which can be attributed to specifically educational experiences and which is therefore to a large extent common to all the products of the same (national) educational system or, in a more specified form, to all the members of the same discipline at a given time. It is what explains why, beyond differences linked in particular to the disciplines, and in spite of the competition between them, the products of a national education system present a set of common dispositions, often attributed to 'national character', which means that they can understand each other with a nod and a wink, and that, for them, many things go without saying which are crucial, such as what, at a given moment, does or does not deserve discussion, what is important and interesting (a 'beautiful subject' or, or the contrary, a 'banal' idea or 'trivial' theme).

To take as one's project the exploration of this academic unconscious (or transcendental) is nothing other than turning anthropology
against itself, as it were, and engaging the most remarkable theoretical and methodological discoveries of anthropology in the reflexive
analysis of the anthropologists themselves. I have always regretted
that those responsible for the most extraordinary advances of cognitive anthropology – I think of Durkheim and Mauss analysing 'primitive forms of classification' or of Lévi-Strauss dismantling the workings
of the 'savage mind' – never applied (with the partial exception of
Durkheim's *The Evolution of Educational Thought*, and scattered
programmatic remarks by Maurice Halbwachs) to their own universe
some of the scientific insights that they provided about societies
remote in space and time.[10] Since I have mentioned Durkheim and
Mauss, I take the opportunity to recall that they explicitly aimed to
implement in their research the Kantian programme of knowledge
which I myself evoke when speaking of the 'academic transcendental'.
This reminder seems to me all the more necessary when, among the
many obstacles to understanding between 'continental' anthropologists and sociologists and their English-speaking colleagues, one of
the most daunting seems to me to be, on this precise point, the gulf
between the research 'programmes' that each side owes to its immersion in very profoundly different academic and philosophic traditions
and to the different academic transcendentals to which they are each
unknowingly wedded.

It is such a programme of *reflexive cognitive anthropology* that I
endeavoured to carry out when I sought, for example, to objectivize
the 'categories of professorial understanding' (in its contemporary
French form), based on a corpus made up of cards on which a teacher
of French at an elite school had recorded the grades and assessments
awarded over the course of a school year to the whole set of his pupils
characterized by their age, sex, and occupation of their parents.[11]
Thanks to a technique adapted from graphical semiology, I uncovered
the unconscious classificatory schemata, or principles of vision and
division, that French teachers (but no doubt also British teachers, or
those of any other advanced country) unwittingly implement in their
operations of categorization and evaluation, proceeding no differently than the 'natives' of Africa or the Pacific islands do when they
classify plants or diseases. This was based on the hypothesis that
classificatory schemata analogous to the forms of classification or the
cognitive structures which (as Durkheim, Mauss, and Lévi-Strauss
showed) organize 'primitive' or 'savage' thought are also present, in
just as unconscious a state, in scholarly thought, so that, short of
exercising special vigilance, anthropologists and sociologists them-

selves implement them in many of their everyday judgements – especially in matters of aesthetics where, as Wittgenstein pointed out, judgements are often reduced to adjectives, or in matters of gastronomy, and even about their colleagues' work or the colleagues themselves (I think here in particular of oppositions such as 'brilliant' versus 'rigorous', superficial versus deep, heavy versus light, and so on). And it is likely that you will resort to similar classificatory dichotomies to perceive and appreciate, positively or negatively, what I am saying to you at this very moment.

It begins to become clear, or so I hope, that objectivation of the subject of objectivation is neither a mere narcissistic entertainment, nor a pure effect of some kind of wholly gratuitous epistemological point of honour, in that it exerts very real scientific effects. This is not only because it can lead one to discover all kinds of 'perversions' linked to the position occupied in scientific space, such as those spurious theoretical breaks, more or less conspicuously proclaimed, in which some young anthropologists eager to make a name for themselves indulge periodically (especially when they catch the latest strain of what my friend E. P. Thompson acerbically called 'the French flu'); or that kind of fossilization of research and even thought that can ensue from enclosure in a scholarly tradition perpetuated by the logic of academic reproduction. More profoundly, it enables us also to subject to constant critical vigilance all those 'first movements' (as the Stoics put it) of thought through which the unthought associated with an epoch, a society, a given state of a (national) anthropological field smuggle themselves into the work of thought, and against which warnings against ethnocentrism hardly give sufficient protection. I am thinking in particular of what might be called 'Lévy-Bruhl's mistake', which consists in creating an insurmountable distance between the anthropologist and those he takes as object, between his thought and 'primitive thought', for lack of having gained the necessary distance from his own native thought and practice by objectifying them.

The anthropologist who does not know himself, who does not have an adequate knowledge of his own primary experience of the world, puts the primitive at a distance because he does not recognize the primitive, pre-logical thought within himself. Locked in a scholastic, and thus intellectualist, vision of his own practice, he cannot recognize the *universal logu of practice* in modes of thought and action (such as magical ones) that he describes as pre-logical or primitive. In addition to all the instances of misunderstandings of the logic of practices I analyse in *Outline of a Theory of Practice*,[12] I could invoke here Ludwig Wittgenstein who suggests, in his 'Remarks on *The Golden Bough*' that it is because Frazer does not know himself that he is unable to recognize in such so-called 'primitive' behaviour the equivalent of the behaviours in which he (like all of us) indulges in similar circumstances:

> When I am furious about something, I sometimes beat the ground or a tree with my walking stick. But I certainly do not believe that the ground is to blame or that my beating can help anything. 'I am venting my anger.' And all rites are of this kind. Such actions may be called Instinct-actions. And an historical explanation, say, that I or my ancestors previously believed that beating the ground does help is shadow-boxing, for it is a superfluous assumption that explains *nothing*. The similarity of the action to an act of punishment is important, but nothing more than this similarity can be asserted.
>
> Once such a phenomenon is brought into connection with an instinct which I myself possess, this is precisely the explanation wished for; that is, the explanation which resolves this particular difficulty. And a further investigation about the history of my instinct moves on another track.[13]

Wittgenstein is closer to the truth still when, referring again, but this time tacitly, to his own personal experience – which he assumes to be shared by his reader – he mentions some so-called primitive behaviours which, like our own in similar circumstances, might have no purpose other than themselves or the 'Satisfaction' gained in performing them:

> Burning in effigy. Kissing the picture of one's beloved. That is *obviously not* based on the belief that it will have some specific effect on the object which the picture represents. It aims at satisfaction and it achieves it. Or rather: it *aims* at nothing at all; we just behave this way and then we feel satisfied.[14]

One only has to have once performed these psychologically necessary and totally desperate acts that one accomplishes on the grave of a beloved one to know that Wittgenstein is right to repudiate the very question of the function and even of the meaning and intention of certain ritual or religious acts. And he is also right to say that 'Frazer is more "savage" than most of his savages' because, lacking an 'inward knowledge' of his own spiritual experience, Frazer does not understand that he understands nothing about the spiritual experiences that he obstinately attempts to understand. And, lastly, from among a thousand, I will quote this remark of Wittgenstein about the custom of 'shav[ing] the whole bodies of persons charged with sorcery':

There is no doubt whatever that a mutilation which makes us appear unworthy or ridiculous in our own eyes can completely deprive us of the will to defend ourselves. How embarrassed we sometimes become – or at least many people – by our physical or aesthetic inferiority.[15]

This discreet reference to the singular, private self of the analyst is poles apart from certain narcissistic confessions of the apostles of postmodern reflexivity and it has the merit of breaking through the screen of false explanations projected by the anthropologist who ignores himself, as well as bringing foreign experiences closer by allowing us to grasp what is at once familiar and profound about them.

It follows that, while the critique of ethnocentrism (or anachronism) is, at a first level, legitimate to warn against and ward off the uncontrolled projection of the knowing subject onto the object of knowledge, it can, at another level, prevent the anthropologist (as well as the sociologist or the historian) from making rational use of his native – but previously objectivated – experience in order to understand and analyse other people's experiences. Nothing is more false, in my view, than the maxim almost universally accepted in the social sciences according to which the researcher must put nothing of himself into his research.[16] He should on the contrary refer continually to his own experience but not, as is too often the case, even among the best researchers, in a guilty, unconscious, or uncontrolled manner. Whether I want to understand a woman from Kabylia or a peasant from Béarn, a Turkish migrant worker or a German office worker, a schoolteacher or a businesman, or a writer like Flaubert, a painter like Manet, a philosopher like Heidegger, the most difficult thing, paradoxically, is never to forget that they are all people like me, at least inasmuch as they do not stand before their action – performing an agrarian rite, following a funeral procession, negotiating a contract, taking part in a literary ceremony, painting a picture, giving a conference, attending a birthday party – in the posture of an observer; and that one can say about them that, strictly speaking, they do not know what they are doing (at least in the sense in which I, as observer and analyst, am trying to know it). They do not have in their heads the scientific truth of their practice which I am trying to extract from observation of their practice. What is more, they normally never ask themselves the questions that I would ask myself if I acted towards them as an anthropologist: Why such a ceremony? Why the candles? Why the cake? Why the presents? Why these invitations and these guests, and not others? And so on.

The most difficult thing, then, is not so much to understand them (which in itself is not simple) as it is to avoid forgetting what I know perfectly well besides, but only *in a practical mode*, namely, that they do not at all have the project of understanding and explaining which is mine as researcher; and, consequently, to avoid putting into their heads, as it were, the problematic that I construct about them and the theory that I elaborate to answer it. Thus, just as the Frazerian anthropologist will institute an insurmountable distance between his experience and that of his object, for lack of knowing how to appropriate the truth of his ordinary experience of his own ordinary and extraordinary practices by putting himself at a distance from himself, the sociologist and the economist who are incapable of mastering their pre-reflexive experience of the world will inject scholarly thought (incarnated by the myth of *homo economicus* and 'rational action theory') into the behaviours of ordinary agents, because they do not know how to break with the unthought presuppositions of thinking thought, in other words to rid themselves of their inbred *scholastic bias*.[17]

Keeping firmly in mind the irreducible specificity of the logic of practice, we must avoid depriving ourselves of that quite irreplaceable scientific resource that is *social experience previously subjected to sociological critique*. I realized very early on that, in my fieldwork in Kabylia, I was constantly drawing on my experience of the Béarn society of my childhood, both to understand the practices that I was observing and to defend myself against the interpretations that I spontaneously formed of them or that my informants gave me.[18] Thus, for example, faced with an informant who, when I questioned him about the divisions of his group, enumerated various terms designating more or less extended units, I wondered whether one or other of these 'social units' – *adhrum, thakharrubth*, and so forth – that he mentioned had any more 'reality' than the unit called *lou besiat*, the set of neighbours, that the Béarnais sometimes invoke and upon which some French ethnologists had conferred scientifically recognized status. I had the intuition, confirmed time and again by my subsequent research, that the *besiat* was nothing more than an occasional entity, as it were, a 'virtual' grouping which became 'effective', existent, and active only under certain very precise circumstances, such as the transport of the body of the deceased during a funeral, to define the participants and their respective rank in such circumstantial action.

That is only one of a great many cases in which I drew on my native knowledge to defend myself against the 'folk theories' of my informants or of the anthropological tradition. Indeed, it was to carry out a critique of those spontaneous instruments of critique that I undertook, in the 1960s, at the same time as I was doing my Kabyle research, to do a first-hand study of Béarn society, which, my intuition told me, presented many analogies with the agrarian society of Kabylia in spite of obvious differences. In this case, as in my study of the academic staff of the University of Paris reported in *Homo Academicus*, the real object, partly hidden behind the declared and visible object, was the subject of objectivation and even, to be more precise, the effects of knowledge of the objectivating posture, that is, the transformation undergone by the experience of the social world (in the case at hand, a universe in which all the people were personally close to me so that I knew, without having to ask, all their personal and collective history) when one ceases to 'live' it simply and instead takes it as object. This first deliberate and methodical exercise in reflexivity was the starting-point for an endless to-and-fro between the reflexive phase of objectivation of primary experience and the active phase of investment of this experience thus objectified and criticized in acts of objectivation ever more remote from that experience. It was in this twofold movement that a scientific subject was progressively constructed, being at once an 'anthropological eye' capable of grasping invisible relationships, and a (practical) mastery of the self based, among other things, on the gradual discovery of the multifarious effects of the 'scholastic bias' to which John Austin makes passing reference.[19]

I am aware that all this may appear to you both very abstract and also perhaps rather arrogant. (There seems to be something a bit delirious in experiencing the progress that one has made, throughout a lifetime of research, as a kind of slow initiatory pathway. Yet I am convinced that one knows the world better and better as one knows oneself better, that scientific knowledge and knowledge of oneself and of one's own social unconscious advance hand in hand, and that primary experience transformed in and through scientific practice transforms scientific practice and conversely.) But I am referring in fact to very mundane and concrete experiences of which I shall now give a few examples. One day, while working on a study of male celibacy in Béarn which had been triggered by a conversation with a childhood friend about a class photograph in which I appeared,[20] at a time when I was trying to construct a formal model of matrimonial exchanges (this was the heyday of Lévi-Straussian structuralism), I was chatting with a person who had been one of my most faithful and most intelligent informants – she happened to be my mother. I was not thinking about my study, but I must have been vaguely preoccupied with it, when she said to me in passing, about a family in the village: 'Oh, you know, they've become very *kith and kin (très parents)* with the So-and-sos [another family in the village] now that there's a *polytechnicien*[21] in the family.' That remark was the starting-point for the reflection that led me to rethink marriage no longer in terms of the logic of the rule (whose inadequacy I had already realized in the case of Kabylia) but, against the then-reigning structuralist orthodoxy, as a strategy orientated by specific interests, such as the pursuit of the conservation or expansion of economic capital, through the linking of the estates of the families thus allied, and of social capital and symbolic capital, through the extent and quality of the 'connections' secured by the marriage.[22]

But it was my whole way of conceiving the existence of groups – clans, tribes, regions, classes, or nations – which gradually came to be completely transformed in the process:[23] instead of 'real' entities, clearly demarcated in reality and in ethnographic description, or genealogical sets defined *on paper* according to strictly genealogical criteria, they appeared to me as social constructions, more or less artificial artefacts, maintained by sustained exchanges and by a whole material and symbolic labour of 'group making' often delegated to women (here is an example of the to-and-fro movement to which I was alluding a moment ago: I am thinking of the work of an American anthropologist, Michaela di Leonardo,[24] who showed that women nowadays in the United States are great users of the telephone – which earns them the reputation of being garrulous – because they are entrusted with maintaining kinship relationships, not only with their own family but also with their husband's). And I could show similarly how my analysis of the Béarn house as estate and household, and all the strategies whereby it asserts and defends itself over and against rival 'houses', enabled me to understand, in what I think is an innovative way, what was then called 'the king's house' and how, before the gradual invention of the specific logic called *raison d'état*, the logic of the rational bureaucratic state, royal 'houses' could, to conserve or increase their estate, resort to reproduction strategies quite equivalent, both in principle and implementation, to those practised by Béarn 'houses' and their 'household heads'.[25]

I have spoken of honour and, given more time, I might have tried to recall before you the protracted labour of empirical observation, analysis, and theoretical reflection that led me from the ordinary notion of honour – the object of my very first anthropological enquiries, which I presented to those who accompanied and protected my entrance into the profession, Julian Pitt-Rivers, Julio Caro Baroja and John G. Peristiany – to the concept of symbolic capital, which is extremely useful, even indispensable in my view, for analysing the most characteristic phenomena of the economy of symbolic goods which perpetuates itself within the most modern economy, such as, to give just one illustration, the very special policy of symbolic investment practised by major firms and foundations and related forms of sponsoring. But I would like to give you rapidly another example of a particularly fruitful to-and-fro: having discovered in Virginia Woolf's *To the Lighthouse*[26] mythological structures that I would not have noticed had my eye not been sharpened by familiarity with the Kabyle (and more generally Mediterranean) vision of the division of labour between the sexes, I was able, thanks to the extraordinarily subtle analysis that Virginia Woolf develops in that novel of how the dominant masculine is dominated by his domination, to discover in return the limits of the lucidity of an anthropologist who had not managed fully to turn anthropology against itself. I was helped in particular by Woolf's supremely cruel yet delicate evocation of the *libido academica*, one of the specific forms taken by the follies of masculinity, which could and should have figured in a less coldly objectivist version of *Homo Academicus*, that is, one that would have been less distant from the object and subject of objectivation.

A last example of the controlled use of anthropology (which, it should be clear by now, is radically opposed to the wild use that some anthropologists in want of exotic locations now make, especially in France, of ethnological analogies): starting from a redefinition of 'rites of passage' as *rites of institution,* I was able to detect and dissect one of the functions of the French 'elite schools' which remain the most well hidden (in particular by their function of training and selection), namely, that they *consecrate* those entrusted to them, assigning to them a *superior essence* by instituting them as separate and distinguished from common humanity by an uncrossable frontier.[27] But, more broadly, I was able to understand more intimately and, it seems to me, more profoundly, a whole set of rites of the academic tradition, which have the function and effect of giving the solemn sanction of the assembled collectivity to the new birth that the collectivity at once performs and demands – think of the 'commencement' and graduation ceremonies of British and American universities, which solemnly mark the end of a long preparatory initiation and ratify by an official act the slow transmutation that has been operated in and by the expectation of consecration; or inaugural lectures, or even, if you allow me to say so, a rite of aggregation to the invisible college of canonized anthropologists such as I am now performing before you and with you.

I would like to close by discussing another effect of reflexivity, more personal but of great importance, in my view, for the progress of scientific research which, I have gradually come to think – as if in spite of myself and contrary to the principles of my primary vision of the world – has something of an initiatory search about it. Each of us, and this is no secret for anyone, is encumbered by a past, his or her own past, and this social past, whatever it is – 'working class' or 'bourgeois', masculine or feminine, and always closely enmeshed with the past that psychoanalysis explores – is particularly burdensome and obtrusive when one is engaged in social science. I have said, against the methodological orthodoxy sheltered under the authority of Max Weber and his principle of 'axiological neutrality' *(Wertfreiheit)*, that I believe that the researcher can and must mobilize his experience, that is, this past, in all his acts of research. But he is entitled to do so only on condition that he submits all these returns of the past to rigorous scientific examination. For what has to be questioned is not only this reactivated past but one's entire relation to this past which, when it acts outside of the controls of consciousness, may be the source of a systematic distortion of evocation and thus of the memories evoked. Only a genuine socio-analysis of this relation, profoundly obscure to itself, can enable us to achieve the kind of reconciliation of the researcher with himself, and his social properties, that a liberating anamnesis produces.[28]

I know that I run the risk, once again, of appearing at once abstract and arrogant, whereas I have in mind a simple experiment that any researcher can, it seems to me, perform for herself or himself with very great scientific and also personal profit. The reflexive device that I set in motion by carrying out ethnographic research at about the same time in Kabylia and in Béarn, in a faraway colony and in my home village, had the effect of leading me to examine as an anthropologist – that is to say, with the inseparably scientific and ethical respect due to any object of study – my own milieu of origin, at once popular and provincial, 'backward', some would even say archaic, which I had been led (or pushed) to despise and to renounce, or, worse yet, to repress, in the phase of anxious (and even avid and over-eager) integration into the cultural centre. It was no doubt because I found myself in a position to train a professional eye, both understanding and objectivizing, upon the world of my origin that I was able to tear myself from the violence of an ambivalent relationship in which were mingled familiarity and distance, empathy and horror, nay disgust, without falling into the populist forbearance for a kind of imaginary 'people' in which intellectuals often indulge. And this *conversion of the whole person*, which goes far beyond all the requirements of the most demanding treatises on methodology, was at the basis of a theoretical conversion which enabled me to reappropriate the practical relation to the world more completely than through the still-too-distant analyses of phenomenology. This turnaround was not effected in a day, through a sudden illumination, and the many returns I made to my Béarn fieldwork – I carried out my study of male celibacy thrice over – were necessary both for technical and theoretical reasons but also because the labour of analysis was accompanied each time by a slow and difficult labour of self-analysis.[29]

So if I have always worked to reconcile anthropology and sociology, it is because I am profoundly convinced that this scientifically damaging division must be overthrown and abolished; but also, as you will have seen, because it was a way of exorcizing the painful schism, never entirely overcome, between two parts of myself, and the contradictions or tensions that it introduces into my scientific practice and perhaps into my whole life. I used to see a strategic 'coup', which greatly contributed to the social (or salon) success of Lévi-Strauss's *Structural Anthropology*,[30] in the fact that it replaced the French word *'ethnologie'*, presumably too narrow, with the word *'anthropologie'*, which, for an educated French reader, evokes both the profundity of the German *'Anthropologie'* and the modernity of the English 'anthropology'. But I can none the less not prevent myself from wishing to see the unity of the sciences of man asserted under the banner of an Anthropology designating, in all the languages of the world, what we understand today by ethnology and sociology.

Return to the Algerian Experience

For a Sociology of Sociologists

I want to try to pose a very general question – the question of the social conditions of possibility and the scientific functions of a social science of social science – in relation to a specific case, that of the social science of the colonized and decolonized countries. The improvised nature of what I have to say may imply a certain number of somewhat risky positions . . . It's a risk I have to take.

First question: you decided to talk here about the social history of social science, and so on. Now, does that have any interest? That's the type of question that people never ask. If we've met here to talk about it, that's because we think it's interesting. But to say we are interested in a problem is a euphemistic way of naming the fundamental fact that we have vital stakes in our scientific productions. Those interests are not directly economic or political; we experience them as disinterested. The distinguishing feature of intellectuals is that they have disinterested interests, that they have an interest in disinterestedness. We have an interest in the problems that seem to us to be interesting. That means that at a particular moment, a particular academic group – without any one person deciding it – defines a problem as interesting. A conference is held, journals are created, people write articles, books and reviews. That means that it's 'worthwhile' to write on that theme, it brings in profits, not so much in royalties (though that may count) as in the form of prestige, symbolic gratifications, and so on. All that is just a preamble to say that one should make it a rule never to embark on sociology, and especially the sociology of sociology, without first, or simultaneously, undertaking a self socio-analysis (in so far as that is ever completely possible).

What use is the sociology of science? What is the sociology of colonial science for? The subject of scientific discourse needs to be asked the same questions that are put to the object of that discourse. How and by what right can the researcher ask, about researchers of the past, questions that he does not put to himself (and vice versa)?

It is impossible to have a proper understanding of the stakes of the scientific games of the past unless one realizes that the past of science is a stake in present-day scientific struggles. Strategies of rehabilitation often mask strategies of symbolic *speculation*: if you manage to discredit the lineage at the end of which your intellectual adversary is situated, then the value of his shares collapses. That's really what people are saying when they say that Marxism or structuralism or structural Marxism are 'outmoded'. In a word, one needs to ask what interest people have in doing the sociology of sociology, or the sociology of other sociologists. For example, it would not be hard to show that the sociology of right-wing intellectuals is almost always done by left-wing intellectuals, and vice versa. These objectifications owe their partial truth to the fact that one has an interest in seeing the truth about one's opponents, seeing what determines them (right-wing intellectuals are generally materialists when explaining left-wing intellectuals). Except that what is never seen, because that would oblige the analyst to ask what he is doing there, what interest he has there, and so on, is the system of positions from which these antagonistic strategies are generated.

Unless it is assumed that the social history of social science has no other function than to give social science researchers reasons for existing, and that it needs no other justification, we have to ask whether it has any importance for today's scientific practice. Is the science of the social science of the past the precondition for the work that the social science of today has to perform? And, more precisely, is the social science of 'colonial' 'science' one of the preconditions for a genuine decolonization of the social science of a recently decolonized society? I would be tempted to accept that the past of social science is always one of the main obstacles to social science, and especially in the case which concerns us. As Durkheim said in *L'Évolution pédagogique en France*, the unconscious is the forgetting of history. I think that the unconscious of a discipline is its history; its unconscious is made up of its social conditions of production, masked and forgotten. The product, separated from its social conditions of production, changes its meaning and exerts an ideological effect. Knowing what one is doing when one does science – that's a simple definition of epistemology – presupposes knowing how the problems, tools, methods and concepts that one uses have been historically formed. (In that light, nothing is more urgent than to make a social history of the Marxist tradition, in order to resituate modes of thought or expression, which have been fixed and fetishized by the forgetting of history, in the historical context of their production and their successive uses.)

What the social history of 'colonial' 'science' could offer – from the only standpoint that seems to me to be of interest, namely the progress of the science of present-day Algerian society – would be a contribution to knowledge of the categories of thought through which we look at that society. The papers given this morning have shown that the colonizers, in a sense dominated by their domination, were the first victims of their own intellectual instruments; and those instruments can still 'trap' those who merely 'react' against them without understanding the social conditions of their work, since they can easily simply fall into the opposite errors and in any case will deprive themselves of the only information available on some objects. So, in order to understand what has been left to us – corpuses, data, theories – we have to make a sociological study of the social conditions of production of that object. What does that mean?

One cannot do a sociology of the social conditions of production of 'colonial' 'science' without first studying the appearance of a relatively autonomous scientific field and the social conditions of the autonomization of this field. A field is a universe in which the producers' characteristics are defined by their position in relations of production, the place they occupy in a particular space of objective relationships. Contrary to what is presupposed by the study of isolated individuals – for example, in literary history of the type 'the author and his works' – the most important properties of each producer are in the objective relationships with the others, that's to say, outside him, in the relationship of objective competition, etc.

We first need to determine what were the specific properties of the field in which the 'colonial' 'science' of people like Masqueray, Desparmet or Maunier produced its discourse on the colonial world, and how these properties varied at different times. In other words, we need to analyse the relationship this relatively autonomous scientific field had with, on the one hand, the colonial power, and, on the other, the central intellectual power, that's to say the metropolitan science of the day. There is indeed a *double dependence*, and one of them may cancel out the other. This relatively autonomous field seems to me to have been generally characterized (with exceptions such as Doutté, Maunier, etc.) by very strong dependence on the colonial power and very strong independence vis-à-vis the national (and international) scientific field. A whole set of properties of its 'scientific' production flow from this. Then one would have to analyse the variations in the relationship of this field with national and international science and with the local political field, and how these changes were translated in its production.

One of the important properties of a field lies in the fact that it implicitly defines 'unthinkable' things, things that are not even discussed. There's orthodoxy and heterodoxy, but there is also doxa, everything that goes without saying, and in particular the systems of classification determining what is judged interesting or uninteresting, the things that no one thinks worthy of being mentioned, because there is no *demand*. We talked about these self-evidences this morning, and Charles-André Julien described some intellectual contexts that are quite astonishing for us. What is most hidden is what everyone agrees about, agreeing so much that they don't even mention them, the things that are beyond question, that go without saying. That's just what historical documents are likely to mask most completely, because it doesn't occur to anyone to write out what is self-evident; and it is what informants don't say, or say only by omission, in their silences. It's important to wonder about these things that no one says, when one wants to do the social history of social science, if one wants to do something more than distribute praise and blame. It's not a question of setting oneself up as a judge, but of understanding why these people could not understand certain things, could not raise certain problems; of determining what are the social conditions of error – necessary error, inasmuch as it is the product of historical conditions, determinations. In the 'goes-without-saying' of a particular period, there is the *de jure* unthinkable (the politically unthinkable, for example), what is unnameable, taboo, the problems that cannot be dealt with – and also the *de facto* unthinkable, the things that the intellectual tools of the day do not make it possible to think. (And that's why error is not distributed on the basis of good or bad intentions, and why good intentions can make very bad sociology.)

This would lead one to pose quite differently the problem of the privileged relation to the object – native or external, 'sympathetic' or hostile, etc. – in which discussion of colonial sociology and the possibility of a decolonized sociology is normally trapped. I think that the question of the privileged viewpoint needs to be replaced by the question of scientific control of the relation to the object of science, which in my view is one of the fundamental conditions of the construction of a genuine object of science. Whatever object the sociologist or the historian chooses, this object, his way of constructing the object, raises the question not of the historian or sociologist as an individual subject, but of the objective relationship between the pertinent social characteristics of the sociologist and the social characteristics of the object. The objects of social science and the way they are treated always have an intelligible relationship with the researcher as he or she is sociologically defined, that is, by a certain social origin, a certain position within the university system, a certain discipline, etc. I think, for example, that one of the mediations through which the domination of the dominant values is exerted within the framework of science is the social hierarchy of the disciplines, which places philosophical theory at the top and geography right at the bottom (that's not a value judgement but an empirical observation – the social origin of students declines as one moves from philosophy to geography or from mathematics to geology). At every moment, there is a hierarchy of the objects of research and a hierarchy of the subjects of research (the researchers), which make a decisive contribution to the distribution of the objects among the subjects. No one ever says (or only rarely), 'Given who you are, you deserve this subject and not that one, this approach – "theoretical" or "empirical", "fundamental" or "applied" – rather than that one, this way – "brilliant" or "serious" – rather than that way of presenting the results.' Such reminders are quite superfluous, most of the time, because all one has to do is to give free rein to the internal censorships, which are simply internalized social and academic censorships ('I'm not a theorist', 'I can't write'). So nothing is less socially neutral than the relationship between subject and object.

The important thing is to be able to objectify one's relation to the object so that discourse on the object is not the simple projection of an unconscious relation to the object. Among the techniques that make this objectification possible, there is, of course, all the equipment of science; so long as it is understood that this equipment must itself be subjected to historical critique, because at every moment it is inherited from previous science.

To conclude, I will say that the problem of the outsider's or the native's privilege no doubt conceals a very real problem, which arises just as much whether one is analysing Kabyle rites, or what goes on in this room, or in a student demonstration, or in a car factory: it's the question of what it means to be an observer or an agent, in a word the question of what practice is.

Between Friends

I should like first of all to express the great emotion and gratitude that the friendly words I have heard here today have inspired in me. Words that are particularly delicate, since even if they struck me as rather too fulsome in their praise, they were never complacent. They rather expressed a complicity that I find touching and see as important, as it attests to those implicit exchanges on which a human society is built. Exchanges of trifles or almost trifles, but which make possible the building of lasting relationships not weakened by time. The kindness of our statements also contrasts with the harshness of those exchanges that are characteristic of the world of science, which, contrary to the Eden-like image that people generally have of it, is pervaded by confrontations that are often violent, not always fair, elegant or generous.

Allow me to offer you this presentation rather as a series of discontinuous reactions to the intellectual stimuli I have received. Jacques Revel, for example, mentioned an error that several French scholars fell into around the 1970s, even some of the greatest such as Michel Foucault. I have in mind the systematic opposition to institutions that marked the years after May 68, which I have called an 'anti-institutional mood'. I myself belong to a generation of intellectuals who were produced in order to occupy the summit of the university institution at the very moment that this institution was crumbling. An institution that has given you so much, but has also disappointed you so much, leads you quite naturally to adopt an extremely critical attitude towards it. If it promotes a certain lucidity, this anti-institutional mood does not predispose people to adopt a comprehending and scientific attitude.

At the request of Tassadit Yacine, and for the ears of young scholars who are here today, I would like to explain the socio-historical
context in which my work on Algeria developed. The procedure of
studying the characteristic intellectual problematic of an era, in order
to situate one's own work in its genuine context, is a very important
moment in the quest for *reflexivity*, one of the imperative conditions
for the practice of the social sciences. It is also the condition for a
better and fairer understanding of the work of one's forerunners.
Every scholar, in every age, takes as their point of departure what
was the point of arrival of their predecessors, but without always
seeing the path that they had to tread.

In the late 1950s and early 1960s, everything relating to the
study of North Africa was dominated by a tradition of Orientalism.
Social science of that time was hierarchized, with sociology proper
being reserved for the study of Europeans and Americans, ethnology
to so-called primitive peoples, and Orientalism to peoples of non-
European languages and religions. It is unnecessary to say here how
arbitrary and absurd this classification was. In this context, my own
work, dealing with Kabyle society, found itself in rather a strange
position, somewhere between Orientalism and ethnology . . .

As far as Orientalism is concerned, the view at this time was that
knowledge of the Arabic language was both a necessary and a sufficient condition for understanding this society. The Marçais family
offered the example in Algeria of Arabist scholars, lacking any specific training, who reigned over the Algiers faculty, distributing
research topics and representing what was called colonial ethnology.
The University of Algiers enjoyed quasi-autonomy intellectually in
relation to the faculties of metropolitan France, its hierarchies, modes
of local recruitment and reproduction all being to a certain degree
independent. There were Arabist or Berberist linguists who did a bit
of sociology, civil administrators, soldiers, geographers and historians
– some of whom, like Marcel Émerit, rescued something of the
honour of science. Émerit was actually hung in effigy by *pied-noir*
students, for the crime of establishing that the rate of educational
enrolment in Algeria had been far higher before 1830 than after, a
fact that seriously upset the colonial university establishment.

There were independent historians, such as André Nouschi, who
helped me a great deal, as well as Émile Dermenghem, who supplied
a tremendous introduction to the secrets of the bibliography. The
essential point, however, is that with very few exceptions, which I shall
come on to name, the link with the scientific mainstream (previously
very strong, with such people as Doutté, Montagne, Maunier, etc.,
and more recently Thérèse Rivière and Germaine Tillion) had been

broken. This was not just the case with those outside the university, for example the White Fathers, who did extremely useful linguistic and indirectly ethnographic work (Père Dallet, in particular), the Jesuits, military and civilian administrators, but also with academics in the Algiers faculty (such as Philippe Marçais, future OAS deputy, or Bousquet, author of a book on the Berbers in the 'Que sais-je?' series and admirer of Pareto, Yacono, etc.). Hence the importance of the work of people like Jacques Berque, which, though I later discovered its limitations, was an extraordinary guide for the young ethnologist/sociologist that I was at that time. I am thinking of course of his great book *Les Structures sociales dans le Haut Atlas*, the notes being full of extremely fertile indications about North African societies, the role of customary law, relations between Berber and Islamic traditions, etc., as well as his article in *Annales* called 'Cinquante ans de sociologie nord-africaine'; it was he who, with the advice of Émile Dermenghem, enabled me to find my bearings in the immense bibliography, very scattered and uneven, devoted to North African societies.

At this point in time, a number of Algerian intellectuals did ethnology in the form of fiction – what were called 'ethnographic novels'. This is a feature to be found in several colonized countries, the transition from literature to ethnography. We may naturally think here of Mouloud Feraoun, a schoolteacher who described the customs and traditions of the Kabyle mountains, and who read and annotated my first texts on Kabylia; also Malek Ouary or Mouloud Mammeri. This last, whom I later got to know well, taught me a great deal about the *imusnawen* (plural of *amusnaw*), custodians of an incomparable wisdom and poetic art.

The impulse that led to my choice to study Algerian society was civic rather than political. I think in fact that the French of that time, whether they were for or against Algerian independence, all had in common a very poor knowledge of the country, and equally poor reasons for being for or against. It was very important therefore to supply the elements for an adequate judgement and understanding, not only for the French but also for educated Algerians, who for historical reasons were also often ignorant about their own society. (Among the grievous effects of colonization can be mentioned the complicity of certain left-wing French intellectuals towards Algerian intellectuals, a complicity that led them to close their eyes to the ignorance of the latter about their own society. I am thinking particularly of Sartre and Fanon . . . This complicity had very serious effects when these intellectuals came to power after independence and showed their incompetence.) I thus presented a first critical balance-sheet of everything I had gained from my reading and observations in the book *Sociologie de l'Algérie*[1] in the 'Que sais-je?' series, using such theoretical instruments as were available to me at the time, that is, those supplied by the culturalist tradition, but reconsidered in a critical sense (for example with a distinction between the colonial situation as a relation of domination, and 'acculturation').

I steadily became involved in a more ambitious project of economic ethno-sociology. (The opposition between sociology and ethnology is one that I have always rejected.) In order to understand the logic of the transition from pre-capitalist to capitalist economy (which, though accomplished in Algeria under external constraint, was of a kind that could shed light, as I saw it, on the origins of capitalism and the debate between Weber, Sombart and various others, a subject I was passionate about), it was necessary to take into account on the one hand the specific logic of the pre-capitalist economy (with the problem of relationship to time, to calculation, to forecasting, etc., the problem of honour and symbolic capital, the specific problem of non-market exchange, and so on), and on the other hand the logic of changes in the economy and economic attitudes (as I did in *Travail et travailleurs en Algérie*[2] and *Le Déracinement*[3]), as well as that of the household economy (a study that I never published, though some of its conclusions were summed up in *Algeria 1960*).[4]

I also had in mind other problems that were more political. The political question that preoccupied the revolutionary intellectuals of that time was the choice between Chinese and Soviet models of development. In other words, the question to answer was whether the peasantry or the proletariat was the revolutionary class. I sought to translate these almost metaphysical questions into scientific terms. With this object, I organized my study according to INSEE guidelines, with sampling, a statistical questionnaire designed to assess the faculty of calculating, anticipating, saving, birth control, etc. These parameters were correlated in the same study with the capacity to undertake coherent revolutionary projects. It is here that I observed how the sub-proletariat swung between a great desire for change and a fatalistic resignation to the world as it is. This contradiction on the part of the sub-proletariat struck me as extremely important, as it led me to a rather reserved stance towards the revolutionary dreams of the leaders of the time. Unfortunately this was subsequently verified. Algeria as I saw it – and this was far from the 'revolutionary' image given by activist literature and writings of struggle – was made up of a vast peasantry that was sub-proletarianized, but not urbanized, of an immense and ambivalent sub-proletariat, of a proletariat that was basically established in France, of a petty bourgeoisie that was quite out of touch with the realities of Algerian society, and of an intelligentsia whose particular characteristic was a poor knowledge of its own society and a failure to understand anything of its ambiguities and complexities. For the Algerian peasants, like their Chinese counterparts, were far from how they were imagined by the intellectuals of the time. They were revolutionary, but at the same time they wanted to maintain traditional structures, as these gave a certain protection against the unknown. I was also very aware of the potential conflicts that would arise from the country's linguistic division, in particular that the opposition between Arabic and French speakers, only temporarily obscured by the unifying logic of anti-colonial struggle, was certain to find expression.

To be sure, this gave my scientific work a politically committed turn, but in no way would I go back on this orientation. A seemingly abstract analysis can make a contribution to solving political problems, even in their most burning form. Because I took up my position on a terrain that was not really occupied, either by ethnology or sociology (so that French ethnologists acted as if I did not exist), I was able to enter the traditional object of these disciplines from a new angle.

I should also mention here the work I conducted on the Kabyle peasants and those of Béarn. Why Béarn? In order to avoid falling into the error of the compassionate ethnologist, amazed by the human wealth of an unfairly despised population, etc., and place between myself and my informants the distance that familiarity permits. It has often happened to me, faced with a Kabyle informant, to wonder how a Béarn peasant would have reacted in a similar situation. In this way I could guard against both the distance of a cavalier, objectivist positivism, and that of immersion in the sympathy of subjectivist intuitionism.

It is certain that the exceptional, extraordinarily difficult (and risky) conditions in which I had to work were bound to make my gaze that much more sharp, by the constant vigilance they imposed. The quite practical problems that the mere conduct of the study constantly posed, forced a permanent reflection on the reasons and rationales of the study, the motivations and intentions of the researcher, and all the questions that positivist methodology spontaneously takes as settled.

It is perhaps because I have always combined analysis of Kabylia with analysis of Béarn, in a kind of enterprise of socio-analysis, that I was able to change the way of talking about Kabylia and make ethnology acceptable to the Kabyles, even those most recalcitrant and hostile to objectification, by helping to free the Kabyles from the alternative between colonial ethnology and the rejection of ethnology. The culmination of this work, as I see it, was the dialogues I had with Mouloud Mammeri, which were published, one in the first issue of *Awal*, the other in *Actes de la Recherche*, 'Dialogue on oral poetry in Kabylia'.[5] This text shows that there is no antinomy between the intention to rehabilitate, which inspired Mammeri's research into the ancient poetry of the Berbers in Kabylia, and the ethnological intent of interpretation. An ethnology that opens one of the paths necessary for genuine reflexivity, as precondition both for self-knowledge and for exploration of the historical unconscious. This was how Tassadit Yacine, combining the findings of social science, has drawn from her anthropological familiarity with the Berber cultural tradition the instruments of analysis, such as the myth of the jackal, that enable her to interpret the condition and position of Berber intellectuals, people such as Ferauon, Boulifa, Amrouche or Mammeri.

But the transformation of the object of ethnology and sociology that made possible the partly double reading of Kabylia and Béarn also had effects that I believe important for knowledge of the knowledge relationship, for the science of social science which is undoubtedly the main precondition for progress in this science. Convinced that it was necessary to take a distance in order to approach, to put oneself in the frame in order to exclude oneself, to objectivize oneself in order to de-subjectivize knowledge, I deliberately took as the first object of anthropological knowledge this anthropological knowledge itself, and the difference that inevitably separates it from practical knowledge. This led me paradoxically to 'de-exoticize' the exotic, to rediscover in our common practices, once they were adequately analysed, the equivalent of the most foreign behaviours, such as rituals, to recognize the practical logic of strategy in what has been so often described in the theoreticist language of the model, and so on. And I could quickly add that, as soon as we abandon the intellectualist vision that artificially places the scientific truth of our practices at a distance, we are forced to discover in ourselves the same principles of the 'savage mind' that we impute to primitive peoples. I have in mind for example the cognitive-practical principles of the masculine view of the world. It is possible and legitimate to speak of others only at the price of a double historicization, of both the object and the subject of knowledge. This means that the scientist must put himself in the frame in order to exclude the frame, he has to work to know himself to be in a position to know the other; all progress in knowledge of the object is a progress in knowledge of the subject of knowledge and vice versa.

All this means that the ethnosociologist is a kind of organic intellectual of humanity, and as a collective agent can contribute to denaturalizing and de-fatalizing human existence by placing his skill at the service of a universalism rooted in the comprehension of different particularisms. I believe that specialists in Arab and Berber civilizations are not the worst placed to fulfil this mission of *Aufklärung*, inasmuch as they are confronted with an object that is itself confronted today by the most radical questioning. I need only cite Mahmoud Darwich, the great Palestinian poet, who declared in a language that could have been that of Kafka on the Jews of his time: 'I do not believe there is any other people in the world who have been so required each day to prove their identity as are the Arabs. No one says to the Greeks: "You're not Greek", or to the French: "You're not French".'[6] Nothing seems more legitimate to me, both scientifically and politically, nor more fruitful, than to return to the particularity of the Arabs – or, more precisely, of the Palestinians, Kabyles or Kurds – not to fetishize it in any form of essentialism, of positive or negative racism, but rather to find in it the basis for a radical questioning of the particularity of a condition that raises in its most universal form the question of human universality.

For Abdelmalek Sayad

For me, Abdelmalek Sayad was a friend and more than a friend, a kind of brother, and it is hard for me to speak of him without an emotion that he would not have wanted. The last time we saw each other, together with Rebecca, a few days before his death, we spoke quite naturally and without any solemnity of all the problems that preoccupied him, about the continuation of his work, the publication of his texts, the fulfilment of his contracts. And I only understood after the event that he wanted to tell me, without seeming to do so, some of his final dispositions. He was both happy for this moment that we had together, and deeply sad (he had just learned that he would never regain normal sight). I spoke a great deal, in order to make him laugh, and he did laugh a lot, particularly in recalling with ironic pride the sixty boxes of papers and books that he had had to pack up in order to prepare for work on his house.

From the end of 1958, when I met him while he was studying at the University of Algiers (he often reminded me with amused admiration of the philosophy lecture I had given on Kant's notion of God . . .), we had visited together the most remote corners of Algeria: the resettlement centres of the Collo peninsular and the Orléansville plain, the forbidden roads of the Ouarsenis amid bomb warnings and alerts, Great and Little Kabylia, the shantytowns and new housing estates of Algiers and Constantine, and so many other places. We had so many memories in common, often tragic: the evenings of our fieldwork when, with everyone else asleep, we stayed up until two or three in the morning discussing and transcribing the day's observations; the day that we learned of the death of our friend Moulah

Henine, killed by the OAS (it could have been Sayad), to whom we dedicated *Le Déracinement*; the day that we drove up together to a small village in Little Kabylia that I was familiar with, on a road with hairpin bends scattered with the bodies of burned-out cars, with the continual sound of shooting in the distance, passing a partly concealed man who was undoubtedly an armed sentinel and exchanging a simple glance (I never saw him flinch or withdraw), and certainly thinking that we would have to return in the evening by the same road; the time that he visited me in the house of the White Fathers of Djemâa Saharidj, a neutral asylum for my research, where he watched me with some amazement take part in evening prayer before dinner; the day that he nudged me with his shoulder, afraid lest I err from an excess of trust, while I carefully noted the somewhat fanciful statements of a little local prophet, a self-educated *amahbul*, who, in order to convince me that the Arabs had invented democracy, asked me: 'Beni Toufout' – the name of one of the local tribes – 'what does that mean? Beni Toufout? *Tu votes.*'

In fact, and this is the reason why I loved working with him (we conducted dozens of interviews together, perhaps hundreds), he looked at the men and women of his country without either complacency or condescension, casting a gaze that I could call tender or compassionate on their little tricks, their little lies, their little weaknesses of suffering and misery. In contrast to all those falsely radical intellectuals who were so keen on giving lessons in nationalism, and who badly concealed beneath a voluntarist and often ostentatious populism their ignorance – if not their fear or disgust – of the people as they actually were, he was always able to be very close and very attentive, without ever being taken in. People felt this, and as attested by the magnificent interviews he conducted, they granted him the trust that is the precondition for a genuine communication between the sociologist and those he studies.

All this was because he had a genuine attachment, without rhetoric, to what one would like to be able to call the cause of the Algerian people. I say 'without rhetoric', and as with my father, whom he reminded me of a great deal, we did not need to speak in order to agree on essentials (particularly about people who speak too much, especially on things that it would be better to leave unexpressed, such as the right sentiments for the right causes). I brought him to my home, my village in the Pyrenees, where I was investigating the causes of the eldest sons of peasant families remaining unmarried, and he understood immediately, thus helping me to understand myself, as Yvette Delsaut did on another occasion, the roots of my interest in the Kabyle peasants. This established between us a kind of real family bond (my father and mother were very fond of him).

He had deep convictions that he refused to state, particularly vis-à-vis pharisaic defenders of good causes, but which he did indeed know how to communicate without emotional or prophetic professions of faith. This was how, when I formed my first team to go out in the field and study the effects of unemployment (already!), in difficult and dangerous conditions that some people would certainly have deemed a bit dubious, he recruited his best friends, Moulah Henine, who was studying medicine and, as I said, was subsequently killed by the OAS, Ahmed Misraoui, who was studying dentistry, and several others, such as Alain Accardo, who has also remained true to the cause right through to today . . . Though he never said so, he undoubtedly saw his choice to bear witness as the best and certainly the only contribution he could make to a struggle whose many ambiguities he was fully aware of. If I say all these things that he never wrote down, it is because we spoke obliquely about them a hundred times, just as we decided a hundred times, in moments of desperation about Algeria, to do a book of dialogue together on the contradictions and ambiguities of the Algerian situation, before definitively abandoning it – one of the most complex and tragic situations in the whole history of humanity (it is enough to recall all the dramas and hidden crimes of the war of liberation).

I must briefly mention the magnificent work that Abdelmalek Sayad has left us, which is still largely unpublished. It can be organized, as he himself did in the papers he left with me to ensure their publication, under two major headings, emigration and immigration, which, in their apparent simplicity, reveal an essential intention. Through the simple symmetry of this plan, he sought to express his desire to keep an even balance – contrary to what is often done, not just here but also on the other side of the Mediterranean, where emigration (and return) poses extremely painful problems – between the two faces of the phenomenon, as indissociable both in fact and in good theory as the recto and verso of a single sheet of paper.

This means first of all breaking with the Francocentric view of migration flows as simply immigration, which sees Algerians only as 'immigrants', without attachments or roots, whose existence somehow begins with getting off the boat in Marseille, or the plane at Orly. A view that led people to believe, still in the 1970s, that the immigrant was a young single man without a family, who had come on a temporary basis to earn a bit of money to send back to his family before returning to his own country and resuming his former life. In two exemplary articles that have become classic, 'Les trois âges de l'émigration' and 'Un émigré exemplaire', Abdelmalek Sayad offered a social history of a century of Algerian emigration that aimed at giving a differentiated description and a differential explanation of departures to France (who left first, to what destinations, via what networks, etc.). He later returned to this problem, trying to analyse the transition from individual emigration to family emigration (largely bound up with the war of liberation that made it acceptable). A radical change that one of his most lucid interlocutors, Abbas, summed up in a magnificent formula: previously people came to produce for the French, now they come to produce French people.

To understand emigration also means understanding the effects it has produced in Algerian society, the economic effects, of course, but also the social and cultural effects. Effects that people were starting to denounce or condemn. It was necessary therefore to study the accusations made against emigration in Algeria itself – in Algeria, too, we should say. Accusations that were hidden beneath discussions about the 'reinsertion' of emigrants in their economy, their society and their culture, and that hid the tensions between the *temptation* of ethnocentric withdrawal and all the seductions of the surrounding world, starting with those exerted by consumer goods. What was condemned in the 'emigrants', these seeming traitors to the nation and nationalism, was the shameful, bad, guilty part of this that people wanted to eradicate.

And so, in a conclusion that is surprising for those who hold to a one-sided view, emigration raises all these problems, and in part identical problems, on both sides of the Mediterranean, touching on the most deeply buried taboos, the very essence of the two societies, everything that is placed under the vague and dangerous words 'identity' and 'nation'. This is seen from the fact that on both sides these are referred to only by euphemisms, evoking for example, on the Algerian side, the 'sacrifice' of the emigrants or the exploitation of which they are victims.

The second heading is immigration: this is the aspect of Sayad's work that is most familiar, and I can proceed quickly. The emigrant is a worker, labour-power. He is in a way the ideal worker of neoliberalism. He is a worker without qualification who always remains 'unskilled', even if he becomes a foreman, who never has real qualifications and is even illegal. Once deprived of work and unemployed, he no longer exists, he is surplus to requirements and has to be sent home. We should remember again Abdelmalek Sayad's final publications on the immigrant body, this visible image of the individual who, still more than his family name, first name or accent, makes hard if not impossible what is called 'naturalization' and successful access to the naturalness of the 'naturals', the natives, the truly indigenous. But this is only one of the facts that mean that the emigrant-immigrant is always, as one of them puts it, neither here nor there, neither from here nor from there. The most determining thing perhaps, the most insurmountable, is the thinking of the state, that incorporated system of categories of perception and assessment that imposes a national (and nationalist) grid on everything perceived, and throws the emigrant-immigrant back on his foreignness, his alterity, particularly when, for any infraction whatsoever of the rules of good behaviour imposed on non-nationals, who are always in danger of appearing as intruders, it reminds its 'guests' of their foreigner status. By bringing up again the memory of the original sin that lies at the root of his presence, unwarranted, undesirable, unjustified and unjustifiable, he almost inevitably condemns himself to a double penalty, the duplication of the sanction that is logically inscribed in his double fault, the fault of being there, displaced, and the fault of committing a fault instead of making himself forgotten, pardoned for being there.

Research in social science, where analytical procedures are less strictly codified than elsewhere, always depends largely, for better or worse, on the habitus, more or less corrected and controlled, of the person conducting it. Abdelmalek Sayad embodied the correct vision, the gaze both close and distant, intimate and remote, that is proper for the sociologist. Not a spokesperson hogging the limelight, a giver of lessons or an expert, he sought to be a *public scribe* who transcribes and transports a speech that is both intimate and public, confided like a personal message to someone worthy of trust, capable of receiving it and transmitting it to its rightful destination. He conducted himself right to the end as a faithful witness, putting his whole life at stake in his work, everything that a difficult existence as a desperately loyal 'defector' had taught him (although he was a member of a French research institute, the CNRS, and secondarily of the École des Hautes Études, Sayad insisted on keeping his Algerian nationality).

The realistic and measured disposition that constantly inclined him to nuanced statements, complex and comprehensive, equally distant from all extreme position-taking, was already manifest right from the start during the Algerian war, in the calm courage that led him to reject ostentatious commitments, sometimes thereby exposing himself to the suspicions and criticisms of radical absolutists, and making the choice, certainly the riskiest one from any point of view, of going to see what other people were saying, and conducting investigations in the Ouarensis, in Kabylia, or in the Collo peninsular. This was the same modest courage that led him to conduct and support till the end, like the two enormous suitcases he carted around everywhere, even from one hospital to another, a research work that he viewed as a form of both scientific and political activism.

It was in this way that he managed to make us believe he was eternal, even when everything about him expressed weakness, fragility and vulnerability. I shall do everything, along with all his friends, to assure for his work, but also the exemplary figure of the researcher who embodied it, the only form of eternity that men can give.

Seeing with the Lens:
About Photography
Interview with Franz Schultheis

Pierre Bourdieu explains the reasons that led him to do photography in difficult conditions bound up with the war and all the violence that followed from it. Photography enabled the sociologist both to fix extraordinary situations, to adduce evidence about a situation on which few sociologists and ethnologists had written, and moreover to preserve images that were not only connected with the object of his research but also with its subject. In fact, the practice of photography perhaps contributed towards changing or even converting the sociologist's gaze, thus implying a genuine discourse or 'conversation'. Photography would thus be an expression of the distance of the observer that 'records while not forgetting that he is recording'.

Franz Schultheis: At the time that you gave us access to the photos you took during your stay in Algeria, stored in boxes for forty years, you also granted us an interview on your use of photography in the context of your ethnographic fieldwork and your localized sociological research. Can we start with a question that is very down to earth: what camera did you use to take these photos of Algeria?

Pierre Bourdieu: It was a camera that I bought in Germany, a Zeiss Ikoflex. This camera got broken while I was visiting the United States in the 1970s, and I much regretted this. When I have the time, I look in second-hand shops to see if I can get the same model, and I've been told several times that it no longer exists. The Zeiss Ikoflex was at the cutting edge of German technology at that time. I bought it in Germany. It must have been the first year that I had any money of my own (I obtained a teaching post around 1955), and I think that I smuggled it back to France . . . It had an extraordinary lens, that's why it was very expensive, otherwise you had the classic Rolleiflex model with the viewfinder on the case . . . This was very useful for me, as in Algeria there were situations where it was delicate to take photographs, and I could photograph without being seen. For example, I also had a Leica, I had friends in Algeria who were professional photographers, whom I asked for advice, because one of the problems in Algeria is that the light is very, very white, very brutal, very strong, and that completely blocks out the image, so I was obliged to turn to them. These friends mainly used a Leica, which was the professionals' camera, but it presupposed that you had the person to be photographed opposite you. Often that wasn't possible, for example if you were photographing women in a region where that wasn't well thought of, etc. In certain cases I asked permission, for example when I was on the ground in the Collo region or that of Orléansville. Then of course I took a lot of photos and people were very happy. For example, there is a series of photos of a circumcision, which are quite dramatic, and I took them at the request of the father, who said to me: 'Come and take photos.' That was a way of introducing me and of my being well received. Afterwards I sent them the photos.

FS: Did you develop them yourself?

PB: I bought the equipment for developing, but only much later, because all my photographer friends told me: a real photographer is someone who does their own developing, it's in the developing that you see the quality, and you can work on them or reframe. That wasn't possible for me at the time, but there was a laboratory in Algiers where I could ask for more or less what I wanted, I had contact prints done, little images, and then I discussed with the person there and asked for more complicated things. As I took a lot of photos, that interested him, and so I gave him a free hand, but I tried to control things as far as I could.

FS: In a certain sense, you were already gripped by photography from the start, you liked doing it. Was it a project to make systematic use of photography during your stay?

PB: I know that I gave it a lot of importance, I bought drawing notebooks in which I stuck prints, and I also had shoeboxes in which I kept the different films; I bought little celluloid envelopes for keeping the negatives in, I numbered each envelope and the numbers corresponded to the notebook in which the prints were stuck. I was very keen on this. My problem was, should I keep all the films? I tended to keep them, because there were always two functions. There was a documentary function: there are cases when I took photos with a view to remembering, to making descriptions later, or else of objects that I couldn't take away with me and that I photographed; in other cases, it was a way of looking. There is a spontaneous sociology of the petty bourgeoisie (certain petty-bourgeois writers such as Daninos in France) that ridicules people who go off with a camera over their shoulder as tourists and in the end don't even look at the countryside they photograph. I always thought that this was a class racism. As far as I am concerned, anyway, it was a way of sharpening my gaze, I looked at things a lot better, and then, it was often just a way in. I accompanied photographers on their reportages, and saw that they did not speak at all to the people they photographed, they knew practically nothing about them. There were therefore several types of photographs: for example, a marriage lamp that I photographed in order to be able to analyse later on how it was made, or a grain mill, etc. Secondly, I photographed things that struck me as beautiful. I loved the country greatly, I was in a state of extreme emotional exaltation, and I took photos of things that I liked. I can still see a photo in which there was a girl with braided hair and her little sister beside her, almost like a little German Virgin Mary from the fifteenth century; or in another that I like greatly, a very young girl on the edge of a shantytown, some 80 centimetres tall, carrying a loaf of bread tightly against her stomach, which she'd gone to collect and which was almost as big as she was. She was very dark, and stood out against a white wall.

FS: When did you start to take photos systematically,
             was it after your military service?

PB: Yes, it was in the 1960s. I had the idea of taking
             photos of situations that touched me deeply because
             they mingled dissonant realities. There was one I
             particularly liked: a photo I took in Orléansville, in
             bright summer sunshine, one of the hottest places in
             Algeria, where there was an advertising billboard for
             a driving school, showing a road snaking through
             pine trees, and alongside it a poster for Frigidaire.
             This kind of mixture amused me. Another one,
             which I used for the cover of *Algérie 60*, I also saw
             as very typical. There are two men in turbans, old-
             style Arabs, who are sitting on the running board of
             a car (you can see my own car, a Renault Dauphine,
             parked in the background) and having a very serious
             discussion.

FS: The question raised on looking at these photos is as
             follows: it is clear that they're not tourist photos,
             but photos that have been directed or set up. There
             is targeting; you said that you took photos in order
             to objectivize, to create a distance or to put yourself
             outside of the present time for a brief moment. And
             so it is quite logical to think that there is an intrinsic
             relationship between the way of objectivizing by
             means of the photographic gaze and the ethnological
             approach that you were in the process of creating,
             and that both eyes, the eye of the ethnologist,
             anthropologist, and the eye of the photographer,
             must have had an elective affinity.

PB: Yes, you are certainly right. There was in both cases
             that kind of relationship, both objectivizing and
             affectionate, something like what is understood by
             humour. There is a whole series of photos I took in
             the Collo region, in a fairly dramatic situation where
             the people in charge of us had the power of life or
             death over me and the people with me, a whole
             series of photos in which people are under a big olive
             tree, discussing and drinking coffee. Taking photo-
             graphs is a way of saying, 'I'm interested in you, I'm
             on your side, I listen to your stories, I'll testify to
             what you are living through.' For example, there is
             a whole series of photos, not at all aesthetic, that I
             took at a place called Aïn-Aghbel, and at another
             called Kerkera. The soldiers had forced the people,

who had been living until then in a dispersed habitat in the mountains, into houses aligned like a Roman *castrum*, and I went off by myself on foot into the mountains, against the advice of my friends, to the destroyed villages, and I found there houses whose roofs had been removed to force the people to leave. They hadn't been burned, but they were no longer habitable and inside them there were the jars (that is something I'd begun to study in another village, at Aïn-Aghbel: there are places where everything that could be called furniture was made of earth, fabricated and fashioned by women), which in Kabylia are called *ikoufen* (singular: *akoufi*), these big jars[1] in which they put grain, decorated with drawings that often represent snakes, because the snake is the symbol of resurrection. And so I was very happy at being able to photograph these despite the desolation of the situation, and that is very contradictory. I was able to take photos of these houses and that furniture, owing to the fact that they didn't have roofs . . . That is quite typical of my experience, which was something fairly extraordinary. I was at the same time quite overwhelmed, very sensitive to the suffering of all these people, and at the same time there was also the distance of the observer, which is expressed in the very fact of taking photos. I thought about all this on reading Germaine Tillion, an ethnologist who worked on the Aurès, another region of Algeria, and who describes, in her book *Ravensbrück*, how, in the camp, she saw people die and made a tick each time there was a death. She did her work as a professional ethnologist, and said that this helped her to carry on. And I thought about all that, I told myself that I was a funny kind of bloke. It was there, in that village where there was the olive tree, a place where the people, the day we arrived – no, not the first day, it was the second day, the first was more dramatic, I won't tell it, it would sound like heroic emotion – and so the second day, people started to say: 'As for me, I had this, I had that, I had ten goats, me, I had three sheep', they went through all the valuables they had lost, and I was with three other people and I noted everything I could. I recorded the disaster and at the same time, with a kind of irresponsibility (which is really scholastic irresponsibility, I realize that in retrospect), I had in mind that I would study all that, with the

techniques at my disposal. I told myself constantly:
'Poor Bourdieu, you're not up to it, despite all the
instruments you have, you would have to know
everything, understand everything, psychoanalysis,
economics.' I put people through Rorschach tests, I
did everything I could to try and understand, and
at the same time, my intention was to collect rituals,
the rites of the first day of spring, for example. And
these people told me stories, stories about ogres and
the games that they played. They picked olives from
an olive tree higher up, olives that weren't quite ripe,
and this was a game, the olives were thrown, you
had to catch them on the back of the hand, and
depending on the number of olives dropped, you got
three or four blows with the fingers. Beneath this
olive tree, I questioned men who were between
thirty and fifty years old, some of whom had a rifle
hidden beneath their djellaba, they started playing
(if you dropped two olives, you were hit with two
fingers, three, it was three fingers, etc.), and they
really hit very hard, they played like children. That
was typical of my relationship with the country. To
speak in a correct way about all this was very hard:
it wasn't all concentration camps. It was dramatic,
but not in the way people say. And I observed all of
this, which was so complicated, so much beyond my
powers! When they told me – it sometimes took me
two or three days to understand, complicated names
of places or tribes, figures for the losses of cattle and
goods – I was submerged, and anything was good
to photograph, and this was a way of dealing with
the shock of a crushing reality. In a centre quite close
to there, called Kerkera, an enormous centre, placed
in a large marshy plain that the local people didn't
cultivate because they didn't have powerful enough
ploughs or ox teams, these people had been settled
there, it was immense, two or three thousand people,
it was tragic, that kind of shantytown without a
town, and there I did the most crazy thing in my
life: a study of consumption in the INSEE fashion
(a consumption study involves a lot of work, you
arrive with a questionnaire and you say: 'Yesterday,
what did you buy yesterday?' Candles, bread,
carrots, you list them and you put down 'yes', 'no',
you come back two days later and repeat the same
thing three times). It was an enormous task – it
wasn't just me, there were three or four of us – to

organize and carry out an investigation of this kind in such a difficult situation. Nothing extraordinary emerged from this study, except that in this population, who had the air of being completely crushed, homogenized, levelled, reduced to the last degree of poverty, you found a normal distribution, there were all the differences that you find in an ordinary population, a normal scattering.

FS: Listening to you, I get the impression that you didn't pursue a specific project, you wanted to go everywhere and do all the sociology in a short space of time.

PB: Yes, but how could you have done otherwise? What are you to do faced with something like that, a reality so pressing and oppressing? Of course, there was the danger of just getting submerged and writing a hallucinatory diary in which I simply put down everything. That is one of the big mistakes I made, not keeping a diary, I just had bits of scrappy notes. I have to say that it was hard work; we didn't have time, it was tiring.

FS: One concrete question: if in theory you don't have a diary, I am almost certain that on seeing the photos you can locate everything rapidly and in quite a reliable way, and you can certainly say when you see this girl sitting on the ground: 'that's it', no? So as supports for memory they are very . . .

PB: Yes, I can say: 'That was in Orléansville [now El-Asnam], that was in Chéraïa . . .'

FS: So, they are actually very important, these supports for memory, and we should see whether a second time round . . .

PB: That's what should have been done . . . but I didn't have the strength, it was unimaginable, we were working from six in the morning until three in the night, Sayad was the only one who could stand the pace, the others collapsed, it was very very hard.

FS: To return once again to this question of gaze, it's emotion that's right at the centre, and then, there is the break that is very important to you, a break that divides a world that is in the process of disappearing in its familiar and habitual forms, from a new world that is very swiftly imposing itself. So a non-contemporaneity of objects. In your book *Travail et travailleurs en Algérie*, what structures the sociological gaze seems to be the gap between temporal structures and economic structures, and so one can say that the same themes are to be found again in the photos, in the photographic gaze directed at the social world . . .

PB: There is one photo, which I see as very typical, that I put on the cover of [the original edition of] *Travail et travailleurs en Algérie*, it's agricultural workers in the plain of the Mitidja, close to Algiers. They are working in a gang, they're treating the vines with sulphate and are linked by a tube that connects them with a machine that supplies the sulphate, and they move forward in a group of five or six, maybe more. This shows very well the condition of these people, and at the same time this industrialization of agricultural work on the big colonial farms, which was well in advance of French agriculture. I did some short interviews with these people, who, although they earned a wretched wage as agricultural labourers, often cultivated their own fields on the borders of the big estates of the colonists.

FS: Faced with what you are saying on your way of conceiving and making these photos, one wonders how to grasp and present them in an adequate manner. A relationship has to be established with the ethnological research and the books that describe your beginnings, in which you analyse the object that is also to be seen in your photos. To make a connection between the two seems obvious, but one might hesitate a bit, because at first sight it is perhaps a more spontaneous and simplistic manner than to look for descriptions of situations in the texts, accounts, which refer to what is seen in the photos.

PB: It is quite normal to make a connection between the content of my research and my photos. For example, one of the things that interested me most at this time was what I called the economy of misery or the economy of the shantytown. The shantytown was generally seen (not only by the racist gaze, but simply by the naive gaze) as dirty, ugly, disorderly, incoherent, etc., whereas in fact it is the site of a very complex life, a genuine economy, which has its own logic and in which a great deal of ingenuity is applied, offering many people the minimal means of survival, and above all reasons for living socially, that is, escaping the dishonour represented, for any man with self-respect, by the fact of doing nothing, not contributing at all to the existence of his family. I took a large number of photos of this, of all the hawkers and street vendors, and I was really bowled over by the deployment of ingenuity and energy represented by the strange constructions that suggest a shop or a display window, or the arrangements of peculiar objects on the ground (this also interested me aesthetically, as it is very baroque) by the apothecaries whom I questioned, who sold all the resources of traditional magic whose names I recorded, aphrodisiacs, etc. There were also very picturesque butchers (these three large wood pillars joined together on which pieces of meat were hung), a typical subject for the photographer looking for the picturesque, the exotic. For me, I always had in mind hypotheses on the organization of space: there is a village plan with a structure, a structure of the house; similarly, I observed that the structure of the distribution of graves followed by and large the organization of the village by clans: would I find the same structure in the markets? That makes me think of a photo I took in a cemetery: on the tomb, anonymous, a *cassoulet* tin full of water. The seventh day after the death, you have to put water to attach the female soul; in this case, it was a *cassoulet* tin which had contained a taboo product, pork . . .

FS: On your return to France then, you very soon embarked on research into photography.[2] How did you get this idea, did someone outside come and suggest it to you?

PB: I don't remember very well, and I don't want to say anything foolish. I know it was connected with the fact that Raymond Aron had appointed me as general secretary of a research centre he had just set up; I wasn't very sure of myself and I thought that I had to find a way of earning money off my own bat: in that way, if I did anything stupid, it wouldn't be too bad . . . And so I signed a contract with Kodak. Photography was something that interested me. I clearly had in mind that the only practice with an artistic dimension that was accessible to everyone was photography, and the only cultural good universally consumed was also photography. And so, with this approach, I would manage to arrive at a general aesthetic theory. It was both very modest and very ambitious. It is easy to say that everyday photos are frightful, etc., and I wanted first of all to understand why this was the case, and try and explain for example why these images are always frontal, because what they show is relations between individuals, a heap of things that arise from necessity, and by the same token had a rehabilitation effect. And then I began to analyse a collection of photos, that of my childhood friend who was called Jeannot, I looked at them one by one, I really absorbed them, and I think that I found a lot of things in this particular shoebox.

FS: But when you were taking photos in Algeria, you also said that you had observed professional photographers, and said: 'I would not have taken the same photo' or 'I would have taken it differently', sometimes 'I would have done it the same way'. There is already a reflexivity in the use of photography, and so it's like a beginning, an embryonic starting-point of reflexion . . .

PB: That's true. Professional photographers, if they sometimes happen to take photos that I would have liked to take myself, even the most peculiar things, they also do a lot of things that I wouldn't have done, things that are just picturesque. I think that it would not have been easy for them, except by accident, to take an unconventional view of this society without any other grid than the category of the picturesque, the weaver at his loom, women coming back from the well. Among my most 'typical' photos there is one of a veiled woman riding a motor-scooter, which they certainly might have taken. It's the 'easiest' aspect of what I was trying to grasp. I have an anecdote that says a good deal about my experience of this country (a strange country, where I constantly experienced a feeling of tragedy – I was very anxious, I dreamed of it at night – and yet, where I constantly saw funny things, which made me laugh or smile), a story that expresses very well the double experience, contradictory or ambiguous, that I always found it very hard to express or get understood here in France, or even in Algeria, to townspeople of bourgeois origin – I have in mind a young female student, who came from a large family of Kouloughlis,[3] who took part in our investigations in the urban environment (she wrote to me recently) and who could not prevent herself from experiencing a feeling of fear mixed with horror at people whom I found very touching, even in the rather derisory or pitiful strategies by which they tried to present their misery and misfortune, or turn it to account. (That is why I liked the approach of people such as Mouloud Feraoun so much, when he told me of his wrangles with his pupils' parents, or Abdelmalek Sayad, whose gaze on the people we met was often both amused and quite compassionate.) To go back to my story: one day, then, as I was coming out of a car park, a young woman in a veil, seeing that I was hesitating to pass her with my car, turned towards me and called out, from under her veil: 'So, my dear, are you going to run me over?!'

FS: You see, what you are saying here reminds me somewhat of the remark of Günter Grass that you are certainly familiar with. He said: 'Sociology is much too serious!' But that's not true! Not at all, but what he didn't understand is that it would have been out of place to bring laughter into *The Weight of the World*.[4]

PB: *La Déracinement*, which is very similar to *The Weight of the World*, does not offer much room for this amusing side. And besides, if I wanted a literary model for expressing such terrible experiences, even in their funniest aspects, I would rather think of Arno Schmidt. I often regret not having kept a diary. I was focused completely on my 'duty' as a researcher and witness, and I did my best, with the means at my disposal, to convey experiences that were at the same time extraordinary and – alas! – universal, those of all exoduses and all wars of liberation. There was also the fact that I didn't want to rest content with witnessing, in the style of a good reporter, I wanted to reveal the logic and the trans-historical effects of these great forced displacements of population. And then there is a censorship of academic good behaviour which means there are heaps of things you don't even dream of saying. And what I am telling you now, it's likely that thirty years ago I would not have been able to, or else I would

have said it, but perhaps not as I have dared to
say it now.

FS: Now, you can permit yourself, at all events the
work is there, you can go back to it to show the
hidden side.

PB: In fact, the concern to be serious, scientific, led me
to repress the literary dimension: I censored many
things. I think that during the whole initial period
of the Centre de Sociologie Européenne there was a
tacit encouragement, without any express advice, to
censor everything that was philosophical and literary. The tacit rules of the group had to be respected.
The rest seemed impolite, narcissistic, complacent.
And I often regret today not having kept any usable
traces of this experience. It is true that I lived through
many things at that time that separated me from my
intellectual contemporaries. I aged much more
quickly . . . Yes, it's true, I should try one day with
a dictaphone to say what comes to my mind in
looking at these photos . . .

FS: Finally, a personal question: what role did this
Algerian experience play, in your view, in the context
of the personal socioanalysis that you sketched in a
recent lecture at the Collège de France?

PB: Yvette Delsaut wrote a text about me, in which she
said quite correctly that it was Algeria that enabled
me to accept myself. The gaze of the understanding
ethnologist that I applied to Algeria, I could then
apply to myself, to the people of my region, to my
parents, my father's accent, my mother, and recover
without any drama what is one of the great problems of all uprooted intellectuals, trapped in the
alternative between either populism or a shame
about themselves bound up with class racism. It was
to people very similar to the Kabyles, people whom
I had grown up with, that I applied the gaze of
obligatory comprehension that defines the discipline
of ethnology. Certainly my practice of photography,
first of all in Algeria, then in Béarn, made a major
contribution to this conversion of view which presupposed a genuine conversation – I don't think that
word is too strong. Photography is actually an
expression of the distance of the observer who
records and does not forget that he is recording
(which is not always easy in familiar situations, such

as a dance), but it also presupposes the whole proximity of the familiar, attentive and sensitive to the
imperceptible details that familiarity allows and
compels him to grasp and interpret on the spot
(doesn't one say of someone who behaves well, in a
friendly fashion, that he is 'attentive'?), to all the
tiny details of practice that often escape the most
meticulous ethnologist. This is bound up with the
relationship that I have continuously maintained
with my subject, never forgetting that it is a matter
of individuals, to whom I applied a gaze that I would
readily call, if I was not afraid of ridicule, affection-
ate and often compassionate. That is why I never
stopped conducting interviews and observations (I
always began each of my research projects in this
way, whatever their subject), breaking with the
routine of the bureaucratic sociologist (embodied
for me by Paul Lazarsfeld and the Columbia Bureau,[5]
which institutionalized Taylorism in research), who
only makes contact with his subjects through interposed investigators and who, in contrast to even the
most timid ethnologist, does not have the opportunity to see either the individuals questioned or their
immediate environment. Photos that can be looked
at again at leisure, like recordings that can be listened to over and over again (not to speak of video),
make it possible to discover details unnoticed at first
glance, details that, owing to discretion, are hard to
observe during the investigation itself (I have in
mind, for example, the indoor shots of the metal-
worker at Longwy and his Algerian neighbour,
taken during my work on *The Weight of the World*).

Appendices

Letters to André Nouschi

These letters addressed to André Nouschi soon after the appearance of Sociologie de l'Algérie *in 1958 are real historical documents, which bear witness to both an intense political tension (including in the university milieu) and the underlying intellectual and scientific preoccupations. The free tone that is apparent in them is the product of a friendship and mutual understanding that were rare in this atmosphere of distrust and terror. Pierre Bourdieu met André Nouschi in Algiers thanks to Émile Dermenghem, at the library of the Gouvernement Général. Nouschi, who was then preparing a thesis in economic history on the tribes of the Constantinois, was among those who guided Bourdieu in his first studies into the dispossession of the* fellah'in *by the laws imposed in the late nineteenth century (cantonment, the* loi *Warnier, the* sénatus-consulte). *He was also a favoured interlocutor owing to his political background (a militant in the Communist Party) and his commitment to Algerian self-determination. A staunch anti-colonialist, Nouschi was the author of several books on Algerian nationalism and on the Mediterranean.*

My dear friend,

A thousand thanks and more for your letter. I am very aware of the fact that you took the trouble to send me criticisms that were precise and precious. I see this as the best testimony of friendship.

Will it surprise you if I say that I've heard a thousand venomous and bilious remarks? You gather that the Algiers 'specialists' (one has to add 'hem, hem!') have not spared treacherous and mealy-mouthed [*doucereuses*] allusions (an admirable adjective, I'm sure you know what I mean . . .). They rapidly established a standard doctrine (cf. Jean Eiffel's cartoons in *L'Express*!) about my little book: bookish, theoretical (what a vocabulary!), lack of experience immersed in the realities of Algeria, that note on the Europeans, etc. To sum up, this little metropolitan who barges in to talk about Algeria, while so many old specialists (do you know that they're no longer called 'fogeys', but '*son et lumières*'?), etc. etc. It makes you think of the gardener's dog who doesn't eat the lettuces and won't let anyone else eat them either.

By the way, at a faculty meeting I witnessed a diabolical battle in which Émerit came out on top. I've come to find him tremendously pleasant, and would really like to get to know him. But I'm afraid of his criticism, which would be precise and well founded. When the opportunity arises, would you be able to speak to him about me so that I can go to see him and ask his judgement?

I've noted the corrections you suggest. Can I take up a few points with you, without troubling you too much? As far as the 'zone' of Kabyle culture goes, my intention was to show how, in the different groups that comprise it,[1] you can observe the constancy of certain features, though never the same depending on the place, here tile roofs, there tree cultivation, elsewhere grouped villages, etc., and the disappearance of other features together with the introduction of features borrowed from Arabic-speaking cultures. Djurdjura in Kabylia seems to me to form the 'centre' of this cultural zone, since all the features found in isolation elsewhere are combined here. All that has disappeared for lack of space.

I know Bousquet's analyses and have taken them into account. But they do not seem to touch on anything essential.

I've noted the nuance that you point out to me on the subject of *nif* and *horma*. Chelhod (*Introduction à la sociologie de l'Islam*, p. 32 n. 2 and 38) has very interesting remarks bearing on the *nif*.

As far as questions of inheritance are concerned, I am completely lost. I only considered the case of inheritance without a formal will, but I was wrong in this respect. Can you make the facts clear for me: do Arab women inherit *melk* land even *ab intestat*? Isn't the *habous* procedure used in order to disinherit them?

I am counting on you to see this more clearly and correct my stupidities. [. . .]

I shall read (and cite) Larcher and Rectenwald's book, which is not familiar to me. Is your thesis published? I would like to read it as soon as possible and cite it in my next work.

You cannot imagine how grateful I am for the criticisms you have been so kind as to make for me. I have the feeling, despite all the drivellers, of having done something useful (Algiers radio, which pushed my book, spoke recently, at considerable length, about 'Mozabite civilization'), and I would like to improve this work as much as possible so that what is good in it is not spoiled by more or less monumental mistakes.

I'm thinking of coming to Paris for Christmas. I will have a lot of things to tell you. You will have seen in the press how the elections are shaping up. I much appreciated Marçais's candidacy; he's been playing the liberal for some time now. Perhaps you don't know that he has the support of the army (more precisely, of Goussault, Lacheroy and Salan. Goussault said recently: 'We have two ministerial class candidates, Lauriol and Marçais). The latest news suggests that the love match is broken off, with the compère being reduced to his own forces alone. I very much liked the way in which *Le Monde* presented the dear dean: 'Ph. Marçais is the son of W. Marçais, one of the greatest Arabists of the French school.' That says it all. Wonderful. Besides, everything is slowly heading towards a situation completely analogous to that of last May. Of course, one can read *L'Express* and *Le Canard Enchaîné*, but appearances of obedience can't hide the fact that everything is continuing or getting worse.

I will send you as soon as it is published an article I've done for a book to be published by the Secrétariat Social on 'Sous-développement en Algérie'. I am going very much further in my conclusions. The 'caution' of the 'Que sais-je?' book was forced on me by the publisher. I think I can be much firmer in the book for Éditions de Minuit. I hope that before then I'll have been able to read your thesis and find arguments there. I'll show you my manuscript at Christmas. I leave out completely the ethnographic details which, I must admit, often weighed heavily on me, and I take up the questions in a more overall fashion. I think that in this way I'll leave myself less exposed to the acid criticisms of these sly 'specialists' who, in parentheses, understand nothing about sociological analysis.

Are you planning to return to Algeria? I would like this, egoistically. I confess that I have never felt as isolated as just recently. The book was partly responsible for this. People look at me with a kind of aggressive commiseration. To the point that I begin to think that everything I've written is completely worthless and I'd have done better to keep silent. Fortunately I can remember their writings, all those darling geniuses! And then the feeling that I've well and truly got up their noses is a comfort to me. So much for my pleasures; sad, sad.

You've given me great pleasure. I thank you again for this.

My dear friend,
Thanks for this long letter. Your observations touch home. Since the judgements you've sent me on my 'opus minimum', I don't want to rest in peace. Here is what is said about your thesis in Algiers (I have this from the deputy head of the Archives Départementales).[2] Your pessimistic conclusions (fall in the standard of living in particular) are only valid for the Constantine region. What do you say to that? Joking aside, do you believe that the Algiers region, for example, has not seen quite similar phenomena, if not still worse? Besides, I must say that your name is surrounded by the greatest respect but you are very awkward. I also chatted with Émerit, who was very kind and gave me his opinion of my little book. His first opinion was unfavourable because he believed I had not given enough space to historical studies. His second judgement was much more favourable, because, as he put it: 'I basically criticized you for not being a historian, but you're a sociologist.' I rather believe that between the first and the second judgement must have come what you said about me . . . He criticized especially my section on the cities . . . I must absolutely revise it and do something less inappropriate. Thanks for your bibliography. I will work on this point once I have time.

I much appreciated the life-jacket image. It goes without saying that I've replaced it, without citing my sources, and that the boat should now move forward . . . Isn't that bad of me! As for the judgement of dear x., I laughed a lot. But it is so completely in his logic that on reflection I was scarcely surprised . . .

You're right in reproaching me for describing traditionalism in its universality without emphasizing the specific features of Algerian traditionalism. I did this deliberately. Here is why: I plan subsequently to develop the analysis that I sketched in the 'Que sais-je?' book: pre-established harmony between Islam and traditional structures. The object is to put an end to the explanation of all phenomena observed in Algeria in terms of Islam and Islam alone. I'd like to show:[3]

(1) That the traditionalist spirit is to be found in two phases and in all places: Max Weber, for example, describing the attitudes of the German workers at the start of the industrial revolution, discovered features absolutely analogous to those observed in Algeria. Another example, the attitude towards work and wages. And again, Lucien Febvre in his Rabelais book.

(2) That other features customarily explained by Islam – for example, ritualism and (the external character of morality) – are also to be found in different civilizations. For example, Ruth

Benedict studying Japanese civilization (*The Chrysanthemum and the Sword*) makes a distinction between 'shame cultures' and 'guilt cultures'. The characteristic features of the former are valid for Algerian civilization. The same thing is found in the morals of Corneille's heroes, Homeric man, etc.[4]

Hence conclusions:

(1) Islam does not provide a sufficient explanation of Algerian sociological phenomena.
(2) A flexible and reversible relationship, a dialogue or harmony, exists between Islam and the underlying structures. Cf. Christianity in the Middle Ages: in harmony with a traditionalist civilization. When social structures change, there is a reinterpretation of religion and *something new* is discovered in the religious message. A fine example: Luther and Calvin found in the same religious message a morality in conformity with capitalist ethics.

I still have to try and show how Islam and the deep structures have always *reinforced one another*, and how Islam has given Algerian traditionalism its specific character. Idem.

I shall also show (as you point out to me) how the destruction of structures is accompanied by a systematic annihilation of the religious context.

I know that the judgement of V. de Paradis is one-sided and relatively exceptional (although similar things can be found in Shaw, Peyssonnel and Desfontaines, etc.). But do you think it does not deserve to be cited as typical of a certain mindset, a certain attitude? I am keen on it because it enables me to corner both Bousquet and Gautier (the note). What do you think? I could add in the note that, as well as these judgements, other more intelligent ones can be found.

Yes, I agree about the topic for discussion. This expands my analysis and strengthens it a good deal.

I shall try to tone down my more inflexible positions. I must say that I sometimes tend to make polemical exaggerations when I get irritated.

Agree about the anti-colonialism of the left (which *bene amat . . .*) and Germaine Tillion.[5]

I think as you do that G. Tillion did not deliberately *intend* to justify, but this is how she has been understood (I will say this in a note; it remains that it is her full responsibility, she could have foreseen the meaning that would be given to her writings).

I shall get on with the continuation, and if it doesn't annoy you, I'll ask you again to be so kind as to read it through and give me your criticisms.

Here a tense atmosphere (esp. in the army). I fear some stupidities. Delouvrier seems to be doing well (he's dared to get rid of Dorget and Decrept). It seems we are close to an outcome. What do you think? Among the Muslims, an immense expectation and an extraordinary confidence (which disturbs me) in D[e] G[aulle]. In all milieus, from the office worker to the teacher. Where will it lead? The Europeans seem quite resigned, and it seems they will collapse if the army doesn't mess about. But that's what's unknown. Finally, I hope that between now and May something will have happened. Then you can make your decision quite calmly.

Émerit has talked to me about the publication of your great thesis. I thought that, if it might help you, you could perhaps go and see Lindon on my behalf.

I don't think that he will agree to publish this kind of work himself, it's not his style, but I know that he has all kinds of connections and would certainly come up with something.

I thank you again a thousand times.

Chronology of Historical Events

1954

1 November — The start of the conflict is marked by a wave of attacks in Algeria. Dispatch of military reinforcements. The interior minister, François Mitterrand, supports the war. Foundation of the Mouvement National Algérien (MNA) by Messali Hadj. Members of the Mouvement pour le Triomphe des Libertés Démocratiques (MTLD) are arrested.

1955

January — Jacques Soustelle is appointed governor-general of Algeria.

April — Legal promulgation of a state of emergency in Algeria.

May — The forces of the French army in Algeria are increased to 100,000 men.

September — First demonstration in Paris of conscripts refusing to go to Algeria.

November — Creation of the Sections Administratives Specialisés (SAS).

1956

February — Robert Lacoste is appointed resident-general.

6 February	So-called 'tomato day': when Guy Mollet visits Algiers, the European population organize a big demonstration. Mollet abandons his liberal line and applies a repressive policy.
March	Special powers are voted under the Mollet government.
April	Resignation of Pierre Mendès-France, minister of state in the Mollet government.
May	The Union Générale des Étudiants Musulmans d'Algérie (UGEMA) launches an indefinite strike.
July	General strike of Algerians in France and in the Algiers department.
August	The FLN defines its structure at the Soummam congress in Kabylia organized by Abane Ramdane.
October	The French authorities hijack a plane of Royal Air Maroc with FLN leaders on board.
November	The FLN carries out the first bomb attacks in Algiers. French civilians there beat up Arabs.
December	General Salan is appointed commander-in-chief in Algeria. He combines civil and military powers; dissolution of the councils of Algerian municipalities and assassination of the president of the association of mayors of Algeria (Froger).

1957

January	Start of the Battle of Algiers.
January–February	Rise in bomb attacks.
February–March–April	Several FLN leaders are arrested, and some of them murdered.
May	Massacre of civilian population of *douar* Melouza by the FLN.
June	Arrest and murder of Maurice Audin, mathematics teacher at Algiers university.
December	Assassination of Abane Ramdane, chief organizer of the Soummam congress.

1958

February | General Salan orders the bombing of Sakhiet-Sidi-Youssef in Tunisia.

April | Resignation of the Gaillard government, demonstrations in Algiers in support of Algérie française.

May | The Gouvernement Général is seized by Europeans. Massu establishes a Comité de Salut Public and appeals to General de Gaulle. Demonstration in Paris in defence of the republic.

June | The National Assembly transfers power to De Gaulle. He declares in Algiers: 'I have understood you.'

September | Formation of the Gouvernement Provisoire de la République Algérienne (GPRA).

December | General Challe and Paul Delouvrier replace General Salan. De Gaulle elected President of the Republic.

1959

April | Publication of Michel Rocard's report on the resettlement camps.

July–August | Start of operation 'Jumelles', a large-scale military operation of the French army in Kabylia.

September | De Gaulle proclaims the right of the Algerians to self-determination by referendum. Rejection by the GPRA, which demands total independence before any discussion.

November | De Gaulle appeals for a ceasefire. Ben Bella and the leaders arrested in 1956 are appointed by the FLN as negotiators.

1960

January | General Massu is dismissed from his post of commander of the army corps in Algiers. Week of the barricades in Algiers.

March	Resignation of General Challe.
June	Meeting between De Gaulle and Si Salah at the Élysée. Talks with the GPRA in Melun.
September	Trial of the 'Jeanson network' in Paris. 'Manifesto of the 121' on the right of insubordination in Algeria.
October	Round-ups of Algerians in Paris and its suburbs.
November	Louis Joxe appointed minister of state for Algerian affairs.
December	De Gaulle's visit to Algeria followed by violent disturbances in Algiers. The United Nations recognizes Algeria's right of self-determination.

1961

January	In a referendum, 75 per cent of French voters support the Algerian people's right of self-determination. Formation of the Organisation Armée Secrète (OAS).
February	Meeting in Switzerland between Georges Pompidou and the FLN.
April	Failure of the generals' putsch in Algiers. De Gaulle assumes full power.
May–June	The first discussions at Évian, new wave of OAS attacks directed by Salan.
August–September	Several bomb attacks in Algeria by the FLN and the OAS.
October	Curfew in Paris and the Paris region for Algerians alone. Bloody repression of peaceful demonstrations by Algerians in the Paris streets. OAS bomb attacks in Algeria. Arrival of the 'barbouzes' in Algiers.
December	The trade unions and the left organize demonstrations in support of Algeria and against the OAS.

1962

January	Bomb attacks in Algiers and in France by both the OAS and anti-OAS elements.
February	Demonstrations followed by brutal repression (Charonne métro station).
March	Signature of the Évian agreements and announcement of a ceasefire in Algeria.
5 July	Proclamation of national independence.

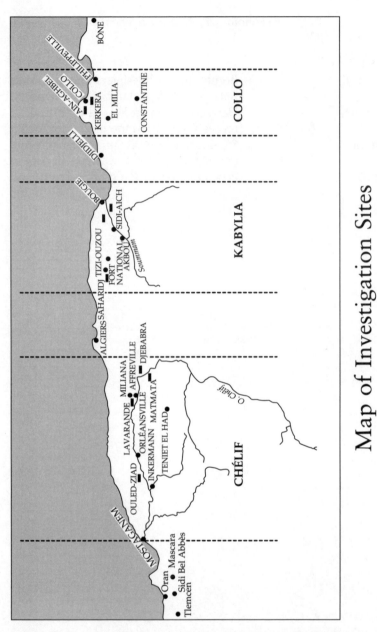

Map of Investigation Sites

The vertical lines mark the three regions where the density of resettlements was greatest (Chélif, Great and Little Kabylia, and Collo). The rectangles indicate the existence of resettlement camps (Ouled Ziad, Lavarande, Matmata, Djebabra, Djemâa Saharidj, Barbacha, Aghbala, Aïn Aghbel, Kerkera).

Source: Pierre Bourdieu and Abdelmalek Sayad, *Le Déracinement. La crise de l'agriculture traditionnelle en Algérie* (Paris: Minuit, 1964).

Publications of Pierre Bourdieu
on Algeria

Sociologie de l'Algérie, Paris: PUF, 1958, revised and corrected 1961. Translated as *The Algerians*, Boston: Beacon, 1962.

'Le choc des civilisations', in *Le Sous-développement en Algérie*, Algiers: Secrétariat Social, 1959, pp. 52–64. Translated as 'The clash of civilizations' in this volume.

'La logique interne de la civilisation algérienne traditionnelle', in *Le Sous-développement en Algérie*, Algiers: Secrétariat Social, 1959, pp. 40–51. Translated as 'The internal logic of original Algerian society' in this volume.

'Guerre et mutation sociale en Algérie', *Études Méditerranéennes*, 7 (spring 1960), pp. 25–37. Translated as 'War and social mutation in Algeria' in this volume.

'Révolution dans la révolution', *Esprit*, 1 (Jan. 1961), pp. 27–40. Translated as 'Revolution in the revolution' in this volume.

'De la guerre révolutionnaire à la révolution', in F. Perroux (ed.), *L'Algérie de demain*, Paris: PUF, 1962, pp. 5–13. Translated as 'From revolutionary war to revolution' in this volume.

'Le hantise du chômage chez l'ouvrier algérien. Prolétariat et système colonial', *Sociologie du Travail*, 4 (1962), pp. 313–31. Translated as 'Haunted by unemployment: the Algerian proletariat and the colonial system' in this volume.

'Les sous-prolétaires algériens', *Les Temps Modernes*, 199 (Dec. 1962), pp. 1030–51. Translated as 'The Algerian sub-proletarians' in this volume.

'La société traditionnelle. Attitude à l'égard du temps et conduit traditionnelle', *Sociologie de Travail*, 1 (Jan.–Mar. 1963), pp. 24–44. Translated as 'Traditional society's attitude towards time and economic behaviour' in this volume.

(with A. Darbel, J.-P. Rivet and C. Seibel) *Travail et travailleurs en Algérie*, The Hague: Mouton, 1963.

(with A. Sayad) *Le Déracinement. La crise de l'agriculture traditionnelle en Algérie*, Paris: Minuit, 1964.

(with A. Sayad) 'Paysans déracinés. Bouleversements morphologiques et changements culturels en Algérie', *Études Rurales*, 12 (Jan–Mar. 1964), pp. 56–94. Translated as 'Uprooted peasants: morphological upheavals and cultural changes in Algeria' in this volume.

'La maison kabyle ou le monde renversé', in J. Pouillon and P. Maranda (eds), *Échanges et communications. Mélanges offerts à Claude Lévi-Strauss à l'occasion de son 60e anniversaire*, The Hague: Mouton, 1970, pp. 739–58; also 'La maison ou le monde renversé', in *Esquisse d'une théorie de la pratique*, in one volume with *Trois Études d'ethnologie kabyle*, Geneva: Droz, 1972; revised and expanded version, Paris: Seuil, 2000, pp. 61–82. Also modified version in *Le Sens pratique*, Paris: Minuit, 1980, pp. 441–61. Translated as 'The Berber house or the world reversed', *Social Science Information*, 2 (1971), pp. 151–70.

Esquisse d'une théorie de la pratique, in one volume with *Trois Études d'ethnologie kabyle*, Geneva: Droz, 1972; revised and expanded version, Paris: Seuil, 2000. Translated as *Outline of a Theory of Practice*, Cambridge: Cambridge University Press, 1977.

'Les conditions sociales de la production sociologique. Sociologie colonial et décolonisation de la sociologie', in *Le Mal de voir*, Paris: Union Générale d'Éditions, 1976, pp. 416–27. Translated as 'For a sociology of sociologists' in *Sociology in Question*, London: Sage, 1993, pp. 49–53, and reproduced in this volume.

Algérie 60. Structures économiques et structures temporelles, Paris: Minuit, 1977. Translated as *Algeria 1960*, Cambridge: Cambridge University Press, 1979.

(with M. Mammeri) 'Dialogue sur la poésie orale en Kabylie', *Actes de la Recherche en Sciences Sociales*, 23 (Sept. 1978), pp. 51–66. Translated as 'Dialogue on oral poetry in Kabylia' in this volume.

Le Sens pratique, Paris: Minuit, 1980. Translated as *The Logic of Practice*, Cambridge: Polity, 1990.

'Mouloud Mammeri ou la colline retrouvée', *Le Monde*, 3 Mar. 1984.

'Du bon usage de l'ethnologie. Entretien avec M. Mammeri', *Awal. Cahiers d'Études Berbères*, 1 (1985), pp. 7–29. Translated as 'The right use of ethnology' in this volume.

'Préface', in T. Yacine-Titouh, *L'Itzli ou l'amour*, Paris: Maison des Sciences de l'Homme, 1988, pp. 11–12.

'Un analyseur de l'Inconscient. Préface', in A. Sayad, *L'Immigration ou les paradoxes de l'altérité*, Brussels: De Boeck-Wesmael, 1991, p. 13.

'La réappropriation de la culture reniée. À propos de Mouloud Mammeri', in T. Yacine (ed.), *Amour, phantasmes et sociétés en Afrique du Nord et au Sahara*, Paris: L'Harmattan/Awal, 1992, pp. 17–22.

'L'intelligence qu'on assassine. Entretien avec E. Sarner', *La Chronique d'Amnesty International*, no. 86 (Jan. 1994), pp. 34–5.

(with M. Virolle) 'Le parti de la paix civile', *Alternatives Algériennes*, 22 Nov. 1995, p. 4.

'Dévoiler et divulguer le refoulé' (Fribourg, 27 Oct. 1995), in J. Jurr (ed.), *Algérie-France-Islam*, Paris: L'Harmattan, 1997, p. 2.

'Hommage à mon ami Abdelmalek Sayad', *Libération*, 16 Mar. 1998, p. 31.

'L'odyssée de la réappropriation', *Awal*, 18 (1998).

'Préface', in A. Sayad, *La Double absence. Des illusions de l'immigré aux souffrances de l'immigré*, Paris: Seuil, 1999, pp. 9–13. Translated as A. Sayad, *The Suffering of the Immigrant*, Cambridge: Polity, 2003.

'Entre amis', *Awal*, 21 (2000), p. 6. Translated as 'Between friends' in this volume.

'The making of economic habitus', *Ethnography*, 1.1 (2000), pp. 17–41. Published in French as 'La fabrique de l'habitus économique', *Actes de la Recherche en Sciences Sociales*, 150 (Dec. 2003), pp. 79–90. Reproduced in this volume.

'Pour Abdelmalek Sayad' (talk at Institut du Monde Arabe, Paris, 1998), *Annuaire de l'Afrique du Nord*, vol. 37 (1998), Paris: CNRS Éditions, 2000, pp. 9–13. Translated as 'For Abdelmalek Sayad' in this volume.

'Entretien avec Franz Schultheis' (Paris, 26 June 2001), in *Images d'Algérie. Une affinité élective*, ed. F. Schultheis and C. Frisinghelli, catalogue for exhibition 23 Jan.–2 Mar. 2003, Institut du Monde Arabe, Arles: Actes Sud/Camera Austria/Sindbad/Fondation Liber, 2003, pp. 19–44. Translated as 'Seeing with the lens: about photography' in this volume.

'Participant objectivation', *Journal of the Royal Anthropological Institute*, ns, 9 (June 2003), pp. 281–94. Published in French as 'L'objectivation participante', *Actes de la Recherche en Sciences Sociales*, 150 (Dec. 2003), pp. 43–58. Reproduced in this volume.

Notes

The Editorial Project

1   Owing to its geographical position as a mountain region and its close-
    ness to Algiers, Kabylia has played a determining role in Algerian
    history. It managed to preserve its political and cultural integrity in
    the face of a number of different invaders. As the region of Wilaya III
    it was the heart of resistance to French colonialism during the war of
    independence [from 1954], and along with the Aurès it was the region
    most affected, owing to the strength of the maquis there and of the
    repression. The FLN (Front de Libération Nationale – National Lib-
    eration Front) drew many of its historic leaders from there. Anthro-
    pologically, it has preserved several cultural practices (language, belief,
    mythico-ritual system) that have aroused the interest of researchers.
    Bourdieu's own interest focused on the very confined social units (vil-
    lages or hamlets) that require direct observation. This made it possible
    to grasp behaviours ('The sense of honour'), social practices ('The
    Kabyle house', 'Kinship as representation and will') and cultural prac-
    tices that a wider sociological investigation extended to numerically
    larger groups does not reveal. Investigation of Algerian society as a
    whole, mobilizing the tools of 'sociology' (statistics, questionnaires,
    investigative techniques) and involving the work of a team, focused
    on the study of a much broader society (rural and urban) faced with
    dramatic social and economic mutations. Observed in the same period,
    these two terrains (in the broad sense) were complementary and shared
    a common experience and history. The same applies to the relationship
    between the ethnological procedure and the sociological approach,
    which, according to Bourdieu, cannot be truly separated.
2   Cf. Bourdieu's research conducted in parallel on the peasant worlds
    in Kabylia and in Béarn.

3   Under the *sénatus-consulte*, a decree-law of the Second Empire, the Algerian tribes were declared owners of the territories that they worked. The law of 28 April 1887 extended the *sénatus-consulte* by proceeding to define the tribes, to form *douars*, and to classify land according to the nature of its ownership; it proved to be 'the most effective war machine against the Algerian social organization'.

4   According to information obtained from André Nouschi, known for his work on the population of the Constantine region and on Algerian nationalism. See 'Letters to André Nouschi', in this volume.

5   The law of 1873, passed under pressure from the colonists after the death of Louis Napoleon, allowed private property to be made official. This procedure was also known as *'francisation'*, as it made a clean slate of the previous 'indigenous' laws and codes, and meant the official transition of 'indigenous' private property to the French legislative regime with definite title. This was a true measure of – legal – dispossession of the Algerian peasants.

6   Cantonment was the system established in order to obtain land for French colonization, cf. Bugeaud's circular of 10 April 1847: 'I believe I have said several times', he wrote, 'that my doctrine towards the Arabs was not to repress them, but rather to blend them in with our colonization; not to dispossess them of all their land and move them elsewhere, but to concentrate them on the territory they possess and have long enjoyed, when this territory is disproportionate to the population of the tribe.'

7   These lectures dwelt particularly on Claude Lévi-Strauss (who had just published his *Structural Anthropology*), James Frazer, Franz Boas, Bronisław Malinowski, Ruth Benedict, George Herbert Mead, Ralph Linton, etc., with very little on Karl Marx, Émile Durkheim, Max Weber or Ibn Khaldun. The rare incursions Bourdieu made into 'ethics' were by way of cultural anthropology, on the theme of the opposition between 'shame culture' and 'guilt culture', for example, as explained by Alain Accardo, a student of Bourdieu at this time.

8   [Translated as *The Algerians* (Boston: Beacon Press, 1962).] The French state refused Algeria the status of a nation: to recognize the existence of an Algerian society was accordingly seen as a provocation.

9   Pierre Bourdieu, *Sketch for a Self-Analysis* (Cambridge: Polity, 2007), p. 40.

10 Cf. Pierre Bourdieu, *Images d'Algérie* (Arles: Actes Sud, 2003). Cf. also Yves Winkin, 'La disposition photographique de Pierre Bourdieu', contribution to Cerisy conference (12–19 July 2001), see *Le Symbolique et le Social. La réception internationale du travail de Pierre Bourdieu* (Liège: Éditions de l'Université de Liège, 2005), pp. 43–51.

11 Cf. Pierre Bourdieu, *Outline of a Theory of Practice* (Cambridge: Cambridge University Press, 1977), and *The Logic of Practice* (Cambridge: Polity, 1990).

12 Ethnology has not always been well seen in politically committed milieus within the social sciences, owing to the connection it has had with the colonial power. It is criticized, for example, for the creation in 1922 of an Académie des Sciences Coloniales by Daladier (minister for the colonies in the coalition of the time), who declared in 1924 that 'only a scientific study of races and peoples, their customs and their history, can truly provide our colonial administration with the flexibility and strength that are indispensable to accomplish the colonizing effort' (in Caroline Martello, 'Germaine Tillion et l'Algérie. De l'ethnologie au politique', mémoire de Master II, history department, University of Nice Sophia-Antipolis, 2005–6). The situation was unfavourable to ethnology in Algeria for a long while after independence. One can understand the reasons why Bourdieu deliberately opted for sociology and not ethnology, even when this was what he practised in the field.

13 This presentation only offers the elements necessary to make the Algerian context intelligible. A more detailed study of the period remains to be made.

14 Jean Sprecher, 'Il se sentait bien avec nous . . .', in *L'autre Bourdieu*, special issue of *Awal*, 27–8 (2003), pp. 298–300.

15 In particular, Guy Mollet.

16 Cf. Lucien Bianco, 'Nous n'avions jamais vu "le monde" . . .', in *L'autre Bourdieu*, pp. 267–77. See also Gisèle Sapiro, 'Une liberté contrainte. La formation de la théorie de l'habitus', in Louis Pinto, Gisèle Sapiro and Patrick Champagne (eds), *Pierre Bourdieu, sociologue* (Paris: Fayard, 2004), pp. 61–3.

17 Pierre Bourdieu, 'Fieldwork in philosophy', in *In Other Words* (Cambridge: Polity, 1990), p. 3.

18 Administrator of the Bibliothèque Nationale, historian, specialist in the history of the Middle Ages and modern times.

19 Bianco, 'Nous n'avions jamais vu "le monde" . . .'.

20 Jean-Pierre Rioux and Jean-François Sirinelli, *La Guerre d'Algérie et les intellectuels français* (Brussels: Complexe, 1991).

21 Unpublished interview with Alain Accardo by Tassadit Yacine.

22 Pierre Bourdieu, Alain Darbel, Jean-Paul Rivet, Claude Seibel, *Travail et travailleurs en Algérie* (The Hague: Mouton, 1963), pp. 251–62.

23 See the connection in *Masculine Domination* (Cambridge: Polity, 2001), and *The Bachelors' Ball* (Cambridge: Polity, 2008).

24 See in particular the foreword to *Photography: A Middle-Brow Art* (Pierre Bourdieu with Luc Boltanski, Robert Castel, Jean-Claude Chamboredon) (Cambridge: Polity, 1990).

25 Bourdieu, 'Fieldwork in philosophy', p. 23.

26 See *Esquisse d'une théorie de la pratique* (Geneva: Droz, 1972), pp. 157–256.

27 *The Logic of Practice*, pp. 1–65.

At the Origins of a Singular Ethnosociology

An earlier and shorter version of this text appeared in the collective work *Travailler avec Bourdieu*, edited by Rose-Marie Lagrave and Pierre Encrevé (Paris: Flammarion, 2003), pp. 333–45, and as Tassadit Yacine, 'Bourdieu in Algeria at war', *Ethnography*, 54 (2004), pp. 487–509.

1   The decision to establish resettlement camps was applied in the Aurès in late 1955, and extended to the Ouarsenis and then the whole of Algeria in 1956. A decree of 17 March 1956 gave full powers to the minister in residence (Robert Lacoste at this time) to 'establish zones in which the stay of persons is regulated or forbidden, with the possibility of delegating this power to the prefects and military authorities'. Marked by the delegation of civil power to the military, this decree also increased considerably the repressive powers of the minister in residence. It indicated a deliberate initiative by the political authority to increase the powers granted to the military authorities, the French parliament having granted the government 'the most extensive powers to take any exceptional measure [. . .] with a view to the restoration of order in Algeria'. Cf. Michel Rocard, *Rapport sur les camps de regroupement et autres textes sur la guerre d'Algérie* (Paris: Mille et Une Nuits, 2003), pp. 231–2.

2   Jean Amrouche, 'A propos des émeutes du 8 mai 1945', in Tassadit Yacine (ed.), *Un Algérien s'adresse aux Français* (Paris: L'Harmattan, 1994), pp. 279–86; Marcel Reggui, *Les Massacres de Guelma* (Paris: La Découverte, 2006); Annie Rey-Goldzeiguer, *Aux origines de la guerre d'Algérie* (Paris: La Découverte, 2006).

3   Lacoste's appointment followed the visit by Guy Mollet to Algiers and the famous 'tomato day' when Mollet was badly received by the European population – a reason that led him to change his policy. Robert Lacoste then embarked on a policy of heavy repression extended to the urban centres (cf. the 'battle of Algiers' of 1957). It was under his authority that political power passed into the hands of the military. The practice of torture and disappearances became generalized (cf. Rocard, *Rapport sur les camps de regroupement*, p. 220). André Nouschi and Jean Sprecher describe the climate of intellectual terror in which research in Algeria was conducted, in André Nouschi, 'Autour de *Sociologie de l'Algérie*', in *L'autre Bourdieu*, special issue of *Awal*, 27–8 (2003), pp. 29–35; Jean Sprecher, 'Il se sentait bien avec nous . . .', in *L'autre Bourdieu*, pp. 295–305.

4   Pierre Bourdieu, 'Between friends', in this volume.

5   Jean Sprecher, *A contre-courant. Étudiants libéraux et progressistes à Alger, 1954–1962* (Saint-Denis: Bouchène, 2000), p. 83.

6   The son of William Marçais, he was professor of Arabic language and North African civilization from 1953. A champion of 'Algérie française', Philippe Marçais was deputy for Algiers from November

1958 to July 1962. On his return to France, he joined Jean-Marie Le Pen's party.

7 Jean Servier was one of the ethnologists most involved in the Algerian war, and certainly the first to entrust indigenous Algerians with weapons (the future *harkis*), according to Alain Maillard de La Morandais. This survivor of 1 November 1954 assumed the improvised command of Arris, in the Aurès; cf. his book *L'Honneur est sauf* (Paris: Seuil, 1990), p. 44. See also Camille Lacoste-Dujardin, *Opération oiseau bleu, des Kabyles, des ethnologues et la guerre d'Algérie* (Paris: La Découverte, 1997), pp. 254–71.

8 The Parti Communiste Algérien was perceived at this time as an appendix of the French Communist Party.

9 This was the Fédération des Libéraux, intellectuals (Emmanuel Roblès, Edmond Charlot, Mouloud Mammeri) close to Albert Camus, who published a newspaper, *Espoir Algérie*, from 1956 until it was banned in 1958.

10 Henri Alleg, *La Question* (Paris: Minuit, 1957).

11 Maurice Audin died under torture on 1 June 1957. Cf. Pierre Vidal-Naquet, *L'Affaire Audin* (Paris: Minuit, 1958).

12 Cf. Sprecher, 'Il se sentait bien avec nous . . .'; Pierre Vidal-Nacquet, *La Raison d'État* (Paris: Minuit, 1961).

13 André Mandouze, a *normalien*, was a Resistance veteran. In 1946 he was appointed professor at the University of Algiers. A Gaullist, close to Duval, the archbishop of Algiers, and to Catholics who supported the FLN (François Mauriac, Louis Massignon, Henri Guillemin, Pierre-Henri Simon), Mandouze campaigned for Algerian independence. He particularly denounced torture in the mainstream press (*France-Observateur*, *Le Monde*, *Témoignage Chrétien*), and founded *Consciences Maghrébines*.

14 Cf. *L'Algérie à l'époque d'Abdelkader* (Paris: Larose, 1951).

15 Cf. Bourdieu, 'Between friends'.

16 Characteristic of Peyrega's action was the publication on 4 April 1957 in *France-Observateur* of a letter to the minister of the interior in which he described the summary execution of a Muslim by a parachutist. This teacher, the dean of the faculty of law, was suspended from lecturing and became the object of violent attack in the Algerian press.

17 Comité Etudiant d'Action Laïque et Démocratique, affiliated to the Comité d'Action Laïque, which had a significant impact.

18 Bourdieu, 'Between friends'.

19 Abdelmalek Sayad, *Histoire et recherche identitaire* (Saint-Denis: Bouchène, 2000), p. 19.

20 Pierre Bourdieu, *Sociology in Question* (London: Sage, 1993), p. 51.

21 Similarly, René Maunier and Robert Montagne, both specialists on the Berber world, produced major work without taking into consideration the colonial phenomenon and its effects on the society they studied.

22 Georges-Henri Bousquet (1900–78) was a specialist in Islamic law and Berber history.

23 Organisation de l'Armée Secrète: a group inside the French army in Algeria formed to sow terror and force the French government to renege on the agreements for Algerian independence. Several Algerian and French figures were assassinated by these militants, on both sides of the Mediterranean.

24 Jean Servier, *Demain en Algérie* (Paris: Robert Laffont, 1959); *Les Portes de l'année* (Paris: Robert Laffont, 1962); *Dans l'Aurès sur les pas des rebelles* (Paris: France-Empire, 1995).

25 See in particular *Structures sociales dans le Haut Atlas* (Paris: PUF, 1955); 'Cent vingt ans de sociologie maghrébine', *Annales* (1957), p. 296. According to André Nouschi, the publication of *Structures sociales dans le Haut Atlas* had the effect of a bombshell in the University of Algiers.

26 In 1955, Germaine Tillion was commissioned by Jacques Soustelle, then governor-general of Algeria. She was the author of a report on the situation in the Aurès, which she described as disastrous (poverty, repression, etc.). It was also under Soustelle that she established the 'social centres' service. The developing political situation in Algeria led her to leave the Gouvernement Général – as also did Vincent Monteil – but without deciding to publicly acknowledge the existing government's logic (and consequent responsibility) for the Algerian disaster. She only came to support the FLN after the battle of Algiers.

27 Jacques Soustelle was a specialist in the Aztec world and a significant figure in the Resistance. In 1943–4 he was already head of the Direction Générale des Services Secrets (DGSS) in Algiers (supported by the Comité Français de la Libération Nationale), minister of information and then of the colonies in the 1945 provisional government. Soustelle was appointed governor-general by Pierre Mendès-France (1955–6), and it was under his aegis that a state of emergency was declared in the Aurès and Kabylia, and the first internment camps created. His policy was to promote the assimilation of Muslims. In 1956 he founded the Union pour le Salut et le Renouveau de l'Algérie Française (ESRAF), then in 1959, with Georges Bidault, Léon Delbecque and Robert Lacoste, the Rassemblement pour l'Algérie Française (RAF), dissolved in 1962. His action in support of maintaining Algeria within the French republic led to his prosecution for undermining the authority of the state.

28 Germaine Tillion, *L'Algérie en 1957* (Paris: Minuit, 1957).

29 Lucien Bianco, Jacques Derrida, François Furet, Jacques Juillard, Jean-Claude Passeron and Marc Augé all did their military service in Algeria during this period.

30 The governor-general, who was both the representative of the French republic in Algeria and the representative of Algeria in acts of civilian life, was appointed by decree of the president on the proposal of the

interior minister. He held very far-reaching powers in matters of internal and external security, as well as in regulatory, administrative and financial affairs. But after the dissolution of the National Assembly on 2 December 1955, the government of Guy Mollet suppressed the Algerian assemblies, and no further election was held in Algeria between 1955 and September 1958.

31 Cf. Émile Dermenghem, *Le Culte des saints dans l'islam maghrébin* (Paris: Gallimard, 1954).

32 Louis Massignon (1883–1962) took a public stand in support of Algeria in 1945. Cf. his articles on the Algerian question and French awareness, published in *Témoignage Chrétien* from 1948 on.

33 Cf. Nouschi, 'Autour de *Sociologie de l'Algérie*'; Sprecher, 'Il se sentait bien avec nous . . .'.

34 A. Honneth, H. Kocyba and B. Schwibs, 'The struggle for symbolic order: an interview with Pierre Bourdieu', *Theory, Culture and Society*, 3.3 (1986), p. 38.

35 See *Sketch for a Self-Analysis* (Cambridge: Polity, 2007), p. 39.

36 Association de Recherche en Sciences Sociales, founded on the initiative of the church, and intended to bring 'Muslim' and European communities together. Bourdieu's first two articles (in the volume devoted to 'Sous-développement') were published thanks to the support of Henri Sanson, a priest and researcher in this same institution.

37 Cf. André Nouschi, *Enquête sur le niveau de vie des populations rurales constantinoises* (Paris: PUF, 1961); Henri Sanson, 'C'était un esprit curieux', in *L'autre Bourdieu*, pp. 279–86.

38 This attitude signalled a political position opposed to the dominant view, in particular to the practices of the army chiefs. Cf. 'L'autre Bourdieu. Ou celui qui ne disait pas ce qu'il avait envie de cacher', interview with Bourdieu by Hafid Adnani and Tassadit Yacine, in *L'autre Bourdieu*, p. 232. See also Michel Froidure, *Où était Dieu en Algérie? Lettres de révolte et d'indignation d'un appelé en Algérie 1956–1958* (Paris: Mettis/Awal, 2006), which recounts the bullying experienced by the recruits. See also Jean Ségura, *Lettres d'Algérie. La guerre d'un appelé (1958–1959)* (Paris: Nicolas Philippe, 2004).

39 See also Sprecher, *A contre-courant*, p. 67. The author offers a poignant testimony: 'I refused the EOR so as not to run the risk of finding myself in a similar situation [i.e. of taking on responsibilities], not out of cowardice but because I challenged the legitimacy of the war we were waging.'

40 Jean-Marie Domenach and Georges Suffert, 'Algérie et renaissance française', *Esprit* (June 1956), pp. 937–48.

41 Cf. Bernard Tavernier and Patrick Rotman's documentary film *La Guerre sans nom*, 1991.

42 The 'insubordinates', as distinct from conscientious objectors who unconditionally rejected armed service, refused to participate in the war, which they deemed contrary to their moral and/or political

conviction. Cf. Jean-Marie Domenach, 'Histoire d'un acte responsable. Le cas Jean Le Meur', *Esprit* (Oct. 1959), pp. 675–7.

43 Ibid.
44 Bianco, 'Nous n'avions jamais vu "le monde" . . .'.
45 Claire Mauss-Copeaux, *Appelés en Algérie. La parole confisquée* (Paris: Hachette 1998), pp. 116–17.
46 Benjamin Stora, *Appelés d'Algérie* (Paris: Gallimard, 1997), p. 45.
47 Ibid.
48 Bianco, 'Nous n'avons jamais vu "le monde" . . .'.
49 Pierre Bourdieu, 'The clash of civilizations', in this volume.
50 Ibid.
51 Ibid.
52 'I began to interest myself in Algeria as a sociologist and ethnologist because I felt that what I saw in Algeria did not correspond at all to what was said on the other side of the Mediterranean. Even those people most well-disposed towards Algerian independence, such as myself, seemed very poorly informed, and to have a rather distant view', interview with Hafid Adnani and Tassadit Yacine, in *L'autre Bourdieu*, p. 232.
53 Bourdieu, 'Between friends'.
54 Pierre Bourdieu, 'Seeing with the lens: about photography', in this volume.
55 Cf. Gilbert Meynier, *Histoire intérieure du FLN* (Paris: Fayard, 2002).
56 Cf. the 'Berber crisis' of 1949, which was a real shock to the Algerian national movement. [This refers to the split between the supporters of the Berber leader Messali Hadj and the majority of what would become the Front de Libération Nationale. – Trans.]
57 Krim Belkacem (1922–70), vice-president of the council of the Armed Forces of the Provisional Government of the Republic of Algeria (1958), was one of the negotiators with France at the Évian conference. He opposed Boumediene, and was assassinated in 1970.
58 Abane Ramdane (1920–57), the main organizer of the Soummam congress held in Kabylia in 1956, developed the broad lines of the revolutionary movement in terms of establishing a state in which politics would oversee the military. A victim of internal struggles, he was assassinated by his own side in 1957.
59 Pierre Bourdieu found himself faced in Algeria with the problems raised in France at the time of the Liberation on the subject of revolution: the connection between the ideas of revolution and its historical avatars, of the 'dictatorship of the proletariat', of the working class and the Communist Party – all of which he had taken his distance from after reading Maurice Merleau-Ponty, in particular *Adventures of the Dialectic* (London: Heinemann, 1974). Cf. Philippe Fritsche, 'Contre le totémisme intellectuel', in Gérard Mauger (ed.), *Rencontres avec Pierre Bourdieu* (Broissieux: Éditions du Croquant, 2005), p. 92. See also Honneth et al., 'The struggle for symbolic order', p. 38.

60 *The Logic of Practice* (Cambridge: Polity, 1990), p. 3.
61 In *Le Sous-développement* (Algiers: Secrétariat Social, 1959), pp. 52–64.
62 Ibid., pp. 40–51.
63 Information obtained from relatives and friends. Cf. also Bourdieu, *Sketch for a Self-Analysis*, p. 53.
64 See Julian Pitt-Rivers, 'Pierre Bourdieu. Anthropologue, sociologue et philosophe', in *L'autre Bourdieu*, pp. 47–8, and Isaac Chiva, 'Pierre Bourdieu. Une ethnographie particulière', in *L'autre Bourdieu*, pp. 39–46.
65 Raymond Aron had also called on Jean Cuisenier, established in Tunisia, at the same time.
66 Tillion, *L'Algérie en 1957*, p. 24.
67 In a subsequent edition, this expression was replaced by that of 'social vivisection'.
68 Pierre Bourdieu, *Sociologie de l'Algérie* (Paris: PUF, 1958), p. 118.
69 Georges Balandier, 'La situation coloniale. Approche théorique', *Cahiers Internationaux de Sociologie*, 2 (1951), pp. 44–79.
70 Germaine Tillion was referring to the increase in the Algerian population (as a cause of its impoverishment), due to a fall in mortality brought about by French medical action. Cf. Tillion, *L'Algérie en 1957*, p. 13.
71 Bourdieu, *Sociologie de l'Algérie*, pp. 117–18.
72 'It is estimated that in the Mitidja', Bourdieu wrote, 'more than 80 per cent of the land belongs to the colonists, and more than 90 per cent in the Algerian Sahel. Similar proportions are observed in the plains of Bône and Philippeville, as well as in certain regions around Oran.' Ibid., p. 109.
73 Jean Amrouche, like Kateb Yacine, had been marked by the bloody repression of 8 May 1945. He campaigned for Algerian independence until 1962, acting as a mediator between the FLN and De Gaulle until the Évian agreements were reached.
74 Jean El Mouhoub Amrouche, 'Algeria fara da se', *Témoignage Chrétien*, 8 Nov. 1957, reprinted in Yacine, *Un Algérien s'adresse aux Français*, pp. 39–48.
75 A law decreeing a state of emergency, in April 1955, then another on special powers, in March 1956, introduced an exceptional regime that applied to Algeria from 1958, despite its being an integral part of the French republic. In actual fact, in order to counter the FLN and the rise of terrorism, 'between the 8th and the 12th of March, the National Assembly, by an almost unanimous vote that included all the Communists, handed the government "terrifying special powers that potentially put an end to any democratic life in Algeria", raising the psychological and moral obstacles for those who sought to continue struggling against the "gangrene" of coercive methods used in police and military interrogations'. In Maillard de La Morandais, *L'Honneur*

est sauf, p. 52. The coup of 13 May 1958, by granting the army a still greater share of civil power, aggravated the situation.

76 This list of informants is far from complete. We only cite here the most important of those who provided information on Kabyle society.

77 Tassadit Yacine, 'Pierre Bourdieu *amusnaw* kabyle ou intellectuel organique de l'humanité', in Mauger, *Rencontres avec Pierre Bourdieu*, pp. 565–74.

78 Cf. Pierre Bourdieu interview by Mouloud Mammeri, 'The right use of ethnology', in this volume.

79 [Institut National de Statistique et d'Études Économiques; Bourdieu worked with its Algerian services. – Trans.] Under the Vichy regime, the NIR (enrolment number on the national register of personal identification), initially known as '*numéro de Français*', a codification invented by René Camille (who died after being deported in 1944), was taken up by General Marie in Algeria to register Jews and Muslims. In reality, however, this initiative consisted in distinguishing Jews from other communities there, as was clearly indicated by a note of 31 March 1941 issued by the Direction de la Démographie and signed by General Marie as administrative inspector, on behalf of the Algiers regional director. 'The application to Algeria of the law of 7 October 1940 and the decrees of 20 November 1940 and 12 February 1941 on indigenous Jews has not yet been the object of any particular instruction on the part of the Gouvernement Général. It is however envisaged that in future censuses, it will be necessary to distinguish this category of inhabitants, who in 1936 were classed together with Europeans. The measures to be taken by the Service de la Démographie for this classification will thus have to be studied without delay. The registering of Europeans, for its part, will begin by checking the civil registers for the surnames, first names and dates of birth of the inhabitants, but Jews are enrolled on the same registers as French people. The first study to undertake is to investigate (1) Jews who benefited from the Crémieux decree [of 1870, granting full French citizenship]; (2) their descendants [. . .]. We shall then be able to distinguish, simply by inspecting the record, a French person from a Jew, as well as from an indigenous Muslim . . .'. Cited in Jean-Pierre Azéma, Raymond Lévy-Bruhl and Béatrice Touchelay, 'Mission d'analyse historique sur le système statistique français de 1940 à 1945', mimeo, INSEE. The management of the NIR was handed over to INSEE in 1946. This note was not without consequence for the situation of Algerian Jews, who were deprived of French nationality.

80 Cf. Michel Cornaton, *Les Camps de regroupement et la guerre d'Algérie* (Paris: L'Harmattan, 1998); Rocard, *Rapport sur les camps de regroupement*.

81 Cf. Pierre Bourdieu, Alain Darbel, Jean-Paul Rivet, Claude Seibel, *Travail et travailleurs en Algérie* (The Hague: Mouton, 1963), p. 13.

82 'Fieldwork in philosophy', in *In Other Words* (Cambridge: Polity, 1990), p. 8.

83 This relationship is a function of the situation of trust established with the subjects investigated: 'Everything that was formerly an obstacle became a stimulus. In this way, the same questions could further the start of a genuine dialogue, because the subjects saw the choice to raise them as indicating a real understanding. For example, it was not the taking of notes that aroused reticence; once trust was extended, the subjects found it quite normal that their answers should be written down, and even sometimes insisted this be done, no doubt seeing it as confirming the seriousness of the investigation and the interest that was taken in their statements', Bourdieu et al., *Travail et travailleurs en Algérie*, p. 261.

84 Ibid., p. 260.

85 Ibid.

86 Sayad, *Histoire et recherche identitaire*, p. 70. 'Roumi' was the indigenous word for Europeans, or Christians more generally.

87 Pierre Bourdieu, *Algérie 60* (Paris: Minuit, 1977), p. 7.

88 Ibid.

89 Cf. Marie-France Garcia-Parpet, 'Des outsiders dans l'économie de marché. Pierre Bourdieu et les travaux sur l'Algérie', in *L'autre Bourdieu*, pp. 139–50; Gisèle Sapiro, 'Une liberté contrainte. La formation de la théorie de l'habitus', in Louis Pinto, Gisèle Sapiro and Patrick Champagne (eds), *Pierre Bourdieu, sociologue* (Paris: Fayard, 2004), pp. 61–3; Frédéric Lebaron, 'Les modèles économiques faces à l'économisme', in Pinto et al., *Pierre Bourdieu, sociologue*, pp. 128–30.

90 'Haunted by unemployment', in this volume.

91 Pierre Bourdieu and Abdelmalek Sayad, *Le Déracinement. La crise de l'agriculture traditionnelle en Algérie* (Paris: Minuit, 1964 and 1977), p. 11.

92 Jean El Mouhoub Amrouche, 'Regroupements ou génocide?', *Démocratie 60*, 28 Apr. 1960, in Yacine, *Un Algérien s'adresse aux Français*, p. 200.

93 Rocard, *Rapport sur les camps de regroupement*, pp. 232–3.

94 Ibid., p. 188.

95 Amrouche, 'Regroupements ou génocide?'.

96 In the aftermath of Algerian independence, this gesture was far from insignificant; its symbolic value went well beyond the dominant perception of the French scientific field, which excluded North Africans. For a bien-pensant elite, the acknowledgement of an Algerian student as possible investigator of Algerian society actually amounted to an eminently subversive stand. This view continued to prevail for a long time after, particularly when Sayad wanted to work on immigration.

97 One of the students who took part in the study of the resettlement camps (Moulah Henine) was subsequently murdered by the OAS. *Le Déracinement* was dedicated to his memory by Pierre Bourdieu and Abdelmalek Sayad, its two authors. On the circumstances of Henine's assassination, cf. Sprecher, *A contre-courant*, p. 97.

98 The expression used in the 1970 edition of *Sociologie de l'Algérie*.
99 Rocard, *Rapport sur les camps de regroupement*, p. 188.
100 Ibid., pp. 24–5.
101 Amrouche, 'Regroupements ou génocide?', p. 199.
102 Cf. Charles-Robert Ageron, 'Une dimension de la guerre d'Algérie. Les "regroupements" de populations', in Jean-Charles Jauffret and Maurice Vaïsse (eds), *Militaires et Guérilla dans la guerre d'Algérie* (Brussels: Complexe, 2002), p. 359.
103 According to sources cited by Pierre Bourdieu and Abdelmalek Sayad. This is not an exhaustive number.
104 In Bourdieu and Sayad, *Le Déracinement*, p. 13.
105 Ibid.
106 General Parlange, 15 Feb. 1960 (p. 2, IH2574/1, SHAT (Service Historique de l'Armée de Terre, Vincennes)), in Amélie Okbi, 'Le camp de regroupement de M'Chounèche, 1955–1962', mémoire de Master II, history department, University of Nice, 2006–7.
107 *Mechta*, the equivalent of *gourbi* ['shelter'], by extension hamlet or village.
108 Bourdieu and Sayad, *Le Déracinement*, p. 12.
109 Cf. for example *Algérie. Naissance de mille villages* (Algiers: Baconnier, n.d.).
110 Interview with Alain Accardo.
111 In the interview published as an appendix to his *Rapport sur les camps de regroupement*, Michel Rocard showed that his brief did not allow access to the camp. An official cover was needed (studying the legal situation of landholding) to distract the attention of the SAS commanders and make direct contact with the occupants.
112 Bourdieu, *Sketch for a Self-Analysis*.
113 Interview with Salah Bouhedja, 'Il était un parmi les dix. Autour de l'enquête sur les camps de regroupement dans *Le Déracinement*', in *L'autre Bourdieu*, p. 291.
114 French people – doctors, nurses, social workers – took part in the Algerians' struggle, as did Bourdieu and his team, by contributing their particular skills.
115 This authorization to circulate had to be requested from the commissariat of one's place of residence, for a definite period of time. All visitors to the resettlement camp had to be known to the military.
116 The special administrative sections were set up by Jacques Soustelle in 1955, and placed under the authority of General Parlange. They were established in regions where the FLN had a strong hold on the population, and were the spearhead of psychological action in the service of pacification. See also Maillard de La Morandais, *L'Honneur est sauf*, p. 44.
117 Bourdieu and Sayad, *Le Déracinement*, p. 47.
118 Interview with Alain Accardo.
119 Interview with Salah Bouhedja, 'Il était un parmi les dix . . .'.
120 Ibid.

121 Ibid.
122 The traditional assembly of adult men.
123 Interview with Alain Accardo.
124 Bourdieu, 'Between friends'.
125 Maurice Halbwachs, *The Causes of Suicide* (1930; Abingdon: Taylor & Francis, 1978), p. 8.

The Clash of Civilizations

This chapter was originally published as 'Le choc des civilisations', in *Le Sous-développement en Algérie* (Algiers: Secrétariat Social, 1959), pp. 52–64.

1 Robert Redfield, Ralph Linton and Melville Herskovits, 'A memorandum on acculturation', *American Anthropologist*, 38 (1936), pp. 149–50 (emphasis in the original).
2 We shall try to give these laws precise expression in a future work.
3 Georges Balandier provides a definition in 'La situation coloniale', *Cahiers Internationaux de Sociologie* (1951).
4 Germaine Tillion, *L'Algérie en 1957* (Paris: Minuit, 1957).
5 Marcelle Faublée-Urbain, 'Les magasins collectifs de l'oued el Abiad (Aurès)', *Journal des Africanistes*, 21.2 (1951), pp. 139–50.
6 'Progrès du réformisme musulman dans l'Aurès' (anonymous), France méditerranéenne et africaine, *Bulletin d'Études Économiques et Sociales* (Paris) (1938), p. 1.
7 Abdelhamid Ben Badis (1899–1940), president of the Association des Oulémas Musulmans Algériens, whose object was to return to the two essential sources of Islam: the Koran and the Sunnah. He was the author of the triptych: 'Algeria is our homeland, Islam is our religion, Arabic is our language'. [Editor's note.]
8 François Perroux (1903–87), an economist who sought a third way between socialism and traditional free-market capitalism; he particularly influenced the social doctrine of the French church. His books include *La Coexistence pacifique* (Paris: PUF, 1958); *Dialogue des monopoles et des nations* (Grenoble: Presses Universitaires de Grenoble, 1982); and *Aliénation et société industrielle* (Paris: Gallimard, 1970). [Editor's note.]
9 Hamza Boubekeur is an ancestor of the rector of the Paris mosque in 2008. His family were well known for having belonged in the past to a major religious confraternity, and having played an important role in the transmission of cultural and religious values in Algeria. [Editor's note.]
10 The Bureaux Arabes were an administrative structure established by France in 1844 after the conquest of Algeria. Their aim was to collect information and help determine policy towards the indigenous

population. They were abandoned under the Third Republic, but revived in 1955 under the name of the Section Administrative Spéciali-sée. [Translator's note.]

11 Albert de Broglie, *Une réforme administrative en Algérie* (Paris: H. Dumineray, 1860).

12 Capitaine Vaissière, *Les Ouled-Rechaïch* (Algiers 1893), p. 90.

13 Xavier Yacono (1912–90), a historian of colonization, was professor at the University of Algiers from 1957 to 1962. *Histoire de la colonisa-tion française* (Paris: PUF, 1973); *Les Étapes de la decolonisation française* (Paris: PUF, 1982). [Editor's note.]

14 The ambiguity of the principles that inspired the *sénatus-consulte* is clearly apparent in the work of Albert de Broglie who, besides the justifications listed above, invoked the following reasons: 'With the communist principle that forms the basis of Arab society, to expect any kind of progress is to give way to a chimera, and to work on this basis means struggling against the impossible. No matter what is done, collective property means permanent and perpetual barbarism; by forbidding man any hope, it discourages him from all work, and by attaching the hard worker and the idle wastrel to the same soil, it has the inevitable effect of also fatally binding the future to the past. There is here a school of laziness and inertia, which will continue to prevail over the most edifying examples and most enlightened instruction that the French administration can give [. . .] It is *always the constitution of Arab society that forms the obstacle*, and this must be tackled at its very root' (*Une réforme administrative en Algérie*).

15 Jean Dresch (1905–94), French geographer with a speciality in desert environments, and a Communist militant actively committed to decol-onization struggles. [Editor's note.]

16 François Perroux, 'L'ordonnance de J. M. Keynes et les pays sous-développés', *Bulletin de l'Union des Exploitants Électriques en Bel-gique* (July 1953).

17 'It is not because in the underdeveloped countries only between 4 and 15 per cent of the population of working age work for wages that other inhabitants are unemployed. The fact that they do not work is something else; they are congregated in agricultural or handicraft production units, or again occupied in unproductive jobs. Egypt counts a surplus agricultural population of at least 5 million (out of a population of 22 million). Unemployment is both everywhere and nowhere. And it is certainly easier to establish employment offices than to change mentality, to create the desire to work and to change habits of life.' André Plantier, in *Encyclopédie française*, pp. 11–12.

18 S. Herbert Frankel, *The Economic Impact of Under-Developed Societ-ies* (Oxford: Basil Blackwell, 1953).

19 Pierre Moussa, *Chances économiques de la communauté franco-africaine* (Paris: Armand Colin, 1957), p. 142. Cf. Journées d'Études des Secrétariats Sociaux d'Algérie, *La Lutte des Algériens contre la faim. Compte rendu* (Algiers: Secrétariat Social, 1955), pp. 19–29.

Traditional Society's Attitude towards Time and Economic Behaviour

This chapter was originally published as 'La société traditionnelle. Attitude à l'égard du temps et conduite traditionnelle', *Sociologie du Travail*, 1 (Jan.– Mar. 1963), pp. 24–44. Part of this article was reproduced in *Algérie 60. Structures économiques et structures temporelles* (Paris: Minuit, 1977).

1 Max Weber, 'Die Grenznutzenlehre und das "psychophysische Grundgesetz"', in *Gesammelte Aufsätze zur Wissenschaftslehre*, cited by Oscar Lange in *Économie politique*, vol. 1: 'Problèmes généraux' (Paris: PUF, 1962), p. 396.

2 Ludwig von Mises, for example, writes: 'The theorems attained by correct praxeological reasoning are not only perfectly certain and incontestable, like the correct mathematical theorems. They refer, moreover, with the full rigidity of their apodictic certainty and incontestability to the reality of action as it appears in life and history. Praxeology conveys exact and precise knowledge of real things.' *Human Action: A Treatise on Economics* (New Haven: Yale University Press, 1949), p. 39.

3 In the collective granary where the Chaouïa used to store their reserves, which was common to the whole fraction, the necessary foresight to distribute a good harvest over time, sometimes over several years, the right of the family head to survey individual consumption, and the privations imposed for fear of scarcity, even in the midst of abundance and for life, were erected into a collective institution. The same went for the *matmura*, the family or clan silo of the Arab-speakers.

4 The resistance to the creation of these terraces was observed throughout rural Algeria. 'The establishment of terraces planted with fruit trees on ground that is sloping and generally mediocre was rejected or accepted only with great reticence by the Islamic occupants, despite the great increase in value it would give their lands and the perspective of significant profits from the subsequent sale of fruit.' Report of the administrator of the mixed municipality of Mascara, in *L'Algérie du demi-siècle* (Algiers: SNLA, 1950). 'The construction of terraces across ploughed land creates (for the peasants) costs of maintenance and an obstacle to their work, with distant profits that they do not conceive.' Ibid., Teniet-el-Haad.

5 Gaëtan Pirou, in *Annales Sociologiques* (1934), p. 71.

6 François Simiand, 'La monnaie, réalité sociale', *Annales Sociologiques*, series D (1934), p. 81.

7 Ibid., p. 80.

8 This is something that merchants are well aware of, especially those who frequent the markets of the South where the nomads live, miserly with their sheep but prodigal with their money.

9   Maurice Violette, *L'Algérie vivra-t-elle?* (Paris: Félix Alcan, 1931), pp. 89–91.

10 Paul Ernest-Picard gives a summary picture of economic life in pre-colonial Algeria, certain essential features of which are worth repeating here: 'The traffic that the movements of transhumant nomads give rise to often assumes [. . .] the form of direct exchanges of goods, barter, rather than genuine commercial negotiations that necessitate recourse to credit or even the employment of money [. . .]. Merchants would give credit to retailers, and Jews and Mozabites, practising direct lending to individuals, in some sense fulfilled the function of bankers. This did not mean that usury was any less.' Paul Ernest-Picard, *La Monnaie et le crédit en Algérie depuis 1830*, collection du Centenaire de l'Algérie (Algiers: J. Carbonel, 1930), p. 21. The most common forms of contract were contracts of association and partnership, lending on the security of landed property (*rahnia*) and *tsenia*. 'It does not appear that commercial paper, either in the primitive form of simple documents noting debts and credits, or that of bills of exchange, was used in the interior of the country as instruments of credit. Local trade, and exchanges between one region and another, were not developed enough to lead to a circulation of commercial paper. Barter and metallic money were the normal means of settlement in internal trade.' Ibid., p. 30.

11 The lack of an ability to handle monetary symbols was often coupled with a pressure of poverty that made anticipation and calculation impossible. 'If he is given a sum of money in exchange for his land, and is unable to find a new use for it immediately, he is obliged to consume his capital in order to live, and in a very short space of time finds himself forced to hire himself out in order to feed his family.' William Marçais, 'L'exode de Tlemcen en 1911', *Rapport de la commission d'enquête*, published by the Gouvernement Général de l'Algérie in 1911, p. 41.

12 To show how society tends to shape economic attitudes from childhood on, one 'ideal type' anecdote is enough (related in the newspapers on 29 October 1959): the children of a middle school in Lowestoft, England, mutually insured themselves against punishment – the insured was paid 4 shillings for a hiding. But faced with abuse of the system, the 13-year-old chairman had to envisage a supplementary clause under which the company was not responsible for voluntary accidents.

13 Adolphe Hanoteau, *Poésies populaires de la Kabylie du Jurjura* (Paris: Imprimerie Impériale, 1867), p. 193, n. 1. These rates, which in many places were still typical in 1954, should be no surprise, given that in Europe in the twelfth and thirteenth centuries they sometimes reached 80%.

14 Or else *wa argaz d wawal*, this is a man, and moreover a word. [Editor's note.]

15　André Leroi-Gourhan and Jean Poirier, for example, write: 'The indigenous, who has perhaps been too readily accused of improvidence but who nevertheless lived and acted in the present for the present, has been obliged to reckon with the future; one could say that the temporal dimension has been definitively introduced into his existence.' *Ethnologie de l'Union français* (Paris: PUF, 1953), vol. 2, p. 921. Does this mean that he was living 'outside of time'?

16　This is how, for example, the implicit description of temporal consciousness specific to Western man, as revealed by Leenhardt's analyses, is precisely that of intellectualism. Perhaps it is because he describes the experience of the Kanaks better than his own that he casts the Kanaks into radical alterity.

17　Perhaps this should be seen as one of the roots of the proscriptions on calculation: you shouldn't count the men present at an assembly, you shouldn't measure the grain reserved for sowing; you don't count the number of eggs laid, but rather the number of chickens born. Is this because counting the eggs or measuring the seed would mean presuming on the future?

18　*D acrik er-Rebbi* in Kabyle.

19　This society develops an entire art of passing time, or better, taking one's time, with politeness and the art of speaking being essential aspects of this. The same indifference towards time, schedules and exactness appears in all behaviour.

20　*Niya* signifies purity of intention, simplicity, uprightness, correctness; pejoratively, stupidity. *Bab niya* or *bou niya* is the simple, candid man. *Aâgun* is the infant who does not yet speak, and by extension the innocent, the naive, the credulous. *Tiâuggant* signifies good faith, innocence, and pejoratively, stupidity.

21　There are still two or three of these *bou niya* in the village of Aghbala where these observations were made. They are the only people for example who still go round barefoot. This joke is attributed to them: 'Why shoes when you still have skin [*tamlikth*, tanned skin]?' Another man goes barefoot, his shoes in his hand, and only wears them on the doorstep, when he enters someone else's house.

22　He may sell dried fruit, or olives, but not oil. [If oil is not sold, it is exchanged for wheat and figs . . . or for products destined for consumption. – Editor.]

23　The watch, as a luxury object, found its way into the countryside a few years ago, but does not govern the whole of life; it simply provides a more precise system of reference than traditional procedures.

24　The behaviour of the Kabyle peasant, and the ethos it reveals, find a symbolic expression in the ritual system whose intention can be grasped by structural analysis: everything happens as if the annual cycle of rituals was inspired by the aim of resolving the contradiction that lies at the heart of agriculture. Nature, left to itself, runs riot, becomes barren and sterile. The fertilizing action of man and his techniques, no matter how necessary and inevitable, is criminal, first of all because it is rape and violence, and secondly because it applies means whose handling is inherently blameworthy and dangerous, i.e. instruments made by fire such as the ploughshare, the loom, the knife and the sickle. The high points of the agricultural year, ploughing and harvest, form the summits of a tragedy played out between two characters, man and nature, the drama of the agriculturalist who is forced to do violence to the land in order to fertilize it and win its wealth. This deeply buried intention, as revealed by analysis, sometimes breaks through to the level of attitudes and ideologies. The land is never treated as raw material, as a brute matter that can simply be exploited. 'The land', people say, 'demands accounts.' It will be able to extract reparation, for example, for ill-treatment inflicted by a hasty and greedy peasant (*al ahammaq*) or a clumsy one.

25 With a geographic environment characterized by uncertain climate and temperatures, and fragility of the soil and its vegetable cover, natural determinisms exert all the greater force given how archaic are the means of production.

26 Karl Marx, *Capital*, vol. 1 (Harmondsworth: Penguin, 1976), p. 175.

27 The descriptions Max Weber gives of traditionalist societies do not totally escape an ethnocentrism that leads to describing them in negative terms: 'Initially,' he writes for example, 'everywhere that traditionalism, the sacred character of tradition, is displayed, what is emphasized is solely activity and economic action as these have been inherited from the ancestors [. . .]. Ineptitude and a general repugnance to emerge from the beaten paths to which one is accustomed form the general reason for the maintenance of traditions [. . .]. What acts still more strongly is the magic stereotyping of activity, the profound *dread* of introducing the least change into the way of life to which one is accustomed, a dread arising from the fear of damaging magic consequences.' Max Weber, *Wirtschaftsgeschichte* (Munich/Leipzig, 1924), pp. 302–3 (my emphasis: P.B.).

28 Given the object of the present article, we have only given here a summary schema of the process of adaptation to the capitalist order and the correlative transformation of the attitude towards time.

29 Cf. Pierre Bourdieu, 'Haunted by Unemployment', in this volume.

30 In January 1960 the French franc was replaced by the '*nouveau franc*', worth 100 old francs. [Translator's note.]

The Internal Logic of Original Algerian Society

This chapter was originally published as 'La logique interne de la civilisation algérienne traditionnelle', in *Le Sous-développement en Algérie* (Algiers: Secrétariat Social, 1959), pp. 40–51.

Notes to Pages 73–80

1 Xavier Jacono, *Les Bureaux arabes et l'évolution du genre de vie indigène dans l'Ouest du Tell algérois (Dahra, Chelif, Ouarsenis, Sersou)* (Paris: Larose, 1953), p. 386.
2 Ibid., p. 387.
3 Adolphe Hanoteau and Aristide Letourneux, *La Kabylie et les coutumes kabyles*, 3 vols (Paris: Imprimerie Nationale, 1872–3). [Editor's note.]
4 A traditional form of sharecropping in which the tenant receives a fifth of the crop. [Editor's note.]
5 *Lazarillo de Tormes*, a book published anonymously in 1554, portrays typical characters of the Spanish 'golden age' through the eyes of its picaresque protagonist. [Translator's note.]
6 The various types of contract, always combining complementary wealth and poverty, should be listed and analysed; their number and diversity is so large that all possible combinations seem to have been realized, according to the law that 'the cultural focal point' gives rise in every culture to the most numerous collective inventions.
7 Secteurs d'Amélioration Rurale; Société Algérienne de Prévoyance. [Editor's note.]
8 The 'stereotype' (part of the universal mythology of racism) according to which 'Arabs are lazy' means nothing, any more than does its pure and simple negation, which is certainly well-meaning, but does not take into account the phenomena described here. Instead of entering the logic of the pre-capitalist mind and considering that the lure of profit and the cult of labour are not universally recognized values, but particular to our own civilization, the result is to be locked in a sterile debate which can only be concluded by a compromise solution according to which there are 'hard workers alongside others who are lazy'. Michel Leiris, *Contacts de civilisation en Martinique et en Guadeloupe* (Paris: UNESCO-Gallimard, 1955), p. 94. Concepts such as 'hard-working' and 'lazy' only have a meaning for an 'activist' view of the world such as our own.
9 Éric Weil, *Philosophie politique* (Paris: Vrin 1956), p. 6.
10 Ibid., p. 71. It is clear that this definition only includes certain features that may be viewed as dominant.
11 Octave Mannoni, *Prospero and Caliban: The Psychology of Colonization* (Ann Arbor: University of Michigan Press, 1990).
12 An Islamic religious feast for which a sheep is sacrificed. [Editor's note.]
13 Jean-Gabriel Magnin, 'L'épargne et l'ouvrier rural', Institut des Belles Lettres de Langue Arabe, Tunis, 1954, pp. 93–8.
14 Anthropologists observe that in phenomena of cultural borrowing, the 'non-symbolic' elements are transmitted more readily than the 'function'. This law should be kept in mind by educators and technicians, who may otherwise find themselves severely disappointed. Thus, it has often been observed that young girls instructed in different techniques (knitting, mending, budget management, etc.) apparently 'forget' these

when they return to their traditional environment. The fact is that these behaviours are relatively easy to acquire in comparison with the psychological structures underlying them.

15 Charcoal burning was a current practice in the 1940s. [Editor's note.]
16 Germaine Tillion, 'Dans l'Aurès, le drame des civilisations archaïques', *Annales* (July–Sept. 1957).

From Revolutionary War to Revolution

This chapter was originally published as 'De la guerre révolutionnaire à la révolution', in François Perroux (ed.), *L'Algérie de demain* (Paris: PUF, 1962).

1 For an analysis of the different aspects of this mutation, see 'Revolution in the revolution', in this volume.
2 These resettlements of population were undertaken by the French army, as part of the policy of military repression. [Editor's note.]
3 This can be seen in the testimony recorded in an agricultural cooperative on the Chéliff plain: 'Were you forced to come here?' 'No, not exactly. Some families, yes. Even with the soldiers, we refused to let the old farmworkers leave here; other [families] are here just like that, they don't know why, they were told to leave, they left and they are quite happy here to find a house, land to work, they are here and the fathers, sons and brothers are in a resettlement centre. That's it. We are waiting. What I tell you here, very few have understood.'
4 The Algerian people are fully aware of the need to invent new educational techniques. People are heard to say, for example, in Algiers: 'The cafés should all be requisitioned and used for schools.' What is desired is a practical teaching, directly adapted to the concrete needs of everyday life, using effective methods capable of obtaining rapid results.
5 For simplicity's sake, the term 'proletariat' is used here for all permanent wage-earners in the modern sector, among whom have to be counted those working in France.
6 What is expected of a job is above all security, the level of wages being a secondary matter, likewise the nature of the work. The status of government employee is desired above all else.
7 The income at which rational management of the budget, a future-oriented and calculating attitude, savings, in sum a complete rational conduct of life, make their appearance is estimated at 70,000 francs per month [i.e. twice the official minimum wage in the 1960s, about £70 in English money of the time. – Trans.].
8 Apart from executives and officials, the highest level of bilingualism and the most coherent opinions are found among the workers; it is also in their case that the gap between opinions and attitudes is narrowest.

9   It is in this context that analysis of the irreversible mutations deter-
    mined by the resettlements acquires its full importance.
10 It will be possible, for instance, to measure the realism of the govern-
    ment by the way that it tackles and resolves the problem of the resettle-
    ments. Although it is right to see these as a continuation of colonial-
    ism, and the majority of those resettled aspire only to return to their
    old land, their home and their former way of life, it may be that the
    resettlements offer an opportunity for a revolution in agrarian
    structures.
11 The attitude that the government adopts towards Europeans, and that
    it encourages the masses to follow, risks coming up against popular
    sentiment, exasperated by years of war and suffering.
12 The issue is to find and train the lower executives who will be the first
    precondition of success for the policy of renovation, especially in the
    rural world. The former social hierarchy has been challenged by the
    war. The former authorities, often discredited by their complicity with
    the old order, have made way for leaders of a new type, whose author-
    ity does not rest on any of the traditional foundations – name and
    renown, religion or even culture. The war has effected a genuine
    democratization, and ensured discipline. But are the authorities born
    out of the war prepared for the new function that falls on them in
    time of peace? Will they be able to give their power new foundations,
    or instead cede their place to men better able to ensure the training of
    the masses? What principle of selection will be needed? Formal educa-
    tion, or participation in the milieu?

Revolution in the Revolution

This chapter was originally published as 'Révolution dans la révolution',
Esprit, 1 (Jan. 1961), pp. 27–40.

1   Raymond Aron, *Esquisse d'une théorie des relations internationales*
    (lecture course given at the Sorbonne in 1958).
2   Ferhat Abbas, (president of the provisional government of the Algerian
    Republic), speech of 17 February 1960.
3   Letter from the Front de Libération Nationale to the French people;
    cited by Charles-Henri Favrod, *La Révolution algérienne* (Paris: Plon,
    1959), p. 174.
4   This analysis also draws on Raymond Aron's lecture course cited
    above.
5   This distinction and these definitions are also borrowed from Raymond
    Aron's lecture course.
6   The fact that the National Liberation Army has to some extent taken
    over these institutions or techniques by raising taxes, running the
    population registry, sometimes opening schools, etc., has made a major
    contribution to furthering this dissociation.

7 The fourteenth century by the Islamic calendar began in 1883 CE. It was a popular belief that this would see the return of al-Mahdi. [Translator's note.]

War and Social Mutation in Algeria

This chapter was originally published as 'Guerre et mutation sociale en Algérie', *Études Méditerranéennes*, 7 (spring 1960), pp. 25–37, and reprinted in *Images d'Algérie. Une affinité élective*, exhibition catalogue edited by F. Schultheis and C. Frisinghelli, Institut du Monde Arabe (Arles: Actes Sud/ Camera Austria/Sindbad/Fondation Liber, 2003), pp. 19–44.

1 Pierre Bourdieu, who has published a *Sociologie d'Algérie* in the 'Que sais-je?' series, is currently working on an analysis of Algerian society as this is being reshaped by the war. The text published here is an early draft of one of the chapters of this book. [The book referred to was never published, though Bourdieu would publish several further texts on Algeria. – Editor.]
2 The generals' coup in Algiers on 13 May 1958, leading to De Gaulle's return to power, was perceived at the time as a setback for the liberation movement. [Translator's note.]
3 A poll carried out in a library in the suburbs of Algiers showed that adults read a good deal, and particularly read works of high literary quality. The reading of French newspapers (*Le Monde* in particular), originally motivated by a desire for political information, contributed much to developing this thirst for learning, which perhaps provides the key to a phrase from an Algerian child that Robert Daveziés reported: 'If Algeria is free and I can't read, there's no point': *Le Front* (Paris: Minuit, 1959).
4 The same is true the other way round. Many European Algerians have told me how amazed they were on their first visit to France to see French people working as labourers or street sweepers, even living in shacks 'like Arabs'.
5 'La Femme musulmane' [propaganda text], Algiers, 1958.
6 Agreements are made between the refugees and the former inhabitants of the village over such things as the distribution of harvests.
7 See 'Revolution in the revolution', in this volume, at n. 6. [Translator's note.]

Uprooted Peasants

This chapter was originally published in collaboration with Abdelmalek Sayad as 'Paysans déracinés. Bouleversements morphologiques et changements culturels en Algérie', *Études Rurales*, 12 (Jan.–Mar. 1964), pp. 56–94. The photographs and drawings that originally accompanied this text are not reproduced here; see Pierre Bourdieu and Abdelmalek Sayad, *Le Déracinement. La crise de l'agriculture traditionnelle en Algérie* (Paris: Minuit, 1964).

The verse in the epigraph is from A. Hanoteau (ed.), *Poésies populaires de la Kabylie du Jurjura* (1867).

1 So as not to complicate the analysis excessively, we shall generally focus here on only the pertinent data. It must be noted however that the elementary social unit is larger in the Collo region than in the Chéliff. In the former, the *zriba* (structurally homologous with the *farqa*) which groups between 100 and 500 individuals who see themselves united by a tie of kinship (real or mythical) has remained very much a living social unit, with its own traditions and strongly endogamous. The tribe has long since ceased to be the framework of social activities, but subjects are all familiar with the traditions that attach them to it. In the Chéliff, units based on a mythic genealogy, such as the tribe or the *farqa*, have broken up into a scattering of autonomous family units, each with its separate territory: if the sense of belonging to the same *farqa* is still alive (until recently, certain *zardat* contained all their members), the tribe is for the majority of subjects only a vague abstraction, and some people are even unaware of its name.

2 A resettled man from Chéraïa remarked: 'Previously, you came back from France for the harvesting and left after ploughing, now you come to build a *gourbi*.' Another added: 'Before we lived in big houses where each person had their room, now we are forced to build two *gourbis* for each family head. That means additional costs for families with a large number of married men!'

3 Allocations of food (for example, when wheat from the harvest was distributed) and gifts were always designed for the household.

4 *Khammès*, agricultural labourers and other peasants who have not inherited any land recognize that in their case there is neither *zaddi* (union) nor *bat'tu* (division); because they have nothing to divide, nothing can divide them: 'Nothing unites us, nothing divides us, there is only what is better.'

5 Just before resettlement, the Aïn-Aghbel *zriba* counted four groceries, a butcher's shop and a *café maure* [Moorish café]; one of the grocers also served as an outlet for bread left on deposit by a Collo baker, and another had a mill on its premises. All the region's artisans were also concentrated there, including a blacksmith, a shoemaker, a taxi driver, two bus drivers and five tailors.

6 Besides the French school opened in 1902, Aïn-Aghbel had a Koranic school that remained open until 1957, when the *taleb* left for the maquis, and that counted some sixty pupils (parents paid the *taleb* 300 francs per month for each pupil). There was also a place of prayer.

7 Peasant mistrust of 'papers' is clearly highest in a population almost totally illiterate; the written word is a 'trap' that the townsman, expert in bureaucratic ruses, extends to the ignorant peasant to dishearten him and steal from him; but, because it holds a determining place in

relations with the administration, the paper is invested with a sacred value.

8   'Kilomètre 10', where the resettlement is located, was no more than a milestone on the road from Collo to Constantine. This crossroads marked by two groceries, a café and a petrol station was the starting point of a whole network of tracks and mule paths leading to the foothill and mountain *zribat*. The houses of the Kerkera *zriba* were less than 500 metres away on the slopes overlooking Lahmar *oued* (a tributary of *oued* Guebli), and for the same reasons as Aïn-Aghbel (presence of the road and of Collo, presence of a school, emigration to France) this was highly urbanized. The majority of houses, for example, were built of stone, some had two floors, several wide apertures, doors and windows with casements, a ceiling, a tiled parterre, a stable or barn separate from the part of the dwelling reserved for people. Some even had their own well in the courtyard.

9   [The widely used word *oued* is often translated as 'river' but does not imply the permanent presence of water. – Trans.] Water is one of the points of opposition between mountain and plains existence. The mountain water, running 'free' and abundant, belongs to each family or each *zriba* whose land it irrigates; the plains water, drawn from wells or springs, is stagnant and reputed to cause diseases such as fever and diarrhoea. Indeed, in both Tamalous and Kerkera the water is highly polluted, with both dysentery and fever attacks being very common.

10 It is not the place here to examine the logic of this system of matrimonial exchange. We simply note that such exchange is not independent of economic and social hierarchies: the underlying principle is that a man can take his wife from a lower position, but not vice versa.

11 The new habitat was established on private land belonging for the most part to the Djebabra (3.5 hectares of this belonged to the Haloui-Zitouni family and 1 hectare to the Merzoug family). The Medjdabi family, from Merdja, also ceded 1.3 hectares. An expropriation procedure had been commenced, with loans provided by the municipality for the compensation of the proprietors, but the legal situation was still not cleared up in 1961, since among other difficulties, none of the reputed owners could produce a property title (with the exception of two plots precisely identified, no. 40 that belonged to a European and no. 42 that its present owner, Haloui-Zitouni, had bought from a French soldier).

12 The mountain people generally suffer most from resettlement and in the resettlement. At Kerkera, for example, natives of the Oued-El-Afia, El-Bir and Djenan-Hadjem *zribat* had their *gourbis* right at the top of the hill overlooking the resettlement, on terraces built by the DRS. In order to find water, women had to travel 4 kilometres, including 1 kilometre with a 45 degree slope. 'This water is illicit (*h'ram*),' said a man from Oued-El-Afia, not just 'because it is made from the sweat

356 *Notes to Pages 125–128*

of women', but also because it can only be obtained at the cost of violating several taboos. In the *zriba*, every family has its own spring, and the common well is always accessible by paths built specially for women and at times fixed by tradition. In the resettlement, the well is often placed at the heart of the male space, and men find it hard to take on the job of water supply, which is a specifically female task.

13   The Medjdabi were divided into six groups cultivating between 20 and 25 hectares of undivided property; after the resettlement, only one Medjdabi remained a farmer.

14   Their territory, i.e. between 80 and 100 hectares of cultivable land and 50 hectares of woodland, has been abandoned.

15   In the resettlement, this family only had one farmer working about one hectare, the others having rented out their land.

16   The present names of these towns are Sidi-Lakhdar, Aïn Defla, Hadjout and Khemia-Miliana. CAPER is the Caisse d'Accession à la Propriété et à l'Exploitation Rurale. [Editor's note.]

17   Another old man said 'Only the dead remain here, the living have all gone elsewhere'; and a man in the Aïn-Aghbel resettlement, originally from Bekoura, declared, probably thinking of the emigrants in France: 'Only women and old men are left, those who are no good for work either here or over there.'

18   Thus the Merdja and Djebabra were well acquainted before being resettled together: they might meet up in a *café maure* at the crossroads of the paths leading to the two *farqat*, initially on market days (Monday and Friday), later more often also on Sundays. In winter, when they were unable to go to their cemetery (located 2 kilometres from Sidi-Moussa), the Djebabra buried their dead in the Sidi-Abdeslam cemetery, on Merdja territory. In the same way, the Matmata market was traditionally a meeting place for peasants from the Béni-Fathem and the mountain-dwellers from the Djebel Louh and Tighzirt, both of whom were resettled on the same site.

19   It seems that the perception individuals have of the group (and its size) promotes the proliferation of shops: above a certain threshold, individual customers give way to a clientele. This proliferation is one of the most indicative symptoms in the development of shantytowns.

20   The role that women have played in the war, the open or hidden responsibilities they have had to take on, both because of the absence of the family's men and out of tactical considerations, have contributed to transforming traditional modes of civility and giving rise to new types of sociability.

21   Expenditure on tobacco makes up only 1.3% of the personal budget in Djebabra, as against 9.9% in Kerkera; similarly, food and drink outside the home (i.e. essentially at the café) comes to 0.8% in Dje-babra and 3.5% in Kerkera: the café and its particular sociability seem connected with the size of the resettlement and the degree of shanty-town development.

22   Three-quarters of the men allotted land here who were interviewed had previously drawn on the aid of their wife. Traditionally, when

women from outside were recruited by the family for certain agricultural work, they were paid in kind; money payment was only made for modern handicraft tasks (sewing, mattress repair, etc.).

23 To a French investigator who hesitated to enter a courtyard where the women of the house were gathered, a man in his fifties from Aïn-Aghbel said: 'What! The soldiers come in here and you don't want to!'

24 The same phenomenon is found in the town among the peasants who have fled, known as *rifij* (refugees). [Editor's note.]

25 'The law does not permit the solitary to have a house.' [In tales and legends, the jackal is condemned to wander, being incapable of establishing a household: *ad iâmer axxam*. – Editor.]

26 For example, a 62-year-old labourer who, on the day of the survey, had just been dismissed by the SAS, explains that he had worked nine days in the past month for a payment of 45 francs; two of his children are in France, the third aged 17 has attended primary school and would like to train for a profession. A 34-year-old labourer defines himself as such, even though he has been dismissed and at the time of the study sells melons on the Kerkera square (thus proving that he knows the illusory character of this activity). A former *fellah*, who owns land in the Tokla *douar*, defines himself as a labourer although he was only employed for a few days by the SAS and does seasonal work in agriculture.

27 In Barbacha, the majority of those with primary education are employed outside of agriculture (16 out of 25), as workers.

28 Service de la Défense et de la Restauration des Sols. [Editor's note.]

29 As well as the losses due to displacement, resettlement has involved new costs, sometimes considerable, and unequally borne by the various categories. Those family heads who were absent at the time of resettlement, for example, chiefly those working in France, have had (when they were not compelled to return specially) to pay 300 francs towards the work needed to construct a single *gourbi*, made of branches sealed with mud and covered with *diss*. But because access to the forest has become very difficult, materials were often lacking and it was necessary to buy wood (a main beam costing up to 100 francs), baked earth bricks (0.13 francs each) and tiles (0.37 francs each). A small brick dwelling covered with tiles comes to nearly 1,000 francs. A *gourbi* of 5 metres by 3.5, with a height of 2 metres, built of *toub* and covered with *diss*, can cost 600 francs. If it has been impossible to recover the tiles from the house abandoned in the *zriba*, it is seen as more economic to cover the *gourbi* with metal sheets; but twenty-two sheets are needed at 10 francs a sheet. The help granted the resettled population is selective here, as elsewhere: homes on the estates are reserved by priority for *harkis* and *mokhazni*, then for certain privileged individuals. To obtain a one-room maisonette with a kitchen on the '*mokhazni* estate' you have to pay 400 francs, or 200 francs plus twenty-one days' work on the construction site. Shop premises are allocated against payment of 450 francs. It is not hard to imagine how,

given the scarcity of ready money, these advantages are accessible only to a minority of well-to-do families. [*Mokhazni* were indigenous members of the colonial police. – Trans.]

30 According to the study of family consumption.

31 The houses of these people in positions of responsibility have every modern comfort (water, electricity, etc.). The mayor likes to show visitors his bedroom, his dining room with its sideboards, chests of drawers and cupboards, and his living room.

32 The few families that were able to attain a certain comfort before resettlement, thanks to funds from emigrants, and had established small shops or handicraft businesses (flour mills, oil mills, transport, etc.), were generally greatly impoverished by resettlement and sometimes completely ruined if they refused to offer the civil or military authorities their full complicity.

33 'Exile is at home'; 'our house has become something foreign to us'.

34 In previous times the rich peasant, rich from land and in terms of land, put his wealth at the service of peasant values, for example prestige expenses such as grain distribution in times of scarcity, sumptuous festivities and *zardat*, donations to the *zawiyat*, etc., fulfilling the demands of peasant morality. Today's parvenus, whose wealth rarely derives from land, prefer to imitate townsfolk and do everything to mark their distance from the peasants.

35 This man was criticized only for paying attention to other people's wives.

36 Many examples have already been seen of transgressions of peasant morality, especially in the economic domain: consumption habits, buying at the market, attitude towards illness and all behaviour implying economic calculation, for example paying a wage to a son or a brother, etc.

37 The standard of living in Djebabra is notably higher: annual consumption per family there is 5,492 francs (845 francs per head) as against 2,290 in Kerkera (350 francs per head); in Matmata, it is 4,260 francs. The figure for Algeria as a whole is 3,750 francs. The families of Algerian farmers have an annual consumption of 4,150 francs, and those of agricultural workers 3,320 francs. Another indication is the consumption of meat and cereals; if in both cases recourse to the market is necessary (cereals make up 29.9% of the budget in Djebabra and 26.7% in Kerkera), the total amount of purchases is much higher in Djebabra, i.e. 1,644 francs per family as against 612 francs in Kerkera. We must add to this that self-sufficiency generally makes up a much higher share in Djebabra (where agriculture has held up better), both because agricultural products are proportionally greater there and undoubtedly also because the imperative of self-sufficiency (and the accompanying ban on buying from the market) has remained more in force than in Kerkera. The family's own production accounts for 15% of cereal consumption in Djebabra as against 1.8% in Kerkera,

74% of milk in Djebabra as against 45% in Kerkera, and 21% of fruit in Djebabra as against 12% in Kerkera.

38 Sections Coopératives Agricoles du Plan de Constantine. [Editor's note.]

39 Kerkera is the only one of the resettlement centres studied to have these *gargotes*.

40 *Casse-croûte*, a snack.

41 It is the same system of values that inspires in emigrants the feeling that their food, being too rich, is 'illicit' (*h'ram*), because it is not *shared* with all their people. 'Here we're eating meat, while our children may be going without bread! Our work won't "rise" [in the sense that dough rises] because we're eating "white bread" [*thaâzults*, privilege, favour] in comparison with our wives and children.' In this logic, work is incapable of fulfilling its prime and increasingly sole purpose, i.e. providing all members of the family with the comfort that it normally assures in France, and it tends to appear as vain and absurd. This explains, among other reasons, the ever more marked tendency since 1956 for entire families to emigrate.

42 It was the traditional custom not to eat meat without a particular reason, except in certain circumstances, religious or secular festivals (marriage, circumcision, funeral, distinguished guests). [Editor's note.]

43 The *bou niya*, naive peasants still stubbornly rural, who refuse to go to the *gargote* and do not dare to face ridicule by carrying their provisions, abstain from food altogether, even when they go to the market on foot.

44 In fact, the whole peasant attitude towards the town and its people has changed. In Collo, the market used to be held each Friday: many peasants from the region came to sell, buy, meet someone, settle a personal or administrative matter, including legal cases held before a large *jamâa*, etc. With the move of mountain people to the foothills, the opening of new paths and roads and the appearance of new needs, visits to the town have become easier and more frequent. Resettlement has put an end to the habit (bound up with peasant activity and the need to sell the fruits of the soil) of going to the weekly market. In the absence of products to sell, people now go to town rather than to the market, and can go any day of the week. The weekly market no longer sets the rhythm for the life of the *fellah'in*; it is frequented less, certain goods such as cereals and beans are no longer found there, being sold instead in shops, and animals are also rare.

45 A man of honour, out of a concern for prestige, can spend a large amount on clothing for himself, but not on food. 'If he is well dressed,' people say, 'he looks good and everyone sees him, he's improved the look of his family; but if he's eaten well, no one knows', or again, 'too big a stomach has never done an honourable deed'.

46 Resettlement brings nothing, not more land, not more work, not even a different organization of existence. This is one of the sources of the

revolt it inspires: 'Before, when we were in the *zriba*, several kilometres away from the school, we didn't think of sending our children there. Now that we are so close, we would like to send them, but there are no places' (a mountain dweller resettled in Aïn-Aghbel).

47 'I am the space where I am,' says Noël Arnaud, cited by Gaston Bachelard, who writes: 'But over and beyond our memories, the house we were born in is physically inscribed in us. It is a group of organic habits. After twenty years, in spite of all the other anonymous stairways, we would recapture the reflexes of this "first stairway", we would not stumble on that rather high step. The house's entire being would open up, faithful to our own being. [. . .] The word habit is too worn a word to express this passionate liaison of our bodies, which do not forget, with an unforgettable house.' Gaston Bachelard, *The Poetics of Space* (Boston: Beacon, 1994), pp. 14–15.

48 The traditional family house with an inner courtyard. [Editor's note.]

49 The *dukan*, in the *zribat* of the Collo region (known as *lakdhar* in Little Kabylia), is the essential element in household equipment. Made from the same material as the wall, i.e. from baked earth, and more or less sculpted into it, it had to be abandoned (and sometimes destroyed) at the same time as the houses. The same goes for most of the grain jars. The *dukan* was used to keep foodstuffs such as galettes, couscous and other dishes, and in particular the various utensils such as cooking pot, galette board, etc.

50 'We are in reed cages' (old woman resettled in Béni-Mansour). 'We're piled in like sardines in a can' (resettled man, Kerkera). 'We are forced to build our own houses with our own hands. Of course we're fed, just as prisoners are' (resettled man, Kerkera). 'We don't know where we are, we don't know where we're going, we are like people passing in the night' (former shopkeeper, Kerkera).

51 The metaphors used to express the dizziness experienced at the wide empty spaces are significant: 'I was like a small grain' (*gad h'abba*), i.e. lost in an immense space; or again, 'like a man swallowed up in a flow of water' (*ghamaq*).

52 The unity of these rhythms is one of the foundations of the group's cohesion, and is felt as a reprimand by those who go against it; it also ensures a form of predictability of technical and social behaviours, the foundation of the sense of *familiarity*.

53 Ignorance of economic calculation and the quest for output or profitability in labour is implicit in the unquestioned submission to the time of traditional routine.

54 The proliferation of bureaucratic relationships has familiarized everyone concerned with the dates, years and months that have replaced the seasons and divisions of the traditional calendar. There is no longer any family head who does not know his own age and the ages of his people.

55 Faced with the failure of this collective transport, the military authorities decided to provide individual passes each day. But this measure aroused the same defiance and had to be abandoned. The peasants of

the CAPER or the SCAPCOs rebelled against the fact that, *like women,* they were not allowed to decide anything.

56 To understand the impatience and revolt of the *fellah'in* in the CAPER or the SCAPCOs, as well as in certain of the management committees, it is necessary to understand that what counts for the peasant, far more than his ownership of the soil, is *the freedom to organize his work as he chooses.*

57 Shopkeepers tend increasingly to give up agricultural activity, leaving their fields to a brother, a son or a *khammès.* They now 'sit on their chair all day', 'in the shade', thereby arousing the irony of the peasants who see them as lazy ('they don't have to make an effort', 'they don't have callouses on their hands'); the shop premises are separated from the home, with the result that the shopkeeper cannot count on the help of his family and has to adopt regular opening hours. This is the rhythm of the little shops in the big towns and their suburbs. Some shopkeepers eat in their shops, leaving the door ajar and taking their meal in the heat of the day. Others return home, leaving their shop closed.

58 Is it not significant that peasants start using such expressions as 'killing time', 'wasting one's time', 'passing time', and that the only people not to get bored are the *bou niya* who spend their time 'watching the land'?

59 For example, the widening of the field of matrimonial exchanges, which the convergence of groups formerly at a distance from one another might well have promoted (to judge by appearances), but which statistical study (of the *farqat* resettled in Matmata and Dje-babra) does not confirm.

60 Everything separated the agricultural workers from what they called the '*farqa* people': a language invaded by borrowed words, the concerns and subjects of their conversation, and religious traditions marked by magical formalism. Evidence that the unity of the group is no longer defined by anything more than cohabitation in the same space, and the identity of conditions of work and existence, is that the currents of matrimonial exchange were stronger among the colonies of agricultural workers, even at a distance, than between these workers and their community of origin.

The Algerian Sub-Proletarians

This chapter was originally published as 'Les sous-prolétaires algériens', *Les Temps Modernes,* 199 (Dec. 1962), pp. 1030–51.

1 This was *Travail et travailleurs en Algérie* (with A. Darbel, J.-P. Rivet and C. Seibel) (The Hague: Mouton, 1963). [Editor's note.]

2 Is it not significant that villagers today, as witnessed by observations made in Aghbala during the summer of 1962, have discovered boredom, that expressions appear such as 'killing time', 'passing time'?

And that the only people not to get bored are the '*bou niya*', vestiges of the past, occupied in 'watching the land'?

3 Analysis of family budgets shows that the share spent on food rises in parallel with income up to a certain threshold.

4 Schumpeter has shown the function of savings very well: 'The role played by savings' (he is speaking of entrepreneurs) 'is to free them from the necessity of the everyday routines imposed by the concern to earn a living from day to day and to give them the leisure to survey the horizon, to make plans and assemble resources' (*Capitalism, Socialism and Democracy*). But one must be careful not to forget that saving itself requires at least a little distance from the necessity of everyday routine. With only three exceptions, an unskilled worker whose income was only 213 new francs and two café proprietors who gave their incomes as between 300 and 400 new francs, everyone who said they had savings had a permanent job and an income higher than 500 new francs.

5 Protests against weekly payment are also encountered. Because employment stability in Algeria varies with the length of payment period, the preference for monthly payment is necessarily strengthened.

6 The peasant's aversion to credit, inseparable from the whole system of values and particularly the morality of honour, is expressed in this testimony from a peasant of the Ouled Hamida (Affreville) fraction: 'I don't manage to make ends meet [. . .] Now there's the problem of credit. I don't like borrowing, as I feel uneasy, and when I owe something, it embarrasses me with the person I owe, and then people here do not give credit to newcomers because they don't offer any guarantee: no wage or income of any kind. The grocer doesn't want to give credit, he's afraid that everyone will disappear once peace returns, and he won't be able to get the money repaid. He only gives credit to those who have animals, or to his cousins from the same *ferka* [fractions], whom he knows.'

7 The amount of debt is sometimes very high. A home help in Oran, for example, who earns 18,000 francs a month, has a debt of 60,000 francs with her grocer. A clerical worker with a Tlemcen cloth merchant owes 50,000 francs. 'I have debts of at least 65,000 francs,' declares a painter from Saïda, 'two months' work [. . .] I ran up debts because of my daughter's marriage. In an Islamic marriage, you have to have a trousseau, jewels. All this is expensive. I save on everything in order to repay my debts. I don't eat well. Even cigarettes, I buy from the grocer on credit.'

8 The testimony of a *fellah* recently displaced to the small town of Carnot makes clear why recourse to credit is almost unavoidable: 'My expenses here are higher than in the *douar*. Having children at school leads to additional costs, clothing, entertainment, educational items. I buy bread, I have many costs and expenses that I did not have previously. My needs are greater from every point of view, vegetables and fruit, milk and meat, etc.; I also have new needs, housing, clothing,

schooling for the children. You have to live as it's usual to live in town, but without having the means for this. My only recourse is credit, I'm fortunate that my father knew a lot of people. I get credit from a shopkeeper that we've known for a long time, who comes from the same village as we do. I owe him 3,500 to 4,000 francs that I'm not able to settle. It's a favour when a grocer agrees to give you credit, this means he trusts you; he has to be a friend or someone from your village, then he can't refuse. But the shopkeepers don't give credit to everyone, they'd have to give credit to the whole population. No one today is in a position to pay for all their purchases in cash, not even the rich. The poor now are experiencing the greatest destitution; there is no longer the help that they previously received from people who were richer than them, and even they, now that they're in the town, are forced to buy the little that was given them in the past. The rich today are impoverished, and share the misfortune of the poor. No one likes credit, but everyone is happy to find someone ready to offer it.'

9   Among shopkeepers, 78.5% don't have any qualification, 20.3% completed primary school and 1.1% finished secondary school. A detailed examination of the survey results (the small sample) enables us to estimate the rate of illiteracy at over 70%. One may suppose that this figure is even higher for the smaller shopkeepers.

10 The ellipses here and elsewhere are original, in so far as this text is precisely presented on its first publication as an 'extract from a work in progress'.

11 Small shopkeepers expect nothing more from their activity than what they need to subsist. 'I don't keep accounts,' one of them says. 'What I earn, I eat.' In this way they obey the traditional principle of maximizing security. The lack of specialization in retail trade is inspired by the concern to reduce the share of risk and chance to a minimum, by having a finger in every pie, so to speak. The same goes for opening hours. As shops become larger and more modern, they tend to specialize and their opening hours are more precise.

12 Another unemployed man from Constantine combined the most contradictory assertions as to the future of his daughters: 'I'll only send the boys to school. The daughters each need a guardian.' And later: 'Oh! If she has education, she'll have to work; she can refuse, that's her business. But now, even if my wife and I are starving, I won't let her work.'

13 Unemployed or unskilled men whose wives work are the exception, in that they express certain reservations; the categorical imperative that forbids women's work is toned down to a hypothetical imperative: 'They shouldn't work if their husband gets enough,' as one Constantine worker (unskilled and unemployed) put it.

14 The French word *piston* overlaps in meaning with the English 'connections', implying unknown workings that can assist a person. But as Bourdieu explains below, it has here a rather more mystical tinge. [Translator's note.]

15　A whole series of explanations along the same lines can be heard: 'Only connections make it possible for people to work. How do you expect a man without connections to find work?' (garage watchman, Oran). 'You have to be well connected, in North Africa, to find a good job. [. . .] You can't get anywhere without connections' (unskilled worker, Oran). 'To find a good job you have to have connections. My son can read and write, but he can't find work' (mattress maker, Sidi-Bel-Abbès). 'You don't get any job without connections' (unemployed man, Tlemcen). 'You can't do anything without connections' (porter, Philippeville, now Skikda). 'Here, I swear to you, without connections you can run your feet off and don't get anywhere' (worker, Constantine). 'In Algeria, it's connections above all that count, it's rare to get anywhere without connections' (shopkeeper, Oran).

16　The most lucid of the sub-proletarians have, as opposed to the petty bourgeois, an explicit awareness of the incoherence of their ideology.

17　It is well known how words like *mana, manitu, mulungu* are used as exclamations in the face of anything that is unusual, surprising, marvellous or terrifying. We have noted how invocation of 'connections' most commonly assumes the form of an interjection. In the great majority of cases, this notion, taken either as a noun, in the sense of a power, or as an adjective, in the sense of a property that some people have, remains as indeterminate as possible (it is most often preceded by the indefinite article), and refers to significations that are different but confused: discrimination, baksheesh and 'acquaintances' – the support given by a relative or friend may be understood either as expression of traditional fraternity or as defence against colonial oppression. For example, an Oran painter successively listed the different meanings without clearly distinguishing them: 'To get a good job, you have to be connected!' (with an energetic wave of the hand). 'You have to have strong shoulders!' (he raises his hand to his shoulders). [. . .] 'Remember, there's a second way if you have a mate, a relative who can help you. But what works best is the money connection.'

18　Everyone knows more or less clearly that the same necessity weighs on the great majority of their fellows. When they are asked whether they know anyone who's been successful, they most often answer: 'No, I don't.' 'No, I don't know anyone.' 'No one that I know.' 'We are all the same.' 'Everyone I know is like me.' 'I don't know them, no one in my trade has got on', and so on.

19　In a general manner, affective political consciousness is ahead of rational political consciousness, and particularly so among women, who have experienced the war more passively and passionately than actively and rationally. For them, political sensibility often has no common measure with political consciousness and culture. Generally less educated than men, less in contact with the modern economy and life, they are less prepared to view their situation rationally. This is why, for example, when they contribute to interviews, it is women who most commonly invoke 'connections' or chance, whereas it is not so rare that their husband attributes success to education or merit.

20 The expectation of paternalistic relationships that is manifest among many sub-proletarians must undoubtedly be understood by reference to the model of interpersonal relations specific to traditional society; but it is certainly also encouraged, in the case of sub-proletarians, by the material conditions of existence in which they are placed, and that promote an attitude of dependence. In a general sense, the cultural tradition often contributes to the miserabilism of rationalizations and a specific language. 'There are not many jobs, the population has doubled and the people from the *douars* are here in the town; perhaps if there weren't all these people there would be work. Someone who lies will never make anything of his life, it's not good to lie. God wants the truth' (former ambulant charcoal-seller, Sidi-Bel-Abbès). 'A serious and polite man finds work' (grocer's delivery man, Algiers).

Haunted by Unemployment

This chapter was originally published as 'Le hantise du chômage chez l'ouvrier algérien. Prolétariat et système colonial', *Sociologie du Travail*, 4 (1962), pp. 313–31.

1   This article presents a part of the results arising from a study carried out in Algeria in the summer of 1960, in collaboration with the Algerian services of INSEE; cf. *Travail et travailleurs en Algérie*, vol. 1: *Données statistiques*, by Alain Darbel, Jean-Paul Rivet and Claude Seibel; vol. 2: *Étude sociologique* by Pierre Bourdieu (The Hague: Mouton, 1963). The sociological study took 150 subjects drawn at random, in a survey plan established by A. Darbel, out of the sample of 3,000 individuals who participated in the statistical study.

2   Among Algerians over 14 years old, 57% were in work on the day of the study. The persons questioned showed a very marked tendency to overestimate the levels of non-employment. 'Eight out of ten men are unemployed' (shoemaker, Algiers). 'Ever since machines have come in, eight out of ten are unemployed, I'm telling you' (unemployed man, Saïda). This overestimation is partly explained by the fact that anyone without 'proper' work, such as street vendors, watchmen, etc., is spontaneously classified with the unemployed.

3   Although the research procedure was the other way round, and the existence of an acute awareness of non-employment inductively appeared as the objective foundation of attitudes and opinions, it seemed preferable to proceed deductively here, and show how the awareness that subjects have of the subjective and objective obstacles to obtaining work determines attitudes and opinions.

4   The quarterly survey of employment in a certain number of businesses for April 1960 showed that Algerians made up 94% of unskilled workers, 96% of skilled workers, 82% of semi-workers, 76.5% of workers in category 1, 69.5% of workers in category 2, and 60.5% of uncategorized workers. This study counted 48,483 workers, including 7,324 Europeans and 41,159 Algerians (i.e. some 85% of the total).

5   In Arabic, *el ktef* (pl. *el ktaf*) means shoulder, a push with the shoulder, hence 'connections'.

6   *El kahwa*, another name for baksheesh, the sum paid to obtain a job. The French word *pourboire* is also used.

7   It often happens that, being obliged to meet their needs when they have no work, he has the same interest in finding work for them as they do themselves.

8   In the case of Europeans, this attitude is explained first of all by the fact that they form a society united by a tie of oppositional solidarity. This solidarity is expressed in all circumstances of life, including of course employment. A generalized wariness leads to reserving for Europeans positions of confidence and responsibility, a 'caste' solidarity to allocating them authoritative functions, while the notion of 'Arab labour' does the rest. Thus the Europeans show spontaneous solidarity with one another, not so much against the Algerians as 'behind' the Algerians. Europeans from one town (particularly the smaller ones) also form a group of true or at least mediated inter-acquaintance; this means that any European can approximately locate himself vis-à-vis any other European (at least of the equivalent social category) in a network of acquaintances and relationships. If we add that the whole administrative staff of the country is practically concentrated in Algiers, a city that counts around 350,000 Europeans, there is hardly a European who does not know someone at some level in the hierarchy of the central administration. It is rare therefore to address oneself to the administration without a mediator or intercessor. The simplest procedure, for example the renewal of a passport or obtaining an aircraft seat, operates by the mediation of a known individual. This fosters the belief that relationships can do everything.

9   This proportion was 21% even for executives and government employees.

10 Little clusters of this kind (counting from five to ten persons) are even found in the civil service; for example, there are clusters of people hailing from Sidi Aich at the Crédit Municipal, the Fonds National Vieillesse, the Caisse de Solidarités des Départements et des Communes, and the Caisse des Allocations Familiales.

11 Resentment towards the foreman is often violently expressed. This man, often a 'poor white', is charged with directly exercising authority while the boss or engineer remains more distant. He crystallizes all discontent, all the more so as his appointment to this position is seen as the most manifest effect of discrimination. 'Oh, the foreman!'

(*akontr'mitr* [from the French *contremaître*]). 'He'd really like me to give him presents! But that, never! He's on his chair and I'm working, and still after that he's not happy!' (worker in a timber company, Oran). 'A works manager earns 240 to 260 francs an hour. He does nothing and sometimes even gets 300 francs, it depends on how long he's been working there. Let's be frank: an Algerian can't earn the same as a European. And yet! The European, if he keeps his head down like me earns 180 francs, even less' (painter, Oran).

12 Paternalism, as a combination of familiarity and distance, is not just characteristic of European bosses. As witness this response from an Algerian boss (Tlemcen): 'My employees are better than friends, they're like sons . . . No, I never meet them outside of work.'

13 The existence of a great stability in work is also confirmed by the statistical sample of 3,000 subjects.

14 The statistical study showed that incomes did not significantly vary with age.

15 Only 5.4% of labourers and workers say that they hope to rise in their trade, as against 55.2% of executives and civil servants.

16 For the lower categories, mobility between generations is scarcely any higher.

17 Here is a significant index of this break with the past and family traditions: while the peasants from regions little disturbed by the war can reconstitute their genealogies back five generations, and sometimes six or seven, 50% of labourers cannot say what their grandfather's occupation was. Among the unemployed, street vendors, casual workers, and labourers without permanent employment, this figure reaches 82% (as against 25% for middle and higher executives). 'They are exaggerating,' one of these replies. 'I don't even remember my grandfather. That was another century.'

18 Unemployed, labourer, street vendor, may be successive states of the same individual; they are in any case interchangeable conditions.

19 This analysis is verified by the fact that aspirations become increasingly realistic as stability of employment rises.

20 The resettlement of population produces the same effects. Whether or not it determines an objective rise in the rate of unemployment, it fosters in any case an awareness of being without work.

21 'All the Europeans have work'; this assertion, repeated a hundred times, attests to a concrete awareness of the notion of full employment. The form and content of this awareness can only be understood by reference to the situation and occasion of its emergence. The full employment of the Europeans is viewed, comparatively, as a privileged over-employment; hence the theme often met with in the course of this study, that among Europeans all members of the family work, women included, whereas the male heads of Algerian families are unemployed.

22 The need to be considered, and the demand for dignity, are strongly and frequently expressed through this theme, which can take different forms:

1 We live like animals ('Look at my house. It's not a house, it's a stable').
2 Not getting education is like being an animal.
3 We're treated like animals (*zayla*, pl. *zouail*: beasts of burden).
4 In France, at least I was treated as a human being.
5 By not educating us, by not giving us work or housing, they make us into animals, so that they can treat us like animals.

In fact, though such reasoning is not thought through in a perfectly clear fashion, and is never fully elaborated, one finds even among the most frustrated and least educated subjects a kind of affective systematization that resembles a dialectical description of the colonial situation. Here are two further examples: 'We (the Muslims) have been forced to steal, so they can then put us in prison' (retired public transport worker, Algiers). 'Previously, Algeria lived primarily from the land; that's been taken from us, and nothing has been done to help us develop, all the better to dominate us' (unemployed man, Kerkera).

The Making of Economic Habitus

This chapter is a translation by Richard Nice and Loïc Wacquant which appeared in *Ethnography*, 1.1 (2000), pp. 17–41; the text was also published as 'La fabrique de l'habitus économique', *Actes de la Recherche en Sciences Sociales*, 150 (Dec. 2003), pp. 79–90.

1 Pierre Bourdieu, *The Algerians* (1958; Boston: Beacon, 1962).
2 The places, conditions and objectives of the inquiries to which this article returns are set out in detail in two books published simultaneously in the early 1960s: *Travail et travailleurs en Algérie* (with Alain Darbel, Jean-Pierre Rivet and Claude Seibel) (Paris: Minuit, 1963), on the transformation of economic dispositions and social structures concurrent with the spread of emigration, urbanization and wage labour throughout Algeria, and (with Abdelmalek Sayad) *Le Déracinement. La crise de l'agriculture traditionnelle en Algérie* (Paris: Minuit, 1964), on the upheaval of rural society, mainly in Kabylia, resulting from colonization and above all from the policy of forced resettlement or 'regrouping' by which the French army sought to destroy the social basis of the armed wing of the nationalist movement. The main results of this research are reported in highly compressed form in the first chapter of *Algeria 1960*, 'The Disenchantment of the World' (1977; Cambridge: Cambridge University Press, 1979).
3 For a representative sample of this current, issued from the reappropriation of Polanyi and Weber in US sociology and the development of 'network' analyses designed to move away from an atomized conception of economic agents, see Richard Swedberg (ed.), *Explorations*

in Economic Sociology (New York: Russell Sage Foundation, 1993); also Mark Granovetter, 'The old and the new economic sociology: a history and an agenda', in Roger Friedland and A. F. Robertson (eds), *Beyond the Marketplace* (New York: Aldine de Gruyter, 1991), pp. 89–112, and Granovetter, 'Economic institutions as social constructions: a framework for analysis', *Acta Sociologica*, 35.1 (1992), pp. 3–12; for a proposal to reinscribe economic sociology within 'rational choice theory' narrowly defined that discloses the utilitarian and individualistic philosophy of action common to both, read James A. Coleman, 'A rational choice perspective on economic sociology', in Neil J. Smelser and Richard Swedberg (eds), *The Handbook of Economic Sociology* (New York: Russell Sage Foundation, 1994), pp. 166–80; for a contrast with the same problematic posed in ethnological terms, see Stuart Plattner (ed.), *Economic Anthropology* (Stanford: Stanford University Press, 1989).

4   Pierre Bourdieu, 'Le champ economique', *Actes de la Recherche en Sciences Sociales*, 119 (Sept. 1997), pp. 48–66.

5   I have shown elsewhere that a similar repression of strictly 'economic' interest comes to govern the field of artistic production as it constitutes itself historically: *The Rules of Art: Genesis and Structure of the Artistic Field* (1993; Cambridge: Polity, 1997).

6   For a converging analysis from the standpoint of information theory, see Clifford Geertz's dissection of the functioning of the Moroccan bazaar of Sefrou: 'The bazaar economy: information and search in peasant marketing', *American Economic Review*, 68 (May 1968), pp. 28–32. A similar mechanism for eliminating uncertainty in economic exchange is depicted in Charles W. Smith's ethnography of auctions: *Auctions: The Social Construction of Value* (Berkeley: University of California Press, 1990).

7   For a similar analysis of the factors that prevent land from becoming a pure commodity in the countryside of the Béarn in south-western France that helped me better decipher the Algerian pattern at the time, see Pierre Bourdieu, 'Célibat et condition paysanne', *Études Rurales*, 5–6 (Apr. 1962), pp. 32–136, and *The Logic of Practice* (1980; Cambridge: Polity, 1990), pp. 147–61.

8   Karl Polanyi, Conrad M. Arensberg and Harry W. Pearson, *Trade and Market in the Early Empires* (New York: Free Press, 1957).

9   Bourdieu and Sayad, *Le Deracinement*.

10 *Harkis* = native-born Algerians enrolled as soldiers in the French Army. [Translator's note.]

11 In the absence of such conversion, the whole set of reproduction strategies becomes derailed and eventually blocked, and reconversion becomes impossible, leading the group into demoralization, even self-extinction, as can clearly be seen in the case of the French peasantry; Pierre Bourdieu, 'Reproduction interdite. La dimension symbolique de la domination economique', *Études Rurales*, 113–14 (Jan.–June 1989), pp. 15–36.

12 The same anamnesis can be provoked by the historical recovery of economic beliefs and practices effaced by economic history, that is, the transmutation of collective representations and dispositions that then become literally unthinkable for us, such as that caused by the symbolic revolution (in the sphere of religion, statistics, the family and the firm) that 'put death on the market' and made possible the invention of the life insurance industry; Viviana Zelizer, *Morals and Markets: The Development of Life Insurance in the United States* (New York: Columbia University Press, 1979). It may also be fostered by the sort of brutal economic involution that suddenly renders obsolete the formally rational economic habitus of an ordered economic cosmos, as analysed by Burawoy et al. in the case of post-communist Russia; Michael Burawoy, Pavel Krotov and Tatyana Lytkina, 'Involution and destitution in capitalist Russia', *Ethnography*, 1.1 (2000), pp. 43–65.

13 Max Weber, *Gesammelte Aufsätze zur Sozial- und Wirtschaftsgeschichte* (Tübingen: Mohr, 1924); Werner Sombart, *The Quintessence of Capitalism: A Study of the History and Psychology of the Modern Business Man* (London: Unwin, 1915); R. H. Tawney, *Religion and the Rise of Capitalism* (London: John Murray, 1926).

14 Gary S. Becker, *The Economic Theory to Human Behavior* (Chicago: University of Chicago Press, 1976); and *A Treatise on the Family* (Cambridge, MA: Harvard University Press, 1984).

15 Many North African emigrants residing in France for decades still keep their telephone numbers ex-directory to escape solicitations and demands from their family; Abdelmalek Sayad, *La Double absence* (Paris: Seuil, 1999).

16 Bourdieu, *Algeria 1960*, pp. 1–94.

17 The same moral condemnation, in the pseudo-technical idiom of 'underclass' in America and 'exclusion' in Europe, fuels many seemingly impeccably positivistic analyses of the predicament of the declining fractions of the working class in advanced societies whose 'mismatched' dispositions (with respect to the requirements of the new polarized service economy) repeat, at a different stage of development, the experience of the formerly agrarian sub-proletariats of cities throughout the Western colonial world.

The Right Use of Ethnology

This chapter was originally published as 'Du bon usage de l'ethnologie. Entretien avec M. Mammeri', *Awal. Cahiers d'Études Berbères*, 1 (1985), pp. 7–29. The introduction is by the editor.

1 S. A. Boulifa, a teacher, was one of the first known Kabyle researchers in the late nineteenth century. He produced in particular *Recueil de*

poésies kabyles (Algiers: Awal, 1990, reissue), *Cours de deuxième année de langue kabyle*, and a history of Kabylia. [Editor's note.]

2 The French anthropologist Émile Masqueray (1843–94), whose *Formation des cités chez les populations sédentaires de l'Algérie* was published in 1886, and his *Souvenirs et visions d'Afrique* in 1894. [Translator's note.]

3 The White Fathers (Pères Blancs), now the Society of the Missionaries of Africa, was founded in 1868 by Cardinal Lavigerie, then archbishop of Algiers, and adopted an indigenous costume. [Translator's note.]

4 The Kanak are the indigenous people of New Caledonia, formerly referred to as Canaque. See below. [Translator's note.]

Dialogue on Oral Poetry in Kabylia

This interview was recorded on 17 February 1978 and published as M. Mammeri and Pierre Bourdieu, 'Dialogue sur la poésie orale en Kabylie', *Actes de la Recherche en Sciences Sociales*, 23 (Sept. 1978), pp. 51–66. The introduction is by the editor.

1 The village that the two enemies were fighting over.
2 Letter from M. Mammeri to Pierre Bourdieu, 22 Apr. 1978.

Participant Objectivation

This chapter is the revised text of the Huxley Memorial Lecture delivered by Pierre Bourdieu at the Royal Anthropological Institute, London, on 6 December 2000; the final version was prepared and translated from the French by Loïc Wacquant and published in the *Journal of the Royal Anthropological Institute*, ns, 9 (June 2003), pp. 281–94. It was published in French as 'L'objectivation participante', *Actes de la Recherche en Sciences Sociales*, 150 (Dec. 2003), pp. 43–57.

1 C. Geertz, *Works and Lives: The Anthropologist as Author* (Stanford: Stanford University Press, 1988), p. 89.

2 G. Marcus and M. Fischer, *Anthropology as Cultural Critique* (Chicago: University of Chicago Press, 1986); K. Rosaldo, *Culture and Truth: The Remaking of Social Analysis* (Boston: Beacon, 1989); Geertz, *Works and Lives*.

3 J. Clifford and G. Marcus (eds), *Writing Culture: The Poetics and Politics of Ethnography* (Berkeley: University of California Press, 1986); S. Woolgar, 'Reflexivity is the ethnographer of the text', in S. Woolgar (ed.), *Knowledge and Reflexivity: New Frontiers in the Sociology of Knowledge* (London: Sage, 1988), pp. 14–34; A. Gupta

and J. Ferguson (eds), *Anthropological Locations: Boundaries and Grounds of a Field Science* (Berkeley: University of California Press, 1997).

4 A. Gouldner, *The Coming Crisis of Western Sociology* (London: Heinemann, 1971).

5 P. Bourdieu, *Science de la science et réflexivité* (Paris: Raisons d'Agir, 2001).

6 L. Wittgenstein, *Philosophical Investigations* (Oxford: Blackwell, 1967), para. 415.

7 P. Bourdieu, *Homo Academicus* (1984; Cambridge: Polity, 1988).

8 C. Soulié, 'L'anatomie du goût philosophique', *Actes de la Recherche en Sciences Sociales*, 109 (1995), pp. 3–21.

9 D. Garnett, *Lady into Fox and A Man in the Zoo* (London: Chatto & Windus, 1960), p. 111.

10 É. Durkheim and M. Mauss, *Primitive Forms of Classification* (1903; Chicago: University of Chicago Press, 1976); C. Lévi-Strauss, *The Savage Mind* (1963; Chicago: University of Chicago Press, 1969); É. Durkheim, *The Evolution of Educational Thought: Lectures on the Formation and Development of Secondary Education in France* (London: Routledge & Kegan Paul, 1977).

11 P. Bourdieu and M. de Saint Martin, 'The categories of professorial understanding', *Actes de la Recherche en Sciences Sociales*, 3 (May 1975), pp. 68–93; repr. as appendix to *Homo Academicus*.

12 P. Bourdieu, *Outline of a Theory of Practice* (1972; Cambridge: Cambridge University Press, 1977).

13 L. Wittgenstein, 'Remarks on Frazer's *Golden Bough*', in L. Wittgenstein, *Philosophical Occasions 1912–1951* (Indianapolis: Hackett, 1993), pp. 119–55, at pp. 137–9.

14 Ibid., p. 123.

15 Ibid., p. 155.

16 P. Bourdieu, 'Understanding' (1993), *Theory, Culture, and Society*, 13 (1996), pp. 13–37.

17 P. Bourdieu, 'The scholastic point of view', *Cultural Anthropology*, 5 (1990), pp. 380–91; P. Bourdieu, *Pascalian Meditations* (1998; Cambridge: Polity, 2000).

18 P. Bourdieu, *The Bachelors' Ball: The Crisis of Peasant Society in Béarn* (2002; Cambridge: Polity, 2008).

19 J. L. Austin, *Sense and Sensibilia* (Oxford: University Press, 1962), pp. 3–4.

20 P. Bourdieu, 'Célibat et condition paysanne', *Études Rurales* 5–6 (Apr. 1962), pp. 32–136.

21 A *polytechnicien* is a graduate of the École Polytechnique, one of France's foremost elite schools and a major recruiting ground for top corporate leaders and state managers; see P. Bourdieu, *The State Nobility* (1989; Cambridge: Polity, 1996). [Translator's note.]

22 P. Bourdieu, 'From rules to strategies' (1985), *Cultural Anthropology*, 1 (1986), pp. 110–20.

23   P. Bourdieu, 'Social space and the genesis of groups' (1984), *Theory and Society*, 14 (1985), pp. 723–44; reprinted in *Language and Symbolic Power* (Cambridge, Polity, 1991).
24   M. di Leonardo, 'The female world of cards and holidays: women, families, and the work of kinship', *Signs*, 12 (1987), pp. 410–53.
25   P. Bourdieu, 'De la maison du roi à la raison d'état. Une modèle de la genèse du champ bureaucratique', *Actes de la Recherche en Sciences Sociales*, 188 (1997), pp. 55–68.
26   V. Woolf, *To the Lighthouse* (1929; New York: Harvest, 1990).
27   P. Bourdieu, 'Rites as acts of institution', in J. G. Peristiany and J. Pitt-Rivers (eds), *Honor and Grace in Anthropology* (Cambridge: Cambridge University Press, 1992), pp. 79–89; Bourdieu, 'Understanding'.
28   Bourdieu, *Science de la science et réflexivité*.
29   Bourdieu. *The Bachelors' Ball*.
30   C. Levi-Strauss, *Structural Anthropology* (1958; Harmondsworth: Penguin, 1968).

For a Sociology of Sociologists

This chapter appeared in Pierre Bourdieu, *Sociology in Question*, trans. Richard Nice (London: Sage, 1993), pp. 49–53. It was originally a contribution to a colloquium on Ethnology and Politics in the Maghreb, Paris, June 1975, reprinted as 'Les conditions sociales de la production sociologique. Sociologie colonial et décolonisation de la sociologie', in *Le Mal de voir* (Paris: Union Générale d'Éditions, 1976), pp. 416–27.

Between Friends

This chapter was originally a talk given at a conference, 'Autour de l'anthropologie au Maghreb', organized by Tassadit Yacine at the Institut du Monde Arabe on 21 May 1997, with Maurice Aymard, Emmanuel Terray, Jacques Revel, Isaac Chiva, Abdallah Hammoudi and Julian Pitt-Rivers. A first version was printed in *Awal*, 21 (2000), pp. 5–6, and reprinted in *L'autre Bourdieu*, special issue of *Awal*, 27–8 (2003).

1   *Sociologie de l'Algérie* (Paris: PUF, 1958).
2   *Travail et travailleurs en Algérie* (The Hague: Mouton, 1963).
3   With Abdelmalek Sayad, *Le Déracinement* (Paris: Minuit, 1964).
4   *Algeria 1960* (Paris: Minuit, 1977).
5   See 'The right use of ethnology' and 'Dialogue on oral poetry in Kabylia', both in this volume.
6   Mahmoud Darwich, *La Palestine comme métaphore* (Arles: Actes Sud, 1997).

For Abdelmalek Sayad

This chapter was originally a talk at the Institut du Monde Arabe on 2 April 1998, in the context of a meeting in memory of Abdelmalek Sayad; it appeared in *Annuaire de l'Afrique du Nord*, vol. 37 (1998) (Paris: CNRS Éditions, 2000), pp. 9–13.

Seeing with the Lens: About Photography

This interview took place at the Collège de France, 26 June 2001; the text appeared in *Images d'Algérie. Une affinité élective*, exhibition catalogue edited by F. Schultheis and C. Frisinghelli, Institut du Monde Arabe (Arles: Actes Sud/Camera Austria/Sindbad/Fondation Liber, 2003). The introduction is by Franz Schultheis.

1 Jars of different sizes in dried earth, in which the Kabyles keep cereals, figs, salt, salted meat, etc. [Editor's note.]
2 P. Bourdieu, L. Boltanski, R. Castel and J.-C, Chamboderon, *Un art moyen. Essai sur les usages sociaux de la photographie* (Paris: Minuit, 1965).
3 Descendants of Turks and 'indigenous' Algerians. [Editor's note.]
4 P. Bourdieu, *The Weight of the World: Social Suffering in Contemporary Society* (Cambridge: Polity, 1999); originally *Le Misère du Monde* (Paris: Seuil, 1993).
5 The Bureau of Applied Social Research at Columbia University. [Translator's note.]

Letters to André Nouschi

The introduction is by the editor.

1 In the margin: 'Atlas mitidjien, Cehnoua, Miliana range, Ouarsenis, Trara'. [Reference to the Berber-speaking regions in general. – Editor.]
2 Bourdieu gives here observations that he gathered here and there.
3 In the margin: 'This chapter will be called "The Algiers school and Islam"!'
4 In the margin: 'I also believe that arguments could be drawn from the study of regions that are little or recently Islamized, e.g. Kabylia, etc. (I am less sure about this and would welcome your opinion).
5 In the margin: 'tone down'.

Bibliography

Addi, L., *Sociologie et anthropologie chez Pierre Bourdieu. Le paradigme anthropologique kabyle et ses conséquences théoriques*, Paris: La Découverte, 2002.

Ageron, C.-R., *La Guerre d'Algérie et les Algériens*, Paris: Armand Colin, 1997.

Ageron, C.-R., 'Une dimension de la guerre d'Algérie. Les "regroupements" de populations', in *Militaires et guérilla dans la guerre d'Algérie*, Brussels: Complexe, 2002.

Ageron, C.-R., *Algérie. Naissance de mille villages*, Algiers: Baconnier, n.d.

Alleg, H., *La Question*, Paris: Minuit, 1957. Translated as *The Question*, Lincoln, NE: Bison Books, 2006.

Amrouche, J., 'Algeria fara da se', *Témoignage Chrétien*, 8 Nov. 1945, repr. in *Un Algérien s'adresse aux français*, Paris: L'Harmattan, 1994.

Amrouche, J., 'A propos des émeutes du 8 mai 1945' (1945), repr. in *Un Algérien s'adresse aux français*, Paris: L'Harmattan, 1994.

Amrouche, J., 'Regroupements ou génocide?' *Démocratie 60* (1945), repr. in *Un Algérien s'adresse aux français*, Paris: L'Harmattan, 1994, pp. 198–201.

Azéma, J.-P., Lévy-Bruhl, R. and Touchelay, B., 'Mission d'analyse historique sur le système statistique français de 1940 à 1945', mimeo, n.d.

Balandier, G., 'La situation coloniale. Approche théorique', *Cahiers Internationaux de Sociologie*, 11 (1951), pp. 44–79.

Benokba, A., 'Le camp de regroupement de M'Chounèche, 1955–1962', Master II, University of Nice Sophia Antipolis, 2006–7.

Bensa, A., 'L'exclu de la famille. La parenté selon Bourdieu', *Actes de la Recherche en Sciences Sociales*, 150 (Dec. 2003), pp. 19–26.

Berque, J., *Structures sociales dans le Haut Atlas*, Paris: PUF, 1955.

Bianco, L., 'Nous n'avions jamais vu "le monde"', interview with Tassadit Yacine, in *L'autre Bourdieu*, special issue of *Awal*, 27–8, pp. 267–77.

Bouhedja, S., 'Il était parmi les dix. Autour de l'enquête sur les camps de regroupement', in *L'autre Bourdieu*, special issue of *Awal*, 27–8, pp. 287–93.

Bourdieu, P., *Sociologie de l'Algérie*, Paris: PUF, 1958; 8th edn rev. and corrected, 2001. Translated as *The Algerians*, Boston: Beacon, 1962.

Bourdieu, P., 'Le choc des civilisations', in *Le Sous-développement en Algérie*, Algiers: Secrétariat Social, 1959, pp. 52–64. Translated as 'The clash of civilizations' in this volume.

Bourdieu, P., 'La logique interne de la civilisation algérienne traditionnelle', in *Le Sous-développement en Algérie*, Algiers: Secrétariat Social, 1959, pp. 40–51. Translated as 'The internal logic of original Algerian society' in this volume.

Bourdieu, P., 'Guerre et mutation sociale en Algérie', *Études Méditerranéennes*, 7 (spring 1960), pp. 25–37. Translated as 'War and social mutation in Algeria' in this volume.

Bourdieu, P., 'Révolution dans la révolution', *Esprit*, 1 (Jan. 1961), pp. 27–40. Translated as 'Revolution in the revolution' in this volume.

Bourdieu, P., 'Célibat et condition paysanne', *Études Rurales*, 5–6 (Apr. 1962), pp. 32–136.

Bourdieu, P., 'De la guerre révolutionnaire à la révolution', in F. Perroux (ed.), *L'Algérie de demain*, Paris: PUF, 1962, pp. 5–13. Translated as 'From revolutionary war to revolution' in this volume.

Bourdieu, P., 'Le hantise du chômage chez l'ouvrier algérien. Prolétariat et système colonial', *Sociologie du travail*, 4 (1962), pp. 313–31. Translated as 'Haunted by unemployment: the Algerian proletariat and the colonial system' in this volume.

Bourdieu, P., 'Les relations entre les sexes dans la société paysanne', *Les Temps Modernes*, 199 (Dec. 1962), pp. 307–31.

Bourdieu, P., 'Les sous-prolétaires algériens', *Les Temps Modernes*, 199 (Dec. 1962), pp. 1030–51. Translated as 'The Algerian sub-proletarians' in this volume.

Bourdieu, P., 'La société traditionnelle. Attitude à l'égard du temps et conduit traditionnelle', *Sociologie de Travail*, 1 (Jan.–Mar. 1963), pp. 24–44. Translated as 'Traditional society's attitude towards time and economic behaviour' in this volume.

Bourdieu, P., *Esquisse d'une théorie de la pratique*, preceded by *Trois Études d'ethnologie kabyle*, Geneva: Droz, 1972. Translated as *Outline of a Theory of Practice*, Cambridge: Cambridge University Press, 1977; revised and expanded version, Paris: Seuil, 2000.

Bourdieu, P., 'Les conditions sociales de la production sociologique. Sociologie colonial et décolonisation de la sociologie', in *Le Mal de voir*, Paris: Union Générale d'Éditions, 1976, pp. 416–27. Translated as 'For a sociology of sociologists' in *Sociology in Question*, London: Sage, 1993, pp. 49–53, and reproduced in this volume.

Bourdieu, P., *Algérie 60, structures économiques et structures temporelles*, Paris: Minuit, 1977. Translated as *Algeria 1960*, Cambridge: Cambridge University Press, 1979.

Bourdieu, P., *Questions de sociologie*, Paris: Minuit, 1980. Translated as *Sociology in Question*, Thousand Oaks, CA: Sage, 1994.

Bourdieu, P., *Le Sens pratique*, Paris: Minuit, 1980. Translated as *The Logic of Practice*, Cambridge: Polity, 1990.

Bourdieu, P., 'The struggle for symbolic order', interview with A. Honneth, H. Kocyba and B. Schwibs (translated from the German), in *Theory, Culture and Society*, 3.3 (1986), pp. 35–51. Translated into English as 'Fieldwork in Philosophy', in *In Other Words*, Cambridge: Polity, 1990.

Bourdieu, P., *Raisons pratiques. Sur la théorie de l'action*, Paris: Seuil, 1994. Translated as *Practical Reason: On the Theory of Action*, Cambridge: Polity, 1995.

Bourdieu, P., 'Structures, habitus and practices', in *The Polity Reader in Social Theory*, Cambridge: Polity, 1994, pp. 95–110.

Bourdieu, P., *La Domination masculine*, Paris: Seuil, 1998. Translated as *Masculine Domination*, Cambridge: Polity, 2001.

Bourdieu, P., 'L'Odyssée de la réappropriation', *Awal*, 18, 1998, pp. 5–6.

Bourdieu, P., 'Pour Abdelmalek Sayad' (Institut du Monde Arabe, Paris, 1998), *Annuaire de l'Afrique du Nord*, vol. 37 (1998), Paris: CNRS Éditions, 2000, pp. 9–13. Translated as 'For Abdelmalek Sayad' in this volume.

Bourdieu, P., 'Entre amis', *Awal*, 21 (2000), p. 6. Translated as 'Between friends' in this volume.

Bourdieu, P., 'The making of economic habitus', *Ethnography*, 1.1 (2000), pp. 17–41. Published in French as 'La fabrique de l'habitus économique', *Actes de la Recherche en Sciences Sociales*, 150 (Dec. 2003), pp. 79–90. Reproduced in this volume.

Bourdieu, P., *Science de la science et réfléxivité*, Paris: Raisons d'Agir, 2001. Translated as *Science of Science and Reflexivity*, Cambridge: Polity, 2004.

Bourdieu, P., *Interventions (1961–2001). Science sociale et action politique*, ed. F. Poupeau and T. Discepolo, Paris: Agone, 2002.

Bourdieu, P., 'L'autre Bourdieu. Celui qui ne disait pas ce qu'il avait envie de cacher', interview with Hafid Adnani and Tassadit Yacine, in *L'Autre Bourdieu*, special issue of *Awal*, 27–28 (2003), pp. 229–47.

Bourdieu, P., 'Entretien avec Franz Schultheis' (Paris, 26 June 2001), in *Images d'Algérie. Une affinité élective*, ed. F. Schultheis and C. Frisinghelli, catalogue for exhibition 23 Jan.–2 Mar. 2003, Institut du Monde Arabe, Arles: Actes Sud/Camera Austria/Sindbad/Fondation Liber, 2003, pp. 19–44. Translated as 'Seeing with the lens: about photography' in this volume.

Bourdieu, P., 'Participant objectivation', *Journal of the Royal Anthropological Institute*, ns, 9 (June 2003), pp. 281–94. Published in French as 'L'objectivation participante', *Actes de la Recherche en Sciences Sociales*, 150 (Dec. 2003), pp. 43–58. Reproduced in this volume.

Bourdieu, P., *Esquisse pour une auto-analyse*, Paris: Raisons d'agir, 2004. Translated as *Sketch for a Self-Analysis*, Cambridge: Polity, 2008.

Bourdieu, P. and Mammeri, M., 'Du bon usage de l'ethnologie', *Actes de le Recherche en Sciences Sociales*, 150 (1985), pp. 9–18. Translated as 'The right use of ethnology' in this volume.

Bourdieu, P. and Sayad, A., *Le Déracinement*, Paris: Minuit, 1964.

Bourdieu, P. and Sayad, A., 'Paysans déracinés. Bouleversements morphologiques et changements culturels en Algérie', *Études Rurales*, 12 (Jan–Mar. 1964), pp. 56–94. Translated as 'Uprooted peasants: morphological upheavals and cultural changes in Algeria' in this volume.

Bourdieu, P. and Wacquant, L., 'The organic ethnologist of Algerian migration', *Ethnography*, 1–2 (Fall 2000), pp. 173–82.

Bourdieu, P., Darbel A., Rivet, A. and Seibel, J.-P., *Travail et travailleurs en Algérie*, The Hague: Mouton, 1963.

Bourdieu, P., Boltanski, L., Castel, R. and Chamboderon, J.-C., *Un art moyen. Essai sur les usages de la photographie*, Paris: Minuit, 1965. Translated as *Photography: A Middle-Brow Art*, Cambridge: Polity, 1996.

Cornaton, M., *Les Camps de regroupements et la guerre d'Algérie*, Paris: L'Harmattan, 1998.

Delsaut, Y. and Rivière, M.-C., *Bibliographie de Pierre Bourdieu*, Paris: Les Temps de Cerises, 2001.

Dermenghem, É., *Le Culte des saints dans l'islam maghrébin*, Paris: Gallimard, 1954.

Domenach, J.-M., 'Histoire d'un acte responsable. Le cas Jean Le Meur', *Esprit* (Oct. 1959), pp. 675–7.

Domenach, J.-M. and Suffert, G., 'Algérie et renaissance française', *Esprit* (June 1956), pp. 937–48.

Dresch, J., *Réforme agraire au Maghreb*, Paris: Maspero, 1963.

Droz, B. and Lever, E., *Histoire de la guerre d'Algérie (1954–1962)*, Paris: Seuil, 1982.

Émerit, M., *L'Algérie à l'époque d'Abd-el-Kader*, Paris: Larose, 1951.

Fritsch, P., 'Contre le totémisme intellectuel', in *Rencontres avec Bourdieu*, Broissieux: Éditions du Croquant, pp. 79–100.

Froidure, M., *Où était Dieu en Algérie?* Paris/Metz: Awal/Mettis, 2006.

Garcia-Parpet, M.-F., 'Des outsiders dans l'économie de marché. Pierre Bourdieu et les travaux sur l'Algérie', in *L'autre Bourdieu*, special issue of *Awal*, 27–28 (2003), pp. 139–50.

Harbi, M., Le FLN, *mirage et réalités des origines à la prise du pouvoir, 1945–1962*, Paris: Bourgois, 1980.

Jauffret, J. and Vaïsse, M., *Militaires et guérilla dans la guerre d'Algérie*, Brussels: Complexe, 2002.

Julien, C.-A., *L'Afrique du Nord en marche*, Paris: Omnibus, 2002.

Lacoste-Dujardin, C., *Opération oiseau bleu, des Kabyles, des ethnologues et la guerre d'Algérie*, Paris: La Découverte, 1997.

Lagrave, R.-M. and Encrevé, P. (eds), *Travailler avec Bourdieu*, Paris: Flammarion, 2003.

Lebaron, F., 'Les modèles économiques face à l'économisme', in L. Pinto et al., *Pierre Bourdieu, sociologue*, Paris: Fayard, 2004, pp. 128–30.

Lévi-Strauss, C., *Tristes Tropiques*, Paris: Plon, 1955. Translated as *Tristes Tropiques*, London: Penguin, 2012.

Maillard de la Morandais, A., *L'Honneur est sauf*, Paris: Seuil, 1990.

Mammeri, M. and Bourdieu, P., 'Dialogue sur la poésie orale en Kabylie', *Actes de la Recherche en Sciences Sociales*, 23 (1978), pp. 51–66. Translated as 'Dialogue on oral poetry in Kabylia' in this volume.

Martello, C., 'Germaine Tillion et l'Algérie. De l'ethnologie au politique', Mémoire de Master II, University of Nice Sophia-Antipolis, 2005–6.

Mauss-Copeaux, C., *Appelés en Algérie. La parole confisquée*, Paris: Hachette, 1998.

Merleau-Ponty, M., *Les Aventures de la dialectique*, Paris: Gallimard, 1955. Translated as *Adventures of the Dialectic*, Northwestern University Press: Evanston, IL, 1973.

Meynier, G., *Histoire intérieure du FLN*, Paris: Fayard, 2002.

Nouschi, A., *Enquête sur le niveau de vie des populations rurales constantinoises*, Paris: PUF, 1961.

Nouschi, A., 'Autour de la sociologie de l'Algérie', in *L'Autre Bourdieu*, special issue of *Awal*, 27–28 (2003), pp. 29–35.

Perroux, F., *L'Algérie de demain*, Paris: PUF, 1962.

Pinto, L., *Pierre Bourdieu et la théorie du monde social*, Paris: Albin Michel, 1998.

Reggui, M., *Les Massacres de Guelma*, Paris: La Découverte, 2006.

Rey-Goldzeiguer, A., *Aux origines de la guerre d'Algérie, 1940–1945*, Paris: La Découverte, 2006.

Rioux, J.-P. and Sirinelli, J.-F., *La Guerre d'Algérie et les intellectuels français*, Brussels: Complexe, 1991.

Rivière, T., *Aurès-Algérie, 1935–1936. Photographies*, Paris: Maison des Sciences de l'Homme, 1995.

Rocard, M., *Rapport sur les camps de regroupement et autres textes sur la guerre d'Algérie*, Paris: Mille et Une Nuits, 2003.

Sanson, H., 'C'était un esprit curieux', in *L'Autre Bourdieu*, special issue of *Awal*, 27–28 (2003), pp. 279–86.

Sapiro, G., 'Une liberté contrainte. La formation de la théorie de l'*habitus*', in L. Pinto et al., *Pierre Bourdieu, sociologue*, Paris: Fayard, 2004, pp. 61–3.

Sayad, A., *Histoire et recherche identitaire*, Saint-Denis: Bouchène, 2000.

Ségura, J., *Lettres d'Algérie. La guerre d'un appelé (1958–1959)*, Paris: Nicholas Philippe, 2004.

Seibel, C., 'Travailler avec Bourdieu', *Awal* (2005), pp. 91–7.

Servier, J., *Demain en Algérie*, Paris: Robert Laffont, 1959.

Servier, J., *Les Portes de l'année*, Paris: Robert Laffont, 1962.

Sibeud, E., *Les Sciences sociales en situation coloniale*, introduction to special issue of *Revue d'histoire des Sciences Humaines*, no. 10 (2004), pp. 3–7.

Simonin, A., 'Les éditions de Minuit et les éditions du Seuil', in J.-P. Rioux and J.-F. Sirinelli, *La Guerre d'Algérie et les intellectuels français*, Brussels: Complexe, 1991.

Sprecher, J., *A contre-courant. Étudiants libéraux et progressistes à Alger, 1954–1962*, Paris: Bouchène, 2002.

Sprecher, J., 'Il se sentait bien avec nous', in *L'Autre Bourdieu*, special issue of *Awal*, 27–28 (2003), pp. 295–305.

Tillion, G., *L'Algérie en 1957*, Paris: Minuit, 1957.

UNESCO, *The Race Question* (statement drafted by leading experts, including C. Lévi-Strauss), Paris: UNESCO, 1950.

Vatin, J.-C., *Connaissance du Maghreb. Sciences sociales et colonisation*, Paris: Éditions du CNRS, 1984.

Vidal-Nacquet, P., *La Raison d'État*, Paris: Minuit, 1961.

Winkin, Y., 'La disposition photographique de Pierre Bourdieu', contribution to the Cerisy conference 'Le symbolique et le social. La réception internationale du travail de Pierre Bourdieu' (12–19 July 2001), Liège: Éditions de l'Université de Liège, 2005, pp. 43–51.

Wolf, E., *Peasant Wars of the Twentieth Century*, New York: Harper & Row, 1969.

Yacine, T., 'Genèse de la domination masculine', in L. Pinto et al., *Pierre Bourdieu, sociologue*, Paris: Fayard, 2004.

Yacine, T., 'Pierre Bourdieu *amusnaw* kabyle ou intellectuel organique de l'humanité', in *Rencontres avec Pierre Bourdieu*, Broisseux: Éditions du Croqant, 2005, pp. 565–74.

Index

abstract future 55, 58, 60, 62, 63–5, 71, 78–9, 153
academics 14, 15, 20, 268, 290
Accardo, Alain 10, 26, 31, 33, 34
accounting 63
acculturation 8, 20, 23, 39–40, 47–8, 118
  laws of 41
acquaintances 165, 167
aesthetics 271
'affective quasi-systemization' 88–9, 158, 160
afsih 232, 233
Aghbala 183
agrarian policy 45
agriculture 72, 120–1, 177, 183–4
  credit 64
  economy 57
  work 78, 124, 127–8
Aïn-Aghbel 120–1, 132, 134, 140–1, 184–5, 304, 305
Aït-Yenni tribe 228, 238, 250
Algeria 5–6, 312
  census of population 27
  diaspora 98, 109
  family 102

and French 96–7, 290
government by Algerians 85–6
independence 11, 15, 17, 21, 24–5, 29, 146–7, 206–7, 290
military service 10
society 29, 41, 43, 44, 46, 52–3, 54, 72, 74, 82, 85, 91, 92, 100, 102, 104, 113, 146–7, 191–2, 285, 290, 292, 298
sociology in wartime 8, 41
war of national liberation 85
working life 26
Algerian war (1954–60) 5, 8–9, 13–14, 16, 18–20
Amlikec, Mohammed Saïd 237–8
Amrouche, Jean 24, 29, 30
amusnaw 226, 227, 228, 229, 231, 232, 235–6, 246, 247–8, 250, 251, 252, 253, 255–6, 257, 258
anthropology 22, 25, 218, 265–7, 269–71, 277, 279, 293
apprenticeship 227, 236, 246
  informal 231
Arabic 253
  language 289, 292

Arabs 45, 95, 294
arbitrariness 165, 167, 174
Aristotle 188
Armée de Liberation Nationale
    (ALN) 108
artisans 228, 229–30
    status 229
    and travel 230
assimilation 40, 46
Aurès 41, 42, 80–1, 305
autochthonous civilization 43–4
autochthonous informant 211
autonomy 98, 108

baksheesh 164, 165
Balandier, Georges 23
barter 41, 59
Barthes, Roland 266, 268
Béarn 12, 204, 205, 207, 208, 209,
    216, 274, 275, 276, 278,
    279
    peasants 210–11, 292
    society 215
behaviours 71, 78–9, 97, 107, 123,
    142, 152, 162, 186–7
    comparison 121
    economic 67, 181
    honour 56–7
    'primitive' 271–2
    and signs 104–5
    stereotyping 70
    temporal consciousness 64
belief 64
Ben Badis, Abdelhamid 42
Benedict, Ruth 320–1
Berbers 42, 204, 218, 219, 254, 293,
    294
    discourse 224
    language 26, 222, 251
    mutual aid 75
    philosophy 226
    poetry 239, 252–3, 293
    society 220, 290

tamusni 254
    unity of 218
Berque, Jacques 80, 290
    *Les Structures sociales dans le
    Haut Atlas* 290
Bianco, Lucien 9, 19, 20
black Africa 39
blacksmiths 183, 205–6
Bloch, Marc 41
books 253
Boulifa 205–6
Bourdieu, Pierre 11, 21–2, 22–3
    Algeria 1960 11, 25, 291, 295–6
    Le Déracinement 25, 29, 291,
    311
    Études Rurales 29
    Homo Academicus 267–8, 269,
    275, 277
    The Logic of Practice 11–12, 25
    *Outline of a Theory of
    Practice* 11–12, 271
    Sociologie de l'Algérie 6, 22, 25,
    291, 317
    *Travail et travailleurs en
    Algérie* 10–11, 191, 291, 308
    The Weight of the World 311,
    313, 374
Breil, Jacques 31–2
budgets 136
Bureaux Arabes 44, 73

café society 127, 130, 136
calculations 71, 80–1, 90, 119,
    189
    spirit of 188
cameras 301–3
cantonment policy 46
capital 50, 75, 81, 82, 191, 192
capital and labour 49, 75
capitalism 53, 153
capitalist behaviour 69–70
caste divisions 93, 94, 95, 97–8
censorship 253–4, 312

Chaouïa society 41
civil servants 195–6
civilizations 86, 100, 105, 111, 141
    clash of 39, 92
    indigenous 96
clans 118–19
classification 270–1, 286
clothing 136
    attachment to 61, 79, 96, 104
cognitive anthropology 270
collective granaries 42
collective possession 119–20
colonialism 7, 8, 9, 13–14, 14, 17,
    24, 40, 44, 87, 89–90, 91, 207
    repression 25
    system 92–3, 94–5, 96, 97, 104,
    162, 179
    violence 21
colonization 7, 9, 10–11, 14, 20, 31,
    53–4, 90, 111, 180, 210, 283
    centres 124–5
    self-determination of peoples 23
community rules 63
competition 174
competitive economy 50–1
connections 157–8, 159–60, 165,
    276
consciousness 65, 160–1, 162, 221
    new 109
    popular 102
consumption 55, 82, 136, 306
    habits 136–7
    urban 133
conversion of gaze 7
cooperation 58
    Algerian peasants 59
counter-gifts 75, 181, 189–90
credit 46, 62, 80–2, 150–1, 189–90
    and gifts 63
    and sub-proletarians 150
    sureties 63
cultural apprenticeship 66
cultural identity 21–2

cultural mutation 85
cultural systems 74, 86, 102, 167
culture 8
    contagion 109
    disintegration 100, 111
    esoteric 234–5
    European view of 224
    oral 254
culture change 40, 44
    restructuring 50, 51

day-labourers 173
debt 150
decolonization 7, 15–16, 98, 108,
    283
deculturation 39, 40, 43
demagogy 88, 90
democracy 219–20, 296
Derrida, Jacques 10, 19
Desparmet, Joseph 65–6
dialogue 91
diffusion 40
direct goods, reserves 55, 59, 60
disaggregation 43, 48, 50
discourse 210–11, 234, 246–7, 260,
    266
    Berbers 221
    men of 230–1
    neighbours 212–13
    oral 247
    wisdom 235
    and words 257
discrimination 93, 163, 165
disintegration 90–1
    of family 102
disorientation 173–4
division of labour 58, 128–9, 277
Djebabra 123, 124, 125, 129, 130,
    133, 134, 136, 144
    resettlement 143
Domenach, Jean-Marie 19
dominant caste 93, 94, 98, 108,
    160

dominant discourse, censorship of 253–4
dominated caste 106, 107, 108
dominated society 97–8, 105
domination effect 43
douars 41–2
duration 147
Durkheim, Émile 270, 284

economic behaviour 54, 69
economic habitus 180–1, 192
economic theory 53
economics 50
  consciousness 53
  decision 55, 57
  deregulation 49
  dualism 89
  individualism 42
economy 8, 42, 43, 48, 75
  Algerian 27, 72, 146, 187
  barter 41
  capitalist 11, 25, 49–50, 52, 69, 78, 291
  good-faith 189
  market 41
  underdevelopment 82
economy of practices 181, 185–6, 188, 190
education 86–7, 90, 91, 102, 106, 112–13, 156–7, 167, 176, 179, 198–200, 227
elders 101, 112
emancipation 102, 112–13
emergency credit 62
emigration 183, 297–8
employment 119, 133, 166, 175–7, 178–9
  lack of 88
  stable 89, 174, 190
  unstable 175–6
enterprise threshold 71
equity 181–2
ethnocentrism 65, 273

ethnology 6, 7, 8, 10, 11, 16–17, 23, 24, 34, 65, 204, 230, 279, 289, 291, 292–3, 312, 313
  as fiction 290
  right use of 203, 205, 206–9, 211–12, 215, 218
ethnosociologists 294
ethnosociology 13
European civilization 39, 43–4
European society 92
existence 147–8, 156, 158–9, 160, 173, 175, 249
  ambiguity 130
  identity 118
  and unemployment 162
expenditure 151–2

family 188, 217–18
  disintegration 102, 113, 118–19, 124–6
  extended 118
  head of 174
  income 71
  solidarity 189
Fathers of the Church 69
fellah'in (smallholders) 28, 46, 49, 54, 55, 57, 59, 64, 65, 70, 76, 80, 138, 144, 152, 183–4
fiduciary money 59
folk theories 274–5
food purchase 138–9
foresight 54, 56–7, 58, 69, 70, 78, 80, 175–6
France 28, 94–5, 105, 110, 291–2, 298, 309
  intellectuals 20–1
Frankel, S. H. 50
fraternity 109, 119, 129–30, 150–1, 165
French 292
friendly agreement 63
future 78, 153–4, 155, 175, 176–7, 190

gargote (cheap restaurant) 137–9
Garnett, David 268–9
Geertz, Clifford 266
gifts 75, 79, 150, 181, 189–90
  exchange of 62, 181
girls, education of 106
goals, hierarchy of 153
God 65, 178, 218, 248–9, 254
  and future 66
  and Islam 251–2
  word of 252
goods 55, 63
  exchanged by barter 60
  and prices 63
gourbis 99, 123, 141
groups 214, 222–3, 276

habitat 141, 142–3
Halbwachs, Maurice 34, 270
Hanoteau, Adolphe 75–6, 213
harmonious social orders 103
harvests 56, 82
hierarchies 102
Homeric poetry 225, 228
honour 75, 77, 100, 111, 119–20,
    128–9, 181, 182, 189, 276
  code of 212, 235–6
hope 170
household 118, 120
household economy 62, 151, 291
human relationships 77
Huxley Medal 265

ideologies 102, 155
  revolutionary 113
immigration 297, 298
imperialism 91
incomes 154, 172, 176, 190
indirect goods 55
individualism, emergence of 43, 119,
    138, 139–40, 153, 160, 179
industrialization 50
inequalities 92–3, 123–4, 177–8

inheritance 318
initiation 236, 245, 246
innovations 70, 102
  of West 105
insecurity 174
instability
  absence of 169–70
  deliberate 170
institutions 288
interest 62
intermediaries 91, 166, 182, 191,
    255
invention 256, 257, 258
investment, symbolic 277
Islam 102–3, 113, 158, 251, 320–1

jobs 132–3, 148, 154–5, 156–7,
    166–7, 168–69
joint possession 45–6, 61
justification for existing 47

Kabyle being 253
Kabyle country 233
Kabyle society 25, 55–7, 58, 59, 65,
    75, 101, 111–12, 118–19, 172,
    177, 181, 186, 187, 188–9, 191,
    195, 203, 206, 207, 210,
    214–21, 228, 230, 236, 252,
    253, 274–5, 289, 292–3, 318
  and censorship 253–4
  oral poetry 204, 227, 293
Kabylia 5, 6, 7, 12, 24, 31, 32,
    109–10, 143, 180, 183, 189,
    205, 207, 213, 218, 220, 221,
    258, 274, 292–3, 305
  oral poetry 224–5
kairos 247
Kanak 221
Kasbah 28, 110, 150
Kerkera 122–3, 126, 127, 128, 129,
    132, 133, 136–7, 139, 140–1,
    142, 304, 306
Keynes, J. M. 79

khammessat 76–7
kinship 25, 129, 130, 167, 204, 207,
    212, 219, 222, 275–6
Koran 251–2, 253

labour 10, 186, 191
    forced 169
    market 71, 75, 76
    reduction in quantity 77
labourers 167
land 46, 102–3, 119
    dispossession 5, 45, 46, 48, 61,
        62
    work on 124, 144
language 214, 234, 239–40, 248
    common 86
    meaning of 240, 245–6
    Occitania 220
    reduction of 244
    ultimate antimonies 249–50
law 254
Le Meur, Jean 19
learning 106
legitimacy 93–4
lending at interest, ban on 62–3
Letourneux, Aristide 75–6
Lévi-Strauss, Claude 270, 279
lifestyles 112–13
linguists 289–90, 292, 294
living from day to day 153
loans 109
logic of practices 271, 287
loi Warnier 46

Maghreb 44, 61
magic, belief in 157–8
Mammeri, Mouloud (MM) 203, 204,
    206, 207, 208, 209, 210–11,
    212, 213, 214, 215–23, 224,
    225, 226, 227, 228, 229–30,
    231–56, 290, 293
A Man in the Zoo (Garnett) 268–9
manual workers 170

marabouts 198, 230, 247, 251, 252,
    253, 254–6
marginal utility 52
market economy 41
marketplace 182
markets 227, 231
marriage 275–6
Marx, Karl 67, 69, 219, 284,
    285
mass and elites 90, 91
mass politicization 102
materialism 50–1
Matmata 126, 129, 144
Mauss, Marcel 270
medicine 106
Mediterranean mythico-ritual system
    8
Merdja 123, 124, 125, 129
migration flows 297
military action 128–9
milling 183–4
miserabilism 160
modality 65
modern economy 46, 49, 57–8, 79,
    120, 177, 189, 276–7
Mohand, Sheikh 256
monetary exchanges 59, 119,
    185–6
money 59–60, 79–80, 135–6, 151
    circulation 76, 80
    economy 147
    income 133, 148
    use of 60–2
moneylenders 109
morality
    honour 63
Moussa, Pierre 50
Mozabite civilization 318–19
Mozabite miracle 75
mutual aid 58, 75–6, 77, 129,
    166–7
    fraternal 63, 77, 151
mutualist associations 77

national fraternity 98
National Liberation Front (FLN) 14, 20, 21, 33, 95, 108
nature 67, 77–8
  dependence on 66
  gift of 190–1
negation 105
neologism 99–100
nepotism 165
nomadism 48, 61
non-Keynesian economic theory 50
North Africa 103, 290
North American Indians 39
Nouschi, André 317, 318

objectivation 275, 284, 287, 293
Occitania 220
occupational training 163
occupations 171–3, 174–5, 177
oral literature/poetry 224, 225–6, 232–3, 237, 240–3, 293
Orientalism 289

Parlange, General Gaston 30
participant objectivation 265–7, 268
paternalism 97, 107, 168
patriarchal family 101
patrimony 56
pauperization 92–3
payment, mode of 149–50
peace 93, 113, 124
peasants 56, 59, 78, 81, 87, 99, 102, 120, 228, 229–30, 251, 291
  and craftsmen 183
  'de-peasanted' 27
  'de-ruralized' 134
  and money 59
  rural 121–2
  society 135, 137
  tasks 58
  uprooted 25, 117, 140, 151
  virtues 66–7
Perroux, François 43, 49

personal dependence 162
personal relations 165–6, 167, 168, 181, 182
phenomenology 278–9
photography 301–4, 306, 307–10, 312, 313
pilgrimages 231
Pirou, Gaëtan 59
plan of life 70, 89, 152, 153, 173, 175–7
poems 241–5, 258–9
poetry 236–8, 240, 258
poets 231–2, 251, 260–1
  apprentice 258
  function of 232–4, 234, 238, 239
  relationship with audience 257–8
Polanyi, Karl 183
politics 87, 90, 291
  rational 91
populations 41–2, 72, 307
  displacements 109
  resettlement 98–9, 117–18, 120, 126
poverty 61, 82, 99, 119, 133, 149
pre-capitalist economy 143, 180
  some properties of 181–5, 187
pre-capitalist societies 69, 216, 291
pre-Christian religions 69
pre-perceptive anticipation 64
prediction 54–5, 57, 71, 80
  rational 78, 90
prestige 75, 76, 77
price fluctuations, seasonal 41
'primitive thought' 271
primogeniture 207
production 57–8, 136
  cycles 57
projects 64, 66, 155–6
proletariat 162, 291–2
property 42, 48
prose 240
'protection' 165, 166, 167–8
proverbs 250–1, 255, 257, 258

racial discrimination 95
racism 64
radicalism 91, 101, 179
rational action theory 180–1
rational forecast 80
rationalization 52, 53, 54
realism 85
reciters 235
recruitment 167
    through cooption 166
    procedures 165
reflection 161
reflexive cognitive anthropology
    270
reflexivity 266, 267, 268, 277–8,
    289, 293, 310
reintegration 48
relations of war 182
religion 75
repression 95
    and army 95–6
reserves 55–6, 150
resettlements 120, 122–4, 125,
    132–3, 140
    camps/centres 26, 28–31, 86, 100,
        109, 110, 111, 137
    high surveillance 31–2
    policy 117
    and women 128, 129
revolution 88, 93–4
revolutionary class 291
revolutionary rationalization 90,
    91
revolutionary war 85, 88, 92–4,
    101
revolutionizing revolution 85, 113
risks 69, 75, 76, 79
'rites of passage' 277
Rocard, Michel 29, 30
rural communities 100
rural populations 109–10
rural society 45
    economic practices 186

savings 78–9, 149, 153
Sayad, Abdelmalek 16, 25–6, 29, 30,
    31, 32, 213, 217, 295–6, 297,
    298–300, 307, 311
scholastic bias 274, 275
Schultheis, Franz 301
science 284–5
scientific objectivity 267, 269
security 174
Seibel, Claude 27
self-sufficiency 77
sénatus-consulte 41–2, 45, 46, 87
serfdom 76
services 181–2, 183
sexes, relations 128–9
shantytowns 28, 86, 99–100, 118,
    130, 136, 137, 308
    rural 110, 126
shopkeepers 150–1, 184–5, 196
    and customers 189
simple reproduction 67
skilled workers 167, 198–9
smallholders see *fellah'in*
social advance, lack of 170
social sciences 283, 287, 289, 293
social status 210
social world 219, 222
science, past of 284
society 46–7
sociologism 219
sociology 17, 34, 218, 219, 269,
    270–1, 279, 283, 284, 285,
    286–7, 291, 307
    colonial 286
    and ethnology 212
    mutations 104
    of science 283–4
solidarity 58–9, 95, 98, 99, 109,
    118, 121, 129–31, 140, 150–1,
    189, 190, 217
    collective 183
space 140–1, 142–3
spatial rhythms 69

speech 224, 231
Sprecher, Jean 15
Stalinism 9
structuralism 8, 11, 25, 284
sub-proletarians 27–8, 70, 146, 148,
    150, 155–6, 157, 159, 179,
    291
  revolt of 160
  urban 88
subversive warfare 95
symbolic future 78–9
symbols 105

tamusni 220, 221, 222, 224, 226,
    227, 228, 229, 231, 235, 236,
    246, 247, 253–4, 255, 256
  and God 252
  and Koranic tradition 251
technical innovations 186
Tell 56, 72–3
temporal consciousness 53, 54
  pre-capitalist man 65
  structure of 64
  and traditional economy 54
temporal rhythms 69
temporality 144, 145
terrorism 95
text 266
theory of practice 8
Tillion, Germaine 17, 23, 24, 41,
    305, 321
  L'Algérie en 1957 22
time 52, 54–5, 143–4, 173, 190
  awareness 175–6
  discovery of 147–8
  and peasants 143
  value of 62, 80
total war 95
Touaba territory (Oued el
    Abiod) 41–2
trades 168, 173, 178, 193–4
traditional behaviour 70, 98–9,
    256–7

traditional culture 90
traditional economy 17, 50–1, 62,
    67, 72, 81
  North Africans 80
traditional society 69, 77, 100–1,
    111
  as integrated system 72, 121
  spirit of 75, 77, 81, 320
traditionalism 67, 68–9
  of despair 70, 152
traditions, renunciations 105–6
tribe 240
  words of 245
Turks 233–4

underdeveloped countries 50
unemployed 27, 148
unemployment 69, 70, 131–2,
    146–7, 152, 162, 173, 175,
    176
  degrees of awareness 177–9
United Nations 105
University of Algiers 14–15, 18,
    22
unskilled workers 163
urban sub-proletarians 90
  and credit 150
urbanization 99–100, 102, 150
usury 62–3, 64, 80
utilitarian vision 189
utopianism 219

Vaillant, Marshal 46
value in time 63
value of values 81–2
veil 105–6, 127
verbalism 156
vertical mobility 170
village assembly 231
village units 118–19
violence 96, 102–3, 113
Violette, Maurice 61
'vulgarization' 245

wage-labour 48–9, 132, 190, 191
wages 60, 61, 120–1, 168, 179
  assured 89
  rise in 77
war, sociological consequences
    of 104
war of liberation 95, 96, 180, 210
wealth 82
Weber, Max 52, 77, 228, 278, 320
Western civilization/culture 96
  and Algeria 103, 104–5
White Fathers 206, 290, 296
wisdom 66, 67
Wittgenstein, Ludwig 267, 271–2
wives, repudiation of 108
women 87, 126–7
  disinheritance 254, 318
  and men 112
  role of 128, 199–200
  and veil 106, 128
  and war 101–2
  and work 161
Woolf, Virginia 277

work 67, 68, 77, 78, 145, 147–8,
    157, 169, 171–4, 175–6, 192,
    194–5, 199, 226, 233
  capitalist view of 144
  competition for 162–3
  lack of 88
  search for 173
  and wages 144, 320
  and women 128
world
  adaptation to 74, 99
  end of the 113
  new 102
  view of 81, 86, 89, 110

Yacono, Xavier 72–3
young people 177
Yusef-i-Kaci 233, 238, 239, 258–9,
    261

zribat 118, 120, 121, 122, 132, 140,
    141